THE
Richard Rodgers
READER

READERS ON AMERICAN MUSICIANS
Scott Deveaux, Series Editor

THE

Richard Rodgers

READER

EDITED BY

Geoffrey Block

OXFORD

UNIVERSITY PRESS

2002

OXFORD
UNIVERSITY PRESS

Oxford   New York
Auckland   Bangkok   Buenos Aires   Cape Town   Chennai
Dar es Salaam   Delhi   Hong Kong   Istanbul   Karachi   Kolkata
Kuala Lumpur   Madrid   Melbourne   Mexico City   Mumbai   Nairobi
São Paulo   Shanghai   Singapore   Taipei   Tokyo   Toronto

and an associated company in

Berlin

Copyright © 2002 by Oxford University Press, Inc.

Published by Oxford University Press, Inc.
198 Madison Avenue, New York, New York 10016

Oxford is a registered trademark of Oxford University Press

Library of Congress Cataloging-in-Publication Data
The Richard Rodgers Reader /
[compiled and edited by Geoffrey Block].
p. cm. (Readers on American Musicians)
ISBN 0–19–513954–2
1. Richard Rodgers, 1902–1979—Criticism and interpretation.
I. Block, Geoffrey Holden, 1948– II. Series.
ML410.R6315 R53   2002   782.1'4'092—dc21   2001037505

1 3 5 7 9 8 6 4 2

Printed in the United States of America
on acid-free paper

For My Family Anthology

PART I: Parents and In-Laws
Mother (Ruth) and Dad (Stanley); Lucille and Bennett

PART II: Their Children
Norma; Barbara, Jacqueline, and Craig

PART III: Their Grandchildren
Jessamyn and Eliza; Bernard, Julie, and Claire

PART IV: Cousins, Brother-in-law, and Aunts
Harriet, Rich, and Jo; Peter; and my two Dorothys

contents

part ii. Rodgers and Hammerstein, 1943–1960

part III.   Rodgers after Hammerstein, 1960–1979

part IV.   The Composer Speaks, 1939–1971

acknowledgments

Like many Americans growing up in the 1950s, I spent my childhood under the spell of Rodgers and Hammerstein. Aside from a few songs and televised renditions of "Slaughter on Tenth Avenue," however, Rodgers and Hart was a later, albeit equally joyous, discovery. In the process of researching and writing *Enchanted Evenings: The Broadway Musical from "Show Boat" to Sondheim* (Oxford, 1997) my fascination with Rodgers and Hart, Rodgers and Hammerstein, and even Rodgers after Hammerstein, continued to grow exponentially. Consequently, when Oxford University Press asked me to contribute a Reader on a Broadway figure, the choice was an easy one. The readings that follow will reveal a man, universally recognized by critics, colleagues, and a vast public as a master melodist, who throughout his long and prosperous career almost invariably placed these melodic gifts at the service of specific characters and dramatic situations to make a show work. With rare exceptions from the 1920s to the 1970s, Rodgers tried to say something new, and in the balance, more often than not, I think it is fair to say he managed to demonstrate his formula for success: "Don't have a formula" and "don't follow it up."

Throughout the preparation of this collection, the University of Puget Sound, especially the staffs of Collins Memorial Library and the School of Music, contributed greatly to the efficiency and pleasantness of the hunting, gathering, and administration process. Maribeth Payne, Executive Editor, Music, my able production editor, Joellyn Ausanka, and others at Oxford University Press provided encouragement and a high level of professionalism at every stage. I would also like to thank Graham Wood for providing a sounding board in my efforts to refine my original choices, and to the anonymous outside reviewers who offered helpful suggestions in response to my proposal and final draft.

It is a pleasure to report that it was possible to secure rights to all the selections considered for inclusion—although in one or two cases the asking price was prohibitive—and I thank all individual authors and rights holders for responding to my queries and granting me permission to include their valuable contributions. Special thanks are due Richard Adler, Arthur and Barbara Gelb, Catherine Green, Jean Kerr, Jane Sargeant, Craig Tenney, and to Ronald J. Grele and Alexander Freund of the Oral History Collection of Columbia University.

Ted Chapin, president of the Rodgers and Hammerstein Organization, read all the selections, and after consulting Mary Rodgers Guettel, graciously granted permission to reprint the many articles and other source materials controlled by R&H. I am especially grateful, not only for Ted's interest in this project, but for his willingness to endorse the collection even when he questioned the fairness and balance of two entries. Robin Walton and Flora Griggs, also of the Rodgers and Hammerstein Organization, helpfully guided me through the complicated rights process.

From the beginning Robin Boomer served as a capable and good-natured factotum, photocopying articles and tracking, writing, phoning, faxing, and in some cases nagging (politely) various rights holders. Derek Johnson typed the readings competently and swiftly, and Jeremy Briggs Roberts carefully proofread the introductions prior to final review and the entire typescript prior to production.

These acknowledgments provide a welcome opportunity to thank my wife, Jacqueline, and my daughters, Jessamyn and Eliza, for filling our home with activity, laughter, and the sound of music, and for giving me a context and perspective to my work.

Tacoma, Washington
December 2001

THE
Richard Rodgers
READER

§

Richard Rodgers (1953)

INTRODUCTION

Richard Rodgers (1902–1979) was one of the most successful popular composers of his era and arguably the most successful, productive, diverse, and influential American composer for the musical stage of the twentieth century. As a songwriter, Rodgers was about as popular as a popular song composer can be. In fact, no fewer than nine Rodgers songs are featured among *Variety*'s Golden 100 songs of Tin Pan Alley (reprinted in Charles Hamm's *Yesterdays*), a figure that equals the great Irving Berlin among all the songs copyrighted between 1918 and 1956.* Rodgers's songs are universally praised for their versatility, craft, and memorability as well as their emotional and dramatic qualities. In his influential survey of Rodgers songs in *American Popular Song: The Great Innovators—1900–1950* (portions of which are excerpted in *The Richard Rodgers Reader*), Alec Wilder introduces his subject with unequivocal ardor: "Of all the writers whose songs are considered and examined in this book, those of Rodgers show the highest degree of consistent excellence, inventiveness, and sophistication."

Although most of the shows with Lorenz Hart (1895–1943) are remembered primarily for the songs, it needs to be said that from the earliest stages of his career Rodgers was concerned with their careful dramatic placement in his shows and films. More consistently than other outstanding songwriting composers of his era, including Berlin, Jerome Kern, George Gershwin, Cole Porter, and Harold Arlen, Rodgers, especially in his collaboration with Oscar Hammerstein (1895–1960), created a repertory of songs that have retained a credible attachment to their staged origins.

After six years largely confined to amateur theater, Rodgers and his first collaborator became overnight sensations in 1925. The catalyst was a benefit performance of *The Garrick Gaieties*, a revue that introduced

---

*In chronological order: "My Heart Stood Still" (*A Connecticut Yankee*, 1927); "With a Song in My Heart" (*Spring Is Here*, 1929); "Lover" (*Love Me Tonight*, 1932); "Blue Moon" (*Manhattan Melodrama*, as "The Bad in Every Man," 1934); "My Funny Valentine" (*Babes in Arms*, 1937); "Bewitched" (*Pal Joey*, 1940); "You'll Never Walk Alone" (*Carousel*, 1945); "It Might As Well Be Spring" (*State Fair*, 1945); and "Some Enchanted Evening" (*South Pacific*, 1949).

the song "Manhattan." For the next three years Rodgers and Hart would enjoy another six hit shows on Broadway and several in London. Nearly all of these shows, now mostly forgotten, contained one or more songs that remain standards. Returning to Broadway in 1935 after several years of a Hollywood diaspora, Rodgers and Hart began a seven-year period in which they created one success after another (nine hits in ten tries), many more memorable songs, and at least a quartet of revivable shows, *On Your Toes, Babes in Arms, The Boys from Syracuse,* and *Pal Joey.* With the death of Gershwin in 1937 and Kern's move to Hollywood their only consistent competition during this period was Porter. Four of Rodgers and Hart's final shows rank among the top twelve hits of the 1930s (*I Married an Angel, On Your Toes, I'd Rather Be Right,* and *Babes in Arms*), and two of their musicals in the early 1940s, *Pal Joey* and *By Jupiter,* ran longer than any of these.

When Hart was unwilling and probably physically and mentally incapable of working on what would eventually become Rodgers and Hammerstein's *Oklahoma!,* Rodgers began a second long-term partnership in 1942. With its record-shattering run of 2,212 performances (a record unsurpassed until *My Fair Lady*), *Oklahoma!* (1943–48), Rodgers's influential first effort with Hammerstein, launched a new Broadway era of thoughtful and convention-shattering musicals with well-constructed central plots, imaginative and sometimes serious subplots, credible stories populated with believable and complex characters who spoke in an authentic vernacular, and songs and ballets that advanced the action. Also during these early years with Hammerstein, Rodgers produced several critically successful and profitable plays and musicals, including a non–Rodgers and Hammerstein hit, Berlin's *Annie Get Your Gun* (1946). Rodgers and Hammerstein were responsible as creators—or in the case of *Annie Get Your Gun,* as producers—for four of the five greatest hit shows of the 1940s and four of the six longest-running shows that premiered before the 1960s. The film version of *The Sound of Music,* released in 1965, became the top-grossing musical film of all time.

Rodgers and Hammerstein popularized the "integrated" musical as the dominant aesthetic ideal and permanently changed the direction of the genre. For seventeen years the second R. and H. produced an extraordinary body of work, including a succession of shows that remain at the center of the Broadway repertoire: *Oklahoma!, Carousel, South Pacific, The King and I,* and *The Sound of Music.* They also wrote a popular film musical, *State Fair,* and a widely viewed television musical, *Cinderella,* both of which have been popularly adapted for the stage. Shortly after Hammerstein's death in 1960, Rodgers completed work on his first major television score since *Victory at Sea* (1952), a program about Winston Churchill called *The Valiant Years* (1960); two years later he composed several new songs, lyrics as well as music, for the film remake of *State Fair.* Also in 1962 the indefatigable Rodgers managed to write his own lyrics for one last bona fide Broadway hit, *No Strings*. His work would continue in four remaining shows with a series of other distinguished lyricists: Stephen Sondheim for *Do I Hear a Waltz?* (1965), Martin Charnin for *Two by Two* (1970) and *I Remember Mama* (1979), and Sheldon Harnick for *Rex* (1976). To varying degrees these last shows were marred by conflicts with collaborators and actors, shorter runs, and Rodgers's own diminished artistry. After the quick demise of *I Remember Mama*, his fortieth Broadway musical in fifty-four years, Rodgers lived to see the opening of a brilliant Broadway revival of *Oklahoma!* three weeks before his death on December 30, 1979.

Not surprisingly, the literature on Rodgers is vast. In addition to several full-length biographies of Rodgers, separate biographies of Hart and Hammerstein, and studies of Rodgers and Hammerstein in which Rodgers naturally figures equally or prominently, the Rodgers bibliography offers dozens of essays and chapters of books, hundreds of reviews, and seemingly endless interviews and profiles. Rodgers himself contributed more than fifty articles that complement both his indispensable published autobiography *Musical Stages: An Autobiography* (New York: Random House, 1975; repr. by Da Capo Press, 1995) and the comprehensive, systematic, and refreshingly candid (yet unfortunately less accessible) series of interviews from late 1967 and 1968 contained in the Columbia University Oral History Collection.

Naturally, I have tried to include the most important and most interesting Rodgers material, favoring sources that can be anthologized without obtrusive cutting. I have also tried to present a balance among the three major creative periods—Rodgers and Hart (1919–1943), Rodgers and Hammerstein (1943–1960), and Rodgers After Hammerstein (1960–1979)—as well as a representative and generous sampling of Rodgers's own writings. To orient readers less familiar with Rodgers and his work, informative, perceptive, and stylish biographical and critical overviews by Ethan Mordden, Gerald Mast, and Winthrop Sargeant will introduce the three central phases of his long career.

Part I. Rodgers and Hart, 1919–1943: Working against the desire for balance is a literature skewed in quantity and quality toward Rodgers's years with Hammerstein—with exponentially still more material after Hammerstein's death—rather than the Rodgers and Hart years. Although several articles from the early 1930s emphasize Hart's lyrics, it was not until about the fifth successive hit show after their return from Hollywood in 1935 that high-profile magazines took serious notice of Rodgers *and* Hart. Part I reprints the most prominent of these, both from 1938: *Time* magazine's "The Boys from Columbia," a cover story that appeared in anticipation of the first major Shakespeare musical on Broadway, *The Boys from Syracuse*, and Margaret Case Harriman's two-part profile in

The New Yorker (produced here as it was modestly updated in Harriman's essay collection, *Take Them Up Tenderly*, six years later). The following readings round out Part I:

- a multi-authored exploration of the genesis, lyrics, and music of a Rodgers and Hart hit song, "My Heart Stood Still," from the anecdotal to the analytical;

- two reminiscences from Dorothy Rodgers: an introduction to the letters Dick Rodgers wrote to her from early in their courtship in 1926 until 1937, the year "finances took an upward turn and daily long-distance calls replaced the letters," and the recollections of her husband's personal and professional relationship with Hart excerpted from her autobiography, *A Personal Book* (1977);

- four letters that Rodgers wrote to Dorothy in 1928 in connection with *Chee-Chee*, Hart's explanation of *Chee-Chee*'s importance and artistic merits, and Rodgers's retrospective view of his major failure with Hart (from *Musical Stages*);

- a famous mixed review of *Pal Joey* by Brooks Atkinson, the principal *New York Times* critic from 1924 to 1960, who reviewed all but three Rodgers shows, usually favorably, between *The Girl Friend* and *The Sound of Music*;

- an overview of Rodgers's film musicals and their departures from staged sources by Stanley Green, one of the leading Rodgers authorities of his (and Rodgers's) generation, and the editor and compiler of the indispensable *Rodgers and Hammerstein Fact Book: A Record of Their Works Together and with Other Collaborators* (New York: Lynn Farnol Group, 1980);

- an affectionate and informative autobiographical essay by Oscar Hammerstein on his meeting and friendship with Rodgers and Hart and his appreciation for their songs.

Part II. Rodgers and Hammerstein, 1943–1960: After Mast and Mordden survey the scope and significance of Rodgers and Hammerstein, readers in this section will encounter the recollections of Lawrence Langner, founding member and coleader of the Theatre Guild, the organization that gave Rodgers his first break with Hart in *The Garrick Gaieties* in 1925 and two decades later produced Rodgers's first trio of musicals with Hammerstein, *Oklahoma!, Carousel,* and *Allegro*. Readers can next revisit choreographer Agnes de Mille's vivid recollection of *Oklahoma!* rehearsals. Several major players in *South Pacific* also wrote quotable memoirs. Two appear here: the autobiographies of director and co-librettist Joshua Logan and leading lady Mary Martin (Nellie Forbush). In Part II readers will again hear from leading critics: Atkinson's reassessment of Rodgers and Hart's *Pal Joey* in the wake of the Rodgers and Hammerstein era and samples from the critical writings of

Eric Bentley and George Jean Nathan, who, in marked contrast to Atkinson, expected less rather than more from a musical, namely the old-fashioned "simple virtues" of "singable tunes and sheer showmanship" as embodied in Rodgers and Hart and neglected in Rodgers and Hammerstein.

Part II also contains five selections that illustrate the range of writings on Rodgers and Hammerstein: Engel's examination of Rodgers and Hammerstein's successful transformation of literary sources into *Oklahoma!, Carousel, South Pacific,* and *The King and I*; Leonard Bernstein's demonstration of Rodgers and Hammerstein's craft and the new maturity of the American musical, evident in *South Pacific*; Alec Wilder's idiosyncratic survey of his favorite passages in the songs of Rodgers and Hammerstein; Cleveland Amory's profile of Rodgers and Hammerstein, a worthy and representative example chosen from the many that appeared in popular magazines in the 1950s; and David Ewen's introduction to the first full-length, but necessarily incomplete, Rodgers biography, published in 1957.

Part III. Rodgers after Hammerstein, 1960–1979: The death of Rodgers's second partner precipitated a flood of articles about what Rodgers would do next. Sargeant's thoughtful assessment in *The New Yorker* of Rodgers's special gifts admirably sets the stage for this final phase. Both this *New Yorker* profile and the following article by Arthur and Barbara Gelb in *Esquire* report on Rodgers's projected collaboration with *My Fair Lady* and *Camelot* librettist-lyricist Alan Jay Lerner (which we now know would soon collapse). Both Sargeant and the Gelbs examine Rodgers's decision to create the lyrics as well as the music for *No Strings*, Rodgers's last critical and popular success.

Again in Part III we meet people who played important roles, however briefly, in the last phase of Rodgers's career: Diahann Carroll, the leading female character in *No Strings*; lyricist Stephen Sondheim, librettist Arthur Laurents, and others associated with *Do I Hear a Waltz?*; and Richard Adler, the co-lyricist-composer of *Pajama Game* and *Damn Yankees*, who produced Rodgers's *Rex*.

In Part III we also hear from more critics. In two selections from the 1960s Walter Kerr looks at a revival of *The Boys from Syracuse, Oklahoma!* twenty-five years later, and the new *Do I Hear a Waltz?* More recent writings include Ken Mandelbaum's analysis (excerpted from his engaging and perceptive study, *Not Since Carrie: 40 Years of Broadway Flops*) of three rare Rodgers failures, *Pipe Dream, Rex,* and *I Remember Mama*, and one "missed opportunity," *Do I Hear a Waltz?*, and William G. Hyland's introduction to the first modern full-length biography of Rodgers. Mary Rodgers Guettel, Rodgers's elder daughter and a successful Broadway composer in her own right, most notably of *Once Upon a Mattress*, will have the last word in her personal and candid introduction to the reprinted edition of Rodgers's *Musical Stages*.

Part IV. The Composer Speaks, 1939–1971: The final section of this *Reader* features thirteen Rodgers articles and interviews (including a self interview) distributed over more than thirty years, 1939 to 1971. The selections originally appeared in sources as diverse as *Theatre Arts, The Rodgers and Hart Song Book,* the *New York Times* and *New York Times Magazine, This Week, The Rodgers and Hammerstein Song Book, Opera News,* and *Dramatists Guild Quarterly.* Collectively they elucidate Rodgers's interpretation of American musical theater history and his values and goals as a composer of popular theater music. In one essay he conveys his ideas on the distinctions between operas and musicals; in another he offers a posthumous tribute to Jerome Kern, the composer who inspired Rodgers as a teenager to attain a high artistic standard; and in another he vigorously defends "the right to revive." In several essays and interviews Rodgers recalls his two principal lyricists, Hart and Hammerstein, as men and as artists. One autobiographical essay attempts to assuage fears and encourage detection of cancer.

The longest excerpt in this anthology is not a reprint. For the first time in published form readers can peruse Rodgers's recollections on the origins, critical issues, and overall assessments of his work from *Pal Joey* to *Do I Hear a Waltz?* as they appeared in the Columbia University Oral History Collection interviews in 1967 and 1968, *Reminiscences of Richard Rodgers,* a source previously available only on microfiche. Although these *Reminiscences* do not replace *Musical Stages,* they do arguably offer Rodgers in a more spontaneous and less guarded forum.

Toward the end of her introduction to the reprint of her father's *Musical Stages* Mary Rodgers wrote: "Theatre was his hobby. And his life." In the final interview included in this collection Rodgers equates retirement as "a kind of not living." He goes on to say that he likes "the actual work," that he likes "being given a lyric, and taking it and trying to work out the problem, trying to get a good idea for a song," that he likes rehearsals and watching his songs take on new life "from my head to somebody else's throat," and that he likes "even the terror of taking the thing out of town. . . . the whole process."

The readings collected here shed light on the man who could say all this after fifty years of unceasing activity and accomplishment. They also reveal how Rodgers's life and music affected several generations of critics, historians, collaborators, performers, and his own family. His elder daughter wrote that her daddy "was an extremely complicated man and deeply unhappy much of the time." This same man left a legacy of mostly uncomplicated (albeit sophisticated) songs in the hearts of millions and provided incalculable happiness, both in his own time and long after his own heart stood still.

I
Rodgers and Hart,
1919–1943

Richard Rodgers and Lorenz Hart, *Time*, September 26, 1938

The Age of Rodgers and Hart

Within a few months of their initial meeting Rodgers and Hart managed to get one of their songs interpolated into a professional show, "Any Old Place with You" (*A Lonely Romeo*, 1919). The following year they discovered on opening night that their first Broadway score, *Poor Little Ritz Girl*, had been reduced to about a half dozen songs (the rest, by the well-established Sigmund Romberg, had been inserted surreptitiously). For the next five years Rodgers and Hart endured a discouraging apprentice period in which they composed twelve amateur shows, most of which disappeared after a single viewing. On the brink of quitting, they scored a surprise success with the Theatre Guild's fund-raiser revue, *The Garrick Gaieties* (1925), a show that also introduced their first hit song, "Manhattan," originally composed for the unproduced *Winkle Town* in 1922. For the next three years Rodgers and Hart surpassed all other teams in productivity and popular runs.

The prolific and insightful Broadway historian Ethan Mordden sets the stage for the present collection with a survey of Rodgers and Hart's principal shows among the fourteen that appeared in the last half of the 1920s, the first decade of what Mordden designates "the golden age" of the American musical (1920–1970). Mordden waxes enthusiastically about Rodgers and Hart's first book show, the Revolutionary War costume drama, *Dearest Enemy* (1925), "a comedy of contemporary manners burlesquing a comedy of bygone manners," the strikingly original *Peggy-Ann* (1926), which "typifies the musical's unending quest for new forms," and *Heads Up!* (1929), where "the inventions simply tumble over themselves." He also perceives dramatic infelicities in shows that offered fine scores, for example *The Girl Friend* (1926) and *A Connecticut Yankee* (1927).

Mordden notes that Rodgers and Hart "avoided a straight-out love song" years before Rodgers and Hammerstein's *Oklahoma!* In fact, in songs like "I'd Like to Hide It" from *Dearest Enemy* Rodgers and Hart were "already tapping an odd vein: that of a young woman as much alarmed as invigorated by her first romantic stirrings." In extolling the virtues of *Peggy-Ann*, Mordden points out that, while numerous previous musicals had omitted the opening chorus (an innovation frequently attributed to this show), "what was unknown was a musical's starting without music of any kind," fourteen years before *Lady in the Dark*. He also refutes the "myth of *Chee-Chee*" (1928): "that the critics recoiled from its subject matter and fell on it like the fold on the wolf," thereby dooming its run to thirty-one performances and causing the formerly innovative team to artistically retrench in *Spring Is Here* (1929).

ETHAN MORDDEN

If Kern and Berlin marked the start of the new music some time before the 1920s, and if Gershwin and Youmans signaled the arrival of younger voices eager to develop the new style, still others arrived in their wake yet outstayed them by a wide margin. Richard Rodgers, of all these giants the last to continue as a working Broadway composer, presented his last show, *I Remember Mama*, forty-two years after Gershwin's death.

One other thing about Rodgers: he was the only major Third-Age composer who spent an entire generation working with a single lyricist, Lorenz Hart. [Ed. Earlier in *Make Believe* Mordden offered the following explanation of the Four Ages of the American musical: "The American musical has undergone four ages of development. The First, taking it from obscure origins to the end of the nineteenth century, is the primitive age. The Second Age, a flowering under distinctly European influences, comprised the first two decades of the twentieth century. The Golden Age lasts from 1920 to 1970, and the present, Fourth Age, that of the dark musical play, when joyous musical comedies seem like throwbacks and when the tourist-attraction pop operas from England threaten to monopolize Broadway real estate with endless runs, is still under way. *Make Believe*, 53.] As with the wandering Youmans, the names of Kern's and Romberg's collaborators would fill a paragraph; Rudolf Friml counted twelve lyricists on his twenty shows; and George Gershwin claimed a goodly number of partners before settling down with Ira (and even then slotted in Harbach and Hammerstein on *Song of the Flame*, teamed briefly with Howard Dietz on *Oh, Kay!* while Ira was in the hospital, worked equally with Gus Kahn and Ira on *Show Girl*, and let DuBose Heyward assist Ira on *Porgy and Bess*).

But "Rodgers and Hart" seemed so immutable, prolific, and unique that it was probably their work more than any Aeolian Hall manifestation that announced the arrival of a native art. The pair were comparable to what "Kern, Bolton, and Wodehouse" had signified in the late 1910s. Indeed, Rodgers and Hart had a house librettist in Herbert Fields, who wrote the book to six of their ten story shows staged on Broadway from 1925 to 1929.

The late 1920s could have been named after Rodgers and Hart; they never turned out fewer than two shows a year and, in 1926, came up with five, including one in London, *Lido Lady*. Oddly, their first professional credit dated back a full five years, to *Poor Little Ritz Girl* (1920). This strangely troubled piece, about a chorus girl who inadvertently rents an apartment occupied by a young bachelor, suffered one of the most remarkable tryouts in Broadway history. It opened in Boston (as the first

Source: Ethan Mordden, *Make Believe: The Broadway Musical in the 1920s* (New York: Oxford University Press, 1997), 114–19, 197–200.

attraction of the Wilbur Theatre) with a book by Henry B. Stillman and William J. O'Neil and the Rodgers and Hart score, with Victor Morley and Aileen Poe in the leads. Seven weeks later, in Stamford, Connecticut, Gertrude Vanderbilt was in the lead, and producer Lew Fields was commissioning some rewriting. After a week in Atlantic City, *Poor Little Ritz Girl* came in with Charles Purcell and Eleanor Griffith in the leads (Aileen Poe was still in the show, in a different role), with a book by George Campbell and Lew Fields and with a score by Sigmund Romberg and Alex Gerber *and* Rodgers and Hart (with one lyric, to Rodgers's music, by Herbert Fields, Lew's son). As Rodgers later put it, "Fields simply obeyed the ancient show-biz dictum that is still all too often followed today: If something is wrong, change *everything*."

Rodgers was eighteen and Hart twenty-five, and if the surviving *Ritz Girl* songs seem a little raw, one nevertheless sees their style emerging, in Hart's slyly Freudian lyric to "You Can't Fool Your Dreams" or Rodgers's zestfully syncopated and artfully harmonized verse (just for fun, it jumps from D Major to the extremely foreign G Flat Major) to "Love's Intense in Tents." A kind of tryout for "Mountain Greenery," this last number also offers a Hart fairly bursting with wicked jest:

> My lady, pay your rent
> With love to your grand lord.
> I've a lease from Cupid, the landlord!

Oddly, Rodgers and Hart were virtually out of work for the next four years—this in a Broadway swelling with young talent and new ideas! It was the flash success of *The Garrick Gaieties* that saved the partnership in 1925. As so often with utterly unheralded shows, it dazzled critics wary of reputations and pretentiousness. The *Gaieties*, a semi-amateur benefit revue for the Theatre Guild put on by Guild underlings with an eleven-piece orchestra, had the air of a college entertainment. But "Manhattan" utterly proclaimed Rodgers and Hart. It was the cleverest lyric since Wodehouse's "Cleopatterer" in 1917, and Rodgers's sunbeam of a melody simply had not been heard before.

Three months after the *Gaieties* opened, the first Rodgers-Hart-Fields show, *Dearest Enemy* (1925), found the team on Broadway in a thoroughly professional staging. Better, the spotty *Gaieties* score had given way to a honeycomb of songs. "A baby-grand opera," Percy Hammond called it; also "a deluxe kindergarten." Burns Mantle found it "mannerly, melodious, sane and charming." E. W. Osborn praised it for lacking "even a touch of that heard-that-before feeling," and Arthur Hornblow thought it "very akin to a genuine comic opera."

Fresh. Tuneful. Enchanting. Perhaps the critics were disarmed because Rodgers's craftsmanship, Hart's twinkle, and Fields's earthy, even smutty attitude were serving a period piece. *Dearest Enemy* is set during the

American Revolution, when colonial women loyal to the Cause detain English soldiers while Our Boys strategically regroup. The show had the air of a comedy of contemporary manners burlesquing a comedy of bygone manners, as when the aged General Tryon (Detmar Poppen) sings "Old Enough To Love" in defense of the seasoned campaigner ("Methusaleh could choose a *la petite* of twenty-two") or when he and Mrs. Robert Murray (Flavia Arcaro) make a flirtation out of "(What do all) The Hermits (do in springtime?)," complete with a Gilbert and Sullivanesque patter section and climaxing on "They can't hold a tree as you're holding me."

Dearest Enemy enjoyed a handsome production, partly because John Murray Anderson supervised it, bringing in his *Greenwich Village Follies* designers, Reginald Marsh and James Reynolds, but also because the star, Helen Ford, was sleeping with the producer—her husband, George Ford. Helen, who passed into legend by making her first entrance wearing only a barrel (she'd lost her clothes while swimming nude in the river), got in on the show's major ballads, "Here in My Arms," "Bye and Bye," and "Here's a Kiss," all duets with Charles Purcell as the English captain she loves. But her solo with the women's chorus, "I'd Like To Hide It," shows us the richness of Hart's view of love in all its ambiguities and discontents. Critics celebrate how, much later, Rodgers and Oscar Hammerstein avoided a straight-out love song by skewing the angle of approach, in "People Will Say We're in Love," "If I Loved You," or "We Kiss in a Shadow." But here's Hart already tapping an odd vein: that of a young woman as much alarmed as invigorated by her first romantic stirrings.

Dearest Enemy was a hit, and the very next Rodgers-Hart-Fields entry, *The Girl Friend* (1926), ran even longer. But *The Girl Friend* shows what can go wrong in its creators' particular format. *Dearest Enemy*'s strength was a good story, *Romeo and Juliet* with a wartime background. *The Girl Friend*'s strength was headliners, the married couple Sammy White and Eva Puck. *The Girl Friend* had no story. It had one of those novelty backgrounds: the craze for six-day bicycle racing. White wants to race, and Puck helps him do so. That's the plot. The score was fine, featuring the title song and "Blue Room," both for the stars, along with a comic waltz for Puck, "The Damsel Who Done All the Dirt," another review of historical figures in modern terms. (Pharaoh made the Hebrews "pay the price" because he couldn't "make a date with Fanny Brice.")

The Girl Friend seemed such an evocative twenties title to Sandy Wilson that, as I've said, he used it to certify *his* twenties musical, *The Boy Friend*, in the 1950s. But it was only the original show's two hit songs that had survived. *The Girl Friend* itself was by then long forgotten. In fact, when it was first brought over to England, in 1927, the feckless Herbert Fields script was simply junked. The producers substituted a new book, based on one written for a musical called *Kitty's Kisses*, which had opened on Broadway two months after *The Girl*

Friend. The *Kitty's Kisses* songs, by Con Conrad and Gus Kahn, were combined with those of *The Girl Friend.* Bizarrely, a regional English tour of this pastiche in the late 1980s (with yet another book, still based on *Kitty's Kisses*) advertised it as "Rodgers and Hart's *The Girl Friend.*"

"Not even a furtive-breath of jazz" was critic Frank Vreeland's comment on *Dearest Enemy*, and he meant it as a compliment. But "I Need Some Cooling Off" is a cry raised in Rodgers and Hart's Bea Lillie vehicle, *She's My Baby* (1928). The song is prefabricated jazz, impervious to mauling by dance bands because it was *composed* mauled, a berserk Charleston with a highly ambivalent message, for the more Hart begs for respite, the more Rodgers jives. This, of course, was their unique quality: Hart's anxieties enriching Rodgers's lyricism, Rodgers's merry melody redeeming Hart's despair. Hart is a philosopher and Rodgers a poet, yet both are ironists—that's where they meet. Let Rodgers compose a sprightly love tune, and Hart will fit something a little nervous to it, as in "If I Were You," dropped during *She's My Baby*'s tryouts but reinstated after the New York opening, for Irene Dunne and Jack Whiting. Another dropped number, "Morning Is Midnight," enjoys the seamless logic of a melody by Schubert but bears a lyric almost Schopenhaurischly metaphysical.

But Rodgers and Hart could plunge into a comedy lyric with relish. They'd have to, in a Bea Lillie show. "Whoopsie" catches her ability to ridicule anything, even a positive attitude toward life, unfortunately in a really rather awful number that must have taxed Lillie's powers. "When I Go On the Stage," however, gave all three of them something to work with: a no-talent scheming to become famous. Hart names the great and near-great—Marilyn Miller, Marion Talley, Mae West, Ernestine Schumann-Heink, Gatti-Casazza, Irene Bordoni, Amelita Galli-Curci, producer Dillingham himself, and *Hit the Deck!*'s Charles King and Louise Groody (who'll "look like Punch and Judy"). This spendthrift cataloguing of celebrities, unheard of before the mid-1920s, was like a verbal jazz, improvisations by youngsters eager to blow their elders away. Hart used it best. Ira Gershwin thought it a little vulgar; his idea of celebrity was Heinrich Heine. Cole Porter was a thoroughly committed adherent, though he adulterated the mix by citing also his frou-frou society friends. Who was the Duke of Verdura, anyway?

Rodgers, at this time, was making his name as a founding member of Third-Age composition more consistently than any of his predecessors, including Kern. Both were supreme melodists, but Rodgers was also an astonishing harmonist. Let one example suffice. In *Spring Is Here* (1929), there is a torchy ballad sung by two sisters (Inez Courtney and Lillian Taiz), "Why Can't I?" Rodgers's tune is simple, even repetitive. But his harmonic structure is so dense that the chord breakdowns printed in the sheet music were beyond anything seen in pop music before, with a $B^{\flat7-9}$ here and an f^{7-5} there. One chord, $b^{\flat7}/E^{\flat}$, was so beyond the day's ken that it was marked without the bass, as if the editor had simply given up.

For his part, the mid- and late-1920s Hart would have to be called the most advanced lyricist since P. G. Wodehouse in his Princess prime. Cole Porter was his only rival, but Porter didn't really get going till the very end of the 1920s; and Ira Gershwin, stylistically somewhat close to Hart, never truly challenged Hart's brilliance, especially in exploring how closely one's self-esteem depends on one's success in love. One thinks of many famous titles—"Little Girl Blue," "It Never Entered My Mind," "Nobody's Heart," say. These are more than torch songs; the singer keens for confidence lost when romance rebuffs him or her. But an obscure number written for an unproduced project during Rodgers and Hart's Hollywood sojourn in the early 1930s recalls to us the true distinctiveness of Hart's worldview. "Tell Me I Know How to Love," the singer pleads, admitting to a poor self-image that love with someone admirable can improve. "Tell me I know how to love," the singer concludes, "and I'll know."

Ira develops forms; Hart creates them, as in *Heads Up!* (1929), an Aarons-and-Freedley Coast Guard-versus-rumrunners show. The inventions simply tumble over themselves: "Sky City," a tribute to New York in terms of its soaring architecture; "(I Behave) As Though You Were There" (these two dropped during tryouts); "Knees," on the chorus girl's anatomy, laid out as a spoof of Rudyard Kipling's "Boots"; "Ongsay and Anceday," in Pig Latin; the opening chorus, "You've Got to Surrender," which starts with an homage to the opening chorus of Gilbert and Sullivan's *Patience*; "Mother Grows Younger," a battle among naval cadets on the dance floor. And *Heads Up!*'s big ballad, the properly nautical "A Ship Without a Sail," was the first torch song not only to pose but to build on a metaphor—and, what's more, it went to the *man* in the case, Jack Whiting. Despite the beauty of the refrain, the climax hits at the second lead-in *verse*, where "You tell your grief to no girls" is despairingly rhymed with "Your smile is like a show girl's."

If the Marxes (and Eddie Cantor) mark a culmination of the twenties idea of a comic musical, Rodgers and Hart are the exponents of musical comedy. Their colleagues either stepped over into operetta now and again or simply could not compete in terms of sheer output. De Sylva, Brown, and Henderson wrote five musical comedies; Rodgers and Hart wrote fourteen (through 1930). Moreover, while De Sylva's gang stuck to formula, Rodgers and Hart sometimes invented new kinds of shows.

Peggy-Ann (1926) typifies the musical's unending quest for new forms. Here was another Rodgers-Hart-Fields title, based on the 1910 musical *Tillie's Nightmare*, in which a boardinghouse matron's daughter (Marie Dressler) dreams of glorious adventures. Fields's updated script drew on trendy expressionism to create absurdist versions of those adventures, as his heroine (Helen Ford) dreams herself out of Glens Falls, New York, onto Fifth Avenue, into a department store her small-town boyfriend (Lester Cole) suddenly owns, onto the sea in a yacht, and off to Havana before she wakes up back in Glens Falls. There was no plot. Peggy-Ann quarrels with her boyfriend and then makes up with her boyfriend. The fun lay in the odd look of her dream—policemen with pink moustaches, a talking fish, family members taking control by wearing giant hats—and in the score, one of the team's liveliest. As always when Fields wrote the book, critics complained of the salty nature of it all. One song, "Give This Little Girl a Hand," applauded prostitution, and "A Little Birdie Told Me So" offended the prurient. Grow up, whiners. This was a first-class show and a first-class hit, lasting 333 performances, albeit at the Vanderbilt Theatre, little more than twice the size of the Princess.

Over the years, *Peggy-Ann* developed a reputation as being the first "daring" musical, with no opening chorus and a very quiet finale, a dance in the dark. (The show ends on the evening of the day on which it began.) Now, its fantasy action is certainly unusual. But plenty of musicals before this one had begun without a chorus. What was unknown was a musical's starting without music of any kind, something that, to my knowledge, was not attempted till *Lady in the Dark* (1941), which lacks even an overture. As for *Peggy-Ann*'s dance-in-the-dark finale, it wasn't the finale. After it, the company trooped on stage to reprise "A Tree in the Park."

That company took in a chorus of nine girls and five boys, a complement fit for the Vanderbilt. But note the extra women. Broadway choruses were not cast on an even boy-to-girl ratio because the musical was to an extent still playing out a history that began with the Girls as a major element in production. The boys were hired to do time steps; the *girls* were the thing. To choose one big show as an example, *Golden Dawn* balanced a chorus of thirty-five men against fifty-four women. That was the musical in the 1920s.

One exception was Rodgers and Hart's *A Connecticut Yankee* (1927), another huge hit at the little Vanderbilt and, because Mark Twain's novel put such emphasis on round-table knights, a rare show with twelve chorus women and *sixteen* chorus men (and mostly male principals on top of that). Here was another Fields book, this one as dull as *Peggy-Ann*'s is surprising, founded on a voyage back to Camelot by a modern-day American (William Gaxton) whose termagant fiancée (Nana Bryant) beans him with a champagne bottle. Like *Peggy-Ann*, he dreams the whole thing. And, as in *Peggy-Ann*, all the contemporary characters reappear in the imaginary adventure, along with some newcomers. At length, Gaxton awakes, now aware that he loves The Other Girl (Constance Carpenter).

The score is fine, counting two standards, "My Heart Stood Still" and "Thou Swell," and two also-rans, "I'd Feel at Home with You" and "On a Desert Island with Thee." Oddly, the one genuine comic song, Carpenter's solo, "I Blush," was cut out of town, though its references to Tristan and Isolde (very *d'après* Wagner, and not only in the spelling of the names—one line runs, "Oh dear, how they yodeled of love and death") richly denote Hart's erudite side. All the great Third-Age lyricists were well read, but Hart had given himself an outstanding education and was one of the smartest men in New York.

Tryout adjustments also played heck with Nana Bryant's role, giving one of her songs to June Cochrane and cutting the other. This left Morgan Le Fay without a single line of music, even in the first-act finaletto, surely a mistake for a musical's second woman lead. It's especially ironic considering that, sixteen years later, Rodgers produced a revival of *A Connecticut Yankee* with six new songs, and *this* show was virtually built around the Morgan, Vivienne Segal, the only star in the cast. Of the six added numbers, three were for Segal, and one of these, "To Keep My Love Alive," has joined "My Heart Stood Still" and "Thou Swell" as the show's three survivors.

This 1943 revival was not a success, and it's hard to know why the original was, for Fields's book reduces Twain to the one-joke culture shock of anachronism:

> LE FAY: Merlin, act thy age. Methinks thou art in thy second childhood.
> MERLIN: Aye, and methinks I do enjoy the second better than the first.
> LE FAY: Merlin forgets that I, too, am no mean sorceress.
> MERLIN: Sauceress . . . Ah, thou art the whole set of dishes!

The team grew adventurous in *Chee-Chee* (1928), after *Rose-Marie* and *Golden Dawn* our third twenties musical to claim too densely integrated a score to list more than a handful of song titles in the program. In truth, this show did toy with the use of fleeting ditties in the manner of *The Beggar's Opera*: script pauses, ditty is sung, script continues. While *Peggy-Ann* demonstrates the musical's delight in innovation and *A Connecticut Yankee* its sense of commercial self-preservation in convention and shtick, *Chee-Chee* reveals the musical's salacious side, the erotic component in Offenbach's *gai primitif*. It was based on Charles Petit's novel *The Son of the Grand Eunuch* and told of the succession of this noble position of old China, from father to son. Problem: Number One Son doesn't want to.

The myth of *Chee-Chee*, which lasted a month and then vanished, is that the critics recoiled from its subject matter and fell on it like the fold on the wolf. In fact, it got five pans, two half-and-halfs, and six raves. The *Daily Mirror* called it "a revolutionary musical show," the *Evening World* saw "a rousing tale of stage adventure with a finale that was greeted by rousing cheers," and the *Sun* found "quality, novelty, a merrily made score, and an utterly charming mounting." But the book, almost all felt, was slow going, and, indeed, the subject gave more than a few view-ers the feeling that the musical had become not so much liberal as pointlessly smutty.

Rodgers and Hart retrenched in their next offering, *Spring Is Here* (1929). For one thing, Herbert Fields was busy elsewhere—Owen Davis adapted his own quite innocent play *Shotgun Wedding*—and, for another, this was an Aarons-Freedley production: high twenties, Arden and Ohman in the pit, quick jokes, fleet plot, fast fun, and easy on the risqè. "Spring Is Here (in person)" runs the second number's refrain: everyone's young and cute, so what else matters? Here was the musical comedy made of interchangeable parts that had been stock-in-trade throughout the decade. A spring show, young and dizzy. Let's dance. Betty thinks she loves Stacy but eventually realizes that it's Terry whom . . . what nonsense. But then, this was the history of musical comedy in the 1920s: every now and then a dart into the unknown, but mostly one size fits all. None of our Great Men—not even Kern and Hammerstein, the outstanding pioneers of this decade—showed consistently progressive work. Still, one does have to let the public catch up with the revolutions. That takes time, even in a golden age.

"My Heart Stood Still"

Most writers become notably silent when it comes to discussing the musical craft and substance of popular songs. Rodgers himself rarely goes beyond anecdotal history (see, for example, the "Introduction" to *The Rodgers and Hammerstein Song Book* included in Part IV). Several authors from the 1930s to the present, including Margaret Case Harriman in the profile that follows, and Rodgers, do, however, seriously address Hart's lyrics. Among recent studies, interested readers might turn to Philip Furia's chapter on Lorenz Hart in *The Poets of Tin Pan Alley* excerpted here.

For meaningful musical discussions of individual Rodgers songs one can fortunately point to two quite distinguished exceptions to the above generality: Alec Wilder's classic study, *American Popular Song: The Great Innovators—1900–1950,* and Allen Forte's more recent *The American Popular Ballads of the Golden Era, 1924–1950.* In an idiosyncratic survey packed with copious musical examples, Wilder usually offers a provocative personal reaction to the music of a Rodgers and Hart song. On the final six pages of a sixty-page chapter reprinted in Part II, however, he takes a surprisingly dismissive glance at the songs Rodgers wrote with Hammerstein. Since Wilder wants to discuss many melodies, which he tends to view as autonomous and wordless musical entities, he devotes relatively little space to any given song. Taking the opposite tack is Forte, who, in his pioneering effort to apply to popular song the kind of rigorous analysis heretofore reserved for European art songs, examines only six Rodgers ballads: two songs from *A Connecticut Yankee*, "Thou Swell" and "My Heart Stood Still," "A Ship Without a Sail" from *Head's Up!*, "You Are Too Beautiful" from *Hallelujah, I'm a Bum*, and a pair from *Babes in Arms*, "My Funny Valentine" and "Where or When."*

The excerpts that follow begin with Gerald Mast's brief remarks in *Can't Help Singin'*, which address one of Rodgers's most ubiquitous musical practices, the creation of strikingly original as well as memorable melody out of simple stepwise scales (Mast's chapter on Rodgers and Hammerstein from the same survey is reprinted in Part II). The remaining passages focus mainly on one Rodgers and Hart standard, "My Heart Stood Still." Rodgers relates the unusual genesis of the song and contrasts Hart's trademark polysyllabic rhymes with his "even rarer ability to write with utmost simplicity and deep emotion" (Rodgers elaborated on this theme in *Musical Stages* and in several of the writings reprinted in Part IV). Furia addresses Hart's subtle and sometimes misunderstood rhyming techniques. Wilder discusses the overall quality and significance of Rodgers's *oeuvre* and briefly touches on Rodgers's predilection for scalar melodies exemplified in "My Heart Stood Still." Even those readers intimidated by detailed analysis (reprinted here in a slightly abbreviated form and minus three technical charts that utilize the influential system of analysis developed by the music theorist Heinrich Schenker [1868–1935]) should nonetheless derive something meaningful from Forte's clear engagement with such seldom considered subjects as the connections between the verse (the generally less tuneful and less remembered introduction to a tune) and the central refrain (the A sections of an A-A-B-A form). Despite his primary attention to Rodgers's music, Forte, unlike Wilder, also pays close attention to Hart's texts, often with considerable sensitivity, and in this case supplies music examples where his predecessor does not.

---

*For analyical discussions that place Rodgers and Hart songs within the context of particular shows see Geoffrey Block, *Enchanted Evenings: The Broadway Musical from "Show Boat" to Sondheim* (New York: Oxford University Press, 1997) [*On Your Toes* and *Pal Joey*] and Graham Wood, *The Development of Song Forms in the Broadway and Hollywood Musicals of Richard Rodgers, 1919–1943* (Ph.D. dissertation, University of Minnesota, 2000) [*Dearest Enemy*, A *Connecticut Yankee*, *Babes in Arms*, and *The Boys from Syracuse*]

GERALD MAST

Rodgers's melodies play a contrapuntal game with all this melancholy. If the two men seemed complementary opposites socially and psychologically, the same can be heard in their theater songs. Rodgers set Hart's biting, cynical, brutal, and intellectual lyrics to lovely, lyrical, sweet, and simple melodies. His favorite musical device was that most elementary of musical maneuvers learned at the parlor piano: marching up or down the major scale. The verse of their first hit song, "Manhattan" (*The Garrick Gaieties*, 1925), simply climbs the major scale, while the refrain of their second hit, "Mountain Greenery" (from the second *Garrick Gaieties*, 1926), first climbs down then up the same scale. Snuggled comfortably within almost every Rodgers tune is a simple scale. The release of "The Blue Room" (*The Girl Friend*, 1926) climbs the scale, just as its lyric climbs to an inviting blue room upstairs. The third and fourth bars of "Have You Met Miss Jones?" and the poignant B section of "Spring Is Here" climb the scales as well. "Johnny One Note" (*Babes in Arms*) alternates the major scale with a repetitive single note to tell its musical story of a singer who rejects every note of the scale but one. Even with Oscar Hammerstein, Rodgers stuck to his scales. The verse for "It Might As Well Be Spring" (the movie, *State Fair*, 1945) ascends and descends the major scale in formless vocalizing to convey the singer's listlessness. The booming refrain of "Oklahoma!" (1943) begins with an indispensable orchestral run up the scale. Appropriately enough, Rodgers's last big hit was a hymn to the musical scale itself—"Do Re Mi" (*The Sound of Music*, 1959).

RICHARD RODGERS

Since it was mid-February and the show [*A Connecticut Yankee*] wasn't to open until sometime in May, Larry and I took off for Paris, primarily to convince Russell Bennett, who was then living there, to do the orchestrations for the score. Russell, even at that time among the most creative arrangers in the theatre, probably has the most amazing powers of concentration of anyone I've ever known. When he eventually joined us in London, I remember walking into his flat one morning to discover

Source: Gerald Mast, *Can't Help Singin': The American Musical On Stage and Screen* (Woodstock, N.Y.: The Overlook Press, 1987), 169–70.

Source: Richard Rodgers, *Musical Stages: An Autobiography* (New York: Random House, 1975; repr. by Da Capo Press, 1995), 101, 103.

him working diligently on the score while listening to music blaring from a radio.

Another reason why we went to Paris was to see if we might not have misjudged it the first time we were there. Somehow, this time the French seemed more friendly, or perhaps it was just that we were getting used to the Parisian way of life. What made our stay doubly enjoyable was that we ran into two girls we had known in New York. With Rita Hayden and Ruth Warner, we made a happy foursome taking in all the expected sights—and a few unexpected ones, too.

While we were escorting the girls back to their hotel one night in a taxi, another cab darted out of a side street and missed hitting us by a matter of inches. As our cab came to a halt, one of the girls cried, "Oh, my heart stood still!" No sooner were the words out than Larry casually said, "Say, that would make a great title for a song." I told him that he was a crazy fool to be thinking of song titles at such a time, but I guess I'm a crazy fool too, because I couldn't get the title out of my head. When the cab stopped at the girls' hotel, I took out a little black address book and scribbled the words "My Heart Stood Still."

One morning in my flat I was looking for a telephone number in my address book and came across the words "My Heart Stood Still." Now what the devil could that mean? Then I remembered that night in Paris. It was early and Larry was still asleep, so I simply sat down at the piano and wrote a melody that seemed to express the feeling of one so emotionally moved that his heart has stopped beating. Later, when Larry came in, I grandly announced, "Well, I've set that title to music."

"What title?" Larry asked.

" 'My Heart Stood Still'."

"Say, that's a great title. Where did you get it?"

He had completely forgotten the taxi incident, but after I played the tune for him he finished the lyric in no time at all. In my entire career this is the only time I can recall in which a specific, totally unrelated incident triggered the creation of one of my songs.

More important than its genesis, of course, is the song itself and the way it illustrates a facet of Larry's talent that has often been overlooked. His ability to write cleverly and to come up with unexpected, polysyllabic rhymes was something of a trademark, but he also had the even rarer ability to write with utmost simplicity and deep emotion. Just look at the lyric to "My Heart Stood Still." With the exception of six two-syllable words, every word in the refrain is monosyllabic. But how direct and affecting it all is with, for example, its tender reference to "that unfelt clasp of hand" and its beautifully contrasting conclusion:

> I never lived at all
> Until the thrill
> Of that moment when
> My heart stood still.

With lovely Jessie Matthews singing it in *One Dam Thing After Another* and Edythe Baker playing it on the piano, this song easily turned out to be the hit of the show.

PHILIP FURIA

Yet Hart has equally clever—and natural—rhymes that are barely audible, noticeable only when one looks at the words on the page. Lehman Engel has praised Hart's shrewd rhyming of syllables in "Blue Room" (1926), where "future" not only rhymes audibly with "suit your" but subtly sets up the key word "blue" with its first syllable. One could go even further than Engel does and note how that *oo* spills over into "*room*" itself, just as the first syllable of "*holiday*" quietly sets up a whole sequence of resounding rhymes: "*ball* room," "*small* room," and, curling all the way back in a homonym, "*hall* room."

Some of Hart's rhymes are so unobtrusive that they elude even Engel, who quotes this passage from another *Connecticut Yankee* song, "My Heart Stood Still":

> A house in Iceland
> was my heart's domain.
> I saw your eyes;
> now castles rise in Spain!

and confesses his puzzlement:

> the only line that contains no rhyme is "A house in Iceland." This fact seemed curious to me since Hart was fond of rhyming and the "house" might have been anywhere. *Except*, the idea is: "Was my heart's domain. (It was cold.)" Afterward, Hart concludes the idea: "I saw your eyes;/Now castles rise in Spain!"*

Yet suspecting Hart of *not* rhyming is as dangerous as suspecting Shakespeare of not punning: in the very lines Engel quotes there is a slant rhyme on *Ice*land and *eyes* and *rise*, then, I believe, a faint tie rhyme: *I saw*.

Such unobtrusive rhyming may have prompted Hart to cite "My Heart Stood Still" and its casually colloquial "I took one look at you—

Source: Philip Furia, *The Poets of Tin Pan Alley: A History of America's Great Lyricists* (New York, N.Y.: Oxford University Press, 1990), 108–9.

*Lehman Engel, *Their Words Are Music* (New York: Crown, 1975), 39.

that's all I meant to do" (instead of "I threw the book at you") to defend himself against the charge of overrhyming. Still, in the climactic line of the song—"un*til* the *thrill* of that moment when my heart stood *still*"— he slips in a patented internal rhyme. Hart's struggle to contain rhyme within the limits of conversational speech must have been fueled by a reviewer of *Connecticut Yankee* who invoked the vernacular spirits of Twain and Mencken and cautioned:

> Occasionally the collaborators seemed to remember that they had been identified as modern Savoyards, and this seemed to please the attendant representatives of Gilbert and Sullivan, who were respectively Alexander Woollcott and Frank Sullivan. But if they want my advice, it's "Be yourselves, kiddoes."*

ALEC WILDER

After playing almost all of Richard Rodgers's published songs, I chose for more intensive examination about one hundred and twenty-five, or somewhat less than half of them. This final choice wasn't easy: there is an extraordinary incidence of inventiveness in practically all of Rodgers's songs. So if I've failed to include a deserving song in my analyses, it's undoubtedly because I happened to choose another which is similar in spirit and intent.

Of all the writers whose songs are considered and examined in this book, those of Rodgers show the highest degree of consistent excellence, inventiveness, and sophistication. As well, they bear the mark of the American song, excepting a few pretentious ballads written in the later years of his career with Oscar Hammerstein II.

I have been aware of Rodgers's work since *The Garrick Gaieties* and have remained highly impressed from then till now. But after spending weeks playing his songs, I am more than impressed and respectful: I am astonished.

As in the case of Jerome Kern and Vincent Youmans, all of Rodgers's songs were written for the theater. And they all bear its stamp. They have that elegance, sophistication, and "created" quality which, until the recent influx of non-theater writers writing for the theater, used to distinguish theater songs from pop songs.

Thou Witty, ed. Dorothy Hart (New York: W. W. Norton, 1976), 58.

Source: Alec Wilder, *American Popular Song: The Great Innovators—1900–1950* (New York: Oxford University Press, 1972), 163–64, 174–75.

His distinction stems more from remarkable melodic sensibility and experimentation than from new departures in song structure. Which is not to say that he wasn't capable of doing structurally startling things as in, for example, "Little Girl Blue." But Rodgers achieved his amazing innovations without resorting to more than an unexpected note here and there, completely startling at first hearing, and ever after a part of one's musical memory.

Though he wrote great songs with Oscar Hammerstein II, it is my belief that his greatest melodic invention and pellucid freshness occurred during his years of collaboration with Lorenz Hart. The inventiveness has never ceased. Yet something bordering on musical complacency evidenced itself in his later career. I have always felt that there was an almost feverish demand in Hart's writing which reflected itself in Rodgers's melodies as opposed to the almost too comfortable armchair philosophy in Hammerstein's lyrics.

Rodgers moved out of the song world only long enough to write a ballet, *Ghost Town*, and a television score, *Victory At Sea*, the former orchestrated by Hans Spialek, the latter by Robert Russell Bennett, both of them brilliant creative craftsmen, and the latter a respected composer. And since Rodgers settled for song writing as his métier, so did he consistently grow creatively from his virtually uninterrupted concentration on it.

Legend has it that somewhere amongst the many radio stations of the United States a Rodgers song may be heard at any time, day or night, the year round. Well, I, for one, hope this is so, though how such a state of musical affairs could still be true at the beginning of the seventies I don't know.

As this chapter progresses it will be seen that, though capable of highly sophisticated harmony, Rodgers never became so concerned with it as to cause it to distort melodic flow. It may well be that the delicate balance between melody and harmony may have had much to do with Rodgers's phenomenally high level of writing.

In 1927, in *A Connecticut Yankee*, there were three splendid songs. The first, "My Heart Stood Still," is one of Rodgers's best known. It's a perfect example of his mastery of step-wise writing. He employs it throughout this song with the exception of cadences and pick-up notes.

Only in the verse, another great one, does he make marked use of unusual harmony. Without disturbing the melodic line, he shifts, in the second measure, to G-flat major from A flat in the first. In the third and fourth measures he repeats this, but moves farther away in the last quarter note of the measure, leading to *a* flat in the sixth measure, supported by an F-flat major chord; then in the seventh measure he works back to *a* flat through B-flat minor and E-flat-dominant-seventh chords. One assumes he will repeat these measures but, instead, he moves from A flat to C major, to a suspended G-dominant seventh, to a G-dominant seventh, to E-flat major. And even more.

It is a verse replete with harmonic invention but only slight melodic chances, such as that in which the harmony moves from A flat to C major.

Rodgers's increasing flair for unusual releases appears in this song. The repetition of the nineteenth measure in measures twenty-one and twenty-three is very effective and very courageous. My impulse would have been to find different notes each time, particularly as there is no rhyme to go with the first repetition.

ALLEN FORTE

"My Heart Stood Still" was the hit song of *One Dam Thing after Another*, which opened at the London Pavilion, May 20, 1927, and ran for 237 performances. The song was also used later that year in *A Connecticut Yankee*, where it came to the attention of American audiences. Rodgers was especially fond of this song, as the many references to it in his autobiography, *Musical Stages*, indicate.

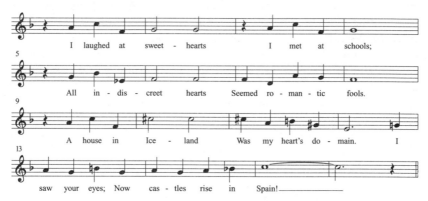

Ex. 1: "My Heart Stood Still," verse

Let us begin with the verse of "My Heart Stood Still," with its ingenious lyric by Lorenz Hart, only the "He" version of which is reproduced in example 1.* From the standpoint of harmony, which includes consideration of the individual chords as well as the unusual harmonic

---

Source: Allen Forte, *The American Popular Ballad of the Golden Era 1924–1950* (Princeton, N.J.: Princeton University Press, 1995), 182–88.

*Rodgers remarks that Hart could write "with utmost simplicity and deep emotion" and cites the lyrics of "My Heart Stood Still" as an instance. He point out that "with the exception of six two-syllable words, every word in the refrain is monosyllabic." Rodgers, *Musical Stages: An Autobiography* (New York: Random House, 1975; repr. by Da Capo Press, 1995), 103.

progression, the verse of "My Heart Stood Still" lies well within the boundaries of the later American popular song tradition. Moreover, the verse has "experimental" features that are often found in the bridges of ballads and that typify Rodgers's penchant for innovation. Foremost among these experimental features is the harmonic design, which involves two symmetric bass motions around the tonic F: the first is the stepwise descent to D♭ in bar 6, which supports the nadir pitch (+1) f¹, and the second is the abrupt leap up to A in bar 10 to support the apex c#², which completes the outline of a large-scale augmented triad: F (bar 1)—D♭ (bar 6)—F (bar 9)—A (bar 10). This symmetric motion about the tonic key F supports the lyric's progression from an expression of the lover's despondency and cynicism (the descent to D♭) to one of burgeoning hope (the upward leap to A).

The A-major key (III#) that accompanies the bass arrival on A at bar 10 stays for exactly two bars, dropping abruptly down to dominant note C at bar 12, whose harmony controls the melodic motion until the end of the verse in bar 16.

In considering any verse in the popular ballad idiom one naturally asks the question, What does its music have to do with that of the refrain, if anything? Often the answer is, "A great deal, but not in an obvious way." Rather, the well-composed verse will suggest features—especially melodic features—of the forthcoming refrain, sometimes in obscure ways, other times in more straightforward fashion. The verse of "My Heart Stood Still" contains instances of each.

Let us consider, first, the piano accompaniment at the end of the verse, bars 15–16: g²-e² and c²-a¹. These two descending minor thirds, a major third apart, are not simply isolated decorations, "fillers" that occupy the bar before the singer begins the refrain; they are two thirds in a cascade of three. As can be seen in example 2, the third descending minor third appears as the boundary notes f¹-d¹ of the first three words of the refrain: "I took one." This third lies a major third lower than those at the end of the verse and occupies the same duration, but it incorporates a passing tone to accommodate the lyric and is thus somewhat concealed.

Ex. 2: "My Heart Stood Still," chorus

But that is not the end of the chain of thirds (example 2): the filled-in thirds create an ascending pattern that occupies the entire first phrase. The pattern changes direction beginning with bar 5 and ends in bar 6 ("heart stood"). This time the "yearning" minor third of the long ascending succession achieves momentary resolution as it descends by step to c^1 on "still," a most affective text-music correspondence that must have touched millions of listeners over the years. . . .

In all these ways the verse prepares the refrain, and, if sung after the refrain, as is often the case in the popular idiom, the motivic connections of the two parts of the song become even more cogent. I have dealt with these connections in some detail here because "My Heart Stood Still" offers fertile musical substance for such discussion and because, in general, the contributions the verse frequently makes to the design of the song are neglected more often than not.

In contrast to the verse, the famous melody of chorus 1 of the refrain, with its virtual absence of emphasized chromatics, still seems to echo the operetta tradition. One striking feature, however, does clearly identify the opening of the song as representative of the "modern" popular ballad: the added sixth.* In "My Heart Stood Still" this first appears in the refrain as d_1 in the initial descending minor third f^1-d^1, discussed previously in connection with the verse. But its most prominent manifestation is at the end of the first period, in bars 5–7, where it is part of the descending arpeggiation and resolves to scale degree 5, the cadential motion that articulates the lyric "stood still."

Now for a closer look at the design of the refrain of "My Heart Stood Still." As it begins, we hear the series of descending thirds, one to each bar, that forms the regular ascending stepwise pattern. In the accompanying parts, elegant chromatic detail supports this diatonic progression as it ascends to its goal, c^2, the primary tone of the song and the beginning of the second phrase of the first period. Particularly arresting is the setting of d^1 in bar 1, certainly the most salient decorative note in the song, together with its octave image d^2 (the apex pitch). This consists of the descending chromatic passing notes $g^\sharp$ and b, which briefly enhance the affect of scale degree 6 in its first melodic appearance in the refrain. Of the remaining two chromatic notes in the first period, passing tones $c^\sharp$ and $d^\sharp$, the former decorates d^1 twice in the inner voice (in bar 3: "I" and in bar 5: "my"), emphasizing both the inner rhyme and the key role of scale degree 6 in this song.

Ex. 3: "My Heart Stood Still," chorus

---

*Although the added sixth occurs in the operetta music, it does not have the structural importance that accrues to it in the American popular song idiom, but rather serves in a decorative capacity.

In rhapsodic arialike fashion the melody of the bridge (example 3) proceeds from nadir pitch c^1 ("though") to apex d^2, which resolves immediately to c^2 ("spoken"), the primary tone of the song and the octave image of the nadir pitch. This motion occurs within the "deepened" harmonic context of the parallel minor key, F minor, the tonic triad of which incorporates the added sixth, the sentient decorative note from chorus 1. . . .

Because of its key role as mode identifier, $A^\flat$, the third of the prevailing F minor key, is particularly salient in the bridge. In specific pitch forms it also occurs at crucial points in the melody. Thus at bar 19, $a^{\flat 1}$ sets "tell," supported by the dominant C-major triad, while two measures further along (bar 21), the half-diminished seventh chord on bass d intensifies $ab1$ forging a musical and semantic link between the unrhymed words, "tell" and "clasp." But the final appearance of $a^{\flat 1}$, in bar 23 ("well"), is again accompanied by the dominant harmony as was "tell" in bar 19, this time linking two rhyming sounds, "tell" and "well." Occurring as it does in this way, just at the end of the bridge, it is possible to regard $a^{\flat 1}$ as an instance of a blue third, but I am reluctant to do so, given the other stylistic features of the song, especially the virtual absence of syncopation and the more complex harmonies found, for example, in the songs Gershwin was writing at nearly the same time. That songwriter's "How Long Has This Been Going On?" (cut from *Funny Face*, which opened just five days before *A Connecticut Yankee*, on November 22, 1927) comes to mind. In the context of "My Heart Stood Still" the minor third fulfills its time-tested role: by invoking a closely related yet far different sonorous domain, it provides expressive contrast to its counterpart, the major third, A-natural.

Ex. 4: "My Heart Stood Still," chorus

The melody of chorus 2 begins like that of chorus 1, with an ascent to a^1 in bar 27 ("Until") but then breaks off with a leap to the apex pitch d^2 ("thrill"). In the most striking way, this special note does not resolve immediately to primary tone c^2 but, as shown in example 4, descends through an arpeggiated G-minor triad (II) until it finds its resolution on nadir pitch c^1 ("heart") at bar 30. This is a striking instance of a prolonged dissonance, whose endpoints set keywords in the lyric and whose pitch components are also of special significance in the song: the melodic coordinates, apex d^2 and nadir c^1.

To sum up, Rodgers's song "My Heart Stood Still," with its elegant deployment of special notes in the melody and its trenchant harmonies, is one of the classic ballads in the popular idiom and one that occupies an interesting chronological position in the decades with which this book is concerned, for it occurs at what might be regarded as the crux—the year 1927, in which the full efflorescence of the American popular ballad began in earnest.

From *Letters to Dorothy, 1926–1937* and *A Personal Book*

In her Foreword to *Letters to Dorothy, 1926–1937* Dorothy Rodgers (1909–1987) reports on the circumstances of her initial meeting with her future husband when she was two months old and Dick seven years old; she also relates her more vivid memories of their five-year courtship that began sixteen years later. Dorothy attributes her husband's success to "tremendous talent, training, and extraordinary self-discipline," and expresses her love for the "wisdom, judgment, compassion, sensitivity, and most of all, the strength" of the private man to whom she was married for nearly fifty years (1930–1979).

Shortly before Rodgers's death Dorothy published her memoirs, *A Personal Book*. In the selection reprinted here she contrasts the professionalism, diligent, and purposeful work habits of Rodgers with the brilliant and witty but cavalier and careless Hart, discloses her resentment at being excluded from rehearsals, and recalls those memorable moments when she was asked to react to a new Rodgers song. The excerpt describes the "lovable" and "difficult" aspects of Hart's personality and actions, acknowledges her awareness of Hart's homosexuality, voices her assessment that Hart was "a deeply unhappy and lonely man," and concludes with an account of Hart's decline and death.

DOROTHY RODGERS

Re-reading Dick's letters after so many years was nostalgic. Reliving the years we went out together reminded me of how much lifestyles have changed since those innocent days.

Source: Dorothy Rodgers, "Foreword" to *Richard Rodgers: Letters to Dorothy, 1926–1937*, William W. Appleton, ed. (New York: New York Public Library, 1988), ix–xiii.

At the time of our first meeting in 1909, the difference in our ages precluded dating—Dick was a handsome seven year old, and I a blonde baby of two months with no hair. The meeting came about because my five-year-old brother, Ben, was recovering from typhoid fever under the care of Dick's father, Dr. William A. Rodgers. Dr. Rodgers had brought his two sons, Mortimer and Richard, to play with the young patient. The Rodgerses were friends of my parents and even our grandparents had been friends.

Ben and Dick saw each other sporadically over the years, but I became more aware of Dick when I was sixteen. It was 1925; Dick was twenty-three and a great deal of excitement had been generated in the theatre world by the arrival of a fresh, irreverent revue with a bright score by Rodgers and Hart. It was playing at the Garrick Theatre. The notices were great, and *The Garrick Gaieties* launched the careers of Rodgers and Hart. Having known Dick for so many years, we were delighted with his success, and my parents took me to see *Dearest Enemy* (perhaps to make up for my having missed seeing the first *Garrick Gaieties*). *Dearest Enemy* was the second successful show with a score by Rodgers and Hart and the plot was based on an episode that took place during the American Revolution. We sat in the first row and Dick, who was conducting, turned around and gave me a warm greeting. I think it was at that moment I realized he was a pretty attractive fellow.

About a year later, my parents and I were returning home on the S.S. *Majestic* after a summer abroad and Dick and Larry happened to be on board, homeward-bound after having written the score for *Lido Lady*, a show produced in London in December of 1926. Dick and I had a marvelous time on shipboard. We spent far more time together than we could have in a month of dating, and I was completely charmed by his delicious, quick wit and his enthusiasm about life in general.

But in September of 1926, with my facing the prospect of four years at Wellesley with no possibility of having the kind of time Dick and I had enjoyed on the *Majestic*, it was not surprising that college turned out to be a serious disappointment. I majored in getting to New York as often as possible to see Dick and making do with his letters in between dates. After a year and a half, I decided to leave Wellesley, thereby qualifying for membership in what would become two generations of the college drop-out club. Dick had left Columbia after he had accomplished his mission of writing the music for two Columbia Varsity shows. (He then went to The Institute of Musical Art, now known as The Juilliard School, to learn the discipline of musical composition.) Years later our two daughters followed the examples set by their parents and left Wellesley and Smith to get married.

Dick's letters in those days were full of buoyant optimism—as well as anxieties. He accepted every job that came his way if it had anything to do with the musical theatre. Most of the shows were amateur, and he wasn't paid anything until *The Garrick Gaieties*, but he learned important things from every show he worked on.

Dick's tremendous talent, training, and extraordinary self-discipline resulted in melodies that captivated a worldwide public. But now, sixty years later, I realize that happy as I was to share the fruits of his talents with millions, it was the private man I loved. I loved his wisdom, judgment, compassion, sensitivity, and, most of all, the strength that sustained him—and me—during the bad times. I had never known anyone like him and there was never a boring moment in his company. It wasn't easy for me to accept the fact that I wasn't the most important thing in Dick's life. His work was. I was, I think, the most important person in his life, but his work was, quite simply, his life.

Most of Dick's letters to me were written between 1926 and 1937, during pre-Broadway tours—out-of-town tryouts. The excerpts that have been chosen are concerned with his professional life, and the photographs that accompany them relate to the same period. They include informal pictures that are personal as well as professional. The letters to me are basically personal, but in these excerpts we have omitted many of the references to family problems, finances, illness, and other everyday matters. I hope the selections will create a feeling of the life and times of this golden period in the Broadway musical theatre. After our marriage in 1930, there were many times when we were separated because Dick was working on shows in New York or London—and an occasional film. In those days of early talking pictures, most of the work was done in the studios in California. After our two daughters were born, Mary in 1931 and Linda in 1935, I would divide my time between New York and wherever Dick's work took him. Sometime around 1936 or 1937, our finances took an upward turn and daily long-distance calls replaced the letters. Dates between the letters became further apart as our separations became less frequent.

This book was conceived and edited by my friend William W. Appleton, who has chosen the excerpts and written explanatory notes to bridge the gaps in time. (Dick frequently dated the letters with a casual "Tuesday, 4 A.M." and Bill has done a brilliant job researching the actual dates by following clues which give the names of people with whom Dick was working on a particular show.) Bill has, I feel, given the reader a glimpse of the Broadway musical theatre in the twenties and early thirties, and of my husband's observations on the exhilarating but often exasperating experience of putting together a musical.

I know my husband would have been as pleased with the book as I am. To have it published by The New York Public Library crowns the effort and does honor to Dick for which I am deeply grateful.

Dorothy Rodgers
New York, July 1988

*   *   *

At any rate, after what seemed an interminable time Dick was on his way home [October 1930]; I felt better—the baby was due in about ten weeks, and Dick and Larry had to go to work on the score and lyrics for *America's Sweetheart*. The boys worked in our apartment—and always in the daytime. Dick likes mornings best for work, and he has never, thank God, felt inspired to write in the middle of the night. He loves writing music more than anything in the world, and he has always been overwhelmingly grateful for being able to do what he loves best. In his work, he is the complete "pro." He works without temperament, without demands, without special trappings. He lets himself off nothing, makes no excuses, gives himself no quarter, is unsparing in his efforts. (Outside of work he's a full-fledged sybarite who has always been spoiled. First by his parents, then by me—and by the people who have worked for him or with him. From them he commands a kind of love and loyalty that stem, I think, from an awareness that he is a kind of living legend.)

Larry, on the other hand, hated working. He had to be caught or trapped or tricked—practically locked up in a room with Dick before he would start. Even then Dick would have to write the tune first to get him going. The boys worked fast, and it seldom took more than four to six weeks to complete a score. Larry was a brilliant but impatient craftsman: not for him the fine polishing—unless Dick insisted on it, and then Larry would make the changes without any fuss or resentment.

After the score was finished, the routine of rehearsals kept Dick busy day and night. I found myself jealous—not of the beautiful girls in the show, but of the time I was shut out of his life. Dick never wanted me to go to rehearsals because he felt that it would be awkward and embarrassing to have a wife—or *anybody* who wasn't actively connected with the show—present. I understood his point of view, but I resented it at the same time. Probably it was the night rehearsals that bothered me the most. Certainly if he had been a lawyer, a businessman or a doctor, I wouldn't have expected to hang around his office, but the theatre was so fascinating that, like most people, I wanted to be a part of it. Besides, I disliked entertaining or going out without him as though I didn't have a husband.

I missed his not working at home. Even though I never stayed in the room with him while he was working, I always knew he was there, and I loved it. I had learned from our London days to keep out of sight until I was invited in to hear the finished song. Dick hates the feeling that anyone is listening to him while he's working, and I have always pretended I couldn't hear even when the lovely sounds came right

Source: Dorothy Rodgers, *A Personal Book* (New York: Harper & Row, 1977), 90–92, 110–17.

through the walls. (Once, when he was working in a living room with no doors, a maid who loved his music kept darting her head around the doorway, much to Dick's irritation. At last she succeeded in catching his eye and, nodding happily, she announced, "I am listening.")

The moment when Dick called me in to hear a song was always terrific. He'd whistle the tune and play the accompaniment, and if Larry was there, he'd sing the lyrics. If not, I'd stand in back of Dick and read the scrawled lyrics that had been propped up on the piano, while Dick played. It has never been possible for me to form a judgment on first hearing, so Dick would play the song several times. Trying to listen to both the tune and the lyrics, and knowing that Dick was eager for my reaction, added to the tension of the moment. It just happened that I was a big Rodgers and Hart fan, and I almost always liked what I heard. Usually it was merely a question of how much. I've never been any good at acting, so Dick always knows how I feel by the expression on my face and the tone of my voice, even more than by what I say. When I really love a song, my eyes get teary for the sheer beauty of the work; when *Dick* is excited by something he has just finished, the hair on his forearms stands on end and his skin is covered with goose bumps. On the rare occasions when I don't like something, I'm dead: my phony enthusiasm never fools Dick. I don't feel qualified to give a negative opinion because I don't trust my non-professional judgment. After all, not only am I not a trained musician, but my parents had always told me I was tone-deaf—a fact that Dick both denied and disproved on one of our first dates, when he took me to see a musical called *Queen High* and I was able to force myself to remember every song in the score. . . .

Because Larry had lived with us in London, I knew that there could be problems. [Ed. During the creation of *Ever Green* Hart occupied the spacious top floor of 11 York Terrace. In March 1930 Hart had joined the newlyweds at this London residence about two weeks after their European honeymoon.] "Lovable" and "difficult" are the two words that come to mind when I think of him. And I think of him often—not only because his work still lives although he died more than thirty years ago, but because I loved him. During the three months he shared the Linden Drive house with us, his genuine sweetness and good humor far outweighed the irritations. But there were irritations. For example, since we wouldn't let him pay rent, he insisted on doing his part by buying the liquor—and tending bar. This proved to be something less than a blessing because when we had guests for dinner, Larry would disappear into the pantry, shake up a batch of cocktails and invite the cook to help him sample them. This could—and often did—have an interesting effect on the dinner.

Although Larry quite often had dinner with us, he always took off afterward to be with his cronies. Where he went, we seldom knew. Our friends, the writers and directors with whom Dick and Larry worked, held little interest for him socially. Most of his friends were chorus boys or women much older than he. I never knew him to have a romantic relationship with a woman, and although I don't think the public was aware of Larry's sexual preferences because the press didn't comment on such things in those days, it was pretty generally accepted by all who knew him that he was a homosexual. I know, too, that Mrs. Hart, Larry's adorable, innocent mother, went to her grave longing for the grandchildren she fully expected Larry to give her.

Fortunately, Larry didn't know how to drive a car—a fact which undoubtedly added years to his life because he was forced to depend on taxis or friends to bring him home. Once Dick and I were awakened at about three in the morning by loud voices and lights that had been turned on in the garden. As Dick opened our bedroom door to investigate, my mother's door opened and at the same time we heard Mary wailing. The whole household had been jarred awake! Dick went downstairs and followed laughter into the pantry, where he was just in time to stop Larry from putting Worcestershire Sauce into the Martinis he was making. His guests were Joan Marsh, a beautiful Wampus Baby Star (who was known in the trade as "Two-Gun" Marsh because of her remarkable breasts), and her date, Jack Oakie, neither of whom had any idea there was anyone besides Larry living in the house. They left quickly and quietly, and Larry—feeling terrible about having disturbed everybody—disappeared for two days. While in hiding, however, he managed to send me a huge basket of orchids as an apology.

Shortly before our lease on 724 North Linden Drive was up, Larry decided to move into a house of his own. [Ed. Larry and Rodgers's family, including Mary (then only ten months old) and Dorothy's recently widowed mother, May Feiner, had moved to their North Linden Hollywood home in November 1931.] Living with us cramped his style a lot, and he wanted to be free to entertain his own friends in his own way. The house he rented was historically famous. Built around 1920 by Norman Kerry, a well-known actor, it was constructed like a ship. Interior walls were wood, stained and polished to bring out the natural grain and beauty; joinings were tongue-and-groove, and wooden pegs were used throughout instead of nails. But, rare and beautiful as all this made the house, the reason for its fame was the fact that it had originally stood downtown on Wilshire Boulevard and had been moved to its Beverly Hills site—rolled majestically up the boulevard, a three-day process during which a non-stop house party went on inside. (I don't know how the guests coped with the disconnected plumbing—maybe they jumped off to use the facilities in houses along the way, then ran to catch up.)

Although to the casual acquaintance Larry seemed to be a party boy, I've always felt that he was a deeply unhappy and lonely man. He spent as little time alone as possible because, I suspect, he didn't like his own company or think much of himself. He was convinced that he was unattractive to women because he was so short—barely five feet tall—and he was the first person I ever knew who wore "elevator" shoes. These may have added a couple of inches to his height, but they weighed so much that they made him walk with a clumping noise and a heavy step. Actually, Larry had a handsome head and his upper torso would have been great had it belonged to a man of average height. His shoulders and arms were powerful, and on the rare occasions when he found himself in a brawl, he usually gave as much as he got. He had a charming kind of shy smile, but in repose his expression was usually unhappy. In the midst of a party, he could be seen brooding and sad, his beautiful dark-brown eyes glazed, and his thoughts obviously far, far away.

Larry had no real hobbies and few interests outside of the theatre, but he was the best-read person I've ever known. He was also a shrewd card-player and he loved to gamble, especially in a casino or gambling house. He loved to eat and drink, too, but his favorite kind of amusement was playing practical jokes. These usually took the form of leaving telephone messages in phony names. One night we'd come home to learn that "Mr. T-c-h-a-i-k-o-v-s-k-y" had phoned, the name carefully spelled out by the poor maid who had had the bad luck to answer the phone. Sometimes it was "Mrs. Polly Adler"—the most famous madam of the thirties—or "Eleanor Roosevelt." But his joking became a real problem when Dick would find a message that "Mr. Schulberg" had called and wanted to be called back. Since Dick and Larry were working for Paramount at the time and Ben Schulberg happened to be the head of the studio, it was distinctly possible that he had indeed phoned, but Dick was never quite sure whether he should return the call or not.

Most of Larry's humor was ribald, raucous or scatological, sometimes tasteless, and always funny, but never at anyone's expense. It was also full of brilliant and witty puns. He loved to make jokes, and when he felt he'd made an especially good one, he'd chortle loudly and rub his little hands together with great satisfaction.

Sloppy as he was about his appearance and the state of his clothes— ashes on the jacket, trousers uncreased, tie usually askew and spotted— Larry was always taking baths, going to the barber or having a massage at the Turkish bath where he often went to sweat out a hangover. He smelled of Eau de Cologne, and his unusually heavy beard was powdered—which, of course, called attention to it all the more. He smoked the largest Cuban cigars made and was seldom without one in his mouth. I remember my anguish as a house-proud bride when Larry, concentrating on a lyric he was working on, stood in front of the huge studio window in our living room, a big cigar protruding from his mouth, and burned a six-inch hole in our new curtain. He wasn't even aware of what he had done. Getting off the elevator at our apartment, I always knew when the boys were at work because of the heavy aroma of cigar smoke that permeated the outside hall.

Larry worked only when he had to—that is to say, when Dick was in the room with him. Usually he wrote standing up, using either the piano or a wall as his desk, with his head cocked to one side and the inevitable cigar jutting up at a sharp angle. He wrote on the backs of envelopes or on yellow foolscap, scribbling obliquely across the page with a soft-lead pencil. If he didn't like what he had done, he'd crush the paper into a ball and toss it anywhere.

Possessions didn't appeal to Larry. I never knew him to own anything of value; he never bought a house, a car, or even a typewriter. His attitude toward money was that it was nice to have so that he could spend it. He loved buying presents for people, and they were always the biggest and most expensive he could find. One year, I remember his telling us that he had sent Dick "a little ashtray" for his birthday. We got home to find our front door blocked by a box that must have been three feet high. In it there was an agate dish, about twenty inches in diameter, out of which rose the bronze figure of a nymph. This was the "little ashtray." Larry had ordered it over the phone from Dunhill, and the salesman had assured him it *was* the most expensive ashtray Dunhill carried. His taste in all things visual was as execrable as it was exquisite in anything aural. And yet, as I write this, I am reminded of the tiny seventeenth-century silver creamer that Larry gave me for my twenty-first birthday—an object so beautiful, so simple and pure in design, that it is one of my favorite things.

In all, he was the most generous person I ever met—to charities and especially to friends who were out of work or, for that matter, to anyone who asked him for a loan. And there were plenty of those. In a restaurant, no one could beat him to a check. His few really devoted friends devised all kinds of ingenious ways to protect him from himself and from the many hangers-on who were constantly taking advantage of him. But, for the most part, he was surrounded by a bunch of freeloaders who were his intellectual inferiors.

I never heard of Larry involving himself in politics or causes, but he had his own strong personal sense of justice for which he was willing—quite literally—to fight. During the rehearsals of one of the shows, Larry learned that the dance director had threatened to fire a chorus boy who hadn't accepted the director's invitation to go out with him. Outraged, Larry waited for a work break in the rehearsal and quietly asked the director if what he had heard was true. The director said, "What's it to you?" and Larry, with scarcely a beat, put down the seat next to the aisle where the guy was standing, hauled his five-foot body up onto it and punched the director in the nose. He then calmly stepped down and rubbed his hands briskly up and down against his cheeks.

Anyone who had ever gone to one of his nightly parties had a permanent claim on him. One of his closest friends was a dentist—a very bad dentist, but Larry went to him for years. Just before Dick and I were married, we were all going somewhere in a cab when Larry announced, "A funny thing happened to me this morning. A tooth fell out." Finally, after a great deal of pleading on our part, Larry reluctantly agreed to go to Dick's dentist. Then, feeling terribly guilty about having been disloyal,

Larry invited his friend and erstwhile dentist to take a trip to Europe with him as his guest. (The two of them joined Dick and me in Cannes while we were still on our honeymoon.) Unless someone had done something awful to him, Larry never made unkind cracks, and he was as generous in his praise of other people's work as he was with his money. Free from prejudice of any kind, he was a true liberal.

Sadly, through the years, the lack of discipline and self-control in every aspect of his life made things increasingly difficult—for him and for those who cared about him. His drinking problem had seriously affected both his health and his work—or at least his capacity to work—and he eventually reached a point where a single beer could knock him out. The eyelids would grow heavy, the eyeballs would roll up and—zonk, he'd had it.

Because Larry wanted so much to work on a show with Dick after Dick had written *Oklahoma!* with Oscar Hammerstein, he managed with tremendous effort to go on the wagon for several months. Willy Kron, Larry's good friend and financial advisor, went away with him for short trips and played endless card games to keep him from drinking. When work with Dick and Herb Fields on the 1943 revival of *A Connecticut Yankee* started, in a flashback to his old brilliance Larry wrote one of his wittiest lyrics, "To Keep My Love Alive"; it was to be his last. When the show went to Philadelphia for its tryout period, Herb even shared a room with Larry so that he could keep an eye on him. Still, unfortunately, Larry slipped out one rainy, cold November night and visited as many bars as he could find. He left his topcoat in one of them and caught a heavy cold which grew worse daily. On the night the show opened in New York, Dick and I were sitting in our usual places—in the last row on the center aisle—when I felt someone's hand brush the top of my head. I looked up to see Larry standing in back of me, but when I reached up to pat him on the arm and to thank him for the orchids he had sent me to wear at the opening, his eyes were glassy and he stared at me almost as if he didn't know who I was. He looked terribly ill. And when the performance started, he moved to the top of the aisle, jingling the coins in his pocket and mumbling so loudly that heads turned and people shushed. Finally someone took him by the arm and led him from the theatre. I never saw him again.

The day after the opening, Larry was nowhere to be found, but the following day he returned to Delmonico's Hotel, where he was staying while his apartment was being repainted. Willy Kron called Dick to say that Larry was back and very ill. The diagnosis was pneumonia in both lungs. He was taken to Doctors' Hospital immediately. Penicillin had only just been discovered, but since the supply was limited, its use was restricted to the armed forces. Dick got in touch with Eleanor Roosevelt, who was most helpful and arranged for some of the wonder drug to be released for Larry. Alas, penicillin was so new and so little understood that in the light of what we know now, the amount given to Larry was so small it couldn't have made any difference. Perhaps he was too ill for anything to have saved him. His poor body had taken such a beating in his short life—he was forty-eight—and his resistance was very low. He remained unconscious all the time he was in the hospital, and on the fourth night, just as the lights went out for a wartime practice blackout, he died. (Later when M-G-M made a movie called *Words and Music* about Dick and Larry, they fictionalized another ending for the story because they said no one would believe what really happened. It was too dramatic for Hollywood.)

Chee-Chee, The Castration Musical

In some respects the forgotten *Chee-Chee* marks a crossroads in the career of Rodgers and Hart. In Rodgers's four letters to Dorothy from September 1 to 17, 1928, the first letter written in New York and the others during the Philadelphia tryouts, he spoke proudly about this innovative work: "No matter what happens to us commercially we've accomplished what we've been after for years." Throughout these letters Rodgers conveys a mixture of enthusiasm and trepidation about how the work would be received. On September 7 he wrote that "there are doubts as to its financial future and its reception by the New York press ... but I know we've done something fine at last." On September 12 he wrote that "the show is the best musical thing I've ever seen." In the final letter he emphasized the varied press response and the views of the letter-writing public.

In contemporaneous remarks to the *Philadelphia Public Ledger* Hart mentions the replacement of musical dialogue "with little songs, some of them not a minute long" and the resulting continuity. Nearly fifty years later Rodgers in *Musical Stages* explains further how these song fragments made music "an essential part of the structure of the story rather than an appendage to the action." From the advantage of hindsight he distances himself from his role in the inception of the work and emphasizes his reservations about the project, describing himself as "the lone holdout." Rodgers concedes that the work appealed to his desire for innovation and uniqueness. Nonetheless he concludes that fundamentally *Chee-Chee* was "a musical about castration," an insurmountable obstacle that "no amount of beautiful scenery, theatrical effects, or musical innovations can hide."

Although no future Rodgers and Hart show came close to matching the popular debacle of *Chee-Chee*, the next three years were marked by less artistic daring (e.g., *Spring Is Here*, 1929), a sharp drop in quantity (a total of four shows), and only one unqualified popular success, the London production of *Ever Green* (1930). In 1931 the team moved to Hollywood and would not have a new show on Broadway until the debut of *Jumbo* toward the end of 1935.

Unless otherwise noted the bracketed material in this selection can be attributed to William W. Appleton, who edited the letters. The ellipses mark places omitted from the published letters, where, as Dorothy Rodgers states in her Foreword (see the previous selection), Rodgers refers "to family problems, finances, illness, and other everyday matters."

RICHARD RODGERS

New York,
Sept. 1, 1928

Dearest Dots,
Somehow or other this has managed to be the most hectic and disturbing last week of rehearsal we've ever had;* not that anything in particular has gone wrong, but things have just managed to be terrific in general. . . .

I pulled my usual pre-opening stunt of becoming good and sick a few days ago. I've managed to do that before every opening except *Present Arms* and that was a flop.** So you see where we stand. It wasn't any more than a nasty cold and a bad throat, but when you have [an] orchestra three days in a row and Helen Ford to contend with, everything is a bad handicap. I'm better now, however, only I can't drive to Philly tonight as I planned. Oh well. . . .

I'm afraid to tell you about the orchestra rehearsals because you're liable to get the idea that I'm raving about the show, but honestly, Dot, it all sounds marvelous. I never realized how deeply I'd gone into it from a musical standpoint until I heard the orchestrations, and now I'm a little afraid that I've gone too far. How much of it will they get? And if they do, will they like it? I don't know. You tell me.

Now we're off for Philly and we'll find out to a certain extent what we have. One thing I do know: we'll never be ashamed of it. . . .

Source: Richard Rodgers, *Richard Rodgers: Letters to Dorothy, 1927–1937*, William W. Appleton, ed. (New York: New York Public Library, 1988), 63–67.

Chee-Chee, with a book by Herbert Fields, and produced by Lew Fields, was preparing to open its out-of-town tryout in Philadelphia.

**It ran in New York for 155 performances.

Philadelphia,
Friday, Sept. 7, 1928

Dearest Dot,
I suppose it's pretty bad not to have written you more than one letter before this, but if you only knew! Well, at least you can guess. It's been a matter of getting to bed between five and six every morning and getting up at eleven for rehearsal. But if you don't mind, I won't complain because the object of your labors, as far as I am concerned, is a success.*

I mean that no matter what happens to us commercially we've accomplished what we've been after for years. We've written and produced a good show! The enclosed notice is one of the milder. (I couldn't get duplicates of any of the others and I don't dare send you my original copies as my old man would never forgive me if they were lost.) All the papers but one raved themselves silly and hailed us as pioneers in glowing and enthusiastic terms. The book, lyrics, and score received equal praise, so it would seem that we have managed to produce that difficult thing—a unit.** Dot, it really is swell! There are doubts as to its financial future and its reception by the New York press—certainly Philadelphia is greatly bewildered—but I know we've done something fine at last. Gosh, I wish you could see it!

Helen [Ford] gives the most delightful performance of her life, and the cast generally is fine. The scenery is quite bad in spots and is being done over by Norman Bel Geddes. On the other hand, the costumes are glorious. There is a continuous riot of color and lovely line. The orchestra is brutal. There have been so many complaints about it, that, in response to universal demand, I expect to take the baton myself in a few days and keep it until after the New York opening. . . .

Philadelphia
Sept. 12, 1928

Dearest,
Things are very much the same. It's a question of work and worry with quite a few disagreements with our star, and once in a while a party to vary the monotony.

The show is still the best musical thing I've ever seen, and I'm happy to say it's becoming better and more easily understood with the few changes we've made. Of course, Philly is slightly dumbfounded and isn't

---

*The book was certainly novel. The son of the Grand Eunuch of Peking flees with his wife to avoid becoming his father's successor.

**Ed. See p. 46 for program note regarding integration of music and book.

quite sure how to take it. They stay away in large numbers, but those who come stay till the very end and give every sign of enjoying it. Then, too, business is slowly but surely improving. That's a great sign. . . .

The big news is that I'm conducting and will continue with it until after the New York opening. It seems that Roy [Webb] sort of fell apart on us, and there were so many complaints that something had to be done. Much against Larry's desires, I seem to be the only solution to the problem, so I went in at the Saturday matinee and have been leading since. In spite of the fact that the band is horrible, it's loads of fun, and the score gives me endless opportunities to do things. I can hardly wait to get a good orchestra in New York.

Helen is still a bitch of the first water and is causing us our only trouble. She's so fine in the part however that almost anything is worth it. Just wait, though, till we open in town and I don't have to stand in front of her and conduct. She heard plenty from me yesterday, but that's nothing to what's in store for her.

That there [Ed. sic] mental state remains just as was. I'm so busy, and things are revolving so fast that I have little time for my own affairs. So far as you are concerned, what can I say? I can only repeat that I miss you terribly and that there's a curious void where your voice used to be. I think of you so much and see so many of the things going on through your eyes. You know what I mean? . . .

Dick

Philadelphia,
September 17, '28

Dearest . . .
Me, I'm all right. I've lost a bit of weight in the pit each night, but it doesn't seem to matter. It's awfully hard work, but then I've done so little of late that the change is rather pleasant. You know the way I feel: anything to keep the mind occupied is good.

A new number went in last Friday which bids fair to rival any of the others. It's called, "Dear, Oh Dear," and Helen and [William] Williams sing it in the second scene. We're plugging it along with "Must Love You."

Beezness was swell Saturday night, but looks terrible for tonight again. Well, we expected it, and we got it. If I could have the Philadelphia losses for my income I'd be doing nicely, thank you. Nothing discourages us, on the other hand, and Saturday, with the house full of Jews fresh from their New Year revels, the show was a panic. They seemed to understand everything and most of the numbers stopped the show. The piece has created a riot in the press here, and people write letters praising it and damning it in good round terms.* It's such fun to be a storm center, and the whole thing seems to indicate importance. I'm really surprised at our nerve, not because it's dirty (because it ain't) but because the show is so far away from anything else. You'll see for yourself. Herb says he can't wait for you to get a look at it because he claims you're the only one who really understands him. See?

There was no rehearsal last night, so a bunch of us went out to the country to visit some friends of one of the boys in the cast. I folded up immediately in the pure air and went fast asleep. I'm surprised it didn't poison me. . . .

Please come home. All is forgiven and I miss you so much! I swear I do. How do you feel about that? Your answer to my last cable came. We'll swap others, but I do wish you were around.

Give my love to your Mommer and my Love to you.

Dick

LORENZ HART

As *Chee-Chee* took shape, Larry and Dick tried much harder than ever before to integrate the songs into the story. In fact, there were only six fully realized numbers in the show: "I Must Love You," "Moon of My Delight," "Singing a Love Song," "Better Be Good to Me," "Dear, Oh Dear," and "The Tartar Song." The rest of the music, sometimes no more than four bars, was used only to advance the plot. The production itself was lavishly produced and mounted, with settings and costumes that were as colorful and exotic as the locale.

On August 26, Larry, always the advance man, took a reporter from the *Philadelphia Public Ledger* to one side and told him musical comedies were changing style.

> Forty years ago when Vienna was Vienna, Johann Strauss played the tunes in the Prater that were fiddled all over the world. Ten years later Arthur Sullivan's more intellectually nuanced tunes ruled the musical waves for Britannia. Popular music moves in cycles. . . . The American

---

Chee-Chee's reception in New York was equally mixed. It survived for only thirty-one performances. The score pleased most of the critics, but they found the libretto tedious and distasteful.

Source: Lorenz Hart, *Philadelphia Public Ledger,* August 26, 1928, quoted in Frederick Nolan, *Lorenz Hart: A Poet on Broadway* (New York: Oxford University Press, 1994), 120–21.

production has reached a stereotyped form. What is known as the American musical consists most often of the Cinderella legend thinly diluted, with hot chorus dance specialties and low comedy scenes sanctified by age.

It is time for renaissance. The persistently rhythmic unmelodious foxtrot is becoming a bit tiresome to ears that still love music. The wishy-washy legend of the saccharine and poor little heroine who wins a fairy prince has lost its meaning by constant repetition. The Brothers Gershwin with George Kaufman attempted a brave revolt with *Strike Up the Band*. They were a little ahead of their time but they will try again.

Herbert Field[s], Richard Rodgers, and myself were luckier with *Peggy Ann* when we satirized the Cinderella legend out of countenance. . . . We went a lot further with *Connecticut Yankee* where the conventionalized love story was left out altogether and now in *Chee-Chee* . . . we are doing away with the ordinary idea of the musical comedy dance routines and chorus number stencil. Here we dare to write musical dialog not as opera bouffe with recitative, but with little songs, some of them not a minute long.

This new musical technique of Richard Rodgers insures the continuity of our story. The libretto by Herbert Fields is far from commonplace with a heroine who dares to be a sophisticated and even a naughty little baggage. In decor too we shall attempt no garish overloading of the stage, but we shall decorate our stage with pictures that are refreshing in simple and pristine beauty.

Chee-Chee opened at the Mansfield on September 25, 1928. Despite its simple and pristine beauty, it turned out to be the greatest failure any of them had ever experienced. Although the critical reaction was in the main understanding, even supportive, the public's view coincided with that of critic St. John Ervine of London's *Observer*, guest critic for the *New York World*, who headlined his review NASTY! NASTY! and went on to say, "I did not believe any act could possibly be duller than the first— until I saw the second."

For the first time Rodgers and Hart experienced the bitter truth of impresario Oscar Hammerstein's dictum about bad plays. The public stayed away in droves, and *Chee-Chee* died after thirty-one performances. With it died the "family." Although they would inevitably continue to meet in the small world of the theatre, Rodgers and Hart, Lew Fields, Helen Ford, Herb Fields, Alexander Leftwich, and Roy Webb never worked together as a team again.

* * *

One afternoon in the spring of 1928 I was working at the piano at home when suddenly my grandfather appeared in the doorway and said, "Richard, I don't feel well." I got him to his bedroom and phoned down to my father's office on the first floor of the apartment house we lived in. Pop was in our apartment within minutes, and his immediate diagnosis was that surgery was imperative. Grandpa wasn't strong enough to be moved to a hospital, so we had to turn his bedroom into an operating room. But the operation wasn't successful and a week later he died. It hit me terribly hard. I adored the old man, as did my brother and my parents. I knew he had no faith in the theatre as a career, but his hope that I would go into a more conventional line of work was motivated only by his deep concern for what he felt was best for me. When I did achieve a measure of success, he never hesitated to tell me how proud he was of me and of what I'd accomplished.

After Grandpa's death I felt that I had to get away alone for a while, so I took a brief trip to Colorado Springs. While there, I began getting frantic telephone calls from Larry and Herb about a new idea they had for a musical. It was to be based on a novel called *The Son of the Grand Eunuch*, and they were both convinced that it had the makings of a sensational musical. Sensational was right. I bought the book, read it, and thought they were both crazy. The story was about a young man in ancient China who did everything he could to avoid being castrated, a prerequisite for inheriting his father's exalted title. This didn't strike me as a theatrically adaptable subject for the musical stage, but Larry and Herb had already talked Lew Fields into producing it, and I found myself in the uncomfortable position of being the lone holdout.

When I returned to New York, we continued thrashing the matter around until I finally agreed to go along. They were all so sure of themselves that I didn't want to be the one to torpedo a project they all believed in so deeply. One factor that helped influence me was that while I found the story distasteful, I had to admit that it was a daring departure from the average Broadway musical-comedy subject. Maybe we could shock people into liking it. *Present Arms* had turned out to be a fair success, but there was nothing out of the ordinary about its theme and I certainly didn't relish hearing people compare it to *Hit the Deck*. With *Chee-Chee*, which was the name of our castration musical, there surely wouldn't be any danger of its being compared to anything. Furthermore, from a strictly creative standpoint it offered the challenge of introducing an entirely new concept within the framework of musical theatre.

Larry and I had long been firm believers in the close unity of song and

Source: Richard Rodgers, *Musical Stages: An Autobiography* (New York: Random House, 1975; repr. by Da Capo Press, 1995) 117–19.

story, but we were not always in a position to put our theories into practice. *Chee-Chee* gave us that chance. To avoid the eternal problem of the story coming to a halt as the songs take over, we decided to use a number of short pieces of from four to sixteen bars each, with no more than six songs of traditional form and length in the entire score. In this way the music would be an essential part of the structure of the story rather than an appendage to the action. The concept was so unusual, in fact, that we even called attention to it with the following notice in the program:

> NOTE: The musical numbers, some of them very short, are so interwoven with the story that it would be confusing for the audience to peruse a complete list.

Chee-Chee also brought up a specific problem about the actual writing of the score. With the exception of *Dearest Enemy* and about three quarters of *A Connecticut Yankee*, all our other previous musicals had had modern settings, mostly in or around New York City. For *Chee-Chee*, my job was to compose music for a story set in ancient China. Obviously it would have been inappropriate for me to write typically "American" music, but equally obviously, even if I could have written "Chinese" music, Broadway audiences would have found it unattractive—to say nothing of the impossibility of Larry's finding the proper words to go with it. The only solution was to compose my own kind of music but with an Oriental inflection, reproducing a style rather than creating a faithful imitation. Frequently composers try to reproduce the musical sound of a specific age or locale, often with some success, but I think it's a mistake. It leaves the writer wide open to comparison—usually unfavorable—with the real thing, and at best only reveals re-creative, rather than creative, skills.

One special pleasure I derived in composing the score for *Chee-Chee* was a musical joke that I used toward the end of the second act. As the son of the Grand Eunuch was being led off for his emasculation operation, he was accompanied by a triumphal march, in the middle of which I inserted several bars of Tchaikovsky's *Nutcracker Suite*. I found it gratifying that at almost every performance there were two or three individuals with ears musically sharp enough to appreciate the joke.

But no matter what we did to *Chee-Chee* it was still a musical about castration, and you simply can't get an audience at a musical comedy to feel comfortable with such a theme. If I learned anything from this experience, it's that if there's a basic problem with a show—and *Chee-Chee*'s was as basic as you can get—no amount of beautiful scenery, theatrical effects or musical innovations can hide it. We opened in New York late in September 1928 and were greeted by a barrage of critically ripened fruit, though there were a few posies tossed at the music and the imaginative way it melded into the story. The production remained on Broadway for exactly thirty-one performances, and achieved the distinction of having the shortest run of any musical I've ever written.

Including *Chee-Chee*, I had composed twelve theatre scores in four years—ten in New York and two in London. Since successes outweighed failures by about three to one, I was able to be somewhat philosophical about my latest disaster. I had developed enough self-confidence in a field notably lacking in this quality to realize that failures are an inevitable part of the game, and that they need not prove fatal if you learn from your mistakes. If you don't, you have no business being in the theatre—and you won't be for long.

Cover Story: "The Boys from Columbia"

In 1925 George Gershwin gained the distinction as the first composer, and first American, to make the cover of *Time* magazine, then only two years in existence. By September 1938 Gershwin had been dead a little over a year. From their return to Broadway in 1935 with *Jumbo* until their final show seven years later, *By Jupiter*, the only consistent challenger to Rodgers and Hart was Cole Porter (who never did get his picture on the cover of *Time*). Although the Depression had so debilitated Broadway that the number of shows had ground to a virtual halt in 1937 and 1938, Rodgers and Hart had enjoyed an impressive run of consecutive hits, including *On Your Toes* in 1936, *Babes in Arms* and *I'd Rather Be Right* in 1937, and *I Married an Angel* earlier in 1938. "The Boys from Columbia" naturally focuses on *The Boys from Syracuse*, then on the eve of its November opening—it even includes previously unpublished lyric samples from three songs. In its sketch of Rodgers and Hart's career from *Garrick Gaieties* through the recent Hollywood years, *Time* emphasizes the team's originality and innovation and concludes that "nobody ever fused words and music more effectively than Rodgers & Hart." The profile also introduces the Credo that Rodgers would espouse for the rest of his career: "The one possible formula was: *Don't have a formula*; the one rule for success: *Don't follow it up*."

Time misspoke when it reported that George Abbott had "pitched out every line of Shakespeare's dialogue, because he likes his own better." Abbott did, in fact, retain several lines from Shakespeare, most famously near the end of the evening when the Seeress proclaims that "the venom clamours of a jealous woman poisons more deadly than a mad dog's tooth." Rodgers writes in *Musical Stages* (p. 191) that "Lest anyone unfamiliar with the classics accept this as a sentence he had thought up all by himself, George had Jimmy Savo follow it by sticking his head out from the wings and proudly announcing to the audience: 'Shakespeare!'"

The *Time* cover is reproduced on page 9.

TIME MAGAZINE

A thousand years hence, when historians gravely chronicle the 20th Century U. S. theatre, diving now & then into their glossaries for light on "strip-tease" or "meat show," they may wonder why, for a time, the theatre harped on human frailties—Follies, Vanities, Scandals—and then suddenly ceased to harp. They may perhaps write learned, ingenious essays describing the rise and fall of the morality play on Broadway, never dreaming that what they chronicled was the rise and fall of the musical show.

Post-War Broadway blazed with such names-in-lights as Ziegfeld, George White, Dillingham, Hammerstein, Carroll. Of a warm summer night buyers from the cornbelt flocked with their women to the New Amsterdam roof; winter after winter the Music Box ground out its medley of tunes. It was an age of Ann Pennington and Marilyn Miller, Jerome Kern and Vincent Youmans, "When It's Moonlight in Ka-lu-a," "Rose-Marie, I Love You." In the season 1924–1925, to pick a sample year, there were 46 musical shows on Broadway.

Then the radio went on the air and the cinemusical on the screen. Tastes changed, repetition cloyed, purses flattened. Gradually the number of musicomedies on Broadway dwindled. Last year there were six.

Of those six, the two biggest hits carried the names of Richard Rodgers and Lorenz Hart. Indeed, during the past three years they have continuously—except for one lone week—had a smash hit on Broadway. Last week, their *I Married An Angel*, entering its fifth month, grossed over $28,681—a new high—and averaged 80 standees a performance. This week, road-show rehearsals will start on *I'd Rather Be Right* after its summer holiday. A week or two hence rehearsals will start on a third Rodgers & Hart show, *The Boys from Syracuse*, which they are doing with Playwright-Producer George Abbott. Their tunes are whistled in the street, clunked out by hurdy-gurdies on the curb. The press, fumbling for a phrase to describe them, invariably ends with one that is glib but nevertheless significant: the U. S. Gilbert & Sullivan.

Their services to musicomedy can be exaggerated, but hardly their success. That success rests on a commercial instinct that most of their rivals have apparently ignored. As Rodgers & Hart see it, what was killing musicomedy was its sameness, its tameness, its eternal rhyming of June with moon. They decided it was not enough just to be good at the job; they had to be constantly different also. The one possible formula was: *Don't have a formula*; the one rule for success: *Don't follow it up*. Their last five shows explain what they mean. *Jumbo* was circus set to music, *On Your Toes* a spoof at ballet, *Babes in Arms* about kids in a depression world, *I'd Rather Be Right* a rubdown of F.D.R., *I Married An Angel* a pure extravaganza that started in Heaven and ended in Radio City.

Source: "The Boys from Columbia," *Time* (September 26, 1938), 35–39.

Three Men on a Farce

It follows that their new show, opening in November, will be another leap in a new direction: this time, over 300 years backward. On a train going to Atlantic City they hit on the idea of putting Shakespeare to music, decided to swipe his *Comedy of Errors*, the farce about the two sets of twin brothers and their women who couldn't tell them apart, which Shakespeare himself swiped form the *Menaechmi* of Plautus (who in turn swiped it from parties unknown). They are leaving the plot as they found it—"If it's good enough for Shakespeare, it's good enough for us"; but they have changed the title to *The Boys from Syracuse*. George Abbott, who has written the book, has pitched out every line of Shakespeare's dialogue, because he likes his own better.

The raw, rowdy tale, as filled with Abbott wisecracks as an amusement park with lights, gives Rodgers plenty of chance for pedal in his tunes, Hart plenty of chance for pepper in his rhymes. The score runs the whole anachronistic gamut from waltzes to hotcha; the lyrics vary from the smart patter of a prison song, listing the advantages of jail:

> You're privileged to miss a row
> Of tragedies by Sophocles
> And diatribes by Cicero

to the sly patter of a He and She song:

> He told her this, on the very day he met her;
> She said the wish is the father to the sport;
> He built a house, in the nursery he set her;
> She helped the stork make an annual report;

to the forthright bang of:

> I want to go back to Syracuse:
> Wives don't get divorces there,
> The men are strong as horses there.

Cast for the roles of the Dromio twins are Comedians Jimmy Savo (*Almanac Parade*) and Hart's brother Teddy (*Three Men on a Horse, Room Service*), two shrimps who look uncommonly alike. (Savo, 5 ft. 4 in., at present weighs 180 pounds, and all through October must diet as well as rehearse.) *The Boys from Syracuse* will be the first Rodgers & Hart show in which Teddy Hart has appeared. Said Brother Larry: "He had to be a star, and this is the first star part that ever fit him." *The Boys from Syracuse* will be the second Rodgers & Hart show in which Rodgers & Hart have an investment; the other was *I'd Rather Be Right*.

The Boys from Syracuse is the 25th show that Rodgers & Hart have worked on together. Since they first met in 1919, when Hart was 23 and just out of Columbia, and Rodgers 16 and just going in, they have never done a stick of work apart. They met, and that decided it. Nor was there any stern parent storming about the house, or lean wolf hanging round the door, to menace their plans. "For the sake of color," says Rodgers, "I should have been a singing waiter at Nigger Mike's. Unfortunately, I was a doctor's son and very well-fed as a kid." Similarly well-fed, Hart was the son of a promoter.

Their first musicomedy was the Columbia Varsity Show of 1920 written in Rodgers's freshman year. Soon after Rodgers quit Columbia, and for five years the two of them plugged along, getting a few shots at Broadway, but no lucky ones. Then in 1925 the Theatre Guild, wanting some tapestries for its new theatre and a chance to give its understudies a workout, decided to put on an informal little revue, engaged Rodgers to write the music. Hart came in on the lyrics. The show, under the title of the *Garrick Gaities*, opened May 17, 1925, ran for 211 performances. People hummed "Sentimental Me" and "Manhattan," music publishers enthusiastically bought from Rodgers & Hart the very songs they had sniffed at a year before, and Broadway producers yelled for shows.

Words & Music

Good taste and an unquenchably romantic point of view are the common denominators of most of the 1,000 songs Rodgers & Hart have written together. Larry Hart did not originate sophisticated lyrics. William Schwenk Gilbert was 48 years and many a smart jingle ahead of him. Richard Rodgers is not the first man to write melodies that get inside of people and do something to them. Franz Lehár could still give him a lesson in *Schmalzmusik*. But a song is words and music, and nobody ever fused words and music more effectively than Rodgers & Hart. When Rodgers's melodic line expresses gaiety, sadness, humor, Hart's lyrical line invariably complements and fulfills it. The lyrical slant may not be as sophisticated or clever as Cole Porter's. The melody may resort to chromatic tricks that such a perfect craftsman as Vincent Youmans would reject as unsound. But a Rodgers & Hart song usually has the power of a single musical expression which not even such a pair of individual talents as P. G. Wodehouse & Jerome Kern could ever quite pull off.

There is one further quality that Rodgers brings to his music which perhaps give him the edge over such peers as Irving Berlin, Arthur Schwartz, Walter Donaldson, Kern, Youmans and great and gaudy Hollywood hack teams like Warren & Dubin and Robin & Rainger. Richard Rodgers is not only the master of a tonal palette filled with surprise and delight, but he is constantly at search for new forms across the known boundaries of his medium. The dream music for *Peggy-Ann*, and twelve years later for *I Married An Angel*, the "Slaughter on Tenth Avenue" ballet music for *On Your Toes*, the march of the clowns in *Jumbo*, while probably causing Richard Strauss no alarm for his laurels, are imaginative and charming beyond the accepted standards of musicomedy music.

In the 13 years since the *Garrick Gaieties*, Rodgers & Hart have livened Manhattan with such hits as *Dearest Enemy, Peggy-Ann, The Girl Friend, A Connecticut Yankee,* and the five-in-a-row of the last three years. They have livened the whole U.S. with such songs as "My Heart Stood Still," "Ten Cents a Dance," "Blue Moon," "I've Got Five Dollars," "There's a Small Hotel," "With a Song in My Heart" (Rodgers's favorite composition), "The Lady is a Tramp." In the 13 years their shows have played everywhere from Wales to New South Wales. And they themselves have gone, more than once, to Hollywood.

Grand Tour

They have, in fact, made the grand tour of Hollywood—Warner Bros., Paramount, United Artists, M-G-M. This assortment of alliances comes from their disliking to sign for more than a one-picture contract. Of their six pictures they, like the public, vote *Love Me Tonight*, with Jeanette MacDonald and Maurice Chevalier, the best. There pours out of them an old familiar tale—of a Hollywood cockeyed, imbecile, exciting, exasperating. The medium: marvelous. The methods: terrible. "Music," they insist, "must be written for the camera. People can't just stand around and sing songs." For Rodgers, the usual experience was to hand in a score and, when the picture was produced, to find the score either missing or massacred. Once they worked for 15 months at M-G-M, and turned out only five songs. Says Rodgers: "In New York we often write five songs in one week. In three weeks we did the entire score of *I'd Rather Be Right*."

According to Rodgers & Hart, Hollywood's trouble is stupidity, not malice. "And you can no more resent stupidity in a movie director than in an elevator boy." Headline boner where they were concerned came when, in the sheet music made for *Mississippi*, "Swanee River" was credited to "Rodgers & Hart."

They differ concerning Hollywood's financial rewards. Hart believes they could make more money there than on Broadway, but prefers to forgo it because he loves the theatre. Rodgers feels that a Hollywood income may be more certain but that only in the theatre can musicomedy writers really strike oil.

They have struck oil in the theatre often enough, but there have been a few spills. There was *Betsy*, the flop they did for Ziegfeld. "Ziegfeld should have been a movie producer. He didn't know the first thing about music, yet he constantly butted in on the scores." "Ten Cents a Dance," the biggest plum they got out of another Ziegfeld show, *Simple Simon*, they "practically slipped in over Ziegfeld's head."

And there was *Chee-Chee*, the musicomedy made from Charles Pettit's witty, bawdy *Son of the Grand Eunuch*, which Lew Fields produced in 1928. Lew Fields's son Herb, who wrote the books of several of their early hits, was sold on the *Son of the Grand Eunuch*, talked Hart into liking it, the two of them talked Herb's father, all three talked Rodgers. Rodgers believes it had the best score he ever wrote, that what killed it was the idea itself: "You just can't talk about castration all evening. It's not only embarrassing, it's dull."

Rodgers & Hart enjoy today that special blessing which befalls successful songwriters, of having money rain in from all sides—from royalties on shows, from the sale of shows to Hollywood and foreign countries, from sheet music, from gramophone records, from radio recitals, from having their music played by bands. On shows they get 6 percent of the gross, which means about $750 a week apiece if a show is a hit. Their biggest money-maker was *The Girl Friend* which played all over the world. In Hollywood they got $50,000 to $60,000 a movie. And from the American Society of Composers, Authors and Publishers (ASCAP), which collects the royalties for public performances of copyrighted music, and grades royalties on a basis of the composers' musical importance— Rodgers & Hart, like Jerome Kern, Cole Porter, Irving Berlin, are graded AA or tops—they each get about $18,000 a year. In a good year, their total income is upwards of $100,000. They insist they are not the biggest moneymakers in their field, though they have no idea who is.

Method and Madness

True to the best tradition of collaborators, Rodgers & Hart are not at all alike. Trim, affluent-looking, father-of-a-family Richard Rodgers (who at 36 is getting grey) supplies the method in their work; tiny, swarthy, cigar-chewing Bachelor Lorenz Hart (who at 43 is getting bald), the madness. Dick Rodgers lives with his attractive wife in a duplex apartment in Manhattan's swanky East 77th Street, summers at smart Sands Point, Long Island, gives formal dinner parties, draws a bid to the famed Charles Shipman Paysons' (the former Joan Whitney) Fourth of July parties, hobnobs with socialite Margaret Emerson, the Herbert Bayard Swopes, Noël Coward.

Hart lives with his mother, whom he describes as "a sweet, menacing old lady" on middle-class Central Park West, scowls at white ties, gives manners-be-damned, whiskey-by-the-case, all-night free-for-alls, gets bored with people and keeps picking up new ones. Rodgers takes the world in his stride; Hart is tempted to protest, fume, explain, deprecate— argues, for example, with the desk-clerk of a Khartoum hotel because it does not carry *Variety*.

On the surface Rodgers, living by the clock, managing his own financial affairs and holding Hart in leash, seems to be the businessman of the pair. But Hart, who employs a business manager, who "runs a temperature" when he does not feel like working, who has to be yanked out of bed late in the day by a determined Negro servant girl, and who prefers to meet a question with a wisecrack rather than an answer, very likely knows to the fourth decimal place the dollars-and-cents value of his "temperament."

Aside from Jerome Kern years ago, Rodgers does not feel that anyone has influenced him musically. He hates swing, and so does Hart: "It's old stuff. Benny Goodman only does better what Ted Lewis did years ago." Both Rodgers & Hart hate having swing bands play their stuff—Hart because the subtlety, and even the grammar, of his lyrics is apt to be outraged; Rodgers because his melodies get buried.

Hart has never studied versification, never uses a rhyming dictionary. Rodgers disparages himself as a pianist, though he is extremely pleased at having once made some Ampico player-piano rolls of some of his song hits. Ampico still contributes something to his income. From time to time it sends him long, involved, incomprehensible royalty statements, with royalty enclosed. The enclosure: a ten-cent postage stamp.

"Words and Music: Rodgers and Hart"

Margaret Case Harriman's two-part *New Yorker* profile, originally published in 1938, appears here as it was modestly updated in *Take Them Up Tenderly*, a collection of Harriman's essays published several months after the death of Hart. Harriman offers the most substantial contemporary introduction to Rodgers and Hart, already "regarded in their profession as musical dramatists rather than as songwriters." Like most writing on Broadway songwriters, then and now, technical discussion is reserved for Hart's lyrics, including brief explanations of such matters as exterior (male), interior (female) rhymes, and dummy lyrics. Little is said about Rodgers's music other than a remark about an alleged resemblance between "Here in My Arms" and the African-American spiritual "Nobody Knows the Trouble I've Seen."

Harriman emphasizes Rodgers and Hart's "belief that a musical comedy should be as well constructed as a straight drama" and notes their recently successful integration of songs into stories in *On Your Toes* and *Babes in Arms*. Rodgers himself remarked on several occasions in *Musical Stages* that his concern with, and sensitivity to, dramatic action did not begin with *Oklahoma!* Harriman also introduces several anecdotes that remain in wide circulation, for example, the story of how "Blue Moon" belatedly evolved into its present title and lyric to take its place among popular song perennials.

MARGARET CASE HARRIMAN

There's a dame next door
Who's an awful bore,
It really makes you sore
To see her.
a. . . . .
b. . . . .
c. . . . .
d. . . . .
By and by, perhaps she'll die,
Perhaps she'll croak this summer;
Her old man's a plumber,
She's much dumber.

The above incantation is part of what is called, in the songwriting business, a dummy lyric. It is a hasty assortment of words thrown together by the lyric-writer while a song is being composed, generally loony and often bawdy, but always carefully accented to follow the rhythm. Fortunately for the lyric-writer, a frenzied toiler, he seldom has to fill in the second stanza, since it repeats the rhythm of the first. The sentimental words that finally grew out of the tale about the dame next door and plumber were written by Lorenz Hart and accompanying the melody by Richard Rodgers, became a song hit in *On Your Toes*:

There's a small hotel
With a wishing well;
I wish that we were there
Together.

There's a bridal suite;
One room bright and neat,
Complete for us to share
Together.

Looking through the window you
Can see a distant steeple;
Not a sign of people,
Who wants people?

Source: Margaret Case Harriman, "Words and Music: Rodgers and Hart," in *Take Them Up Tenderly* (New York: Alfred A. Knopf, 1945), 166–85. Originally printed in *The New Yorker* (May 28 and June 4, 1938), 9–23 and 21–25.

This seems to be an answer to the ancient question with which the layman badgers songwriters; "Which do you write first, the music or the words?" But Rodgers, who writes the music, and Hart, who writes the words, say that there is no answer to that. Sometimes it happens one way, sometimes another. One day in Paris, in 1926, the collaborators were riding in a taxi with two girls; the cab skittered into a truck and one of the girls, fluttering, cried, "Oh, my heart stood still!" From the floor of the taxi, where the collision had flung him with his hat jammed over his eyes, Larry Hart mumbled, "Hey, Dick, that's a title for a song." The rest was fairly simple (after they got out of the wrecked cab), and "My Heart Stood Still," originally presented in a Cochran revue in London and introduced to New York in 1927 in *A Connecticut Yankee* (which was revived this year), has come to be known reverently in the trade as a "standard"—a song kept on file for continual use and amounting to about the same thing as a "classic." The reverence is due partly to the emotions a good song honestly rouses in the hearts of everybody in the songwriting business, partly to the fact that "My Heart Stood Still" earned around fifty thousand dollars during the seventeen-year lull between the first performance of *A Connecticut Yankee* and its revival.

Rodgers and Hart have been collaborating for twenty-four years, since Rodgers, then sixteen years old, met Hart, who was twenty-three. Rodgers is poised, immaculate, and humorous. He is under five feet seven inches in height, but he seems tall in comparison with the exact five feet of his partner, a small, tumultuous man, rumpled and amiable behind a large cigar which he takes out of his mouth only in order to make excited gestures with it. Hart's carefree attitude toward his appearance sometimes worries Rodgers, and then, he says, "I take Larry by the hand, lead him into the children's department of any good store, and have him fitted out from head to foot—a short distance." The only other thing about his collaborator that used to furrow the Rodgers brow, until he became used to it, is Hart's gift for getting away from wherever he is. When, for instance, the two are walking along a street, conversing pleasantly, Hart abruptly disappears. "You find yourself talking to yourself" is the way Rodgers describes it. He has learned now to walk along slowly until Hart reappears and chattily resumes the conversation where it was left off. Generally it turns out that Larry has darted into a store for one of his big cigars or to a newsstand for a copy of *Variety*. Several years ago Rodgers came upon Hart in a hotel lobby, fiercely denouncing the manager, who was trying to explain, with outspread hands, why he had not been able to procure the latest issue of *Variety*. His reason, which Hart was finally forced to accept, was that the hotel was in Khartoum.

Nothing about Dick Rodgers worries Hart except his own conviction that Rodgers encourages the orchestra to play too loud at rehearsals and performances. "So you want to drown out my lyrics?" he wails. Rodgers regards him peacefully and inquires, "Do you want the audience to go out whistling the lyrics?" All of this bickering is strictly affectionate, the kind that can go on for twenty-four years between two men who are friends although their lives are curiously different. Rodgers married Dorothy Feiner fourteen years ago and now lives rather formally with his wife, two daughters (aged thirteen and nine), and three servants in a pleasant apartment on East Seventy-fourth Street and in the summers at their farm in Fairfield, Connecticut. A drawing of Central Park which hangs on one wall of the New York apartment was given to Rodgers one Christmas by his wife, who bought it when she saw that it happened to include the towers of the apartment building on Central Park West where Larry Hart lives. Larry is a bachelor and his home life is a happy pandemonium shared by his mother and Black Mary, the general maid, who had been with the Harts some twenty years. One time, when Josephine Baker came to dine with the Harts after her elaborate triumphs in Paris and elegantly requested *"une tasse de café noir,"* it was Mary who stared at her for a long moment and demanded somberly, "You talk out of your mouth, you, the way you was born."

Geographically separated (and everyone knows how great is the distance between Central Park West and Fifth Avenue), Larry Hart and Dick Rodgers also differ in their social tastes. Mr. and Mrs. Rodgers, gay, attractive, and sociable, are frequently seen with fashionable friends at first nights, in restaurants, and at parties. Larry likes company, too, but the thought of a white tie dissolves him and he prefers to give parties at home, always loudly and almost tearfully proclaiming any soirée of his a failure if even one guest has departed sober. In spite of this sartorial and social gap between them, the Rodgers family frequently invades the Hart apartment for a visit, and the Rodgers home setting generally includes Larry, waving his cigar from the depths of an armchair and talking rapidly in a high, slightly husky voice. Both men speak softly in conversation, and Rodgers's singing voice, like that of a good many composers, is true but faint.

Except for the agonized periods before the opening of a new show, when Hart flees to Atlantic City to revise the lyrics or to write new ones and Rodgers locks himself into his study in the Fairfield house to score the melodies, they always work together in Larry's apartment or in Dick's. In one or the other of these sharply contrasted surroundings, Rodgers and Hart have turned out over a thousand songs, many of them notable hits, including "Thou Swell," "With a Song in My Heart," "I've Got Five Dollars," "The Blue Room," "Ten Cents a Dance," "Falling in Love with Love," "I Didn't Know What Time It Was," "Lover," and "The Most Beautiful Girl in the World." Another song, "Have You Met Miss Jones?" was in the musical commentary *I'd Rather Be Right*, for which the book was written by George S. Kaufman and Moss Hart, the music and lyrics by Richard Rodgers and Lorenz Hart. Moss Hart and Lorenz Hart are not related, except by mutual consternation in the production of *I'd Rather Be Right*. One scene, in Central Park, included the President of the United States sitting on a bench, members of the cabinet and justices of the Supreme Court gathered around a long table, and a young man in love. The plot required the young man to proclaim his love at this point, and it was mechanically impossible to shift the president, cabinet, and Supreme Court off the stage and whist them back again for the number with which they immediately followed the love song. So the boy was obliged to fetch his girl, Miss Jones, from the wings and introduce her to the president in song, in the presence of a sizable section of the United States government. "Have You Met Miss Jones?" an engaging number, never achieved popularity outside of New York. Dealers in phonograph records and sheet music throughout the country must, when they buy songs, implacably follow the dictates of the average customer's heart; an embrace, implied or accomplished, is fine for the trade, and so is frustration, as expressed by a slow wrenching apart of persons or by a kind of gay defiance of the face of heartbreak. "Have You Met Miss Jones?" lacking all of these qualities, and suggesting merely a formal acquaintance, left the dealers baffled. "Who is this Miss Jones?" one of them demanded when he was approached with the song. "And why do I want to meet her? Did she do something to somebody?"

Both Richard Rodgers and Lorenz Hart were born into comfortably established middle-class families in New York. Rodgers's father was a doctor, with home and offices on West Eighty-sixth Street, and his mother was a merry, musical woman, who liked to sing and to play the piano. She would sing songs from *The Merry Widow* and *Mlle. Modiste*, and when Richard was four he was able to pick out the melodies, by ear, on the piano. Dr. Rodgers didn't play or sing, but he loved music and his house was full of it. During the Doctor's business hours, Richard, temporarily distracted from the piano, ran errands around his father's office, helping with the bandages and iodine, but when the Doctor set out on a round of professional calls, it was Mortimer, Dick's older brother, who was allowed to go along with him and carry his bag while Richard was once more retired to the piano stool in the parlor. His family encouraged him endlessly, as he grew older, to write music, and Richard responded with an enthusiasm that dropped only when they suggested that his music might have some commercial value and that he should leave the home piano long enough to go out and try to get a job composing for money. Mortimer Rodgers, who has never been able to carry a tune, faithfully pursued his father's profession and is now an obstetrician, with offices on Park Avenue. His career is no surprise to his father and mother, but they are occasionally stirred to a slow wonder by Richard, the dreamer.

Dick Rodgers turned out his first song, "My Auto Show Girl," when he was fourteen. In the same year, 1917, Larry Hart was a student at Columbia University and had abandoned his regular course there to study journalism. Rodgers and Hart were not to meet for another two years, and in the meantime Rodgers became precociously active in the amateur-show business. He wrote the music and some of the lyrics for shows put on by the Akron Club, a social organization to which his brother belonged, and for various other benefit performances around town. Between shows he peddled mimeographed copies of his songs to music publishers, one or two of whom listened to a couple of numbers without emotion and then, rising, said, "Thank you very much." This, a courteous phrase, always courteously spoken in the show business and in the song-writing business, is generally a death verdict, and it had a violent and healthy effect upon Rodgers. He entered Columbia University in the fall of 1919 with the determination to write the music for the Varsity Show the next spring. The show was called *Fly with Me*, and Rodgers was the first freshman ever to compose the score of a Columbia Varsity Show. After this achievement he was acclaimed a prodigy by the Columbia faculty and the New York press to such an extent that he never went back to Columbia—partly because he feared an anticlimax, partly because through *Fly with Me*, he had met Lorenz Hart.

Hart, a descendant on his father's side of Heinrich Heine, had grown up on West 119th Street, playing with such boys as Edwin Justus Mayer and Morrie Ryskind, who were both to become playwrights. Larry's father was a promoter, but in spite of the fact that he generally promoted the wrong thing, the Hart household was a lively and a genial one. At Columbia, Larry Hart and Morrie Ryskind entertained themselves by writing verses and passing them around in class, and both became locally famous as versifiers. Although Hart left college in 1918, he was recalled to Columbia to write the lyrics for the Varsity Show for which Dick Rodgers was to compose the music. Another Columbia student who had a hand in its production was Herbert Fields, a son of Lew Fields, the comedian. Herbert Fields knew Larry Hart, and some months before work on the Varsity Show began, he took Rodgers to call at the brownstone house on 119th Street where Hart was at that time gloomily translating German plays and musical comedies into English for the Shuberts. Of that meeting, both Rodgers and Hart say now it was love at first sight. After the considerable triumph of the Varsity Show, they had a small flurry of success on Broadway. Their first professional collaboration was on a song called "Any Old Place with You," which was interpolated in a Lew Fields comedy, *A Lonely Romeo*. The lyric included the lines:

> I'll go to hell for ya
> Or Philadelphia

and proved that Lorenz Hart was on his way toward stamping out the prevalent June-moon kind of lyric. Next, they wrote the words and music for two more Lew Fields shows and a musical comedy called *Winkle Town*, which was never produced. *Winkle Town* had a song the boys liked, however, and they put it aside for future use; it was called

"Manhattan." Their work in those days was signed Herbert Richard Lorenz, in fairness to all three, and for the next eight years Herbert Fields continued to collaborate with them, writing the books for such Rodgers and Hart successes as *Dearest Enemy, The Girl Friend, Peggy-Ann,* and *A Connecticut Yankee.*

In spite of the brief Lew Fields connection, the early 1920s were for Rodgers and Hart mainly a long and futile period of hanging around Broadway. They wrote songs and submitted them to Edward B. Marks, who had published the music written for Lew Fields; when Marks turned them down, they went to see Max Dreyfus, who was then with the T. B. Harms Co. Dreyfus, who had been in the music-publishing business for twenty-five years, told them that they had talent but were too young for the business, and advised them to go somewhere to study. Hart starkly resumed translating plays and musical comedies into English suitable for the Shuberts, and Rodgers went to the Institute of Musical Art to study under Frank Damrosch. Damrosch, George Wedge, and Henry Krehbiel opened up to him a whole new field of music—Wagner, Beethoven, and Debussy—and the young Rodgers traveled passionately, week after week, to concerts at Carnegie Hall. At the end of the year he was chosen, as one of the Institute's most promising pupils, to write the music for its annual show. He speaks of this nowadays with pride, but it is not hard to believe that after a year of listening for the first time to Beethoven and Wagner he was depressed by being asked to write a few catchy melodies for another amateur show.

When Rodgers left the Institute he found once more that, in spite of his success with amateurs, there was nothing for him on Broadway. With Larry Hart, he put on some twenty amateur shows in the next year or two for girls' schools, churches, and synagogues. He lived at home and his father gave him an allowance, but Dick liked to take girls out dancing and, to indulge this mild luxury, borrowed five dollars at a time from a friend, one Earl Katzenstein, until he owed one hundred and five dollars. In something of a panic, he went to his friend's office and said, "I'm through trying to get anywhere in music. I want a job." Mr. Katzenstein led him across the hall to a Mr. Marvin, engaged in the children's-underwear business. Marvin wanted to retire in a few years and was looking for a young man he could train to succeed him; he was impressed with Dick's appearance and by the fact that he had gone to college, and offered him fifty dollars a week on the spot. It was a swift solution of Dick's financial problem, but, confronted with actually giving up music, he hesitated. He told Mr. Marvin he would let him know the next day and went home for dinner. During dinner he was called to the telephone by Benjamin Kaye, whom he had come to know during his amateur career. Mr. Kaye was a lawyer who wrote sketches and plays in his spare time, and he now told Rodgers with some excitement that the Theatre Guild needed some new tapestries and was planning to put on a small amateur show Sunday nights, and matinees, maybe, to pay for them.

How would Dick, he asked, like to write the music for it? "Positively no," said Rodgers. "No more amateur shows for me." Kaye explained that it wasn't exactly amateur, that most of the cast would be Theatre Guild understudies, and then he went on to speak familiarly of "Terry" Helburn. The thought that if he did the show he might meet Miss Theresa Helburn, a director of the Theatre Guild, decided Rodgers. "But," he said, "I'll have to have Larry Hart to write the lyrics." Hart, with the money he had earned from translations, had gone into the producing business with two fairly spectacular failures: one a play starring Vera Gordon, and another chiefly notable because Tom Powers and the late Clare Eames were the only people in the cast. The Guild had tentatively hired another lyricist, but after some maneuvering Hart was engaged to collaborate with Rodgers on the Junior Guild show, which was called *The Garrick Gaieties*. *The Garrick Gaieties* opened on a Sunday night in May, 1925, to the hosannas of public and critics, and soon became a riot at the Garrick Theatre, with nightly performances and two matinees a week. People went around humming "Sentimental Me" and the song the boys had saved from *Winkle Town*:

> We'll have Manhattan,
> The Bronx, and Staten
> Island too . . .

Bidding for the publication rights to the score became noisy among music publishers, and the Edward B. Marks Music Co. got the job. *The Garrick Gaieties* played two hundred and fourteen performances on Broadway; its second edition, a year later, played one hundred and seventy-nine.

One night years afterward when Dick Rodgers and Larry Hart attended one of the Theatre Guild's stately first nights, Larry nudged Dick and murmured, "See those tapestries? *We're* responsible for them." "Hell," said Rodgers, "they're responsible for *us*."

A few years later, when the Theatre Guild had all but succumbed to its own stateliness, it was Rodgers who helped to pull it back to prosperity with *Oklahoma!*, the Guild production that he wrote in collaboration with Oscar Hammerstein II.

On the afternoon in 1919 when Herbert Fields took Rodgers to the brownstone house where Hart lived on the upper West Side, Fields pushed the doorbell and Rodgers waited, smoothing his tie a little and adjusting the brim of his hat. He was a smooth dresser even then, at the age of sixteen, and he was unprepared for the vision that greeted him when Hart opened the door. Mr. Hart, also a very young man, was wearing an undershirt, a checked jacket, dress trousers, and carpet slippers. However, when he led his guests into the parlor and started talking about lyrics, Rodgers, who had written several songs without any cash profit, forgot his host's unusual appearance and listened devoutly. Hart had not sold any lyrics at that time, but he spoke freely of such mysteries as exterior and interior rhymes, and male and female rhymes. A male rhyme is generally exterior and accents the ultimate syllable, a female rhyme accents the penultimate syllable and is usually interior, and both are illustrated by the lyric of a song Rodgers and Hart were to write some time later:

> Thou swell! thou witty! thou sweet! thou grand!
> Would'st kiss me pretty? Would'st hold my hand?
> Both thine eyes are cute too; what they do to me.
> Hear me holler I choose a
> Sweet lollapaloosa
> In thee. . . .

Here, the first two lines are male and exterior, the fourth and fifth female and interior. Hart says nowadays that he has never known much about such things. He has never studied versification, he will tell you, and he has always rejected rhyming dictionaries with the comment that it is more trouble to look up a rhyme than to think up one. Occasionally stirred to some heat by people who try to make a scholar out of him, Larry will wave his cigar dangerously, pull at his explosively patterned necktie, and yell, "Why, I don't even know what onomatopoeia is, or a trope!"

Rodgers and Hart have come to be regarded in their profession as musical dramatists rather than as songwriters. The radio and the phonograph long ago proved equally disastrous to the sale of sheet music and to composers who could turn out single ballads suitable to the sheet-music counters but who were not trained to write an entire score. With a few freakish exceptions such as the "Mairzy Doats" song (a number written by a couple of other fellows that Rodgers, incidentally, liked so much that he went around happily interpreting it to anybody who hadn't yet caught on) most song hits now come from musical comedies or moving pictures, and since *The Garrick Gaieties* Rodgers and Hart have been identified with the theater and with Hollywood. One of their specialties is musical dialogue, which they brought to perfection in *I Married an Angel*, in 1938. In one scene, for example, the Angel said to a visiting sister angel:

> Excuse my lack of hospitality.
> Won't you—sit down?

The dialogue that followed was spoken in a conversational tone to an engaging and allusive musical accompaniment, and it drifted into song only when a plump angel with overtones of a blonde cutie melodiously referred to her archangelic beau:

> Beauty is truth, truth beauty
> Gabriel, blow your rootie tootie!

Faithful to their belief that a musical comedy should be as well constructed as a straight drama, Rodgers and Hart also like their songs centered around [sic] a situation in the plot. In the fifteen shows for which they wrote the music and lyrics in the five years following *The Garrick Gaieties*—including *Dearest Enemy, The Girl Friend, A Connecticut Yankee, Spring Is Here*, and *Heads Up[!]*—they were seldom able to achieve this ideal; most authors of musical-comedy books and most producers had a theory that any sentence implying the presence of the moon, the month of June, or a feeling of frustration was a sufficient cue for a boy and a girl to walk into a spotlight and sing about love. When Rodgers and Hart wrote the book for *On Your Toes*, with the assistance of George Abbott, they came nearer to a reasonable combination of plot and song, but it was not until the two alone wrote the book, music, and lyrics of *Babes in Arms*, in 1937, that they were able to turn out a show in which, as they like to recall, every number was a "plot" number, including the hit song, "The Lady Is a Tramp." Audiences in general, pleased by the song and by the way Mitzi Green sang it, did not think of it as a "plot" song, but Larry and Dick felt that Mitzi had roamed through the play long enough without any explanation, and they are convinced that audiences would have been confused about her if she hadn't sung the song.

Rodgers and Hart wrote "The Lady Is a Tramp" in one day, when they decided that *Babes in Arms* needed it. Another time, they wrote "Ten Cents a Dance" in less than two hours, and they completed the score for *I'd Rather Be Right* in three weeks. Perhaps the fastest long-distance work they ever did was in connection with a Bing Crosby picture, *Mississippi*, several years ago. They finished the score of *Mississippi* on the Coast, and came East to start work on *Babes in Arms*, arriving in New York slightly in advance of a telegram from Paramount frenziedly announcing that the picture needed another song for Crosby right away. Rodgers and Hart turned out the song the day they got the telegram, but then they hesitated. "If we send the manuscript," Hart said, "somebody out there will play it and sing it the way we don't want it." Rodgers said, "If we send a record, they'll play it in some executive's office with the doors banging and the telephones ringing and nobody paying any attention." For a moment the two were baffled by the hellish intricacies of Hollywood art, but at length they brightened and sauntered over to the Paramount Studios on Broadway. With Rodgers at the piano and a radio singer to give the number the sales quality that the composer's small singing voice could never have instilled into it, they made a sound film and rushed it, special delivery airmail, to Hollywood, where they knew that Crosby and the Paramount producers would have no way of hearing it except in the hushed darkness of a projection room. The song, "It's Easy to Remember," was remembered by a good many people after *Mississippi* was forgotten.

* * *

Rodgers, the composer, is more methodical in his work and calmer in his attitude toward it than Hart, the lyric writer. He starts about eleven in the morning. If the collaborators have arranged to work that day in Rodgers's apartment, he puts in a series of telephone calls to Hart, beginning around ten o'clock. Mary, the Negro maid in the Hart household, answers these calls and dutifully rouses her employer, who goes back to sleep again like a little child. Mary is a patient woman up to a certain point, when she becomes picturesque. Once after the third or fourth telephone call, she was heard to slam down the receiver and yell heartily into the bedroom, "Mr. Larry it's goddam time to get the hell *up!*" Most nights there is an impromptu party at Larry's, with old friends pounding the piano, shouting songs, and screaming amiably at each other. Mrs. Frieda Hart, Larry's mother, mingles happily with the guests on these occasions until she feels sleepy, and then goes quietly to bed. Late one evening Dorothy Rodgers, Richard's wife, went into Mrs. Hart's room to say good night and found her in bed, reading. "Doesn't that noise in the living room even bother you?" Mrs. Rodgers inquired sympathetically. Mrs. Hart shook her head and smiled. "No," she said, "it has never bothered me." She reflected a moment, and added gently, "Except, maybe, that night Paul Whiteman's band came in."

Whatever revelry enlivens the evening, Larry Hart generally begins work the next morning while he is dressing, sorting out the crumpled fragments of paper which his mother periodically removes from his coat pockets and places on his bureau. These contain lyrics written the day before, or perhaps a week earlier, and the probability is that Larry has composed them in a traffic jam, or in a Turkish bath, or while waiting for an elevator somewhere. Those that he likes on reading them over go back into the pockets of whatever suit he puts on before setting forth for a day's toil at the Rodgers apartment. By the time he arrives, Rodgers may have polished up one of the songs for the show they are working on, or he may have decided whether another should be written in three-four, four-four, or six-eight time to fit a certain situation. If Hart bursts in with a totally different idea about the same situation, there is no friction between them; that, they point out, is where collaboration comes in. When they have roughly completed the score they separate until the show is ready to go into rehearsal, and their collaboration then becomes, for each man, a matter of grim and solitary labor. Hart takes the first version of the book and lyrics and goes to Atlantic City, the Shangri-La of most authors and playwrights. Rodgers puts on a torn, brown sweater buttoned up the front, to which he has become attached, and shuts himself in his study to write the music. Several copies of the original manuscript are made after the show is in its final form; one goes to Robert Russell Bennett or to Hans Spialek (a volatile Czechoslovakian known to the boys as the Bouncing Czech), who orchestrates it for the show; another is sent to the Rodgers and Hart publishers, Chappell & Co., where one "Doc" Szirmai simplifies it for sheet music; and a third goes to the American Society of Composers, Authors and Publishers, for eventual release to the public, and to radio, night-club, and other orchestras. Arrangements for popular orchestras are approved by Rodgers before release, but this is a fairly hollow gesture. With the growth of individualism among orchestra leaders, any successful dance orchestra has come to be known as a "name band," and the melody it offers is increasingly less important than the manner in which the leader swings it, or "schmalzes" it. Benny Goodman, Guy Lombardo, and Wayne King, for instance, play the same tune so differently that it has little relation to what the composer had in mind, and their respective fans worship the maestro rather than the music. Featured singers with name bands also have their individual ways of kicking a song around. Rodgers, a patient man, says that a composer can do nothing about any of this unless he goes into the music publishing business himself and puts out, say, an album of his music played and sung the way it was written. If the public likes the album, he claims, they won't care much for the radio deviations.

A year or so ago Rodgers went into the music publishing business in partnership with Max Dreyfus and Oscar Hammerstein II. The firm, with offices in Rockefeller Center, is called the Williamson Company, Inc. because both Rodgers and Hammerstein are sons of men named William. The Williamson company's first product was the sheet music of *Oklahoma!* which has also been recorded by Decca with the original company, exactly the way the composer intended. The *Oklahoma!* album of records has sold about 500,000 copies so far, and what pleases Rodgers most about this phenomenon is the knowledge that the half-million people who own the album and play it probably accept it as the best rendition of the songs in the show, and will therefore string along with the composer in sneering at any radio maestro, crooner, or female sobber who tries to make improvements.

Larry Hart had no part in writing *Oklahoma!* but with a team like Rodgers and Hart, one member can disappear for a while without splitting the act. As Hart once said in answer to a frown from Rodgers when he returned from some vague journey or other, "Did Gilbert bawl out Sullivan for giving him the slip and writing 'Onward, Christian Soldiers'?" Larry wrote no hymns and he was often in California or Mexico when Rodgers needed him in New York, but he always turned up in time to write the lyrics that helped to make Rodgers-and-Hart part of the American language.

The long life of Rodgers and Hart songs, and the fact that they continually put out new ones, helped to establish them in the AA class of song writers with the American Society of Composers, Authors and Publishers. AA writers and composers in the Society include Jerome Kern, Cole Porter, Ira Gershwin, and other men who are known in the trade as "smart" song writers, meaning that their work is subtle enough to please the carriage trade and sufficiently engaging to satisfy everybody. The ASCAP grading (from AA to D) is based on the popularity and lifetime of a tune and on the money it has earned, which makes Irving Berlin, though he is not a polysyllabic song writer, an AA member; the late George Gershwin is still listed in the AA class and will remain there as long as his music is played. Proprietors who engage dance orchestras must pay ASCAP from $30 to $2,400 a year—depending on whether the orchestra is a piano, a fiddle, and a saxophone in a beer joint or a name band in a fashionable café—for the privilege of playing numbers written by ASCAP members. At the end of the year, the Society adds up the fees earned by each member and after deducting its own expenses, sends half of the remainder to the composers and authors, half to the publishers. Rodgers and Hart's annual income from ASCAP is about $20,000 apiece. Besides this they get six cents on every copy of their sheet music sold and fifty per cent of the royalties on phonograph records. When they collaborate with one or more authors on a show, their combined royalty is six per cent of the gross box-office receipts—a smaller percentage than they receive for writing an entire show; six percent is frequently adequate, however, as in the case of *By Jupiter*, which took in $24,000 during Holy Week, when nobody allegedly, goes to the theater. Moving-picture companies pay Rodgers and Hart from $50,000 to $60,000 to write the music and lyrics for a film, generally over a period of five weeks. All money paid to them jointly is divided on a fifty-fifty basis; there has never been a written contract between them.

One of Rodgers and Hart's biggest song hits was kicked about for a long time through the whims of a Hollywood producer who saw no merit in it. Metro-Goldwyn-Mayer signed Rodgers and Hart in 1934 to write the score for a Jean Harlow picture. One song, "Oh, Lord, Why Won't You Make Me a Star?," was yanked out of the picture at the last minute; Hart thought up a new title, "The Bad in Every Man," and Metro tried it in another film. Once more it was quietly removed when the rushes were shown. Back in New York, Rodgers and Hart could do nothing with the song through Harms, Inc., who at that time published their work, because good or bad, the song belonged to Metro-Goldwyn-Mayer. Always reluctant to let any number of theirs gather dust, Rodgers and Hart took it to the New York office of Jack Robbins, music publisher for Metro. Mr. Robbins listened and spoke. "Boys," he said, "you've got a beautiful melody there, and I have faith in your song. But boys, boys, give me a title! Something with romance," he pleaded, adding, after a moment's reverie, "like 'The Blue Hour,' maybe, or 'The Hour of Parting.'" Next day the boys came back with the title, "Blue Moon"; Robbins published it as a popular number unrelated to any stage show or movie, and it sold 175,000 copies—their largest sheet-music sale to date.

Auditions for a Rodgers and Hart show generally start while Larry Hart is still at work on the first act. Rodgers attends every audition and he will listen to almost anybody who shows even the first stirrings of talent or personality, but he suffers on these occasions, chiefly because it is his task to say at the end of every number, no matter how deplorable, "Thank you very much"—that polite and fatal phrase which so frequently shattered him in his own early days of trying to sell songs. Sometimes an aspiring act turns out to be so painful that its conclusion leaves Rodgers in a kind of coma, in which he can only grasp at George Abbott, or whoever happens to be sitting next to him, and mutter, "Say something nice, for God's sake." Mr. Abbott, or whoever, then raises his voice toward the stage and says clearly, "Thank you very much." Boys and girls trying out for the chorus are observed with particular care, since all of the principal roles in Rodgers and Hart shows are understudied by the chorus; Rodgers once saw a performance of *On Your Toes* played entirely by members of the ensemble, and he says it was fine. A chorus daisy who had danced in *Higher and Higher* and understudied a specialty dancer in *By Jupiter* turned up at the auditions for *A Connecticut Yankee* last Spring, and Rodgers gave her a part in the show. "You know who she is?" he says, beaming. "Vera dash Ellen!" To anyone who does not immediately recognize Vera-Ellen's name, Rodgers adds casually, "She just signed a contract with Goldwyn for a thousand bucks a week." Like most good showmen, Rodgers likes to see people, including himself, get ahead in the theater. After a couple of ex-officio passes at the producing business in collaboration with Dwight Wiman and George Abbott, in *By Jupiter* and *Best Foot Forward*, he became a full producer with the revival of *A Connecticut Yankee* this year. When anxious friends inquire why he wanted to add the headaches of a producer to those of a composer, Rodgers replies simply, "Look, when I had a producer we used to have to call conferences to decide every little question. Now that I'm the producer I just call a quick conference with myself and the whole thing's decided. It's simpler."

At rehearsals, Rodgers and Hart are quiet or waggish, according to the pressure or comparative relief from the strain which naturally devours them. One time during rehearsal, a leading man announced his decision that the second act was a disaster to which he declined to lend his presence. "You know why, don't you?" Rodgers said to Hart after the actor had passed by with a fearful frown. "He's only got one number in the second act." Hart was reminded of the story about another actor, who, receiving his part, weighed it in his hand and, finding that his arm sagged beneath its burden, exclaimed, "Ah! An excellent play!" At their own opening nights the false calm which traditionally supports authors, composers, and members of the cast during rehearsals and tryouts temporarily deserts Rodgers and Hart. Rodgers sits with his wife in the last row, on the aisle, so that he can get out into the stage-door alley when the tension threatens to tear him apart. Hart wanders around the lobby in a frenzy; if the show seems to be getting across, he rubs his hands together and passes them wildly over his head, his arms, even his back. Of this habit Rodgers says, "Success starts his blood circulating again, and he begins to itch all over."

Rodgers, an educated and honest musician, goes habitually to the opera and to concerts, and his appearance in the front row at Carnegie Hall is generally a signal for the musicians, who have been tuning up their instruments and glancing idly over the audience, to drop briefly what they are doing and come down to the footlights to shake hands with him. Musicians who are good enough to play in the symphony orchestras can play any kind of music, and many have often worked between concert seasons in the orchestra pit at Rodgers and Hart shows. At least once, however, a remark from a long-haired musician has shaken Rodgers to the core. Four years ago he rather tremulously conducted the orchestra of the Metropolitan Opera Company in the first rehearsal of his ballet, *Ghost Town*, which was later presented at the Met, with Rodgers conducting. At the end of the rehearsal the Met's first trumpet stared gloomily at Rodgers and shook his head. "From you I expected hot licks," he said.

Another connection between Rodgers and Hart and the more intellectual realms of entertainment is George Balanchine, former ballet director for the Metropolitan, who has staged all of the Rodgers and Hart ballets since "Slaughter on Tenth Avenue," Ray Bolger's memorable dance in *On Your Toes*. The boys, however, have a knack of mingling their artistic and popular achievements so that the result is pleasing to all customers. The orchestras assembled by Rodgers often include swing harpists and other interesting compromises, and one of the most ambitious Rodgers and Hart numbers, "All Points West," introduced at a Paul Whiteman concert in December, 1936, later became a feature of Rudy Vallee's floor show on the Astor Roof. Mrs. Rodgers suggested the title "All Points West" to her husband, in return for the name he had given her for the profitable business she conducts: Repairs, Inc. Under the direction of Mrs. Rodgers, a slight and graceful blonde, Repairs, Inc., mends everything it is possible for the human hand, the elements, or time itself to break.

No successful song writer can long escape public insinuations that his tunes sound like somebody else's. Some years ago, Gilbert Gabriel, reviewing *Dearest Enemy*, with music and lyrics by Rodgers and Hart, wrote that the song "Here in My Arms" strikingly resembled the Negro spiritual "Nobody Knows de Trouble I Seen." Later another purist remarked that "Where or When," from *Babes in Arms*, was remarkably like certain passages in *La Bohème*, and only a few months ago Walter Winchell nagged Rodgers in his column about the resemblance of some tune to some other tune or other. Both Rodgers and Hart are more interested than distressed by such accusations. They are apt to point out, in the happy discussion that follows, that the army bugle call for assembly is extremely suggestive of the "Ride of the Valkyries" in Wagner's *Ring*, but mostly they are content to explain to skeptics how easy it is for any song writer who wants to write songs the easiest way to think up a melody without treading on sacred ground.

Their favorite method of explanation is the telephone stunt, which consists of asking the heckler's telephone number and then, substituting the note C for 1, D for 2, and so on, rapidly transposing it into a tune. The telephone stunt can be elaborated, for purposes of relaxation, by using the letters of the exchange as well, taking them from the number with which they appear on the dial. The telephone number that has sometimes engaged Rodgers and Hart in their hours of ease is Sp 7–3100 (Police Headquarters), which turns out to be a waltz.

Pal Joey:
Drawing "Sweet Water from a Foul Well"

From *The Girl Friend* (1926) to *Pal Joey* (1940) drama critic Brooks Atkinson (1894–1984) was the man who introduced *New York Times* readers to the originality and pleasures of Rodgers and Hart shows. Atkinson consistently gave these shows high marks. Even when "in one of their workmanlike moods" (Atkinson's characterization of *Higher and Higher*), a Rodgers and Hart musical gave their *New York Times* critic enough to encourage theatergoers to attend. One rare exception was *Chee-Chee*, which Atkinson indicted as "their most pretentious production and the least entertaining." Due to his service as a war correspondent from 1941 to 1946, Atkinson missed the premiere of *By Jupiter*, the revival of *A Connecticut Yankee*, and the debuts of *Oklahoma!* and *Carousel*, but between his return as a drama critic and his retirement in 1960 he reviewed Rodgers and Hammerstein's final seven shows and a return engagement of *Oklahoma!*'s national touring company.

In reviewing *Pal Joey* Atkinson praises the production as "well-staged" and "expertly done," lauds Gene Kelly's "triumphant" debut performance as an actor and a dancer in a musical, and singles out "Bewitched" as "one of Richard Rodgers's most haunting tunes" in a score filled with "wit and skill." But for a reviewer who the previous year found the good-natured *Too Many Girls* "humorous, fresh and exhilarating," the "high class" *Pal Joey* is undermined by its "ugly" topic, a "joyless" book, and depraved characters, and "offers everything but a good time."

BROOKS ATKINSON

If it is possible to make an entertaining musical comedy out of an odious story, *Pal Joey* is it. The situation is put tentatively here because the ugly topic that is up for discussion stands between this theatregoer and real enjoyment of a well-staged show. Taking as his hero the frowsy night club punk familiar to readers of a series of sketches in *The New Yorker*, John O'Hara has written a joyless book about a sulky assignation. Under George Abbott's direction some of the best workmen on Broadway have fitted it out with smart embellishments.

Rodgers and Hart have written the score with wit and skill. Robert Alton has directed the dances inventively. Scenery out of Jo Mielziner's sketchbook and costumes off the racks of John Koenig—all very high class. Some talented performers also act a book that is considerably more dramatic than most. *Pal Joey*, which was put on at the Ethel Barrymore last evening, offers everything but a good time.

Whether Joey is a punk or a heel is something worth more careful thinking than time permits. Perhaps he is only a rat infested with termites. A night club dancer and singer, promoted to master of ceremonies in a Chicago dive, he lies himself into an affair with a rich married woman and opens a gilt-edged club of his own with her money. Mr. O'Hara has drawn a pitiless portrait of his small-time braggart and also of the company he keeps; and Gene Kelly, who distinguished himself as the melancholy hoofer of *The Time of Your Life*, plays the part with remarkable accuracy. His cheap and flamboyant unction, his nervous cunning, his trickiness are qualities that Mr. Kelly catches without forgetting the fright and gaudiness of a petty fakir. Mr. Kelly is also a brilliant tap dancer—"makes with the feet," as it does in his vernacular—and his performance on both scores is triumphant. If Joey must be acted, Mr. Kelly can do it.

Count among your restricted blessings Vivienne Segal, who can act with personal dignity and can sing with breeding. In a singularly sweet voice she sings some scabrous lyrics by Lorenz Hart to one of Richard Rodgers's most haunting tunes—"Bewitched, Bothered and Bewildered." June Havoc applies a broad, rangy style to some funny burlesques of night-club routines and manners. Jean Casto satirizes the strip-tease with humorous condescension. As a particularly rank racketeer Jack Durant, who is a sizable brute, contributes a few amazing and dizzy acrobatics. This department's paternal heart goes out especially to Leila Ernst, who is the only uncontaminated baggage in the cast.

Occasionally *Pal Joey* absents itself a little from depravity and pokes fun at the dreariness of night club frolics, and at the close of the first act

Source: Brooks Atkinson, "Christmas Night Add 'Pal Joey' to the Musical Stage," *New York Times* (December 26, 1940), 22.

it presents an admirable dream ballet and pantomime. Joey's hopeful look into a purple future is lyrically danced by Mr. Kelly. There is a kind of wry and wistful beauty to this spinning figures of Mr. Alton's dance design. But the story of *Pal Joey* keeps harking back to the drab and mirthless world of punk's progress. Although *Pal Joey* is expertly done, can you draw sweet water from a foul well?

"Not a Few of His Songs Were Left on the Cutting Room Floor"

Stanley Green (1923–1990) was one of the leading Broadway historians of his (and Rodgers's) generation. His work on Rodgers ranges from the brief *Rodgers and Hammerstein Story* (New York: Da Capo, 1963) to the monumental, encyclopedic, and indispensable *Rodgers and Hammerstein Fact Book: A Record of Their Works Together and with Other Collaborators* (New York: The Lynn Farnol Group, 1980). Green was also probably the leading researcher in the preparation of Rodgers's autobiography, *Musical Stages*, and appeared with Rodgers in a videotaped program for the Theatre Collection of the Lincoln Center Public Library.

In the somewhat obscure selection that follows Green offers a reliable and comprehensive survey of Rodgers's Broadway shows before 1957 that were adapted into film musicals or originally composed for film. In addition to providing encapsulated plot synopses, production information, and a brief explanation of such idiosyncratic features as the "rhythmic dialogue" in *Hallelujah, I'm a Bum*, Green also documents those Rodgers and Hart songs *not* left on the cutting room floor. Of Green's final predictions and suggestions of future film possibilities, two came to fruition. *South Pacific* appeared the next year, and *Jumbo*, the last Rodgers and Hart filmed adaptation, was released in 1962. *Dearest Enemy, Peggy-Ann*, and *Me and Juliet* still await their film close-ups.

STANLEY GREEN

A 1931 Broadway musical called *America's Sweetheart* was one of the first attempts on the musical stage to satirize Hollywood morals and mores.

The three young men who fashioned that piece—Herbert Fields (book), Richard Rodgers (music), and Lorenz Hart (lyrics)—had shortly before completed their first original motion picture. It was a filmusical called *The Hot Heiress*. Their experiences on that film sharpened the barbs they put in *America's Sweetheart*.

At that time the team of Rodgers and Hart was firmly established on Broadway and had been so for about six years—ever since the first *Garrick Gaieties*.

While Rodgers was still in high school, in 1919, a mutual friend had introduced him to Lorenz Hart, a Columbia University graduate seven years Rodgers's senior. Hart was then trying to crash Broadway by translating German plays. The methodical, well-adjusted Rodgers—his parents were well-to-do—and the volatile, unpredictable Hart, hit it off, and their partnership lasted until Hart's death in 1943.

Rodgers and Hart's first published song, "Any Old Place With You," had been added to the score of *A Lonely Romeo* (1919), by the producer, Lew Fields, father of Herbert. Rodgers was 17 years old. The following year he and Hart wrote their first "book" show, *You'd Be Surprised*, an amateur effort called "an atrocious musical comedy" on the program.

When Rodgers entered Columbia University he and Hart submitted a musical, *Fly with Me*, to the alumni board, which approved it for the Varsity Show of 1920. One of the board members was 25-year-old Oscar Hammerstein II, whose first professional musical, *Always You*, had opened in New York not long before.

Then Lew Fields, about to produce a new musical called *Poor Little Ritz Girl*, decided to let Rodgers and Hart do the songs. However, during the Boston tryout, Fields got nervous and called in veterans Sigmund Romberg and Alex Gerber to divide the musical chores. Rodgers and Hart consoled themselves by writing a second Columbia Varsity Show, *You'll Never Know*, which Hammerstein directed.

With little interest in anything but music, Rodgers quit Columbia after his sophomore year and enrolled in the Institute of Musical Art (now the Juilliard School of Music). He stayed there two years. In 1925 he and Hart wrote the words and music for *The Garrick Gaieties*, a semi-professional revue which the Theatre Guild put on to raise money for some tapestries for the Guild Theatre. The success of this show opened all the

Source: Stanley Green, "Richard Rodgers' Filmusic: Not a Few Of His Songs Were Left on the Cutting Room Floor," *Films in Review* (October 1956), 398–405.

doors previously bolted against young Rodgers and Hart. In the next five years they did the scores for sixteen musical comedies and revues.

Four of the sixteen later became movies. Neither *The Melody Man* (released February 1930) nor *Spring Is Here* (July 1930) were given national distribution. Neither was shown in a first run theatre in New York. The former had been adapted from an unsuccessful non-musical play they had written with Herbert Fields in 1924, under the pen name of Herbert Richard Lorenz. The screenplay was written by Howard J. Green, who had contributed material to the 1925 *Garrick Gaieties*.

Spring Is Here had been a moderate 1929 stage success. The movie version of it used only two songs from the original production ("Yours Sincerely" and "With a Song in My Heart"), and had new songs by Harry Warren, Joe Young and Sam Lewis.

The film version of the two other Rodgers and Hart stage musicals fared better. At least they were presented in first run movie houses. Radio Pictures turned *Present Arms* into *Leathernecking*. Paramount adapted *Heads Up!* Both films were released in the fall of 1930. *Leathernecking* had an interesting cast: Ken Murray, Eddie Foy, Jr., Lilyan Tashman, Louise Fazenda, the John Tiller "Sunshine Girls," and Irene Dunne making her movie debut. Once again songs by other composers were interpolated, and only two from the stage version—"You Took Advantage of Me" and "A Kiss for Cinderella"—were used in the film. And only two were used in *Head Up!*—"A Ship Without a Sail" sung by Charles "Buddy" Rogers, and "My Man Is on the Make," boop-a-dooped by Helen Kane. Victor Moore, repeating his stage role, supplied what little comedy the film had.

Rodgers and Hart went to Hollywood shortly after completing *Ever Green*, the English musical they wrote in the fall of 1930. Herbert Fields wrote the screenplay of their initial film, First National's *The Hot Heiress*. In it Ben Lyons, a riveter, follows a mis-tossed bolt into the boudoir of socialite Ona Munson, with the inevitable falling in love, misunderstandings, and final clinch.

Rodgers and Hart were accustomed to whipping a show into shape, in a couple of weeks, in small hotel rooms on the road, and to writing for singers. Now, supplied with luxurious accommodations, they were told to write for the camera, and to take their time. They did, and the final output was three songs—"Nobody Loves a Riveter," "Like Ordinary People Do" and "You're the Cats." They were not surprised when *The Hot Heiress* turned out to be cold turkey.

After giving vent to their Hollywood feelings in *America's Sweetheart* they returned to the film capital and stayed more than three years.

Some of their best work was written for the first three pictures they then made: *Love Me Tonight* (released August 1932); *The Phantom President* (September 1932); and *Hallelujah, I'm a Bum* (February 1933). These three films did not slavishly imitate René Clair's satirical movies, but they are among the more successful attempts to adapt Clair's approach to American films.

Rodgers thinks *Love Me Tonight* is the best of his cinematic efforts. Rouben Mamoulian, who was to stage the original production of *Oklahoma!*, directed, and the cast included Maurice Chevalier, Jeanette MacDonald, Myrna Loy, Charles Butterworth and Charlie Ruggles. Chevalier was a tailor and Miss MacDonald a princess living in a tower.

This film integrated mood, song and story better than any previous filmusical had. It opened with shots of Paris at dawn, with early morning city noises on the sound track. At first unconnected and discordant, the sounds blend into the song, "That's the Song of Paree," sung by Chevalier as he strolls to work. Another musical number, "Isn't It Romantic?", imaginatively bridges two scenes. First sung by Chevalier in his tailor shop, the tune is picked up by a customer and sung as he walks down the street. A cab driver hears it, sings the melody, which is taken up by his fare, who gets out at a railway station. There some soldiers hear it, and sing it lustily on a train as they pass a gypsy camp. The gypsies join in the chorus, and are overheard by the lovelorn Princess Jeanette as she leans out of her tower, sighing for the man of her dreams. The film had other good songs—"Mimi," "Love Me Tonight" (suggesting "Diamonds Are a Girl's Best Friend" of a later date), "The Poor Apache," and "Lover."

The Phantom President was a vehicle for George M. Cohan, and was his first and only sound film. Despite good reviews, it was not very successful, perhaps because of the widespread rumor that Mr. Cohan was dissatisfied with it. Cohan did nothing to squelch the rumor.

There were only three Rodgers and Hart songs in it—"Give Her a Kiss," "Somebody Ought to Wave the Flag" and "The Country Needs a Man." Cohan played a dual role: a colorless Presidential candidate and his double, a medicine showman. The latter puts on a song and dance campaign to win the Presidency for the former. Jimmy Durante played the campaign manager, and Claudette Colbert was the love interest.

Rodgers and Hart used "rhythmic dialogue" in *Hallelujah, I'm a Bum*. They had toyed with the device in the two previous pictures. By having much of the dialogue spoken in rhyme, music and plot seem more integrated, for the dialogue leads more naturally into the songs, fragments of songs, and background music. In one scene, three hoboes—Al Jolson, Harry Langdon and Edgar Connor—find a pocketbook in the street. Connor takes a gold watch out of it and, holding it to his ear, comments: "Tick, tick, tick . . . Dat sure am slick!" The "tick, tick, tick" theme is then picked up by the orchestra and played as walking music as the trio continue down the street. While they walk they examine the contents of the pocketbook, and when Jolson discovers a postcard, which is important to the plot, he sings its message aloud. S. N. Behrman wrote the screenplay from an original story by Ben Hecht. Lewis Milestone directed. The satire was aimed at the depression—and New York's fun-loving mayor Jimmy Walker, played by Frank Morgan. The songs included "Hallelujah, I'm a Bum," "You Are Too Beautiful," "I'll Do It Again" and "What Do You Want with Money?" In addition to the Clair influence, some detected a resemblance to Kurt Weill's *Die Dreigroschenoper*. In fact the film may have been too self-consciously experimental for its own good. It pleased neither reviewers nor public.

Although Rodgers and Hart wrote many songs for films during the next couple of years, comparatively few were in the pictures after the films had been edited.

In 1933, their "That's the Rhythm of the Day" was used in the finale of MGM's *Dancing Lady*, which featured Joan Crawford and Clark Gable, and introduced Fred Astaire. The following year, Anna Sten gave their sultry "That's Love" the Marlene Dietrich treatment in Samuel Goldwyn's *Nana*. And Hart had time to write new lyrics for Paramount's re-make of Lehar's *The Merry Widow*—the only time he ever wrote lyrics for music not composed by Rodgers.

Metro's *Hollywood Party* (released May 1934) ended up with just three Rodgers and Hart songs—"Hollywood Party," "Hello" and "Reincarnation," the last being a really funny specialty item for Jimmy Durante. The film was loose-jointed, practically plotless, and employed almost all the comics within hailing distance of Culver City. In addition to Durante there were Polly Moran, Charles Butterworth, Ted Healy, Jack Pearl, Laurel and Hardy, and Mickey Mouse. It was produced by Howard Dietz and Harry Rapf, but no director was credited (we ignore the explanation that no one was willing to take the rapf). The reviews were mixed and the public was indifferent. A song intended for the picture but unused was called "Prayer" ("Oh Lord, if you're not busy up there/ I ask for help with a prayer/ So please don't give me the air . . . ") and was written for Jean Harlow to sing in a casting office sequence, which was later eliminated. The melody, with a different lyric, became "The Bad in Every Man" that Shirley Ross sang in *Manhattan Melodrama* and again was left on the cutting room floor. Finally, with a third lyric, the tune emerged as "Blue Moon," the only really popular Rodgers and Hart song unrelated to a stage or a screen production.

Ever Green, their 1930 hit, became *Evergreen* when Gaumont-British filmed it, with a slightly different story. Some old Rodgers and Hart songs ("Dancing on the Ceiling," "Dear, Dear," "If I Give in to You"), and some new ones by Harry Woods, were used. The adaptation had been made by a young man named Emlyn Williams; Jessie Matthews repeated her original stage role; and Victor Saville directed. The film was shown in the US early in 1935, received good reviews, and was moderately popular.

Paramount's *Mississippi* (released April 1935) was the last movie Rodgers and Hart made before their second return to New York (in the spring of 1934). They had written seven songs for *Mississippi*, and three were used (Stephen Foster's "Old Folks at Home" was somehow credited to Rodgers and Hart when the sheet music from the film was released). "Soon," "It's Easy to Remember," and "Down By the River" were crooned by Bing Crosby to almost immediate success.

Their return to New York has been said to have resulted from the line in O. O. McIntyre's newspaper column: "Whatever happened to Rodgers and Hart?"

Rodgers and Hart then had an unbroken string of successful Broadway musicals, beginning with *Jumbo* in the fall of 1935 and continuing to [the revival of] *A Connecticut Yankee*, which opened on November 17, 1943, five days before Hart died of pneumonia.

They went back to Hollywood only twice—in 1936 for *Dancing Pirates* and in 1938 for *Fools for Scandal*. The former was one of the first feature-length pictures using the modern Technicolor process. The plot had to do with a Boston dancing master (Charles Collins) being shanghaied by pirates and taken to southern California. There he escapes hanging by teaching the Alcalde's daughter (Steffi Duna) how to waltz. Two lovely, and neglected, songs made up the "score"—"Are You My Love?" and "When You're Dancing the Waltz."

Carole Lombard and Fernand Gravet were teamed in *Fools for Scandal*, a lightweight tale of temperamental screen star and an impecunious marquis, written by Herbert Fields and his brother Joseph. Although a complete score was written, only three songs were used—"There's a Boy in Harlem," "Food for Scandal" (spoken by the film's principals with a musical background), and the still popular "How Can You Forget?"

The next four movies containing music by Rodgers and Hart were all based on their plays: *Babes in Arms* (released in October 1939), *On Your Toes* (released about the same time), *The Boys from Syracuse* (August 1940), and *Too Many Girls* (November 1940).

More of a vehicle for Mickey Rooney than a film version of the musical, *Babes in Arms* retained only the title song and "Where or When." New songs by Arlen and Harburg, Brown and Freed, Roger Edens and others, were added. Judy Garland and Charles Winninger were also around.

On Your Toes was notable for the dancing of Vera Zorina, who had played the lead in the London stage production, and the elimination of *all* the Rodgers and Hart songs. The music for "Slaughter on Tenth Avenue," was retained. Jerry Wald and Richard Macauley wrote the screenplay, Ray Enright directed, and Eddie Albright played Junior.

For the screen versions of both *The Boys From Syracuse* and *Too Many Girls*, Rodgers and Hart wrote songs not in the stage presentations. For the former, the booming "Who Are You?" sung by Allan Jones, and the minor "The Greeks Have No Word for It" shouted by Martha Raye, and for *Too Many Girls*, the haunting "You're Nearer" sung by Richard Carlson. *Boys* retained "Falling in Love with Love," "He and She," "This Can't Be Love," and "Sing for Your Supper."

Girls was closer to a photographed play than a film adaptation—it was produced and directed by George Abbott, who had staged the original show—and more Rodgers and Hart songs were retained in it than in any other movie.

They Met in Argentina (1941) was an original filmusical, now forgotten, about a Texan sent to Argentina to buy race horses who ends up winning the daughter of the horse owner. It had two directors—Leslie Goodwins and Jack Hively—and their combined efforts could not save it. The Argentine government protested its exhibition before a print had reached South America. But it did have quite a few Rodgers and Hart songs: "Amarillo," "Simpatica" (probably the most attractive in the film), "You've Got the Best of Me," "Never Go to Argentina," "North America Meets South America," "Cutting the Cane," and "Lolita."

During the war Rodgers and Hart wrote the title song for *Keep 'Em Rolling*, a patriotic short consisting of montaged war scenes that was dedicated to the Tank Corps. Jan Peerce sang the song.

In July of 1942 MGM released a film version of a stage version of a Hungarian play called *I Married an Angel*. In 1933 Rodgers and Hart and Moss Hart had prepared a scenario of it for Metro, but the picture was never made. When Dwight Deere Wiman wanted it for a Broadway musical in 1938 he bought the rights and when MGM brass finally decided to make a movie of it, they had to buy the rights back from Wiman.

They needn't have gone to all the trouble, for *I Married an Angel* pleased neither the fans of Nelson Eddy and Jeanette MacDonald, nor those of Rodgers and Hart. Of the original score, the title song and "I'll Tell the Man in the Street" and "Spring Is Here," were retained. The music of the rousing and Rabelasian "Did You Ever Get Stung?" was mated to a more innocuous lyric by Chet Forrest and Bob Wright, and called "Little Work-a-day World."

Higher and Higher (January 1944) was probably the least recognizable Rodgers and Hart musical on the screen. Its sole purpose was to serve as a vehicle for Frank Sinatra's film debut, and special songs were written for him by Jimmy McHugh and Harold Adamson. "Disgustingly Rich" was the only Rodgers and Hart song used for anything more than background music. The cast was rather startling: Michele Morgan, Jack Haley (who was in the play), Leon Errol, Barbara Hale, Mel Tormé, Victor Borge and the Hartmans. Sinatra made it a moderate success.

When in 1943 the Theatre Guild was planning *Oklahoma!*, a musical version of Lynn Riggs's play *Green Grow the Lilacs*, they approached Rodgers and Hart to do the score. Hart was in poor health, however, and Rodgers was persuaded to go ahead with the project with Hammerstein as his collaborator. Unlike Hart, who had achieved fame as the partner of only one composer, Hammerstein had been associated with a wide variety of song writers, including Rudolph Friml, Herbert Stothart, Jerome Kern, Sigmund Romberg, George Gershwin, Emmerich Kalman, Vincent Youmans, Richard Whiting, and Arthur Schwartz.

The rustic charm of *Oklahoma!* was more suited to the warm, lyrical verses of Hammerstein than to the brittle, complicated lyrics of Hart. The new partnership made theatre history—both artistically and financially.

With *Oklahoma!* and *Carousel* such record-making successes on Broadway, it was natural for 20th Century-Fox to get Rodgers to write the music, and Hammerstein the screenplay and lyrics, for a filmusical based on Phil Stong's *State Fair*. It proved very popular and "It Might As Well Be Spring" won an Academy Award. Its other melodic songs included "Our State Fair," "That's for Me," "All I Owe Ioway," "It's a Grand Night for Singing," and "Isn't It Kind of Fun?" The cast included Jeanne Crain (whose singing was done by Louanne Hogan), Dana Andrews, Dick Haymes, Vivian Blaine, Fay Bainter and Charles Winninger.

As it must to all successful song writers, a screen "biography" came to Rodgers and Hart in 1948. Called *Words and Music*, it was tasteless Technicolored hash, and the two dozen or so songs ground into it were the film's only excuse. Those responsible were Arthur Freed (producer), Norman Taurog (director), Fred Finklehoffe (screenplay), Ben Feiner, Jr. (adaptation), and Guy Bolton and Jean Holloway (story). Tom Drake played Rodgers and Mickey Rooney played Mickey Rooney, although he was called Larry Hart in the film.

Rodgers's most ambitious solo undertaking occurred in 1952, when he was commissioned to write the background music for TV [television] clips of Navy film of the major naval engagements of World War II. Called *Victory at Sea*, it was presented on 26 half hour programs over the NBC network, beginning October 26th, 1952. Rodgers's thirteen-hour orchestral score was brilliantly orchestrated by Robert Russell Bennett, and won for Rodgers the Navy Department's Distinguished Public Service Award. In the summer of 1954 the TV series was re-edited and distributed as a movie to theatres.

Along with other theatre notables, Rodgers and Hammerstein appeared in *Main Street to Broadway* (1953), a misguided effort sponsored by the Council of the Living Theatre that was intended to show something of the glories of the legitimate stage. However, its hackneyed story ideas were not worthy of the talents of Robert E. Sherwood who wrote the original story, Samson Raphaelson who wrote the screenplay, and Tay Garnett who directed. In their bit appearance Rodgers and Hammerstein pretended to compose a song, "There's Music in You," sung by Mary Martin.

During the past year the music of Richard Rodgers has certainly flourished on film. Although he contributed no new songs to the movie versions of *Oklahoma!*, *Carousel*, and *The King and I*, those stage successes were so transferred to the screen as to make them seem new.

People all over the world have become so familiar with the Rodgers and Hammerstein plays that it would be suicidal for any motion picture comedy to alter them in any major way. But this very fact poses a problem: how, without essential change, to utilize the advantages of the movie medium so the film will interest those who would not be lured to see a photographed play. The solution, and a sound one, is in the new movie techniques. *Oklahoma!* was filmed in Todd-AO, and *Carousel* and *The King and I* in CinemaScope 55.

Of the three, *Oklahoma!* (released in October 1955 and now just finishing a year's run on a reserved seat policy) was perhaps the most successful transfer to the screen. It was personally presented by Rodgers and Hammerstein, and except for the dream sequence, the locale was real (it was filmed in Arizona). Imaginative camera work at times created an impression of early American primitive painting—exactly right for the story. The cast, for the most part, was chosen with care, and Gordon MacRae, Shirley Jones and Charlotte Greenwood added immeasurably to the film's charm.

Carousel was somewhat less successful, partly because CinemaScope 55 is no Todd-AO, but chiefly because it aimed, in it exterior sequences, at too much realism. Shot in Boothbay Harbor, Maine, the scenery often vied with the story development and the music. When Gordon MacRae sang the "Soliloquy," certainly moving and dramatic in itself, he had to compete with the pounding surf and the beautiful but desolate seacoast. The dancing episodes seemed out of place, and unnatural. Contrast the delightful spontaneity of the "Many a New Day" presentation in *Oklahoma!* with the forced jollity of "June Is Bustin' Out All Over" in *Carousel*. It must be remembered, however, that, of the three plays, *Carousel* was the only fantasy, and consequently the most difficult to film.

The King and I made full use of the wide-angle lens to depict a tenuous tale of East meeting West amid the Oriental splendor of Siam. Except for a few outdoor sequences, most of the picture was shot inside the king's palace, where elaborate decor enhanced the musical numbers, as well as the action. Deborah Kerr's singing, incidentally, was expertly dubbed in by Marni Nixon. The screenplay, by Ernest Lehman, followed the original more closely than did either *Oklahoma!* or *Carousel*.

There are quite a few Broadway shows with Rodgers music that have not been filmed. *Pal Joey*, ignored by film companies after its original Broadway run in 1941, will soon be made for release sometime in 1957. *South Pacific* will eventually be screened. *Me and Juliet* would make a good movie, and so would such earlier efforts as *Dearest Enemy*, *Peggy-Ann*, and the colossal *Jumbo*.

Remembering Rodgers and Hart

The *Rodgers and Hart Song Book* appeared in 1951, eight years after the death of Rodgers's first lyricist. By this time Hammerstein had known Rodgers for more than thirty years. Hammerstein recalls their first meeting, in which his future collaborator on *Oklahoma!, Carousel*, and *South Pacific*, at least as Hammerstein remembered the occasion, was wearing short pants (see "Words by Rodgers" in Part IV for Rodgers's public refutation of this crucial detail). In this fond and thoughtful tribute to Rodgers's work with Hart, Hammerstein castigates himself for possessing neither "the perception nor the courage to predict their professional success." Hammerstein singles out for special praise Rodgers's work for invariably adapting "to the situation for which it was written and the character required to sing it," a trait more commonly attributed to Rodgers's work with Hammerstein. Similarly, in an assessment that predates Joseph Kerman's influential thesis that "the dramatist is the composer," Hammerstein asserts that Rodgers composes "music to depict story and character and is, therefore, himself a dramatist."*

OSCAR HAMMERSTEIN

I met Larry first. We were both actors in a Columbia Varsity Show. He had written a burlesque of the silent movies which had been very loosely interpolated into the story of the play. I don't remember much about this except that Larry played Mary Pickford. This would, of course, be unforgettable. The blonde curly wig didn't go very well with his thick black eyebrows, but it was not meant to. There was nothing subtle about varsity show satire in those days (circa 1915). Imitating the way movie ingenues were chased around trees by playful but pure-hearted heroes, Larry skipped and bounced around the stage like an electrified gnome. I think of him always as skipping and bouncing. In all the time I knew him, I never saw him walk slowly. I never saw his face in repose. I never heard him chuckle quietly. He laughed loudly and easily at other people's jokes and at his own too. His large eyes danced, and his head would wag. He was alert and dynamic and fun to be with.

After the Saturday matinee of this same Varsity Show, while the ball-

---

*Kerman, *Opera as Drama* (New York: Alfred A. Knopf, 1956; rev. Berkeley and Los Angeles: University of California Press, 1988), 91.

Source: Oscar Hammerstein II, "Foreword" to *The Rodgers and Hart Song Book* (New York: Simon and Schuster), 1951), ix–xii.

room of the Hotel Astor was being cleared for the dancing that followed all performances, a fraternity brother, Morty Rodgers, came up to me. He had in tow a boy about twelve years old, a smaller and darker version of himself, his kid brother, Dick. As we were being introduced I noted, with satisfaction, young Richard's respectful awe in the presence of a college junior whom he had just seen playing one of the chief parts in the Varsity Show. I, too, was conscious of my current glory and, realizing what a treat it must be for the child to meet me, I was my most gracious and courteous self—a man about nineteen trying to be a man about town. Whenever I made this effort I always finished far south of Beau Brummell and much nearer Ichabod Crane.

I saw Dick a few more times that year. Morty brought him up to the fraternity house and I heard him play on our bruised and beaten piano. We all liked him—a cute kid. In my memory of him, during this period, he wore short pants. He tells me now that by that time he had already put on long pants. All right, but in my memory he wore short pants. This impression—or illusion—is never quite absent from my current conception of him. Behind the sometimes too serious face of an extraordinarily talented composer and a sensationally successful theatrical producer, I see a dark-eyed little boy in short pants. The frequent overlapping of these two pictures is an element in what I consider to be my sound understanding of Dick and my affection for him.

It is not just my middle-aged weakness for reminiscence that led me to begin my appraisal of Rodgers and Hart by describing them when they were very young. The essence of the work they did together was its youth. They stayed young and adventurous and never lost an attractive impudence that was very much their own. At the outset, lacking a proper reverence for their elders and predecessors, they scorned to imitate Viennese operettas or the products of the local masters—Victor Herbert and Henry Blossom; Bolton, Wodehouse, and Kern; Harbach and Friml. They started something else, a kind of entertainment that soon became known as a "Rodgers and Hart Show." It had an amateur quality—amateur in the sense that its creators seemed to have had fun doing the job. In their extraordinary development as theatrical craftsmen, they never lost this gift for retaining their early character—a couple of lively New York kids, products of their town and their time.

A year or so after I had left law school I was on a Columbia University Players Club committee, appointed to choose the Varsity Show for that year. The script submitted by Dick and Larry won the competition quite easily. From time to time, after that, they would come up to my house and play songs they had written. One of these was "Manhattan." They wrote it several years before it landed on Broadway in the *Garrick Gaieties*. And how it landed! How swift was the welcome, how wide-open were the arms of the town for the newness and brightness of this sassy little revue.

In addition to "Manhattan," the *Garrick Gaieties* had several other songs I knew. I liked them for their original rhymes and gay tunes, but I hadn't the perception or the courage to predict their professional success. They were, in my opinion, too literate, too complicated, to become popular. I wished that the public would accept songs of this quality, but I was quite sure they wouldn't. Now here's the obvious question: if I liked them so much why didn't I assume that a great many other people were as bright and discriminating as I? It was because I hadn't yet learned that I was part of the world, going along with it, improving my taste as others improved theirs. I was pretty young myself, and inexperienced, and trying to get started in the theatre. I might, therefore, be forgiven for underrating the intelligence of the public and placing it far below my own. But I would not forgive myself for making this mistake today. And I do not forgive the hundreds of theatre, picture, radio, and television producers who continue to serve up products deemed "commercial" instead of works which they intensely and sincerely admire. The quick rise of Rodgers and Hart is a perfect illustration of how eagerly the public runs to meet something new and good, surfeited as they are with stale and imitative professionalism.

Climbing down from my soapbox, I will proceed to the business of discussing the music of my friend, Richard Rodgers. Music is a difficult subject—anybody's music. Words are easier to analyze. Everyone speaks and writes words. Few can write music. Its creation is a mystery. There are mathematical principles to guide its construction, but no mere knowledge of these can produce the emotional eloquence some music attains. We are made sad or happy, romantic, thoughtful, disturbed or peaceful by someone else's singing heart. To me this is a most exciting and inexplicable phenomenon. I should hate to be a music critic with the task of telling people what is good or bad in a musical composition or what are its component elements. One might as well try to explain to a group of children at the seaside the chemistry of salt water and sand, and the source of the sunlight or the breeze that romps with them along the shore. Certain experiences have an effect on us quite beyond the capacity of any symbols that can be written on paper, and what music can sometimes do to us is quite beyond the ken and lingo of academicians.

I am not a trained musician. As a librettist I use music as a tool that a kind composer has given me, but I have no idea where he got it. I do have some idea of how music can affect an audience in a theatre, and only within this limited area do I consider myself qualified to discuss the work of Richard Rodgers. He is essentially a composer for plays. He writes music to depict story and character and is, therefore, himself a dramatist. He is not an abstractionist in any sense and, as far as I can see, he has no interest in the mere creation of sound, however unusual or ingenious. He composes in order to make words fly higher or cut deeper than they would without the aid of his music.

He has written songs with only two men, Lorenz Hart and me. This is unusual. In the history of light music, I know of only three instances where an author and composer were permanently and exclusively linked: Gilbert and Sullivan, Rodgers and Hart, and Rodgers and Hammerstein. Before my collaboration with Dick, I wrote with Jerome Kern, Sigmund Romberg, Rudolf Friml, Vincent Youmans, Herbert Stothart, and at least a dozen other collaborators. This promiscuity is more typical of our craft. It is interesting that of the three instances of collaborative fidelity, Rodgers is in two of them. This is significant, I think, because it illustrates a sense of pattern and constructive purpose which never leaves him. This is not just professional habit, but a view of life. He is impatient with people who believe in good luck and bad luck, and he rejects mysticism as an explanation for anything. (In his heart he is far more a mystic than he knows he is. This is my belief, but he would never agree, and we shall never have time to argue it out with each other. We shall always be too busy delineating characters in our plays to spend very much time on ourselves. A good thing, too.)

To write with one collaborator after another, to turn out a series of disconnected theatrical projects, would be unattractive to Dick. He is essentially a planner and a builder. These qualities come out clearly in his music. His melodies are clean and well-defined. His scores are carefully built, logically allied to the stories and characters they describe, No overgrown forests or weed-clogged meadows of music here, but neat rows of tenderly grown flowers on well-kept lawns. Pseudo-artists and dilettante critics might interpret these comments as disparaging. The impulsive creator of "overgrown forests" of music might seem a more powerful and more important and more rugged fellow. Speaking for myself, I am bored with undisciplined talent. The intertwining vines and aimless vegetation that spring from careless genius are of little use to a world which suffers from obscurity, and not from too much clarity. Life is so short that no musician has the right to expect any appreciable number of people to devote any appreciable part of their listening lives to the wild free notes that dribble from his talented but casual fingers. A large number of musical compositions, a large number of grand operas and light operas, are too long, too carelessly put together, and fail for this reason. They are not above the heads of the public. They are just not worthy of the public because the creative artist involved has been too self-indulgent actually to finish off his job.

In his chosen field of light dramatic music, Rodgers's work is never tentative or indefinite. Each melody adheres to the purpose for which it was put into a play. It is romantic, funny, or sad according to the situation for which it was written and the character required to sing it. Most of the songs in this volume are gay and bright and brisk in spirit. Even the music of the love ballads is, for the most part, light-hearted because the lyrics were written in that vein. The stories of the plays for which these songs were written were light stories. It is no accident that the best words I can find to describe these songs are the very words I used in my first paragraph, describing Larry Hart. I said that he was always "skipping and bouncing," and that he was "alert and dynamic and fun to be with." Larry's humor and spryness are matched perfectly by Dick's melodic resourcefulness and the persistent, pulsating beat he puts beneath every tune. He has a way of making a melody appear to be going faster than it is really being played. When a song is actually played at a very fast tempo, the singer is handicapped in projecting the lyric and the listener is handicapped because of the singer's embarrassment. With Dick's appreciation of lyric values he would never permit a song to be played too fast or too loud, yet you think of these songs as fast songs: "Sentimental Me," "Manhattan," "The Girl Friend," "Where's That Rainbow?," "You Took Advantage of Me." Play these in a fairly slow, four-four time. Sing them in that time and yet observe how quickly they seem to be moving. I think it is because of that "pulsating beat," a sustained sharpness of accent in the bass.

Even the love ballads, which perforce must be slower and sung with more sentiment, even these seem to have a pace beyond the speed at which they are actually played and sung. "Here in My Arms," "My Heart Stood Still," "Where or When," "With a Song in My Heart"— these have strong melodic lines, and one line moves on to another without any long pauses between. Composer and lyricist get on with what they have to say, say it clearly and effectively and without interruption, without getting gooey in their sentiment, without becoming ponderous.

In the second decade of their collaboration Rodgers and Hart began to take waltzes more seriously. They had started writing at a time when American composers were dodging theme songs in three-quarter time. Waltzes had been the stock in trade of the Viennese school. Victor Herbert was an American exponent of the Viennese school as were Romberg and Friml. But Jerome Kern, Lou Hirsch, George Gershwin, Vincent Youmans, and Richard Rodgers seceded from these traditions and one of the results of their secession was to reduce the waltz to a minor position in their scores. Every once in a while, however, the natural charm of this tempo would assert itself, and these rebels would write fine waltzes, in spite of their alleged prejudice. "The Most Beautiful Girl in the World," "Falling in Love with Love," and "Lover" are three of the strongest songs in this Rodgers and Hart collection. They have become standard American waltzes played year after year, all over the world. One of my favorites is "Wait Till You See Her," a song that was placed in their last show, By Jupiter, but eventually cut from the score. Read it and play it and sing it and see if you don't agree with me that it should be revived some day to take its proper place in their impressive catalogue of waltzes. Any contemporary, looking through the pages of this book, must feel grateful to Rodgers and Hart for all the joy they have given us. This is a group of lovable songs. It is not alone the writers who can be proud of them. We can all be proud that they were written in our country and in our time.

II
Rodgers and Hammerstein, 1943–1960

Richard Rodgers and Oscar Hammerstein II (1943)

"As Corny as Kansas in August, As Restless as a Willow in a Windstorm"

Gerald Mast offers a rich critical survey that focuses on Rodgers and Hammerstein's popular quintet (*Oklahoma!, Carousel, South Pacific, The King and I,* and *The Sound of Music*) and their film adaptations. He displaces Sondheim with Hammerstein as the primogenitor of the "concept" musical ("Hammerstein was the first American to devise a concept for a musical and to write every show within it"), while at the same time challenging the widely accepted notion that Rodgers and Hammerstein's shows are totally integrated ("their shows do not integrate music and dramatic action so much as music and *character*"). He also shows through example how R&H tie up "a complicated plot" in short second acts "with very little musical twine" and how they modify the standard thirty-two bar song forms and remove "the essential distinction between verse and refrain" in their songs. Throughout his survey Mast addresses the larger cultural contexts and argues that R&H contained "musical debates on the pressing legal and social issues facing the American public and American public policy."

Mast is tough on the first four R&H films, *Oklahoma!* in 1955, *Carousel* and *The King and I* in 1956, and *South Pacific* in 1958, displaying particular antipathy toward *Carousel*, "the worst of the lot." For Mast, "these four Rodgers and Hammerstein films reject the entire history of the filmusical, especially the powerful relationship of space to music." On the other hand he finds much to praise in *The Sound of Music* (1965), crediting director Robert Wise for converting Hammerstein's "verbal poetry into visual imagery, freely intercutting images and telescoping space while characters sang," and making the lives of its characters "inseparable from the scenic surroundings."*

GERALD MAST

If, in Jerome Kern's words, Irving Berlin is American popular music, then Oscar Hammerstein II is the American musical theater—from his collaboration on *Rose-Marie* in 1924 to his spiritual influence on *Sunday in the*

---

*For more detailed musical and dramatic examinations of individual Rodgers and Hammerstein shows see Joseph P. Swain, *The Broadway Musical: A Critical and Musical Survey* (New York: Oxford University Press, 1990) [*Oklahoma!* and *Carousel*] and Geoffrey Block, *Enchanted Evenings: The Broadway Musical from "Show Boat" to Sondheim* (New York Oxford University Press, 1997) [*Carousel*].

Source: Gerald Mast, *Can't Help Singin': The American Musical on Stage and Screen* (Woodstock, N.Y.: The Overlook Press, 1987), 201–18.

Park with George in 1984. He envisioned a totally unified American music drama in which songs define the characters and drive the narrative, translating Wagner's *Gesamtkunstwerk* into American theater tastes and cultural terms. His stage works would be based not on Germanic myths but on homespun American characters, values, and ideals—combining Wagner's mythic seriousness with good old American fun. He also combined two generations of Hammersteins before him—his grandfather Oscar's productions of grand opera, his uncle Arthur's productions of operettas, and his father Willie's vaudeville shows. After his forty years in the theater, Hammerstein had not only demonstrated a theory but had forced everyone to adopt it. His vision of musical theater triumphed for an obvious reason: it represented the noblest imaginable idea for a show that began in 1866 with some songs, some jokes, and a lot of leg.

Hammerstein was also the premier poet of American musical theater. His lyrics strive for a heightened poetic imagery, based on the ordinary, everyday sensibilities of the characters who produce it. From the sun swimmin' on the rim of a hill in "The Surrey with the Fringe on Top" (*Oklahoma!*, 1943) to the canary yellow sky of "A Cockeyed Optimist" (*South Pacific*, 1949), from the buds bustin' outa bushes of "June Is Bustin' Out All Over" (*Carousel*, 1945) to the snowflakes that stay on the lips and eyelashes of "My Favorite Things" (*The Sound of Music*, 1959), Hammerstein transformed the sights and feelings of everyday American life into a heightened but homespun poetry.

He was also the first modernist of the American musical theater, writing with a conscious command of both the conventions and the history of the art he was crafting. Although it is fashionable to draw a distinction between Hammerstein's "realist" musicals and Stephen Sondheim's "concept" musicals, Hammerstein was the first American to devise a concept for a musical and to write every show within it. His concepts lead directly to Sondheim concepts: figuratively, because Sondheim merely shifts Hammerstein's conceptual emphasis; literally, because Sondheim was not only a Hammerstein admirer but his pupil and *protegé.*

Hammerstein dominates every history of American musical theater published over the last three decades. Ethan Mordden's series of deductions is exemplary: "The musical play is the most significant of all developments in the American musical. *Show Boat* was the first musical play. Hammerstein designed *Show Boat.* That makes him the most significant figure in the musical's history."* That significance, however, ignores two corollary losses: the great song hits from Broadway shows (fewer and fewer with every passing season since *Oklahoma!*) and the great top

---

*Ethan Mordden, *Broadway Babies: The People Who Made the American Musical* (New York: Oxford University Press, 1983), 142.

bananas and belting mamas to put them over. Hammerstein's music drama redefined the singer of a song—a specific character living in a specific place at a specific moment in history. While the voice, the I, of a Gershwin, Hart, or Porter lyric is an undefined surrogate for the lyricist himself, the voice, the I, of a Hammerstein lyric is an Oklahoma rancher, or a nurse from Little Rock, or a Victorian British schoolmarm.

Hammerstein's move toward Wagnerian theory demanded a response from Rodgers's music. Songs no longer captured casual moments but great peaks of emotional intensity. An inevitable stage direction in a Hammerstein script describes the music's swelling to "great ecstatic heights," further ecstasized by Robert Russell Bennett's monumental orchestrations. Songs became operatic arias for booming voices or "art songs" for delicate interpreters of *lieder*. The most famous male star of a Rodgers and Hammerstein show, Ezio Pinza, was an opera singer, and the most famous female star of Rodgers and Hammerstein shows, Mary Martin, was capable of singing *lieder*. No belter like Merman, Martin was a head singer with a sweet and willowy but very precise vocal instrument.

Rodgers and Hammerstein scripts also initiated an inescapable pattern: the very long first act, over ninety minutes, and the very brief second act, less than half as long. Their shows do not integrate music and dramatic action so much as music and *character*. Songs introduce characters—their beliefs, values, hopes, intentions—and they depict character interactions—falling in love, arguing each other out of love, feeling empty after the argument. Their songs serve the familiar dramatic functions of exposition (introducing the world of the play and its inhabitants) and complication (chronicling responses to social and emotional problems). The final section of the theatrical pattern—the resolution—is never sung in their shows because it is not singable. Characters perform an action by deed or in dialogue: Curly kills Jud in *Oklahoma!*, Billy Bigelow kills himself in *Carousel*, Lt. Cable dies on a spy mission in *South Pacific*. The first act is the long act (and the entertaining act) because all the songs that introduce and complicate characters are in it. To the second act goes the thankless task of getting the plot over with as efficiently as possible. The second act of *Oklahoma!* slots exactly three new songs and three reprises; the second act of *South Pacific* four new songs and two reprises.

Rodgers and Hammerstein shows build to a dramatic and emotional climax at the end of the first act: the great dream ballet of *Oklahoma!*, "Laurey Makes Up Her Mind"; Billy's soliloquy in *Carousel*, which leads him to join Jigger's plot to rob Bascombe; Nellie's shattering discovery in *South Pacific* of Emile's previous marriage and interracial children. Although the pattern comes from Rodgers and Hammerstein, it has been adopted by everyone else. The first act of Lerner and Loewe's *My Fair Lady*, one hour and forty-five minutes long, concludes with Eliza's triumph at the ball; the first act of Bernstein-Sondheim-Laurents's *West Side Story*, one hour and thirty-five minutes long, concludes with the choreographed "Rumble" that kills Riff and Bernardo.

To build a first act toward a soaring climax of triumph, pain, or doubt is a good way to get an audience back after intermission; it also increases the danger of disappointing them once you do. The structure runs contrary to the oldest adage of the musical show: build toward "the big finish," the "five-to-eleven number," as it was called when shows began at 8:30. The vaudeville bill always saved its headliners until the very end (like the Busby Berkeley films with their bam-bam-bam finales of three consecutive production numbers). No second act of a Rodgers and Hammerstein show (or most others of the last four decades) is as interesting or entertaining as its first. At best, it economically resolves an interesting story and keeps two terrific musical surprises in reserve: like "Happy Talk" and "Honey Bun" of *South Pacific*.

Although the cliché is that weak musicals run into trouble in the second act, all "integrated" musicals do. The difference between utter failure and resounding success is disguising the difficulty of tying up a complicated plot with very little musical twine. Rodgers and Hammerstein disguise their plot-heavy second acts with a sprinkling of new numbers and reprises plus a terrific production number at or near its very beginning ("The Farmer and the Cowman" for *Oklahoma!*, "A Real Nice Clambake" for *Carousel*, "The Small House of Uncle Thomas" for *The King and I*). Richard Rodgers, aware of the problem, began his work on a show by writing the opening number of the second act.

The Rodgers and Hammerstein shows demonstrate their music-drama idea most convincingly in individual scenes of the first act. The most important and carefully constructed of these scenes is the initial one between the two lovers—Curly and Laurey in *Oklahoma!*, Billy and Julie in *Carousel*, Emile and Nellie in *South Pacific*. In both spirit and method, these scenes descend literally from the first meeting of Magnolia and Gaylord Ravenal in *Show Boat*. Songs are not merely slotted into these scenes but whole scenes are built from interwoven songs, talk, and musical motifs. The songs refuse to stay put in specific spots and slots but seep repeatedly into and through the dialogue. This achievement can be traced to a musical development in the work of Rodgers and a verbal development in the work of Hammerstein.

With Lorenz Hart, Rodgers wrote songs, thirty-two-bar refrains preceded by lovely or intriguing verses. Only an occasional Rodgers and Hart song flaunted a structural innovation—like the haunting "A Ship without a Sail" (*Heads Up!*, 1929), structured A (twelve bars)-B (eight bars)-A' (twelve), or the seventy-six-bar "Johnny One Note" (*Babes in Arms*), whose musical extensions permit extended performances of Johnny's big note. With Hammerstein, however, the thirty-two-bar form became a very faint Rodgers skeleton. The essential distinction between verse and refrain disappears: "Out of My Dreams," "What's the Use of

Wondrin'?" and "A Cockeyed Optimist" dispense with the verse altogether. Rodgers regularly extends a refrain's length beyond the basic thirty-two measures with codas, musical interludes between choruses, and other transitional or extensional musical passages. Take, for example, the familiar "There Is Nothin' Like a Dame" (*South Pacific*). Although the song feels like a multichorus catalog of female attractions by a group of comically horny sailors, Rodgers has actually written a single song of precisely 128 measures: A (sixteen bars)-A(sixteen)-B (a four-bar recitative with a torrent of ad-libbed words)-C (the title theme, sixteen bars)-A-B-C-D (a forty-bar coda, listing the "dame's" attractions). There is no way to alter this structure, to add to it or subtract from it, as with a Cole Porter catalog. The male chorus must sing the entire number in precisely this form, no more and no less.

Rodgers is no longer writing verses and refrains but complex musical structures—arias and recitatives. "Some Enchanted Evening" (*South Pacific*), the single biggest popular hit to come out of any Rodgers and Hammerstein show, is hardly a thirty-two-bar song. It is a precise sixty-bar structure of A (sixteen bars)-A (sixteen)-B (a very odd release of six bars)-A (sixteen)-B' (in which the release becomes a six-bar coda). The song cannot be sung any other way. The "Dual Soliloquy" that precedes it is another odd structure—forty-eight bars, in which every eight-bar section is a variation on an identical musical motif (the "song" is A-A'-A"-A'"-A""-A""'). This musical passage depicts two characters, Nellie and Emile, each submerged in his or her own thoughts (a duet that is really two solos), considering the chances of being accepted by the other.

This "Dual Soliloquy" occupies a central place in the all-important first scene for these two characters. It follows, almost immediately, Nellie's view of her own cheery self—"A Cockeyed Optimist," a forty-bar song without a verse but with a coda. It precedes, almost immediately, Emile's view that life's opportunities must be seized (the sixty-bar "Some Enchanted Evening"). The "Dual Soliloquy" is a forty-eight-bar dramatic transition in which two separate people move toward becoming a unified pair of lovers. The entire drama of their swelling emotions evolves over the 148 measures of the three "songs," each representing a particular point in their progressive emotional journey, each with a radically different musical structure. This is not a love scene with three numbers; it is a scene that moves from getting acquainted to falling in love, whose numbers provide the dramatic transportation.

Rodgers could not envision this musical dramatization without the sensibilities of Oscar Hammerstein—particularly his ability to translate a character's dialect from the lines of an original play or novel (whether by Lynn Riggs or James Michener) into the lyrics of songs. The problem for Hammerstein, as for every American theater composer, remained how to make characters sing the way they talk. In *Oklahoma!* and *Carousel* rural patterns of American speech—a-worryin' and a-hollerin' and ascurryin' and a-skeered—skedaddle directly into the songs. Ado Annie "cain't" say no, and her songs burst (or bust) with dialect figures of speech—Nen, Foot! sorta, orta, heared, fergit, turrible, c'n, jist, purty. The New England fishermen of *Carousel*, like the Oklahoma ranchers, sing in their own dialect: "the vittles we et" at the "Real Nice Clambake" were "fitten fer an angels' choir." Hammerstein joins these dialects with images his characters experience in their daily lives: the "bright golden haze on the meadow" and the corn as high as "a elephant's eye" of "Oh, What a Beautiful Mornin'."

Rodgers accompanies these speech patterns with musical patterns that arise from the same personal experience as the dialects. "Oh, What a Beautiful Mornin'" is an old-fashioned waltz with a sixteen-bar verse, structured A-B, and a sixteen-bar refrain, structured A'-A", whose melody is a variation on the opening motif of the verse. The verse and refrain together form an indivisible thirty-two-bar whole, exactly like Stephen Foster's "Camptown Races" and "Old Black Joe." The implication is that Curly makes up this little waltz extemporaneously, merely improvising his honest, simple feelings in a song inspired by the sights, sounds, and smells of the mornin'. He pours his spontaneous experience into a musical form familiar from the songs of the day, hence credible for him to improvise. Like the Gershwins in *Porgy and Bess*, Rodgers and Hammerstein mirrored the feelings of "simpler folk" with simpler and earlier American song forms.

The most stunning effect of this collaboration is their weaving musical sounds and word sounds into perfect blends of feeling and idea. "The Surrey with the Fringe on Top" was their first (and most dazzling) piece of musical onomatopoeia. The song's rhythm mirrors the steady clip-clop-clip-clop of a trotting horse, characterized by five repetitions of a D with five identical quarter notes to begin every line of the refrain. A quarter note becomes the gait of a quarter horse. Hammerstein weds the repeating D's to monosyllables: "chicks and ducks and geese," "watch that fringe and see," "when I drive them high." To conclude the phrase, Rodgers repeats the D once again, this time as a fleeting eighth note, then drops down a note to C [Ed. C$^\sharp$], climbs back to the D and jumps up to a G. To these notes, Hammerstein pins multisyllable verbs to emphasize the musical movement—"better scurry," "how it flutters," "steppin' strutters." Rodgers's music "scurries" and "flutters" when Hammerstein's lyric describes scurrying and fluttering.

The same musical-verbal onomatopoeia created their Academy Award winning song, "It Might as Well Be Spring" (*State Fair*, 1945). The singer's listlessness is mirrored by repetitive musical phrases accompanying soft consonants and vowels: "restless as a willow in a windstorm," dominated by the soft "w" "as busy as a spider spinning daydreams," dominated by the lazy "s." In the next musical phrase, Rodgers deserts his predictable steps to jump up and down the scale in surprising leaps. Hammerstein accompanies the musical jumps with "jumpy" words in both their sounds and meanings: "as jumpy as a puppet on a string," dominated by the alliterative "p's"; "as giddy as a baby on a swing," dominated by the "y" and the consonants "g," "d," and "b." The meanings and sounds of Hammerstein's words are inseparable from the sounds and feelings of Rodgers's music.*

No theater craftsmen constructed these musical-verbal mirrors of dramatic emotion as powerfully or as frequently as Rodgers and Hammerstein. "Many a New Day" (*Oklahoma!*) is a defiant minuet in which Laurey protests (too much) that she cares not a whit about losing Curly. The rhythmically emphatic beat captures her head's tossing with defiance, accented by every repetitive "many," falling precisely on the downbeat of a measure, and the many "d's" of Hammerstein's lyric which alliterate defiantly—day, dawn, die, do. Laurey is defying no one but herself, her own feelings. "A Wonderful Guy" (*South Pacific*) is an exuberantly defiant waltz—this time Nellie defies the friends poking fun at her feelings for Emile with emphatic alliterative sounds on the crashing downbeats: both in the verse ("proud protestations," "person in pants") and refrain ("corny as Kansas"). Rodgers had begun to cherish the waltz, not for its flowing liquidity but for its thumping insistency.

"I'm Gonna Wash That Man Right Outa My Hair" (*South Pacific*) is a white pastiche of the blues, the only song of its kind Rodgers and Hammerstein ever wrote. Like the blues, its lyric and notes repeat identically three times before moving to a musical and verbal variation on the fourth statement. Like Curly in "Beautiful Mornin'," Nellie is making up a simple song as she goes about her everyday business—washing her hair—the equivalent of singing in the shower. She falls back on a kind of song she's heard often before. What makes her comic lament a white blues is that it lacks any surprising syncopation or mournfully flatted blue notes. A bouncy tune in strict "cut" time, with no unexpected departures from either rhythmic or harmonic regularity, this blues isn't blue. It reflects the way a cockeyed white optimist from Little Rock would sing the blues: revealing her own pervasive racial ignorance by unconsciously turning black blues into white bread.

Hammerstein has cleverly used the canary yellow of Nellie's naiveté to provide a moral commentary about the value and mission of America. As he had done two decades before with Kern and *Show Boat*, Hammerstein's books with Rodgers mixed thematic invention with operetta convention, contemporary commentary with Operettaland settings. His basic tool remained the double plot of operetta: the romantic love story balanced and paralleled by the comic love story in *Oklahoma!* and *Carousel*, the romantic love story balanced and paralleled by a tragic love

---

*An early Blossom Dearie recording of "It Might as Well Be Spring" on her first Atlantic album—in French!—proves how lifeless it is without Hammerstein's sensitivity to the sounds of English vowels and consonants. [Ed. Rodgers and Hammerstein briefly discuss the relationship between lyrics and music in their "Introduction" to *The Rodgers and Hammerstein Song Book* reprinted in Part IV.]

story in *South Pacific* and *The King and I*. The multistrand plots carry Hammerstein's moral and political commentary.

In *Oklahoma!* both love stories are triangles in which a "foreigner" invades the romantic territory of true-blooded Americans. Jud Fry stands between Laurey and Curly, just as the comic peddler, Ali Hakim, stands between Will Parker and Ado Annie. Ali, despite his accent, can be assimilated into American society; he belongs in the new state of Oklahoma. Although he is a traveling salesman, that traditional figure of rootless wandering and rampant womanizing, Ali can be very practical when he sees the moonlight shining on the barrel of a father's shotgun. Ali steps out of Will's and Annie's way to marry Gertie and "settle down to run Papa's store" (p. 78).* Like Rodgers and Hammerstein's own ancestors with accents, he is one of those immigrants who belongs in America. After all, he is a salesman.

Jud Fry is morally, not geographically, foreign. Physically dirty and slovenly, he collects lewd *Police Gazette* "pitchers" for the walls of his grimy shack. His masturbatory song, "Lonely Room," compares his creepy sexual behavior to that of mice and spiders.** Jud's difference is a matter of mind and spirit, not of accent and custom, like Ali Hakim's. Curly frees the new commonwealth of this lurking menace by making a practical response, like Ali, to a weapon—Jud's menacing knife rather than Gertie's father's comic shotgun. Curly's is an act of justifiable resistance to unprovoked attack, consistent with both the spirit and the letter of the law. When the Federal Marshal pronounces Curly's killing a justifiable act of self defense, Hammerstein invokes the very rationale for sending American men from states like Oklahoma overseas to kill the Jud Frys of the world, in 1943 called Nazis.

In later Hammerstein scripts, the obstacle is less personal than ideological, not a specific human being in a triangle but mental and spiritual barriers between the lovers themselves. Julie Jordan and Billy Bigelow of *Carousel*, like Magnolia and Ravenal of *Show Boat*, are psychological opposites—she innocent and well-bred, he a brawlingly powerful sexual animal. Their initial scene of meeting and infatuation is a virtual remake of Hammerstein's 1927 scene, complete with a song about "Make Believe," this time called "If I Loved You." Julie responds to Billy's dynamic sexual energy and he tries to bend to her domesticated demands, but the seeds of dissolution have been planted in this impossible marriage from its beginning. In his lengthy "Soliloquy," the single most consciously operatic passage in any Rodgers and Hammerstein show, Billy undertakes

*All quotations are from the Modern Library edition of *Six Plays by Rodgers and Hammerstein* (New York, 1959). This collection of "plays" represents the only musicals ever published by the prestigious Modern Library series of "Great Books."

**This song was not included on the Decca original cast recording of the show, the very first cast recording of an American show. Like the parodic numbers of *Pal Joey*, "Lonely Room" was probably considered deficient in tone for such a historic event.

the robbery that leads to his own destruction because he wants to provide materially for his new daughter, the way any proper middle-class father would. His failed robbery of Bascombe, owner of the town's fisheries—its leading citizen, moral dictator, and robber baron—is both a romantic act of political revolution and an illegitimate attack against the law itself, the basis of Hammerstein's civilization. As in *Oklahoma!*, the political debate in *Carousel* is between the legitimate act of defiance and the essential rule of law.

For comic contrast, Julie's friend, Carrie Pipperidge, snares the sensible businessman Mr. Snow, who has planned his entire life even before he lives it. Snow and Carrie grab their materialistic American rainbow but not without a loss of spontaneity and human compassion, not without becoming Bascombes—prudish, moralistic, bourgeois snobs, who pass these values on to their children. Mr. Snow never escapes the literal or metaphoric stench of fish. Although their comic union contrasts with the tragic incompatibility of Julie and Billy, the luckless, incompatible lovers share a passionate intensity that the bloodless, fishy couple lacks.

The dead Billy descends from his eternal home in heaven to observe the graduation, the coming of age, of his daughter, Louise. Like Kim in *Show Boat*, the daughter combines the spirit of both parents, carrying within her that mixture of physical and moral strength into the future where "You'll Never Walk Alone." Unlike Kim, however, Louise can produce no magical resolutions on earth; mortal consequences cannot be avoided and ultimate reconciliations must await immortal reunions. If *Oklahoma!* developed the moral argument for sending American boys overseas, *Carousel* offered consolation to those wives and mothers whose boys would only return in spirit. The meaning lay not in the tragedy of the present but in the hope for a future where no one walks alone.

While *Carousel* interwove tragic main plot and comic subplot, *South Pacific* reverses the two. The wartime *Carousel* suggested that present sacrifice could produce a brighter future; the postwar *South Pacific* warned of present and future dangers if social inequality could not itself be overcome. The main plot initiates a romance between another apparently incompatible couple—the brightly and brashly optimistic American nurse, Nellie Forbush, and the much older but wiser French planter, Emile de Becque. He reads Proust and Anatole France, while she, in his comic butchery of American slang, is a "hick who lives in a stick." He has seen the world and she has seen Little Rock, Arkansas. He has run away to the South Pacific because he once killed a man to defend his rights—the same reason that Americans like Nellie had come to the wartime *South Pacific*. Nellie can transcend all their differences but one—his former marriage to a Polynesian woman and its result, two "adorable" children who appear Asian not Caucasian. It is she, an American from a Southern state whose laws support segregation, who must overcome her racist assumptions. As in *Oklahoma!* and *Carousel* Hammerstein is testing the idea of law. Of course, Emile is as white as she is, but in Nellie's eventually accepting Emile and his children, *South Pacific* looks forward to a wiser racial future. The marriage between Emile and Nellie produces a union of three generations and three continents, of Old World wisdom and New World hope.

The tragic subplot of the show affirms these values. Its look backward to musical dramatizations of interracial East-West conflict—especially *Madame Butterfly*—suggests that looking to the past will produce tragedy in the future. Lt. Joseph Cable is a Mainline Philadelphia Ivy Leaguer who responds to the sensual power of the Polynesian Liat. The crunch comes for this lieutenant, as it does for Puccini-Belasco's Pinkerton, when the act of lust demands the legal sanction of marriage. Cable knows that his value system is artificial, not natural, a result of being badly but "Carefully Taught." But unlike Nellie, he cannot transcend his "education." In this later retelling of *Madame Butterfly*, it is the man who has "sinned" and must be punished by death. It comes, appropriately enough, at the hands of the Japanese, the enemy race his own white nation has come to fight in the South Pacific. Of course, Cable could never have married Liat and taken her home to his Mainline family; it is not Cable himself who is at fault but his "home"—the narrow values of the world that produced him but which he is dying to defend. Unlike the smug and callous Pinkerton, the lieutenant of *South Pacific* is a nice guy, a smart and sensitive Joe; it is his homeland that is wrong and must be taught otherwise. He becomes Hammerstein's sacrificial lamb on the altar of racial equality.

The King and I continues the clash of cultural values. This time neither mainplot nor subplot produces a conciliatory marriage. The king and the schoolmistress he imports from England cannot marry: she is a properly monogamous widow and he is a lustfully polygamous prince. But the sexual energy of their conflicting values—and the complete foreknowledge that their relationship can produce no sexual or romantic resolution—converts their antagonistic but loving companionship into the most intriguing clash of romantic characters in the four shows. While Julie and Billy, Nellie and Emile are clashing metaphors, Anna and the king of Siam are clashing minds, brilliantly equal and witty opponents. While Hammerstein usually let very little of himself into his characters, masking his own views and values behind theirs, the crusty king of Siam is as close to Hammerstein's dour, curmudgeonly self as he ever created.

Unlike earlier jingoistic operettas of cultural antagonism (say, *The Sultan of Sulu*), Hammerstein does not give his representative of Western civilization all the moral ammunition. Although a spokesperson for "democracy"—opposing the Siamese customs of slavery, possessing wives as property, and subservient kowtowing to the king as to a god—

the moralistic Anna has forgotten a few historical details. Slavery was originally a British mercantile institution; her visit to Siam in the early 1860s occurs at the very moment of the American Civil War, a historical consequence of British commerce. Nor does Hammerstein admire her sexual squeamishness, and he subjects the symbol of that prudery—the Victorian hoop skirt—to considerable derision. Like Billy Bigelow, the king is an admirably healthy sexual animal—and perhaps Hammerstein lets just a bit more of himself slip out of the closet with the king's sexual attack on Anna's blind propriety.* The closest they come to a union is an exuberantly climactic waltz, "Shall We Dance?" a question that returns to the "what if" of "Make Believe" and "If I Loved You." The result of their metaphoric union is, as in every Hammerstein show, a new future with a new law promised by a child. The young prince, a product of the king's tradition and Anna's education, abolishes the law of kowtowing to the king. He does not, however abolish keeping wives as property. Perhaps Hammerstein acknowledges the Marxist argument that in Western democracy monogamous marriage laws also reduce women to property.

If the main plot of *The King and I* is the most crackling of any Rodgers and Hammerstein adaptation, its unhappy subplot is sappy and formulaic. Tuptim, one of the king's many wives, a piece of property he received as a gift from Burma, longs for her true love, Lun Tha. She has been educated in Western ways—well enough to speak Anna's English and to yearn for Anna's romantic monogamy. Her attempt to elope with Lun Tha ends with their executions—like Cable of *South Pacific* and Julie Laverne of *Show Boat*, sacrificed to the misguided mores of a whole culture. Not only do the enslaved lovers "Kiss in a Shadow"; their whole love affair seems a shadowy slave to the Rodgers and Hammerstein formula.

How do Rodgers and Hammerstein inject the variety, the diversity, the "fun" that audiences expect from a musical into these serious-minded shows? With great difficulty. "No girls, no gags, no chance,"

---

*Despite the more normal surfaces of Hammerstein's life, he frequented the same kinds of bars and inhabited the same kind of closet as the more flamboyant Porter and desperate Hart. Jack Richtman, professor of Romance Literature and Gay Studies at SUNY, Albany, reports meeting Hammerstein in Upper East Side gay bars during the period of Hammerstein's greatest public popularity. These personal experiences never get into his shows, although the relationship between Anna and the king of Siam is perhaps a very oblique glimpse at a forbidden and impossible love. "We Kiss in a Shadow," also from *The King and I*, opens another crack in the closet door. The song's gay subtext is especially evident when sung by gay men's choruses. [Ed. It should be noted that neither Jack Richtman's recollection nor Hammerstein's level of awareness about the clientele of Upper East Side bars constitute reliable evidence that "We Kiss in a Shadow" offers a demonstrably gay subtext. See John M. Clum, *Something for the Boys: Musical Theater and Gay Culture* (New York: St. Martin's Press, 1999), for a thoughtful study that explores ways in which gay culture has successfully appropriated gay subtexts from ostensibly heterosexual characters and dramatic situations.]

Michael Todd predicted before the opening of *Oklahoma!** It was easier for *Oklahoma!* than for later Rodgers and Hammerstein scripts to get the gags and the girls into the show. Ado Annie is the classic soubrette, Ali Hakim the classic comic (with a Dutch accent, no less), and Will Parker the comic juvenile. Balancing Laurey's romantic Operettaland yearning to fly "Out of My Dreams" is Annie's comic song of earthly compliance, "I Cain't Say No":

> Fer a while I ack refined and cool,
> A-settin' on the velveteen settee—
> Nen I think of thet ol' golden rule,
> And do fer him whut he would do fer me!

Balancing Curly's poetic sights of the beautiful mornin' are Will Parker's comic sights of "Kansas City":

> With ev'ry kind o' comfort ev'ry house is all complete.
> You c'n walk to privies in the rain an' never wet yer feet!

Balancing Curly and Laurey's romantic "People Will Say We're in Love" is Will and Annie's comic duet, demanding "All er Nothin' ":

> If you cain't give me all, give me nuthin'—
> And nuthin's whut you'll git from me!

Agnes de Mille's dream ballet brings to dancing life the French post-cards and *Police Gazette* "pitchers" of Jud Fry's girls (as well as Will Parker's comic stripper at the burleecue who went about as fer she could go in "Kansas City").

As the shows move from *Oklahoma!*, they move steadily from not only traditional comic material but even from comic opportunity. The soubrette and comic of *Carousel* are more thematic than funny, and there is no soubrette in *South Pacific*. She has been transformed from the perky gal into the character lady, Bloody Mary, alternately bawdy of speech (parroting sailor slang, like "stingy bastard") and dreamy of song ("Bali Ha'i"). Only the comic, Luther Billis, who does not sing, litters the romantic script with bawdy sailor humor. The subplot romance between Cable and Liat is even more poetically inclined than the mainplot romance between Nellie and Emile; in "Younger than Springtime" Hammerstein's imagery converts Cable's arms into a "pair of birds that burst with song."

South Pacific varies romantic and comic material by translating the differing social backgrounds of the characters into different styles of

---

*Quoted in Mordden, *Broadway Babies*. Todd is the showman whose acumen gave us such stinkeroos as Smell-o-Rama.

song: Nellie's upbeat bounce, Emile's romantic wisdom, Bloody Mary's poetry, and American GI humor—whether the longing for dames or Nellie's parody of that longing, "Honey Bun." The comedy of *The King and I* is exclusively confined to the witty script and Jerome Robbins's choreographic parody of Uncle Tom's Cabin. This brilliant production number simultaneously alludes to American slavery, Siamese slavery, the parallels between Eastern and Western social oppression, and the oddity of translating Western mores and stories into an alien style of diction and dance.

In building steadily toward a unity of dramatic tone, musical form, and moral statement, the shows of Rodgers and Hammerstein just as steadily sacrificed the variety, the surprises, the virtuoso performance "turns," the witty songs that had brought audiences to American musical shows for a century. Like *Show Boat, A Connecticut Yankee, Porgy and Bess,* and *Pal Joey,* the four biggest Rodgers and Hammerstein successes were based on source material—two plays, one collection of stories, one novel (that had also been a film). Among their least successful shows were original conceptions: an allegory of Americana small-town life, *Allegro* (1947), and a backstager, *Me and Juliet* (1953). Their successes solidified a trend that they had themselves begun—with different collaborators—in 1927. It became a given that musicals would adapt novels, plays, and, by the mid-1950s, even films that had already been deemed worthy of cultural attention.

The four major Rodgers and Hammerstein shows were as bound to a specific period as they were to the covers of a book. Written between 1943 and 1951, they span the years during and just after World War II. They sought to define exactly what America meant and Americans believed, what its history had been, what moral resources that history provided, what moral lessons of error and inadequacy that history taught, what relationship and responsibility American and Western civilization had to the other sections and peoples of the globe. World War II was global in a way that World War I had never been. The United States, which lay between Europe and Asia, fought in both directions during the same four years. The sequence of Hammerstein shows, from *Oklahoma!* and *Carousel* through *South Pacific* to *The King and I,* suggests a steady expansion of a movement that began in Europe, was formed on both the New England coast and the Western Plains, then crossed the Pacific to less privileged, still enslaved peoples of other races. By 1951, America was fighting yet another war across the Pacific—in Korea, which turned out to be a dress rehearsal for Viet Nam. Though set in an apparent Operettaland, Hammerstein shows were musical debates on the pressing legal and social issues facing the American public and American public policy.

For Hammerstein, voicing the hopes of his generation, America was the beacon of the world, even if that light were sometimes dimmed by a naive optimism, racial prejudice, and sexual prudery. The Rodgers and Hammerstein shows move from the Civil War (the period of *The King and I*) through the 1880s (the period of *Carousel*) and the turn of the century (*Oklahoma!*) to 1943 (the watershed year in the South Pacific and the opening of *Oklahoma!*) and 1951 (when America returned to Southeast Asia). No wonder the United States Navy commissioned Richard Rodgers to write the music for the public telling of World War II—the orchestral score for the documentary television series, *Victory at Sea* (1951). Rodgers had been musicalizing the moral issues of that war for almost a decade. When politicians speak nostalgically of making America "the way she used to be," they are referring less to a reality of what America was than to the vision of what America ought to be in the shows of Rodgers and Hammerstein.

The only other Rodgers and Hammerstein hits came at the end of the decade. *Flower Drum Song* (1958) literally assimilated the exotic East with the modern West, setting the life of San Francisco's Chinatown to American song. Their last show, *The Sound of Music* (1959), was a nostalgic regression. Maria has been hired to educate the Trapp children just as Anna has been hired to teach the Siamese children; Maria and the crusty Baron von Trapp clash with the same willful intensity as Anna and the king of Siam; Maria's innocence, like Julie's and Nellie's, clashes with the baron's worldly and sexual wisdom, like Billy's or Emile's; the show's political backdrop recalls the wartime backdrop of *South Pacific*. *The Sound of Music* also regresses musically—"Climb Every Mountain" is another 4/4 anthem of hope and determination, ripped from the cloth of "You'll Never Walk Alone"; "My Favorite Things" reweaves "Getting to Know You," another interchange between teacher and pupils; "Do Re Mi" whistles a "Happy Tune" with the notes of the musical scale. Rodgers's songs are closer to the simpler structures and spirit of *Oklahoma!* than to the operatic passion and complexity that came later. Written in placid peacetime, between the war in Korea and the war in Viet Nam, the show is too confident that the storms have all been walked through and every mountain climbed.

It is unfashionable to admire this musical show and even more unfashionable to admire Robert Wise's 1965 film* called every parodic name from *The Sound of Muzak* to *The Sound of Mucous*. Wise's film, however, is as good a musical film as there is between 1958 and 1972—the best film version of any Rodgers and Hammerstein show, as good as any film adaptation of a stage musical in the same fifteen years. To understand why requires understanding Broadway's invasion of Hollywood in these same years. Rodgers and Hammerstein converted

---

*Ethan Mordden doesn't even mention *The Sound of Music* in either of his books on the Broadway musical. The film, for Mordden, is "neither all that great nor all that horrible," merely a model of Hollywood blockbustership. Mordden, *The Hollywood Musical* (New York: St. Martin's, 1981), 203–4.

Oklahoma!, Carousel, The King and I, and *South Pacific* into block-buster films in rapid order between 1955 and 1958. Models for every filmusical of the next decade, they represent the personal revenge of Broadway creators on a rival entertainment industry that had treated them shabbily two decades earlier. The industry's subtle retaliation was that these films barely lived on the screen and do not survive apprecia-tively in critical repute.

Richard Rodgers tells the story, with more than a little smug pride, of his triumphant return to Hollywood in 1954 to make *Oklahoma!* He took over Irving Thalberg's private office, the very place where, two decades earlier, he bid his personal goodbye to Thalberg, who did not know (or pretended not to know) who Rodgers was.* Hammerstein had equally bad memories of Hollywood in the 1930s—the most discourag-ing decade of his creative life. Kern had moved to Hollywood, where Hammerstein could never knock out lyrics the way a Lorenz Hart or Ira Gershwin could. Hollywood, which could never get enough of the same old thing, merely expected Kern and Hammerstein to pour old *Show Boat* into new bottles, like Paramount's 1937 *High, Wide, and Hand-some.* When Rodgers and Hammerstein returned to Hollywood in triumph, they held all the cards. They personally produced *Oklahoma!* and *South Pacific,* and they firmly controlled the rights, script, and style of the other two.

These are movies made by theater people, not movie people—lacking in visual style, visual interest, even visual beauty (except for an occasional Todd-AO ride in a surrey). They photograph human mouths in motion, while the notes and words (almost literally from the stage scripts) pour out. They are "opera films"—reverential attempts, in a blockbuster era of Hollywood desperation, to hang decorative sights on important music. They reject one of the earliest discoveries of movie musicals—going back to 1929—that space need not remain constant while characters sing. A striking statistic is that not once in *Carousel, The King and I,* and *South Pacific* does the camera ever desert the singer's space. Only rarely does it even desert a singer's face for the reaction of a listener. The films regress to the leaden visual style of *The Jazz Singer* as a matter of choice not technological limitation. The theory behind the choice must have been that to depart from the lips would distract from the lyrics, from Hammerstein's meanings, images, and sounds.

These four Rodgers and Hammerstein films reject the entire history of the filmusical, especially the powerful relationship of space to music. In *South Pacific* the sailors sing "There Is Nothin' Like a Dame" on what appears to be a real beach: a blue sky blazes overhead, waves roll toward the shore, palm trees offer their leafy shade. The wide CinemaScope frame supplies a vast panorama of visual potential—which Joshua

---

*See *Musical Stages* for Rodgers's tales of Hollywood misadventures.

Logan's direction ignores, duplicating the movements and gestures that might have been performed in his stage production (and probably were). Not once during this number does any member of the male chorus do anything with this scenery: nobody kicks sand, splashes water, climbs a tree. Nobody even gets wet. The real beach might as well be represented by a painted olio drop; the scenery has no organic relationship to the song. The big surprise on stage was Mary Martin's washing that man right outa her hair with real water: a functional shower is a pretty big deal on a stage. This was also the movie's only use for real water during a musical number. Someone forgot the ocean.

As "opera films," not "real movies," how well does each perform the original script and score—with as much visual and cinematic adornment as possible! Twentieth Century-Fox's *The King and I* (1956), directed by Fox's most dependable veteran of musicals, Walter Lang, produced by the movie-wise Charles Brackett, wins this contest hands down. The witty battle of the two characters—their clashing views, values, vision of the world—is genuinely interesting (as it was in the Rex Harrison-Irene Dunne film at Fox a decade earlier). Deborah Kerr and Yul Brynner do more than justice to it. Although the totally studio-bound film (even for the arrival of Anna's ship in Siam's backlot harbor) is as visually heavy as any of the group, the exuberant "Shall We Dance?" spins magnificently within the wide scope frame, and the dazzling "Small House of Uncle Thomas" is the greatest single musical number in any Rodgers and Hammerstein film. Directed, according to rumor, by an uncredited Vincente Minnelli with costumes by Irene Sharaff, the number offers a blazing display of radiant orange and yellow in an abstracted black mental space, a brilliant synthesis of Eastern theatrical convention and Western cinematic dance.

The worst of the lot is *Carousel*, made at the same studio in the same year. The most operatic of Rodgers and Hammerstein's theatrical productions (and Rodgers's own personal favorite), the script is their least dramatic and most metaphoric—from the pantomimic *Carousel* waltz, to a solilo-quized aria, to scenes "up above" in heaven. Henry King's direction captures a styleless visual void—from a *papier maché* forest beside a backlot lagoon for the interminable initial meeting of Julie and Billy; to a tacky electric-blue heaven strung with plastic Stars of Bethlehem; to a real beach where a soliloquizing Billy wanders in thought (but never picks up a pebble, sifts some sand, or touches a rock). The casting (Gordon MacRae and Shirley Jones) usually gets the blame for this film (and the allegedly sexy Bigelow looks pretty potty as MacRae squeezed into a tight striped sweater). But not even a Frank Sinatra, rumored to have wised up and walked out at the last minute,* would have been able to breathe life into this script, score, and decor.

---

*Ethan Mordden, *The Hollywood Musical*, 199.

South Pacific (1958), though not quite as deadly as *Carousel*, has few filmusicals to rival it for sheer bad taste. Joshua Logan's sole visual "idea" for the film was a series of colored filters to convey the poetic imagery of Hammerstein's lyrics. When Bloody Mary sings of "Bali Ha'i," we watch Juanita Hall's lips while her face goes fuchsia. The "Enchanted Evening" turns silver blue, but the faces of the two enchanted lovers, Mitzi Gaynor and Rossano Brazzi, turn ash gray, something between the color of newsprint and the color of death. And for "A Cockeyed Optimist" the sky (and everything else) turns a bright canary yellow. A younger Richard Rodgers had written a parody of conveying emotion by turning colors—"That Terrific Rainbow" for *Pal Joey*. He must have forgotten it when he produced the film of *South Pacific*.

Given Hammerstein's highly imagistic lyrics, and their consciously metaphoric unity with Rodgers's melodies, a Hammerstein film needed visual imagery to evoke the world of the characters in sights as powerfully as their words and music do in sounds. Only after Hammerstein's death could Robert Wise translate his verbal poetry into visual imagery, freely intercutting images and telescoping space while characters sang. *The Sound of Music* is a film in which the action is not only set in the Alps and the characters live in the Alps; Wise makes the Alps live in the characters. Their lives are inseparable from the scenic surroundings— they ride bicycles in it, row boats in it, climb trails in it, eat lunch in it. The film draws powerful visual contrast between being indoors, in the cramped, dark confines of the abbey or the von Trapp mansion, and outdoors, where Maria hears, feels, sees the sound and light of nature's music—and where she teaches others to hear, see, and sing them. The nature that inspires Maria's songs also "sings" in the radiance of Wise's images. The film's score, theme, verbal imagery, and visual imagery are one—sound, space, and light. The light of that outdoor space inspires the sounds that Maria makes into music.

Perhaps Maria is too metaphorically perfect for adult belief, and the children are milked and churned to cutesie-pie butter. But Christopher Plummer's cranky battles with Julie Andrews ignite the same clash of wit and wills as the brittle battles between Kerr and Brynner a decade earlier. The pathetic subplot—teenage Rolf becomes a Nazi, destroying his adolescent romance with Liesl—is as much an absurd understatement as a predictable Hammerstein formula. The use of singing as a political, not just a spiritual, metaphor is nonsense: if the Nazis would only sing, the film implies, if they would hear and make the sound of music as the Trapps do, they would cease to be Nazis. Bob Fosse's 1972 film of *Cabaret* answered that chimera with the revelation that the Nazis did sing; political values can be defined not by whether people sing but by what and why they sing. To make singing itself an act of spiritual, philosophical, and political commitment is a Hammerstein metaphor that goes back to "Ol' Man River." As a metaphor, this musicality may have been four decades and four wars out of date for literate American taste. But the film had more cultural power in the social climate of 1965 than the show did five years before. In those five years, a popular and attractive president had been assassinated, a Caribbean neighbor had become an enemy, blacks were accusing American society of its persistent racism, and American boys were dying in a distant place called Viet Nam. Many who stayed home didn't see any reason for Americans to die there, and said so—loudly. The film of *The Sound of Music*, like the Rodgers and Hammerstein shows from 1943 to 1951, was at the center of cultural debate, even if (like the earlier shows) it seemed an evasion of debate. The film transported a scarred generation of Americans out of the present's lack of political clarity and social cohesion, back to a past when Western moral values and American social purpose seemed clear and coherent. Where and how could clarity and coherency be found again if not back there—in what America was and what Americans believed in the battle against the Nazis?

Oscar Hammerstein would have been an influential figure if he had never written with Richard Rodgers. Co-author of Sigmund Romberg's best shows (*The Desert Song* and *The New Moon*), Rudolf Friml's best show (*Rose-Marie*), Kern's best show (*Show Boat*), and supervising producer of Berlin's best show (*Annie Get Your Gun*), that consistent excellence could have been no coincidence. Hammerstein's firm conception of what a musical might and should be stimulated his collaborators to their very best work.

His current cultural reputation is dimmer than it once was. Like David Belasco of an earlier generation, Hammerstein has suffered the simultaneous fate of institutionalized reverence and cultural contraction. The four films of his most important stage works don't capture their theatrical and cultural vitality. The four original cast recordings, from the era just before high-fidelity and stereo disks, don't sound very lively four decades later. The work of the man who began by translating Wagner's music drama into American terms today seems much more like child's play, much more suitable for children, than the songs of the poisonously playful Porters, Gershwins, and Harts.

"The Work That Changed the Form"

In this excerpt from his survey of 1940s musicals, a volume in a series of comprehensive decade-by-decade surveys from the 1920s through the present, Mordden revisits (and dispels) various legends about *Oklahoma!*'s inception and reception and places the work's artistic achievement within the context of its time and ours.* In Mordden's assessment, *Oklahoma!* fully measures up to the critical and historical hype and hyperbole that has surrounded it over the years, and he clearly and insightfully explores its influential adaptation and treatment of subject matter, its rich and nuanced character development, its innovative dramatic structure, its integration of all musical and dramatic components, and its use of dance to accomplish "what the script and score could not do in words and music." For once the facts fit the legend: *Oklahoma!* was indeed "the work that changed the form."

ETHAN MORDDEN

We know how unsuitable *Oklahoma!* was for the Broadway of 1943; that is what centers its legend. First, it was based on a flop play, Lynn Riggs' *Green Grow the Lilacs* (1931), that was more a study of a community than a story. A dark play, at that, in which a degenerate farmhand menaces a young couple till the boy has to kill the creep. Then think of the decor—flannel, jeans, and gingham against a background of cornfields and barns. A musical wants color, flamboyance, the exotic. And where would the choreography fit in, as square dances? Would wartime audiences, so eager for escapist entertainment, be remotely interested in a piece of history on life in the last territory within the national borders to be granted statehood?

How often legend misleads. In fact, *Green Grow the Lilacs*—the musical's working title, altered to *Away We Go!* by the start of rehearsals and

---

*In addition to his 1920s survey *Make Believe* (excerpted in Part I) and *Beautiful Mornin'* (excerpted here), two other relevant volumes in Mordden's series are now available, *Coming Up Roses: The Broadway Musical in the 1950s* (New York: Oxford University Press, 1998) and *Open a New Window: The Broadway Musical in the 1960s* (New York: St. Martin's, 2001). All of these books prominently feature the work of Rodgers as does Mordden's *Rodgers & Hammerstein* (New York: Harry N. Abrams, 1992). On *Oklahoma!* see also Joseph P. Swain, *The Broadway Musical: A Critical and Musical Survey* (New York: Oxford University Press, 1990), 73–97 and Max Wilk, *OK!: The Story of 'Oklahoma!'* (New York: Grove Press, 1993).

Source: Ethan Mordden, *Beautiful Mornin': The Broadway Musical in the 1940s* (New York: Oxford University Press, 1999), 70–79.

again to *Oklahoma!* just before the New York opening—was a fine idea for a musical in 1943. The story is actually quite strong—not busy, no, but rich in character development. As for decor and choreography, don't think literally; think of panorama, evocation, poetry. Cornfields? How about a *vista* of them, stretching as far as imagination can reach? Consider the costume designer's many options, playing around with the men's great hats, the women's frontier finery, with stripes and colors all zigzagging against each other. And *history*? When better to consider the national pageant than in wartime?

No, the idea itself was a sharp one, however much the usual swamis predicted disaster. What was wrong with *Oklahoma!* right from the start was the writing team, Rodgers and Hammerstein.

What team? Composer Rodgers had spent an entire generation working strictly in musical comedy with the ultra-witty *flâneur* Lorenz Hart. Librettist and lyricist Hammerstein had spent the same years mainly in operetta and its derivations, where waltz mattered more than wit and the *poète* roamed, not the *flâneur*.

All Broadway gaped as these two partnered up, and not only because they were so ill matched. Of Hammerstein's most constant collaborators, Sigmund Romberg was still very much on the scene, and Jerome Kern, though living and working in Hollywood, remained available for stage work—he in fact was to have composed *Annie Get Your Gun* before his sudden death in 1945. Rodgers's Hart, however dejected in his personal life, had just produced the lyrics *and* (with Rodgers) the book for *By Jupiter*, and would work with Rodgers on a revision of *A Connecticut Yankee* (1927) after *Oklahoma!* had opened.

So what did this mating of such opposites mean? SMART WEDS HEART (as *Variety* might have put it)?

But if the Rodgers and Hammerstein coupling hadn't existed, Broadway would have had to invent it. There were simply too many *Walk with Musics* and *Beat the Bands*, too much decrepit genre, junk about nothing. Theatregoing, so reduced during the Depression, had been expanding since the late 1930s. Money was more available, hit shows were running longer, and a huge audience was awaiting a long overdue revolution in the writing and staging of musicals. The form, cautious throughout the 1930s (with few exceptions), was stale by the early 1940s, so 1943 was about as late as the revolution could happen if the musical was to survive. In essence, the Rodgers and Hammerstein show turned out to be the converse of the Aarons-Freedley show: start with a solid story, then let all the showman's arts follow that story.

True, many operettas, the odd musical comedy such as *No, No, Nanette* or *Dearest Enemy*, and the always exceptional *Show Boat* had followed this line back in the 1920s. But the lesson had not taught in any real sense till *Oklahoma!* restated it, on March 31, 1943, in the St. James Theatre, to an opening night audience that had been hearing two very conflicting reports from the New Haven and Boston tryouts. One was

that the show was too . . . well, too cowboy to go over. It was corny and
. . . okay, not *corny* but . . . different. The other report called it the greatest musical that Broadway would ever see.

This is the part that gets left out of the legend. We hear of the Theatre
Guild's financial dismay, of countless backer's auditions to deaf ears. We
hear of Mike Todd's "no gags, no gals, no chance" after the New Haven
opening.* We don't hear from spectators who rushed back to New York
virtually trumpeting, or how Boston audiences screamed and leaped to
their feet in a day when standing ovations were unheard of.

Are we really to believe that, before the New York critics wrote their
reviews, *Oklahoma!*'s audiences didn't know a good thing? In fact, the
reviews varied picturesquely, from comparisons to *Show Boat* and *Porgy
and Bess* to Stark Young's being reminded of a "good college show"—
that cheap production, again, no doubt. *Oklahoma!* has always been an
audience show, whatever the critics think.

Let me point out something special about the piece: the songs pop out
of the script so naturally that the singing is like dialogue, only more so. Of
course, you reply: that's what musicals do. Not in early 1943. Songs
tended to block the action, stop it dead. *Oklahoma!*'s songs convey it. The
conversational nature of such first lines as "I Got to Kansas City on a
Frid'y," "Sposin' 'at I say 'at yer lips're like cherries," or "You'll have to
be a little more standoffish" is something only Hammerstein of all lyricists
ever employed before, and sparingly; in *Oklahoma!* he exploited it. The
times loved genre numbers; Hammerstein wrote none. On the contrary,
Oklahoma!'s opening number is a tiny tone poem on dawn in God's country followed by a cowboy's waltzy hymn to life and love on a lavishly
sunny summer day. *Oklahoma!*'s major courtship duet is contentious,
couched almost entirely in the imperative voice. Don't do this. Don't do
that. It's a bossy love song. Two of the show's major comedy numbers, "I
Cain't Say No" and "Many a New Day," not only make no allusion to
current events or town topics but trouble to oppose two types of woman,
the roughhewn sensualist, with plenty of basic rhymes, and the idealist,
with the poet's devious alliteration, internal rhyme, and metaphor. And
Oklahoma!'s most dramatic number, "Lonely Room," goes to the villain,
in an anguish of sexual appetite and psychopathic rage.

It is especially odd that Rodgers fell right in with Hammerstein's
program—odd because, with Hart, Rodgers wrote the melody first,
sometimes on a lyrical hook ("This can't be love," Hart suggests, and
Rodgers is already composing) and sometimes out of thin air. This had
long been the practice throughout American songwriting. But Hammerstein wanted a chance to initiate an entire lyric for each musical number,
and perhaps the inverted procedure is what called up an entirely new

*Another of Todd's comments, this one seldom quoted, was "I spent more on *Something
For the Boys'* curtain calls." Remember, part of what made *Oklahoma!* so unusual was its
cheap staging, inevitable given the Guild's economic problems and beautifully papered over
by the ingenious designs, but all the same disconcerting in an era that liked its musicals *big*.

sound in Rodgers. Perhaps the material itself did. Certainly, Rodgers had never written anything with Hart that anticipated the stylistic world in which "It's a Scandal! It's an outrage!," "Out Of My Dreams," or "All Er Nothin'" operates in.

Maybe the two authors worked so distinctively here because their characters gave them so much to investigate. Curly (Alfred Drake) and Laurey (Joan Roberts) are bickering lovers, mainly because Laurey is too headstrong and wishful for her narrow frontier culture and Curly is too typical of it. She's a landowner, a free woman—and a hungry one, though she doesn't know what she wants. It *should* be Curly: he's got charm and smarts, and he really loves her. Still, something about him gets on her nerves. His abundant self-confidence? His teasing need to control? She's restless and he's bewildered; so the bad guy, Jud Fry (Howard da Silva), tries to push in and take Laurey to the big social that forms virtually the entire second act. Why would she even consider going with this monster? Is she too terrified of Jud to refuse? Protecting Curly from Jud's rage? Lost in *nostalgie de la boue*? Eventually, Jud attacks Curly with a knife and, in the ensuing fight, gets stuck on his own piece, canceled out.

Thin plot or no, that's already more "there" than most musicals had. But this heavy triangle is lightened by the secondary couple, Will Parker (Lee Dixon) and Ado Annie Carnes (Celeste Holm), he so direct and she so flirty that it takes the ultimate Traveling Salesman, Ali Hakim (Joseph Buloff), and Annie's suspicious, gun-toting father (Ralph Riggs) to firm up the happy romance. Laurey's Aunt Eller (Betty Garde) supervises, as a figure Rodgers and Hammerstein would make generic, the Earth Mother (in Nettie Fowler, *Allegro*'s Grandma, Bloody Mary, *Pipe Dream*'s Fauna, a diaphanous version in *Cinderella*'s Fairy Godmother, and the Mother Abbess), who understands and guides, sometimes in an operatic contralto.

So there's not much in the way of actual events here. It's mostly courtships of various kinds, even imaginary, as Curly proposes to take Laurey to the social in a deluxe hired rig that doesn't exist (the famous Surrey with the Fringe on Top), though it somehow makes an appearance during the finale. The "Surrey" number is another very special thing about *Oklahoma!*: a musical scene rather than a song, using underscored dialogue to maintain the personal interplay between choruses and even changing the nature of the music itself, from braggadocio to lullaby.

The musical scene was not new to the musical. Hammerstein and Rodgers both had employed it throughout their careers. Yet neither had tried anything like "Pore Jud Is Daid," a funereal comedy number in which the hero tries to get the villain to kill himself even while goading him into a fight as the insults helplessly pour out. Like "Surrey," it mingles song with speech and even includes recitative, as Curly pictures the preacher's eulogy. The scene nudges the story along, develops character, and reveals how a primitive culture looks at death. That's a lot to do in four minutes, yet there's nothing apparently artful here, no demonstrations. It's natural.

Better, it's unique, like all the rest of *Oklahoma!*—and that explains this show's overwhelming role in the musical's evolution. One might say that *Cabin in the Sky*'s folkloric tone, *Pal Joey*'s naturalistic character development, and *Lady in the Dark*'s imaginative music-making all saw climax in *Oklahoma!*; but that's no more than a historian's irrelevant symmetry. What really matters here is how, at exactly the historical moment when Broadway needed it to, *Oklahoma!* applied unconventional storytelling arts to unconventional content in a way that seemed, if not imitable, inspirational.

That last statement may seem odd considering how many professional know-it-alls thought the piece would fail. But then, know-it-alls are always perplexed by novelty. Of course *Oklahoma!* could be copied, at least in part. Indeed, its use of choreography was almost immediately influential—specifically in the way the dancing fit into emotional grooves cut by the score. For once, in "Many a New Day," the dance following the vocal was not decoration but extrapolation, the women styling in movement the feminist independence that Laurey had been singing about. At the same time, the scoring of the song's verse ("Why should a woman . . . ") in the dance music uses the rich major seventh and 9/6 chords that we associate with the "heartland" sound pioneered by classical composers in the late 1930s. It's folk ballet.

So is the second-act curtain-raiser, "The Farmer and the Cowman," which might easily have been any banjo-friendly ditty quickly followed by its true *raison d'être*, a lively western dance. Not in this show: Rodgers and Hammerstein carefully twisted the song to highlight the social background, with a touch of range war implied. In fact, a scuffle does break out, ended only when Aunt Eller shoots off a pistol and forces the formidable Carnes to restart the number, a cappella, at gunpoint. When everyone else joins in—and only then—a dance of social harmony can proceed.

Clearly, director Rouben Mamoulian and choreographer Agnes de Mille found a way to mesh their work, to hold all of *Oklahoma!*'s staging in balance the way its authors had matched the score to the book. True, one piece did stand out: the dream ballet, "Laurey Makes Up Her Mind," because of its unusual length, its lyricism corrupted by brutal violence, and because the first act builds up to it so intensely that it makes a tremendously—and unpleasantly—decisive curtain before the intermission.*

This ballet typifies the way Hammerstein used Lynn Riggs's play—

---

*Actually, though *Oklahoma!* revivals do sometimes close Act One with the end of the dream—Jud's murder of Curly and abduction of Laurey—the original production topped off the dream with about thirty seconds of real time, as Jud awoke the drowsing Laurey and led her off to the dance while Curly looked on, "dejected and defeated." This may seem anti-climactic, but to end a dream sequence without ushering the public back into daylight violates one of the theatre's most useful rules. *Lady in the Dark* made no such error. It would be not unlike ending *Follies* after "Live, Laugh, Love." Dreams don't tell what happened; dreams tell *why*.

cutting down dialogue while remaining faithful to the central triangle, wholly inventing Ado Annie and Will Parker out of a bit part and a mere name, and always looking for ways to expand a chance line into music. In Riggs, the peddler tries to sell Laurey something, and she's a willing but difficult customer. Here's the *Oklahoma!* version:

> LAUREY: Want a buckle made outa shiny silver to fasten onto my shoes! Want a dress with lace. Want perfume, wanta be purty, wanta smell like a honeysuckle vine!
> AUNT ELLER: Give her a cake of soap.
> LAUREY: Want things I've heard of and never had before—a rubber-t'ard buggy, a cut-glass sugar bowl. Want things I cain't tell you about . . . Things so nice, if they ever did happen to you, yer heart ud quit beatin'. You'd fall down dead!

That's a wonderful moment, underlining Laurey's impulsive, confused personality; it's very close to what Riggs wrote. But in Riggs, the peddler offers Laurey only perfume. "Smells like the Queen of Egyp'!," he explains.

Hammerstein pounced on that, turning the perfume into the "Elixir of Egypt," a potion to clear muddled minds. "Smellin' salts!" Aunt Eller remarks. "Throwin' away yer money!"

But Laurey believes in it: because she needs to. Later, the elixir cues in a fifteen-minute musical segment, moving from under-scored dialogue to "Out of My Dreams," which starts as an ensemble number, as the girls advise Laurey to consult her own feelings and not the potion, and ends as Laurey's solo. Or does it end? For Curly enters during the chorus, and at the song's final phrase the dancing counterparts of Laurey and Curly come on, in effect taking over for the actors, who drift off. Nothing has ended: something is about to begin.

This is, of course, the dream ballet, designed to explore Laurey's worldview: her love for Curly, her doting friends, the vain, horse-proud cowboys (who dance on bowlegged, as if riding, to a clopping rendition of "The Surrey With the Fringe on Top"), the threatening Jud (also played by a dancer), Jud's "bad" women (three can-can girls, who strut and kick to "I Cain't Say No"), and Jud's solution to Laurey's emotional chaos: a date with Jud, which is murder and rape.

No wonder *Oklahoma!*'s dance plot impressed Broadway so quickly. Here at last was the reason all those ballet people had been choreographing musicals: to do in dance what the script and score could not do in words and music. To consult a character's feelings. Surely, one of the attractions of the forties classics was their choreography, exposing to an uninitiated public the excitement of high-maestro dance.

The designs, as I've said, were limited by the Guild's desperation budget, though costumer Miles White managed to exploit the fantastic possibilities in frontier chic, if such there be. Lemuel Ayers's sets were functional, though he did capture those vistas. At least both men held true to their subject, never sending everyone onstage for, say, a Latin number in rhumba ruffles and capes. Don't laugh—costuming the ensemble in irrelevantly coordinated outfits to dress the stage for a number was routine in the early 1940s, as if shows had not characters but dolls. No, everything in *Oklahoma!* kept faith with everything else. "The orchestrations sounded the way the costumes look" is how Richard Rodgers explained it: integrity.

Didn't earlier shows have it? Yes, at times; but even *Show Boat* contained moments given over to performer's specialties, not to mention a parade of Ziegfeldian beauties in the World's Fair scene. Even *The Cat and the Fiddle* let Odette Myrtil play her fiddle: because she could. Even *Lady in the Dark* gave Danny Kaye "Tschaikowsky." And even *Oklahoma!* had one conventional and even ancient excrescence, the Jewish comic.

This early-twentieth-century stereotype, preserved in many an early talkie, had almost vanished from the musical when Rodgers and Hammerstein revived him for the role of the peddler. In Riggs [*Green Grow the Lilacs*], played by Lee Strasberg, he was simply exotic—"a little, wiry, swarthy Syrian," Riggs tells us. "His speech is some blurred European tongue with middle western variations." But *Oklahoma!*'s Joseph Buloff, a veteran of New York's Yiddish theatre, made Ali Hakim into a throwback to *Rose-Marie*'s Hard-Boiled Herman, a dialect comic, with the gestures and the inflections. It's worth noting that, when Rodgers and Hammerstein superintended the *Oklahoma!* film in 1955, they deracinated the peddler, giving him to the gently all-American Eddie Albert: as if admitting that Buloff's performance was the one piece in the original show that wasn't quite correct.

Oklahoma!'s success was instantaneous, and eventually world-wide. It played New York for 2,212 performances, five years; the national tour (with, at first, Harry Stockwell, Evelyn Wyckoff, Pamela Britton, and David Burns as the peddler) lasted so long that it got back to New York in 1953, after ten years on the road, as *Oklahoma!*'s first revival. The film, though it dropped two numbers, is immensely faithful and brilliantly cast (including a splendid piece of genuine acting from the usually dizzy Charlotte Greenwood, the authors' original choice for Aunt Eller in 1943). Revivals are perennial. The very title of the show has become a summoning term meaning "The work that changed the form."

Well, it did. Its immediate and all-encompassing influence takes in: a cycle of shows with historical American subjects; a fascination with characterful rather than plot-filled stories and with conversational lyrics, leading to a concomitant decline of the genre number; a proliferation of musical scenes, especially in the addition of a few spoken lines between the vocal choruses, thus to keep story tension vital; a layout of long first act and short second act (because the stronger stories need more exposition time and the act break must now arrive at a genuine dramatic climax and not because the candy counter is ready for business); and in a sudden emergence of atmospheric, personalized, narrative dance, not for prestige but to bridge the gap between the script and the score, that place where neither speech nor song quite expresses what we need to know. True, not every choreographer tilling de Mille's field added all that much to his shows, and some of the imitations were embarrassingly slavish. For instance, the once occasional dream ballet would become de rigueur: there were at least four others in the eighteen months after *Oklahoma!*'s premiere. But there were some wonderful side effects as well, not least in a new sophistication in the composition of dance music. Indeed, *Oklahoma!* made dancing so integral to the . . . well, the integrated musical that high-maestro choreography became the fourth Essential.

The Theatre Guild Presents
Oklahoma! and *Carousel*

In his autobiographical *The Magic Curtain*, Lawrence Langner (1890–1962), a founding member of the Theatre Guild, whose fund-raiser in 1925 created the opportunity for the initial success of Rodgers and Hart, expresses his gratitude that the success of Rodgers and Hammerstein's *Oklahoma!* saved the Guild from precarious financial straits brought about by World War II. He also conveys his view that their Theatre Guild sequel, *Carousel*, developed into "the finest American musical play of our time." In one final paragraph Langner addresses the failure of the Guild's third Rodgers and Hammerstein show, *Allegro*, a failure he attributes to the production rather than the essential artistic material.

Langner describes the long and difficult fund-raising process for *Oklahoma!*, surveying the changes made during the out-of-town tryouts and numerous insider details related to the production history of both *Oklahoma!* and *Carousel*. He also offers insights into the working methods and character of Rodgers and Hammerstein, concluding that it is a "generous endowment of friendliness for others which has been at the base of Oscar's poetic quality in his verse, and of Dick's popular appeal in his music." Theresa Helburn (1887–1959), the Theatre Guild's executive director, revisits this material in her autobiography, *A Wayward Quest* (Boston: Little, Brown, 1960), 281–95.

LAWRENCE LANGNER

While the war was proceeding and we were all absorbed, in one way or another, in the war effort, I still had a theatre to keep going with Terry Helburn. And at the Theatre Guild there were crises, prospects of utter disaster and fortunately counter-measures that brought us out of extreme difficulties into the light of victory. The miracle that ensured the latter is no secret: it can be summed up in the magic word *Oklahoma!*, which will long remain a legend in the annals of the American theatre.

In our twenty-fifth season, that of 1942–43, our fluctuating fortunes were again at a low ebb. In December and January we had about thirty thousand dollars in the bank; our plays of the season before had lost a great deal of money, and because of the way the war was going, it was difficult to raise capital. This was the time which Theresa Helburn chose to launch her project to produce the new musical play called *Oklahoma!*, and it looked as though the gods were against us from the start.

Green Grow the Lilacs, the original play from which *Oklahoma!* was fashioned, was originally produced by the Guild in the season of 1930–31 and, as written by Lynn Riggs, it called for a colorful chorus which sang cowboy songs to cover the changes from scene to scene. Terry and I had long admired the musical genius of Dick Rodgers, and often tried to persuade him to write a musical play for the Guild. About four years earlier we had called on him at his home and suggested that *Lysistrata* by Aristophanes would make an excellent musical, and might be suited to the talents of the redoubtable Ethel Merman. Dick turned down the idea on completely practical grounds, but I remember remarking at the time, "Dick, I think you ought to write something for posterity," to which he replied, "I'd like to, Lawrence, but I have a family to support."

When Dick Rodgers came to live near Westport, Terry Helburn suggested to him that *Green Grow the Lilacs* would make an excellent story for a musical play. At the time, Lorenz Hart, who had been Rodgers's collaborator in *The Garrick Gaieties* and a great number of other musicals, was in poor health, and this made it difficult for them to continue collaborating. Terry talked over a number of lyric and book writers with Rodgers, and he suggested as his first choice working with Oscar Hammerstein, whom Dick admired greatly. Terry agreed enthusiastically to his being engaged by the Guild, thus forming the association between these two which has since made history in the musical theatre and resulted in such inspiring works as *Oklahoma!, Carousel, South Pacific* and, I hope, many others. To Terry goes the full credit for having conceived the idea of producing *Oklahoma!* and for bringing together these two artists to create the work. In doing this she provided them with

Source: Lawrence Langner, *The Magic Curtain* (New York: E. P. Dutton, 1951), 368–77, 390–93.

an American folk story which stimulated their creative energies in a direction away from the normal musical comedy field, in which both of them had been active for so many years. They, on the other hand, were quick to realize that in this American material, written by a genuine poet of the soil, Lynn Riggs, was a story and characters worthy of the very best they could create. Dick and Oscar, both of them poets, took this story and made it their own, and with such songs as "Oh, What a Beautiful Mornin'," "The Surrey with the Fringe on Top" and "Oklahoma!," a magnificent contribution to the folk music of America was made in their first collaboration.

I remember my first interview with Oscar Hammerstein after he had written the script. He is a big, slow-moving man with a broad kindly face—slow moving but quick thinking. Unlike so many men I have met in the musical field, his interests are wide, his reading extensive and his knowledge of philosophy, economics and world affairs, greater than almost any other man I have met in the theatre. Richard Rodgers is quick and volatile, a practical man of the theatre, and an excellent business man. Nevertheless, both men have this in common, that they are essentially artists in their approach to their work, have a simple, direct humanity, and take a warm personal interest in the lives of the dozens of men and women who work in the plays with which we have been associated. I think it is this generous endowment of friendliness for others which has been at the base of Oscar's poetic quality in his verses, and of Dick's popular appeal in his music.

The book of *Oklahoma!* was completed in the late summer of 1942, and all through the fall and winter thereafter, we held auditions in the Guild Theatre for singers and actors. It was soon decided that Alfred Drake, who had appeared in the Guild's production of *Yesterday's Magic* the year before, and had an excellent singing voice, would make a good Curly, and Joan Roberts who had appeared in a small part in one of Oscar's musicals was selected as Laurey. While we were auditioning actors and actresses for these roles, we were also engaged in financing the musical. As our own treasury was so depleted, it was obvious that we could not produce *Oklahoma!* without outside capital. It was also obvious, when we got in touch with our usual backers, that during this dolorous period in the history of the world it was going to be no easy matter to raise the money. We needed $90,000 to $100,000, and as I was often away in Washington, Terry bore the greater part of the task of raising this money. Indeed, our morale at the Guild was fairly low, for in addition to our failure with *Mr. Sycamore* (which ended in an arbitration with the author, which we lost), we also lost the services of our highly efficient business manager, Warren Munsell, who was invited by the Air Force to return to the Army, so that we were operating the Guild without a Business Department.

Marcus Heiman and Lee Shubert agreed to put up part of the money, but they themselves felt it would be necessary to secure considerable outside backing. We decided the best way to do this would be to have Dick, Oscar, Alfred Drake and Joan Roberts attend a number of tea parties or cocktail parties to which prospective backers would be invited, and then to play and sing the songs to them so that they would not be buying a pig in a poke. We took a studio in Steinway Hall on several occasions, and one of our first visitors, Joseph Swan, came with his young daughter, and they were so delighted with the music that he decided to invest 10 per cent of the capital needed.

We also tried to interest another friend, Mrs. Vivian Spencer, who had backed some of our other plays, but her own finances would not allow her to invest in this musical at the time. She generously gave us a large party, inviting guests who were in the habit of backing plays, and Dick, Oscar, Alfred and Joan—like a little band of itinerant musicians—played and sang the songs while Oscar explained the story of the play. Speeches were made about the fortunes which would result from a small investment in the new musical. Alas, neither the songs nor the speeches were persuasive, for among all those present, only two persons were found to invest in the play and this only to the tune of $2,000.

The money needed came in very slowly indeed, and I became very pessimistic, but Terry kept her chin up and continued to seek investors.

More cocktail parties were given, one in the home of Jules Glaenzer, a friend of Richard Rodgers's, and little by little in checks of $1,000 to $5,000, we gradually raised the necessary amount. S. N. Behrman, whom Terry persuaded to invest in the play, told me later that he did it only as a gesture of good will, feeling his money would be lost, but that he owed the Guild something for being the first to present his plays!

Finally came the question as to who should direct the play and design the scenery and costumes. Rouben Mamoulian, the hero of *Porgy* [the 1927 play] and *Porgy and Bess* [the 1935 opera], came to town from Hollywood, and he was engaged as the director on our suggestion. Miles White, the costume designer, and Lemuel Ayers, the scenic artist, had been discovered by Alfred Lunt and Lynn Fontanne, and were used in our joint production with the Playwrights's Company of *The Pirate*, which was very beautiful and colorful to look at; it seemed a very natural move to engage them for *Oklahoma!* When the question of a dance director arose, there was some difference of opinion as to the style of production and the kind of dance director needed. It so happened that Agnes de Mille, remembering that I had wanted to use her for the choreography in my production of *The School for Husbands*, wrote me asking if we could use her in the new musical project. I passed her letter on to Richard Rodgers, and later on I learned that Agnes was in rehearsal with her ballet *Rodeo* for the Ballet Russe de Monte Carlo. She invited us to see this, and Terry Helburn took Dick and Oscar to the opening performance. They were enraptured with Agnes's work, and indeed I have always felt that her creation of *Rodeo* greatly influenced the style of the ballets of *Oklahoma!*

Richard Rodgers contributed an experienced musical comedy stage manager, Jerome Whyte, who had been a "hoofer" in his young days and had successfully worked as Stage Manager for George Abbott and on some of the Rodgers and Hart musical plays; we contributed John Haggott, our Technical Director, and Elaine Anderson our Assistant Stage Manager. Early in January, we went into rehearsal at the Guild Theatre, every inch of space of which was thereafter crowded with activity. I remember particularly the ballet rehearsing in the lobby, with an impish-looking sprite named Joan McCracken who played "The Girl Who Falls Down," leaping through space in a tightfitting, black jersey practice costume, while every evening on the stage, as the shadows began to fall and the tired company went home, one became aware of the presence of a weird-looking individual named Eric Victor, who, long, lean and bearded, practiced leaping goat-like from the stage at unexpected moments, and scaring the lights and liver out of anyone he happened to take unawares.

Oklahoma! was a new form of musical, for it included both the elements of the musical theatre and of the dramatic theatre, as well as the ballet. The marriage between the musical elements and the dramatic elements in the staging of this unique combination, was due to the genius of Rouben Mamoulian who held to the same kind of integrated production he had established for *Porgy and Bess* and welded the varying elements together.

This was not an easy matter, and resulted in a number of controversies. For instance, it was the custom at the time for all musical plays to have so-called "specialty" dance numbers, and the original manuscripts called for one or more dancers to appear in what were called "spots" in the play to interrupt the action with the dance. For this reason the lively leaper Eric Victor was engaged without there being any particular "spot" for him. As the style of the play evolved, it became apparent that no place could be found for such "spots" either in the play action or the choreography, with the result that the necessity for using the talents of Victor, who had a "run-of-the-play" contract (which meant that he could not be discharged for several months) weighed heavily on our shoulders. On the opening night in New Haven, he fell off the trellis work and fractured a wrist. This would have been enough to deter any other dancer. Not so the leaping Victor! He went to the New Haven Hospital, had a plastic cast made for his wrist, and turned up the following week in Boston. It was suggested that he might hide in a barrel in Act 1 attired in cowboy costume, and after the musical number "It's A Scandal," he could jump out and perform his anti-gravitational antics. Victor, wearing large green gauntlets to hide the plastic cast on his wrist, was introduced into the play, but with disastrous results. His appearance was so unexpectedly frightening, that it took ten minutes before the audience would laugh again, and moreover it so hurt the production stylistically, that we paid off his contract. I happily record that he has since made a great success in other musical plays and revues which were more suited to his talents.

While *Oklahoma!* was in rehearsal at the Guild Theatre, Oscar and Dick were writing new songs without any apparent effort during the rehearsals, whenever they were needed. Terry and John Gassner, our play reader, suggested that some kind of rousing song of the earth would be helpful in the second act, and one day Dick and Oscar appeared at the theatre, sat at the piano where we surrounded them on benches and chairs, while they played for us the rousing melody of the song "Oklahoma!" Further excitement was provided when we went to the Brooks Costume Company and saw the costumes for the play. Both Rouben and I, along with the rest of the men, thought that the women were far too covered up, as their costumes stretched from the tops of their necks to the tips of their toes. So while the designer, Miles White, was not looking, we persuaded the cutter to reveal a little more of the girls' necks and bosoms, especially in the costumes of Ado Annie which were worn by the beautiful and talented Celeste Holm.

At the final dress parade on the stage of the Shubert Theatre in New Haven, we were somewhat appalled by the shirts which the cowboys were wearing; they included a number of fancy colors and designs, which would have been greeted by true cowboys with shouts of derision, and it was necessary to tone these down considerably before we could possibly open the play. "Can't you get rid of those 'bitch-pink' shirts," asked Lem Ayers. "They're killing my scenery." "They're killing our cowboys, too!" was the response.

After the dress rehearsal, there were a number of small adjustments, and the play opened with the title *Away We Go* on the evening of March 11, 1943, to an audience made up of New Haven play-goers, Yale students, a considerable number of New York managers, and finally the investors who came out of curiosity to learn the fate of their investment. The first half of the play flowed like a dream; indeed, except for a certain amount of cutting, it opened in New Haven very much as it is being played today.

The second act did not play so well, but when the final curtain fell, the play received warm applause from the audience. As I went backstage after the cheering had subsided and the house had cleared, the curtain was raised and I stood at the footlights with Elaine Anderson, our attractive Assistant Stage Manager, whose eager face was glowing with delight. "Imagine, Lawrence," she said, in her rich Texas accent, "Ah've bin in nothing but failures with the Theatre Guild, and this is mah first reel success!" Being superstitious, I rebuked her. "Don't say it's a success until after our opening night in New York." "But ah just know it's a hit, Lawrence," she said. "Ah absolutely know it!" And she was right.

As the crowd of managers, backers, friends of the actors, the composer and author chatted on the stage after the play was over, a well-known musical comedy producer who seldom talks in tones quieter than a resounding shout, informed everybody present that Oscar would have to rewrite the second act completely. Another important musical comedy producer called me on the telephone the next day and spent twenty minutes arguing with me that the perverted farm hand Jud should not be killed in the second act, because, in his experience of twenty-five years of producing musical comedies, there had never been a killing in one of them! I stated gently but firmly that this was essential to the play, and we would have to let it go at that. So pessimistic were the reports that came out of New Haven regarding the second act, that we decided to sell some additional interest in the play in order to be prepared for staying out of New York longer, if that were necessary, or to take care of losses in New York.

After the play opened in New Haven, Theresa Helburn whose courage and ideas had been so largely responsible in bringing *Oklahoma!* through its period in swaddling clothes, was taken ill with a severe throat infection due to overwork, and during a considerable part of the Boston engagement we had to conduct our conferences at her bedside. Notwithstanding this handicap, she continued to keep her fingers on the pulse of what was going on throughout the many ramifications of production. I applied myself particularly to organizing the changes in the second act, taking charge of the rehearsal timetable, which made me unpopular with everybody, and attending the conferences with the authors and director which were held nightly after the performances.

By a rearrangement of the material in the second act, and with very little rewriting, within ten days of the opening of the play in Boston, it was in excellent shape, and in practically the exact condition in which it opened in New York. During the Boston engagement there was an outbreak of German measles in the company, but fortunately for us, this took a mild form; it did look, however, for a moment that we might lose Agnes de Mille for quite some time. One morning while she was rehearsing her dancers, I met her in the lobby of the Colonial Theatre and remarked, "I've managed to get you an extra half-hour today, and I expect a kiss for that!" "Very well," she said, pecking me reluctantly on the forehead. Three hours later she came to me and said, "The doctor says I have German measles and I guess you're going to get it, too. This'll teach you not to collect bribes from choreographers." She was laid up for two or three days, but I escaped.

I was impressed during the rehearsals with the extraordinary resourcefulness of both Rodgers and Hammerstein. One of the chorus girls remarked to Rodgers, "Why isn't there more chance for us singers to use our singing voices? We have a wonderful chorus, and not very much to do." At that time, the number "Oklahoma!" was being sung mainly by Curly and Laurey, and we were all calling for more excitement at this part of the play. Dick immediately conceived the idea of using the entire chorus for the number with explosive effect. Oscar had a similar ability to think on his feet. When he was asked for an additional verse for the song "All or Nothin'" I remarked, "You have such a wonderful second verse, I don't see how you can ever improve on it." "I shall have to, Lawrence," was his reply. "It's my job to write a topper." "What does that mean," I asked, thinking vaguely that it had something to do with silk hats which had been called "toppers" in my youth. "Just a verse that will be better than the one that goes before," he replied. And sure enough, a few hours later he came out of his room with a third verse, definitely a "topper" to the other two.

Mamoulian was equally brilliant in integrating all the talent involved in the production, and merging them into the final form of *Oklahoma!* This was illustrated not only in the way the songs were directed by him, rather than, as customarily, by the dance director, but also in the way the play was lighted. In the beginning, the scenery was lit in accordance with current so-called "musical comedy lighting," but as the play progressed in Boston, it was supplemented with the kind of lighting which is used in the dramatic theatre. Every day more and more lighting equipment would arrive at the Colonial Theatre, in order to produce the effects of dramatic lighting called for by Mamoulian. When we moved to New York, to my horror, on the dress rehearsal night, we found that the front of the stage of the St. James Theatre was inadequately lit, and that the moment we turned on the very strong front lights which hung from the balcony, we had shadows all over the ballet drop which completely destroyed the effect of the end of the first act. We held a council of war and the following morning at eight o'clock John Haggott and I were working at the theatre with the electricians who constructed booms which were placed in the boxes, and were left there for the entire five-year run of *Oklahoma!*

When we were in Boston, a musical play called *Dancing in the Streets*, produced by Vinton Freedley with the adorable Mary Martin in the lead, and with scenery and consumes by Robert Edmond Jones was playing against us, and there was quite a question as to whether we should not try to race in to New York ahead of this play. Rudolf Kommer, Max Reinhardt's shadow, the roly-poly gentleman whose name has appeared now and again in these pages, came to Boston and saw both *Oklahoma!* and *Dancing in the Streets*, and he was as loud in his praises of the latter as he was pessimistic about the fate of *Oklahoma!* I myself had been worried as to what would happen in New York, because *Oklahoma!* was so different from any of the musicals which were running at the time. Many of the New York musical producers were either graduates of burlesque, or produced slick musical shows, done with great professionalism, which by this time had hardened into a formula. Except for *Show Boat*, there was absent from them any of the poetry or mood of Americana which characterized *Oklahoma!*

One objection which had confronted us when we asked for capital to back *Oklahoma!* from the professional Broadway investors, was that the play was "too clean." It did not have the suggestive jokes, the spicy situations, the strip-teasers and the other indecencies which too often went with a successful musical of those days. Some of these objections must have been in my mind when on the last matinee, the immaculate Vinton Freedley, producer of *Dancing in the Streets*, came to see *Oklahoma!* at the Colonial Theatre. "What do you think are its chances?" he asked me as he came in. "Well," I replied, "I don't know. A great many people think it's 'too clean' for Broadway." After the play was over, Vinton walked up the aisle and remarked, "I think this play will be a tremendous success! And," he added, "I don't think it's so clean either." There is, of course, a certain amount of lusty humor in *Oklahoma!* but it is never lascivious.

When the fateful day arrived for the opening of *Oklahoma!* in New York, we refused to allow anyone to be seated during the singing of the opening number, "Oh, What a Beautiful Morning," and it was apparent to me from the beginning of the play that it had started off on the right foot.* I wondered how a New York audience would respond to the fact that for nearly forty-five minutes, not a single chorus girl appeared on the stage. But as one beautiful song followed another, the audience took the play to its heart, and there was the most tremendous outburst of applause at the end of the ballet, as the curtain fell upon the first act. During the intermission, I noted there was that electric thrill which passes through an audience when it feels that it is attending something of exciting import in the theatre.

During the second act, after the gaiety of the "Cowman and the Farmer" songs and dances, there was no doubt about the outcome. At the end of the play, the applause was overwhelming. A lump came into my throat, for not for many years had any play of ours received such an ovation from its opening-night audience. The next day the newspaper critics wrote column upon column of praise for Rodgers, Hammerstein, Mamoulian and de Mille; there was not a single bad newspaper notice. And then the legend of *Oklahoma!* began to grow.

At first we knew that we had produced a successful musical play, but not one of us—Rodgers, Hammerstein, Mamoulian, de Mille, Terry or myself—had any idea of the popularity which the play was to achieve, and the bright page it was to write in the history of the American musical theatre. It was only as the enthusiasm grew month by month with the impact of the play upon the American public, along with the well-advertised difficulty of securing tickets which became a standing joke in the newspapers, that we began to realize that we had produced a theatre classic. On one occasion, Armina [Ed. Langner's wife, Armina Marshall] lost her little Tibetan terrier Chang, and in desperation, she gave out a story to the newspapers describing her dog, offering as a reward to anyone

---

*The principal members of the original cast of *Oklahoma!* included Alfred Drake, Joan Roberts, Celeste Holm, Betty Garde, Joseph Buloff, Lee Dixon, Howard da Silva, Ralph Riggs, Marc Platt, Katharine Sergava, Joan McCracken, Bambi Linn, Owen Martin, and Vladimir Kostenko.

who found him, two seats to *Oklahoma!* Chang was returned to us the following day!

The queue at the St. James Theatre box office grew longer and longer, the appeals from the ticket agencies grew stronger and stronger, and Fiorello LaGuardia, Mayor of New York City, telephoned for reservations whenever any distinguished visitors came to New York. The visiting European generals were entertained by the stationary American generals from the Pentagon; Mrs. Roosevelt from the White House, Mr. Morgenthau from the Treasury Department, and Mr. Hull from the State Department entertained foreign diplomats and potentates by bringing them to the play. The Duke of Windsor and his attractive wife saw *Oklahoma!* half-a-dozen times, and on one occasion I conducted him backstage where he bashfully made a charming speech to the equally charming company. "There's your favorite," said the Duchess pointing to Joan McCracken, the little dancer who originally fell down, and with whom the Duke shook hands and made some stammering compliments like an admiring schoolboy. . . .

Soon after *Oklahoma!* opened in New York we began to talk with Richard Rodgers and Oscar Hammerstein about the possibility of working on another musical together. Dick Rodgers was very frank in regard to his attitude. "We will work for anyone who brings us a good idea," he replied. Terry and I worked hard to find another good idea for them. She and I agreed that *Liliom* would make an excellent libretto for a musical. However, there were a number of complications. First of all, neither Rodgers nor Hammerstein seemed to find the subject entirely to their taste, while Ferenc Molnar, the author of *Liliom*, was not at all enthusiastic about having his classic of the theatre transformed into a musical play. We decided that the best way to solve the problem was to arrange for Molnar to see *Oklahoma!* and then to make his decision. At an interview with Theresa Helburn and myself after he had seen the musical, he confessed that if Rodgers and Hammerstein could treat the subject of *Liliom* as tastefully and charmingly as they had treated *Oklahoma!*, he would give his consent.

Our only obstacle now was Rodgers and Hammerstein, and they were a tough obstacle, for it took almost nine months of discussion before they finally agreed that a story as foreign to the American scene as *Liliom* could be made into an American musical folk play. It was only when Richard Rodgers thought of using a New England background, that matters began to progress. We were helped in this by the fact that while Armina and I were in Los Angeles a few months earlier, Armina's niece, a young lady considerably taller than Armina who responded to the name of "Little Armina," told her of a very fine singer named John Raitt who sang at their high-school concerts, and had recently won a prize for singing in radio. Armina met this young man in Hollywood at a time when there was no piano available for her to hear him sing, but she had one of her "hunches," and came into the adjoining room where I was engaged in a conference, saying "I wish you would meet a young man, John Raitt, who reminds me of Spencer Tracy in appearance, and is said to have a very good voice." I met John Raitt and was also impressed by his appearance, but had absolutely no idea as to how well he could sing.

Some months later, when we were looking for a replacement for the part of Curly in *Oklahoma!*, Armina insisted that we bring John Raitt from California and have him sing at an audition for Dick, Oscar and ourselves. The morning of the audition, Armina was very nervous. "Good Lord," she said, "supposing he can't sing!"

At the audition, John Raitt, a veritable young giant, came on the stage before the group consisting of Dick Rodgers, Oscar Hammerstein, Theresa Helburn, myself and Armina, who was sitting on the edge of her seat wondering what the outcome would be. Raitt stepped forward on the stage and said, "Do you mind if I warm up by singing the Barber's song from *The Barber of Seville* so that I can loosen up my voice?" He was told to go ahead, and stepped onto the apron of the stage and sang the Barber's song with such zest, execution, beauty of voice and clarity of diction, that we were all carried away by the excitement of the occasion. As he began to sing the second verse, Dick Rodgers, who was sitting behind me, leaned over and whispered in my ear, "There is our Liliom!" From then on the making of a musical play based on *Liliom* was assured.

In due course *Liliom* was transformed into *Carousel* by Rodgers and Hammerstein and with the integrated production by Rouben Mamoulian and ballets by Agnes de Mille, became, in my opinion, the finest American musical play of our time.

An unusual result of the uncanny collaboration of Rodgers and Hammerstein, was to make the musical play considerably deeper than the original play of Molnar, for they carried into it, through the ballet which was worked out with Agnes de Mille, and in the final scene of the play, a story of father-child relationship which is not to be found in the play from which *Carousel* was fashioned. Molnar was delighted with the work done by Rodgers and Hammerstein and attended one of the later rehearsals, sitting in the rear of the theatre. Nobody recognized him, and someone asked, "Who is that white-haired gentleman who is weeping so copiously?" It turned out to be Molnar. Indeed, everyone at the rehearsal was weeping so copiously that as I left to board a train with Terry Helburn, I remarked, "I'm afraid they have made the play far too sad. I doubt whether anyone will pay $6 for tickets to have their hearts completely broken."

The play opened in New Haven and the results were not unlike those connected with the opening of *Oklahoma!* The first act seemed to require the least amount of work while the second act was chaotic. Rodgers and Hammerstein had the idea of using a Mr. and Mrs. God in the proceedings, who turned out to be very gloomy indeed, for one could hardly be jocular on the subject. A number of changes were made in the play, including the elimination of a maternity scene in the ballet, in which Julie gave birth to her child—a scene which Agnes de Mille, not a girl to waste her ideas, promptly put into another ballet. With some excellent suggestions from Molnar and Mamoulian on the book, we arrived in Boston with a second act which was on its way toward the perfection which it later achieved.

Along with Dick Rodgers, I felt that a reprise of the love song "If I Loved You" was necessary toward the end of the play, but I met with considerable resistance to this idea. "Once you do this," said the authorities, "the members of the audience will reach for their hats and will never wait for the end of the play." However, I became quite obstinate on the subject, and to please me, or to silence me by proving their point, the reprise was put in. That evening I stayed in the theatre to watch the effect and I realized as I saw the audience reach for their hats and begin to rise and leave the theatre, that Dick and I were wrong, while the others were unquestionably right. I went backstage afterward to admit my error, when Dick Rodgers came up to me with a happy gleam in his eyes. "What sheet-music song do you suppose has sold the most copies of all those that are being offered in the lobby?" "I have no idea," I replied. "'If I Loved You'! The sales went way up tonight, and it now looks as though it will be the hit song of the show," said Dick. "But you will have to take that reprise out," I said. "It just doesn't work. The people want to go home." "Take it out?" said Dick. "Not at all. We'll find some way to use it so the people won't want to go home." It took a week's work before this was achieved.

Finally, *Carousel* came to New York and was installed in the Majestic Theatre.* Things went quite badly on the dress rehearsal night, and I left the theatre thoroughly discouraged. I went home and the next morning I remarked despondently to Armina, "What an absurd occupation this is. Months have been spent on writing this musical, more months in producing it, $180,000 has been invested in it, yet on the basis of one evening's performance, all this may go down in defeat. This is the very last play I will *ever* do." Armina had heard this kind of talk before, and she knew that in time it would wear off, but nobody could have felt gloomier than I did on the opening of *Carousel* in New York City. Richard Rodgers, whose back had been hurt during the Boston tryout, had to be wheeled into the theatre on a stretcher, and I thought I never saw him look so much the very picture of a composer and artist as when he lay helpless with his hair ruffled on a pillow and listened to the wonderful score of *Carousel*, which I consider to be his masterpiece to date.

This musical play again made history, and although it did not have the universally popular appeal of *Oklahoma!* it nevertheless ran a close

---

*The original cast of *Carousel* included Jan Clayton, John Raitt, Bambi Linn, Jean Darling, Jean Casto, Christine Johnson, Eric Mattson, Peter Birch, Murvyn Vie, Annabelle Lyon, Russell Collins, Robert Pagent, and Jay Veliè.

second and played two successful years in New York at the Majestic Theatre, a considerably larger theatre than the St. James where *Oklahoma!* played for five years. It also toured for two seasons and played later in the Royal Theatre, Drury Lane, London.

After *Carousel*, indeed, it seemed as if the luck of the Theatre Guild was henceforth to be bound up with the fabulous fortunes of Rodgers and Hammerstein. As if destiny wanted to warn us against too much dependence on anyone, however, our last musical venture with Dick and Oscar was less fortunate, as we were to discover in the fall of 1947.

Allegro, the third Rodgers and Hammerstein opus, made by no means as happy a chapter as the earlier two plays. There was an extremely cumbersome scenic investiture, which made it difficult to operate the stage, and moreover Oscar Hammerstein had to devote a great deal of his time to helping the direction of the play. The same teamwork which had resulted in the success of *Oklahoma!* and *Carousel* was missing, and the results were unwieldy and unconvincing. This was unfortunate, because the play broke many traditions, and was moving in the direction of an advanced American musical theatre. Oscar's thesis was really an excellent one, and would have been appreciated by the very critics who misunderstood it, had not his message been obscured by the production.

"R. and H."

In this excerpt, Agnes de Mille (1905–1993), the choreographer of *Oklahoma!* and *Carousel*, and *Allegro*'s director-choreographer, recalls how Rodgers (in contrast to Aaron Copland in *Rodeo*) gave her considerable initiative in determining a detailed scenario for the ballet music in *Oklahoma!* and how Rodgers tacitly approved her decision to set the death struggle of Curly and Jud at the end of the central ballet in silence. Readers also learn that the "dramatic invention" required in *Carousel*'s second act ballet "represented probably the hardest challenge" of de Mille's career to date.*

De Mille focuses on the diverse individual personalities and artistic partnership of Rodgers and Hammerstein. She attributes their unique effectiveness to "their professional watchfulness" as well as their talent, and expresses her admiration for a professionalism and insight that enabled them to dispassionately discard whatever it took to make the second act of

---

*De Mille's other major Broadway success from this period was *One Touch of Venus* (music by Kurt Weill, lyrics by Ogden Nash, book by S. J. Perelman and Nash). *Venus*, which starred Mary Martin and Kenny Baker, opened a few months after *Oklahoma!* on October 7, 1943, and ran alongside its blockbusting predecessor for 567 performances, a smaller but nonetheless impressive popular success.

Carousel work, including half of de Mille's ballet, five complete scenes, and even some good songs. What emerges from the "R. and H." chapter of de Mille's autobiography is a perceptive personal profile of Rodgers, who "fascinates and amuses," but also presents "a figure of some terror," and the more accessible Hammerstein ("one can talk to Oscar about anything at all") based on observation and personal experiences.

AGNES DE MILLE

In March 1945 Rodgers and Hammerstein once more collaborated with the Theatre Guild management, Theresa Helburn and Lawrence Langner, on a musical version of Molnár's *Liliom* to be called *Carousel*. The staff that had produced *Oklahoma!* reassembled, Rouben Mamoulian, Miles White and myself. The only addition to our group was Jo Mielziner replacing Lemuel Ayers as scene designer.

I had had the barest acquaintance with Dick and Oscar when I signed up for *Oklahoma!* but during the rehearsals and afterwards our friendship deepened. By the winter of 1944–1945 I was going to Oscar not only for professional advice but personal reaffirmation. Since every man in my life was far away and unavailable for comfort or council, I began to turn to him as big brother on many nontheatric occasions. The relationship grew to be one of the joys of my life. He had talked for over a year about his plans for *Liliom* and I looked forward to the opportunity of working on a second R. and H. production as the happy reward for being a good girl.

Plans ripened that spring. While the snow fell softly outside his Pennsylvania farmhouse, Oscar talked as only he can, transforming the material of our common craft into hopeful and lyric enchantment.

There have been few lasting collaborations in the history of the theater even though the theater is in essence collaboration. The difficulties involved in sharing responsibility and effort, the trial of work conditions, the apportioning of recognition and rewards have proved more than most friendships could encompass. Preservation of equilibrium implies a restraint rather more subtle than that required, for instance, in marriage. Such a relationship obviously presupposes mutual respect and absolute loyalty, consideration, and steadiness of nerve. Rodgers and Hammerstein have worked together in a team that has lasted longer in friendship (if not yet in business association) than Gilbert and Sullivan. They have been able to do this because they recognize their need of one another and because they practice discipline. I had a ringside seat at their first joint

Source: Agnes de Mille, *And Promenade Home* (New York: Little, Brown, 1956), 232–45.

effort and witnessed their great, their unprecedented triumph. I saw them at work in three productions; I was privileged to work beside them.

In a union like theirs, bound tight by creative collaboration, business involvements, administration and public exposure, they are locked closer than most families. Their interdependence suggests royal dynasty. And although the two households live apart with summer homes in different states, they present a common front to the public. R. and H. appear publicly together, they refer to one another in all interviews, they make decisions jointly, their joint word is pledged on all deals, they receive joint and equal honors. One might think that a double opinion on all questions would cause delay; it does not. They act with dispatch.

They always hold their first conferences privately, and come to staff meetings united and in perfect agreement. They decide quickly and they stand by their decisions. In the field of art this is not easy, the artist's birthright being to reconsider and alter. But in the theater hesitation is not always practical, especially in matters of casting and staff. And therefore R. and H. examine all newcomers personally, even the totally unknown. They can see, no one better, talent or lack of it in a face, they can hear it in a voice. Whatever I had that was good, either professional or personal, held their instant attention and no intermediary was needed to tip them off. For years anyone could appear for an audition and be heard and everyone, even the well known, had to—a precaution, although seemingly arrogant, designed to guarantee high caliber of production. They were like doctors who refused to diagnose until they had personally taken the pulse. From the time of *Oklahoma!*'s opening, every Thursday has been audition day. They saw and heard literally thousands, took note, and when the opportunity came in their great international enterprises, sent for the applicants and placed them.

This attention to detail has always governed their activity. Every audition, every rehearsal was watched by one or the other. They had final word on every set, prop, hat, light, inflection or musical key. Absolutely nothing was overlooked, not even after the openings, when Dick policed his theaters with a zest and concern extraordinary for someone who had seen so very many shows through long runs. During rehearsals, Oscar usually stayed with the actors, absenting himself only for rewrites, while Dick guarded the dancing and singing. Even with a management as experienced as the Theatre Guild and with directors as distinguished as Rouben Mamoulian, Joshua Logan, John Van Druten, Harold Clurman, and Fred Zinnemann, they never slacked their vigilance from the first day of rehearsal. What has made them uniquely effective (beside their talent) is their professional watchfulness. They check every aspect of their productions like mechanics going over an engine prior to transoceanic flight.

The impression on first meeting them was that here at last were the aristocrats of the business. They spoke softly, intelligently and politely. They knew about theatre prior to 1919 and outside of Broadway and

Hollywood. They were courteous and charming. Their interests were manifold.

In appearance they are dissimilar. Dick is moderately short and squarish, with a strong compact torso, the developed hands and forearms of a pianist, a strong short neck on which sets and turns a head almost archaic in its concentrated power. When considering, he becomes fixed and monolithic like a primitive. His piercing black eyes grow as opaque as an Aztec's, his face expressionless. The rest of us wait and hold heartbeat because the decision will be Star Chamber and final. "Well," he will say, throwing down his cigarette and smiling so suddenly and graciously that every subsequent remark becomes illuminated by the unexpected release, "I'll tell you what we'll do," and then he outlines a practical course of action, which may not be what you had in mind at all, but while he talks you will be convinced, or at least you will wish very much to be.

"I want you at the end of the dance," he will say, "to get a big hand— not a cheap hand. I want you in your way, in your own style, to stop the show—without, of course, sacrificing any of the delicacy or tenderness you value. I know you can do this without compromise; you have that kind of technique." The challenge has been thrown by Rodgers, S.J. [Society of Jesus]. And under the spell of his hypnotic persuasion you rush to meet it.

He kids and jokes companionably at all rehearsals, but he is a figure of some terror, through sheer nervous tension, high voltage, and the unforgettable overtones of his world power. His diction and tonality are straight New York, a flat, crisp, didactic voice, something like an instructor. He is the reverse of talky. He does not converse; he pronounces with judgment frequently unexpected and sharp, like summer lightning. Most of his comments are *coups de grâce.*

But at moments of direct personal approach he can be gentle. I suspect he feels in some ways cut off, even yearning; the banter is too constant, the quips too quick and sharp to betoken anything but vulnerability. He moves behind verbal machine guns. But just as the greatest quality in his music is a lilting delicious scherzo with overtones of hovering sweetness, so in his manner and in his eyes (when he is off guard) there is a brooding quiet, a kind of unappeased hunger, a woe.

Oscar seems solider, more the country gentleman, the paterfamilias, the benevolent, genial, eighteenth-century man of letters. He looks too neighborly, too understanding, too philosophic for our gypsy and disreputable trade. Oscar is somewhat older, but his respect for Dick's judgment amounts to veneration. He is a tall, broad, heavy and gentle-faced man with a soft voice, a Yankee twang when excited, and a chuckle that is one of the most auspicious sounds our theater ever housed. He has, for all his size, the quietness and discipline of an athlete. He smokes little, drinks almost nothing at all, and practices daily exercise and massage. Like Dick, he is always immaculately dressed. He wears beautiful custom-made shoes of glove leather that fit over his insteps without laces. He walks quietly; he waits quietly, he watches with attention genial and silent and can enter and leave a rehearsal without being observed or interrupting work in progress; but he will have learned a great deal.

Dick is considerate and quiet too, but always noticed. He takes a chair by the director, or by the piano, or he sits chatting in the auditorium with a member of the cast, or he dictates his entire morning mail. But he misses nothing, not an inflection, not a turn of the wrist or a grace note. And none of us ever misses the fact that he is there watching. In music rehearsals he is, of course, an active participant; he plays well and frequently takes the piano to give pace and dynamics.

When I started rehearsals for *Oklahoma!* I asked for an interview with him about the ballet music and handed him a detailed scenario broken down into seconds as I had done for Aaron Copland. He nodded and stuffed it into his pocket, then proceeded without slackening step into his song rehearsal. "Aren't you going to read this?" I asked. "You have all the songs, haven't you?" he answered. And, smiling, he hurried on.

No further word coming from him, the dance pianist and I began piecing his song tunes together in a kind of sequence—purely as a makeshift—and without warning, suddenly Dick materialized like a chef standing over the piano with pepper and salt, accenting, changing keys, shaping phrases, organizing both pace and music. But when at last we came to the final death struggle at the end of the ballet, we found that the score contained no melody suitable for breaking a man's back. I sent bulletin after bulletin upstairs to Rodgers, but he was coaching songs and too busy to come down. Finally in desperation we set the fight in silence to counts, and showed it this way at the first run-through. At conclusion Dick came tearing up the aisle and grabbed my hands. "It's wonderful and I like the silence. We'll put some tympany underneath to cue in the dancers." And that is how it remained. I was startled by this seeming casualness, but Dick knew it would be all right. He added a coda and the whole piece worked out well. If he had found the effect weak, he would have given prompt orders.

The most noticeable differences between the men are in their habits and methods of work. All matters except the writing and reading of lines are dominated somewhat, I should say, by Dick, but it is Hammerstein who composes first. His incomparable ear and flair for metrical form establish rhythms that are later translated into melody. Oscar works at his farm in Pennsylvania or in his superb Georgian study in New York, slowly and painstakingly, beginning at dawn every morning, writing at his stand-up eighteenth-century desk and pacing the floor, muttering. Dick works anywhere—his home, backstage, the orchestra pit, frequently in a cubicle in Carnegie Hall—rapidly and easily. (The eight-minute aria of Billy Bigelow in *Carousel*, which had taken Oscar many weeks to conceive and complete, was set by Dick in two hours, as fast, in fact, as he could indicate melody and key changes on paper.) Dick seldom revises or alters. His work is virtually complete when we go into rehearsal.

Oscar on the other hand, does considerable editing; the job for the rest of us just begins. So Dick sits watching. Oscar is more relaxed perhaps, because busier, and not so constantly present. Both are available with ideas and time when needed.

Oscar, who has the reputation of being folksy, down-to-earth and more or less cracker-barrel in his style, is actually prone to considerable daring in his search for new forms. He has attempted startling and lovely experiments. His first version of God in *Carousel* as a New England minister and his wife was extraordinarily imagined but shocked Calvinistic New Haven and was immediately and entirely deleted, the two characters becoming one, the star-tender, the keeper of the heavenly back doors, "The Mother-of-Pearly Gates," but the first version had a dry toughness that the second lacked and a quality that Oscar has frequently had to yield before audience hesitation or surprise. This occurred in one of the scenes in *Allegro*.

Dick is more conventional, classic, if you will. He is not so interested in experimenting as in reaching the audience emotionally and he prefers the direct and proven methods for doing this. He thinks the words of a song should be heard and understood, and the best place for the singer is, therefore, standing on the footlights and facing front, all but motionless, surrounded and framed by perfect quiet. To this end the lights are as a rule lowered and the singer picked out by a special spot. This treatment rather handicaps the director and gives small scope to movement invention. It can become monotonous. But monotony to Rodgers is of no concern beside clarity. If the song is good enough there will be no talk about monotony. And under his care the song is generally good enough.

Neither man has an eye for color. And this is strange considering Dick's great love for modern painting. On the other hand, he can grasp the form and idiom of dance movement with the skill of a choreographer and has always been creatively helpful in placing and cutting dances. Oscar has no true visual appreciation; he admits he does not know how to look at painting. Pure gesture communicates nothing to him. But if he recognizes only dramatic content, how sensitive he is with this! My feeling for character, for intimate comedy, for the pattern dictated by situation and mood, even my willingness to forgo the effects that would ensure a final hand were treated by him with gentle and appreciative intelligence.

In setting stage business for their song I strove, without contradiction of text or character, to broaden the author's original intent by adding my own comment. Sometimes quite sly and expressive jokes could be contrived by playing off one medium against another. But they always were keyed to scene and mood. In this way the dances are rooted into the score and dialogue and have become part of the flesh; that is why they are always reproduced no matter who stages the revivals.

The authors were appreciative. Dick's enthusiasm for any subtle rhythmic device or a gay "button" at the end of a piece (the trick that drives the point home sharp and clear), Oscar's joyous and tender excitement when I did something revealing of character, when I added speech to the dances in *Carousel*, for instance (Oscar is in love with language and likes to see it get on), were the rewards of working with them. They were equally vocal when dissatisfied, insisting on eighteen tries and my heart's blood, insisting and persisting until the curtain was up. Then time stopped and they cut. I have seen Dick yank out ten minutes of his own music without an attempt to save it. He has also yanked ten minutes of my dancing, but he put the scalpel into my hand.

In spite of their great skill, the tryout periods for their shows have always been quite as hard as any others; but there were little diversions and encouragements peculiar to association with them. There were the quatrains and parodies Oscar improvised under his breath apropos of rehearsal occurrences. Many a lunch ended with a completed song quite as brilliant as any published. There were Oscar's outrageous and superb puns murmured half apologetically as though not expecting the corroboration of a giggle or even the turning of a head, like his designation of a delicate caress on a cancan girl's bustle as a "gosling," or his wordless comment as when at a particularly stringent moment, having ordered a cut against my bitter opposition, "and don't come out of rehearsal hall until it's done," he sent a tray of twenty cartons of coffee where I sat alone brooding (this was, of course, after coffee rationing had ended), or when he had discussed for days the cutting of another number, the *Carousel* clambake dance, he said, sitting down quietly, "Convince me," and sometime later, "You argue well, but I don't agree."

"I don't agree too," I replied patly.

"That makes us even. But I have the choice."

I answered, "That's candid. I can accept that."

"My dear," he chuckled, "you'd better. You have to."

Or again, when hearing me express extreme dissatisfaction with my own work, he put his arms around me and murmured, "You be careful what you say about de Mille; you're talking about the woman I love."

Both men, wise in this difficult business, are generous with advice. Oscar takes time off to read and consider lengthy manuscripts and gives council and help. But one can talk to Oscar about anything at all. For Oscar one clips items from newspapers and magazines, marks passages in books, reports conversation of adolescents. I have seen him set aside work and spend half an afternoon teaching chess to an eight-year-old. Oscar has given away a dozen young professionals in marriage and stood godfather at a score of christenings. Dick fascinates and amuses, but it is Oscar whose hand they ask to take at solemn moments.

And at moments of need. I went to him once on behalf of Ballet Theatre. It was the first time I had ever approached anyone in his position for money. I had not warned him about what I came for. I sat down in great disquiet in the beautiful Georgian chair, surrounded by the fabulous porcelain and books, and faced him over the mahogany desk with the silver accouterments. He smiled and waited. I squirmed and moistened my lips. He didn't speak.

"It's just this—" I stuttered.

"All right, yes," he cut me short.

"Yes what?"

"Yes a thousand dollars. Never mind the pitch. Do you want Scotch or bourbon?"

Oscar and Dick take on together not only the regulation charities expected of men in their position, but their own foundation and causes, political issues and social reforms. They work hard at them, writing pamphlets and sketches and songs. Oscar devotes a real measure of his time and resources to this.

Both are businessmen in the historic American tradition and combine the drive and power of nineteenth-century empire builders with eighteenth-century politesse and philosophy, living in ducal splendor and maintaining a suite of offices outside of the law firm they all but endow. Seldom in the history of the theater has anyone approached their business success. Their four great plays have been running very nearly continuously in at least three countries for from ten to fifteen years. They each separately have a dozen or so permanent successes that bring in constant royalties. In addition, they have functioned as producers for others' work with enormous return (*Annie Get Your Gun, Happy Birthday*). They publish their own music and print their own books. They are now currently producing their own movies.

Far from exhausting them, these manifold interests and diversions are like catnip; they revel in the multifarious responsibilities and incomes. In this huge zest for affairs and returns they share equally.

Whenever we boarded a train together, Oscar would stop me and, placing a hand on my shoulder, say in his gentle, even voice, "Now, Agnes, what have you forgot this time?" (This was not a frivolous question. I had been known to forget or leave behind suitcases, brief cases, reading glasses, single shoes, music and, once, myself, when the Oklahoma City fire department was dispatched to find me and fetch me to the train.)

What have I forgot? Oh, so much. It is hard in a few pages to sketch these complex, contradictory, fascinating, passionate and gifted men who played such an overwhelming role in my life and of whom I grew so fond, so grateful to for so much, with whom, in fact, I fell in love, yet who, for all the rich and fruitful hours spent together, the miles traveled, the honors and horrors shared, were bent on preserving what in the end could not be shared. For over the years they became more and more concerned with what tragically and inevitably must raise barriers between their ambition and all collaborators.

Carousel was a tough show for the choreographer because it was based on a strong and well-written play and there seemed small need for dances. The ballet in Act II, therefore, represented probably the hardest challenge I'd ever met. It entailed a real job of dramatic invention, close to playwrighting. I struggled and strained, but at last the bosses avowed themselves pleased.

The opening night in New Haven was a real surprise. This was, as Jo Mielziner remarked, the best musical-comedy script he'd ever read and it had been beautifully directed, but almost none of it came off as we had expected. The staff repaired to a hotel room where sacrifice and a cold supper awaited. There followed the kind of conference that professionals seldom see: in two hours we made a plan, throwing out or drastically altering the better part of Act II, half my ballet, five complete scenes (and with one the services and hopes of an elderly actress who had come out of retirement for the first real chance of her life), a couple of good songs and several verses in the remaining ones.

At the end of two hours we were all well exercised.

Although neither of the authors could have foreseen the audience reaction that night, they must have been to some degree prepared, because they set to rewriting with an alacrity and organization that bespoke foresight.

One of the assistants said as we left the room after that dreadful first *Carousel* conference, "Now I see why these people have hits. I never witnessed anything so brisk and brave in my life." And indeed, not three minutes had been wasted pleading for something cherished. Nor was there any idle joking as at the [*One Touch of*] *Venus* conferences. We cut and cut and cut and then we went to bed.

Oscar went earliest, as soon as he could get away, because he would be up at six, working. And he had a list of required lyrics, scenes and liaison bits that would have daunted any lesser theater craftsman. For the next two weeks he was due to put in five or six hours of creative writing every day from dawn on.

Oscar would be alone and quiet in his room with his wits about him. But I was scheduled to begin in public. And into the room with me would drag the slightly soiled and shopworn brutes known as my dance company. They had to pull it out of their backs. I thought I had better be ready to help. Therefore I was also due up at six.

One might with time, one would think, build up a toleration for the tryout period, but working with Rodgers and Hammerstein always seemed more significant than working with others. Their united force was greater, their passions channeled deeper, their intent more noticeably implemented. One could no more think of their failing than of the war effort failing. One always felt that Posterity sat in on all staff meetings and had a good deal to say. Also our old colleague, Box Office, but this time dressed in a silk hat and carrying a gold-headed cane, and this time with voice mellifluous and venerable. There were elements of Patriotism and Mother Love and Honor in what they expected, and what you were privileged to give. Dick had never had a failure, he kept saying. And were you going to be the one to help him to this unprecedented, humbling experience? Oscar had had several, long before, and at the height of his great fame took a full page in *Variety* and advertised his worst notices with the endearing caption, "It happened before; it can happen again." This public penance, this propitiation to Fortune made him the more worthy of serving. It was only human for others to watch with jealous eyes for the misstep in the splendid parade. But we who marched alongside were very proud and minded the music and the step carefully.

All night I minded and counted and planned. All day I rehearsed. Between times I walked the streets alone in the twilight and thought of how someday I would not have to work like this. I would sleep and waste time and think of frivolities. Someday I would look forward to the evenings.

"What Is a Richard Rodgers?"

It is indeed unfortunate that subsequent generations remember Joshua Logan (1908–1988) primarily as the man responsible for the outrageous colors that marred the 1958 film version of *South Pacific*. From the late-1930s through the mid-1950s Logan was one of Broadway's most distinguished directors and producers with numerous major play and musical credits, including *On Borrowed Time* and *Knickerbocker Holiday* (1938), *Morning's at Seven* (1939), *This Is the Army* (1942), *Mister Roberts* (1948), *Picnic* (1953), *Fanny* (1954), and *Middle of the Night* (1956). His association with Rodgers began in 1938 with the Rodgers and Hart hit musical, *I Married an Angel*. Over the next few years Logan would serve as co-librettist as well as director for *Higher and Higher* (1940) and as the director of Rodgers and Hart's last musical, *By Jupiter* (1942). Before co-producing, directing, and co-authoring the original stage production of *South Pacific* (1949), Logan directed another hit show, Irving Berlin's *Annie Get Your Gun* (1946), co-produced by Rodgers and Hammerstein one year after *Carousel*.

In *Josh: My Up and Down, In and Out Life* Logan describes his role in the creation of the *South Pacific* libretto over a ten-day period on Hammerstein's farm, and relates in painful detail how, in his view, the Rodgers and Hammerstein corporate juggernaut deprived him of what he felt to be his legitimate right to share an author's copyright with Hammerstein. At the same time he blamed Rodgers for these decisions, Logan acknowledges that Rodgers did more to establish and maintain his career than any other man. Logan's anguish, hurt, and anger loomed so large after his experience with *South Pacific* that he "politely refused" co-authorship and direction for Rodgers and Hammerstein's next show, *The King and I*.

Note: For the record, the problem with the *South Pacific* film (from Logan's perspective) began when his technical advisers erroneously assured him that the color filters could be removed if deemed unsatisfactory. In the end this proved impossible, at least not without enormous delay and expense. Consequently, Logan would be saddled with the "Inglorious Technicolor" that audiences invariably snicker at when they view *South Pacific* on their VCRs. Logan describes the making of this film in *Movie Stars, Real People, and Me* (New York: Delacorte Press, 1978), 122–39.

JOSHUA LOGAN

I was hoping that Oscar had finished the book of *South Pacific*. Instead, Dick called to say that Oscar, after working for months, had only finished the first scene and an outline.

As for songs, Dick said, "Well, we've done those for the first scene and Oscar's written some scattered lyrics. But God knows where they'll fit." I could feel Larry Hart's old school principal in his voice.

"Aren't you committed to a schedule?"

"You're damned right. We've booked theatres, drawn up ads. Oscar generally works fast. But now we're in trouble. I want you to drive down to Oscar's farm. Maybe you can help him."

I called Oscar, who said, "Josh, I know absolutely nothing about Army behavior or how a sergeant talks to a general, and vice versa. What do sailors do when young Lieutenant Cable comes onto the beach? I had them snapping to attention. But that seemed wrong."

"Good God, yes," I said. "They'd pretend he wasn't there."

"I hate the military so much that I'm ignorant of it."

"I wish I were. It's been shoved down my throat since I started Culver at thirteen. Oscar, Dick thinks I should come down there so that we could work the Army stuff out together."

"Oh, please do, Josh. Dorothy would love for you and Nedda [Ed. Nedda Harrigan, daughter of the playwright–actor Edward Harrigan of Harrigan and Hart fame] to stay here. Come down this afternoon. I need you."

Packing my Dictaphone—which Oscar found as terrifying as a snake—I drove down with Nedda and brought Jim Awe to type.

Oscar and Dorothy owned a large working farm near Doylestown where Oscar raised prize Black Angus with the help of a Norwegian farmer who was also Oscar's masseur. Oscar was forced to raise cattle to keep his masseur happy.

Dorothy Hammerstein was not only warm and beautiful, but had a genius for decoration and for organizing an overflowing household.

Source: Joshua Logan, *Josh: My Up and Down, In and Out Life* (New York: Delacorte Press, 1976), 220–33, 245–46.

I didn't plan to stay long. I would just get Oscar on the right track and dash back to New York to plan the production. But within a day I realized that Oscar was holding onto our talks like a man grappling up a cliff. We talked excitedly through an entire rough structure. Scenes bobbed up that neither of us had expected.

At first, my idea bad been to use the tale "Fo' Dolla'," about the beautiful native girl, Liat, her lover, young Lieutenant Cable, and her repulsive mother, the foul-mouthed Bloody Mary.* But Oscar had been caught by another story, "Our Heroine," in which a middle-aged, sophisticated French planter and a naive American nurse fall in love. The part of the nurse was being written with Mary Martin in mind because of her huge success in *Annie*.** When she finds out that the mother of his children was a Polynesian, she runs away from him, unable with her Little Rock background to accept the relationship. But her love eventually overpowers her prejudice and she returns to him and his family. (This story, incidentally, was so low key compared to the rest that it was eliminated in the paperback edition of Michener's stories, and readers who had seen the play wondered where we got the idea.)

Oscar's great contribution was to combine the two stories, making that of the nurse and the planter the major one. He then planned to use three other stories, the most important being the one about the coast watcher who hid in the hills and reported by radio movements of the Japanese fleet. Oscar had also asked James Michener for more comic material, and Jim wrote him a complete story of the GIs elaborate handling of laundry. Out of this we later got color for the character of Luther Billis.

When I arrived, he had written a lovely first scene which introduced Emile and Nellie, and the start of their love—the "Some Enchanted Evening" scene. He also had a couple of exciting pages somewhat later, on the meeting of Cable and Liat. For Nellie they had written the ecstatic song "I'm in Love With a Wonderful Guy" to be sung to her fellow nurses in an unwritten scene, but otherwise Oscar seemed to be—yes—a bit frightened.

He and I previewed the sequence of scenes, and in two days we had it committed to memory. Just before I left he asked me to stay another day and help him through the difficult second scene on Bloody Mary's beach. I pulled out the Dictaphone and started acting all the roles into it. I was Billis, I was a Seabee, I was Lieutenant Cable. For me, military dialogue flowed easily. Oscar was amazed. When I got to Bloody Mary, suddenly he was talking and I was repeating his words into the mouthpiece. We

---

*[Ed. The musical *South Pacific* is based primarily (but not exclusively) on two stories from James A. Michener's *Tales of the South Pacific* (1947), "Fo' Dolla'" and "Our Heroine." Despite its unusual structure as a collection of nineteen occasionally connected short stories, both Michener and the Pulitzer Prize committee considered the *Tales* a novel.]

**[Ed. Martin had played the title role in *Annie Get Your Gun* with the national touring company in 1947.]

were both so stimulated by each other that we kept on dictating into the night and through the next day. There was no more talk of my going back to New York. I just stayed.

Being Southern, I spontaneously spoke all of Nellie's lines in my Mansfield accent, and he was a very suave Emile de Becque.

The scenes were transcribed by our secretaries, Jim Awe and Shirley Potash, and we would proofread them for the next draft. Our wives collated the pages on the living room floor. After three-fourths of the first act, I realized that Oscar was throwing me lines for Emile de Becque, Bloody Mary, and sometimes for Captain Brackett, and I was doing all the rest.

We were going full out—when we came to a screeching halt. The last scene of the first act, Emile's party for Nellie, stopped us cold. We had imagined Emile would be entertaining his guests with erotic native dancers. We both felt we needed a divertissement here. The stage would be peopled with neighboring French planters and their wives but when we started to write it, the whole tension vanished. Our hearts sank like plummeting lead.

Oscar suggested we go for a walk, and we stalked out the front door. We had not gone twenty paces when Oscar said, "Do you suppose it's those goddamned native dancers? Is that the blockage? What if we begin *after* the party, with the guests calling good-bye in French offstage?"

"That's right," said I, catching fire. "And then Emile pulls Nellie onstage by her wrists. They're both full of wine and he wants to get into bed with her this minute!"

"Exactly! They're high. They're passionate! They've been drinking all evening, and now they're sailing!"

We jogged back to the house, and took the stairs two at a time, waving casually to our dumbstruck wives in passing. In the study, I grabbed the Dictaphone and started rattling off "Bon soirs," and then described Emile pulling Nellie on stage to make love. After some wine-laced talk, Nellie and Emile break into a waltz, with Emile singing— Oscar's spontaneous lyrics:

> I'm in love, I'm in love and the girl that I love—
> She thinks I'm a wonderful guy!

Within a few minutes we had written what we were sure would be a high spot, and had done it in the same time it would take to play it on stage.

We worked hard every afternoon and evening, but I left Oscar alone in the mornings to chisel out the lyrics. We were both working against time.

At night with Nedda, in our room, she would ask, "Why are we still staying? Who's writing these scenes you're reading to us?"

When I described to her how Oscar and I worked, she'd say, "But you're writing again and you only signed a contract to direct. Oscar was to write it by himself."

"I know, but crazy as it may sound, he *can't* write this one. He doesn't understand the military or Little Rock. He needs me."

"Then you must tell him in the morning that you can't continue unless you're his *collaborator*. Don't get into another situation like Tom Heggen [Ed. Tom Heggen (1919–1949) was the author of the novel *Mister Roberts* and co-author (with Logan) of its successful stage adaption in 1948, one year before *South Pacific*], for heaven's sake!"

"I don't think Oscar wants a collaborator."

"Who cares—he's *got* a collaborator—one *he asked for*. You don't like giving away your ideas any more than he does, do you? He's a grown man and a businessman, and so are you. Tell him tomorrow."

But the next morning I dreaded some kind of angry blowup which would destroy the whole undertaking, and so, I didn't have the showdown I should have had then, and we continued to work ceaselessly, though Nedda never stopped telling me to state my attitude or quit writing.

Altogether, including the two days of planning, we took ten days to write the book for *South Pacific*.

Nedda and I drove, a bit shaken, back to New York. Oscar was to come within the next three days with more lyrics.

The intensity of this work was emotionally debilitating. After the writing of the description of Emile and Nellie clasping hands at the end, I had to leave the room because I was so moved. In my mind, I had just seen the first preview of *South Pacific* and I was astounded by its power. A single thought kept drumming through my mind: "It's going to win the Pulitzer Prize and no one will ever know I wrote a word of it." In rehearsal I would be forced to say, "That's not what Mr. Hammerstein meant when he wrote that line."

At night, I found I couldn't sleep. Nedda called our doctor and explained my disturbance. He gave me a sleeping pill and some advice. "You've got to let this man know you're being torn apart. He's a human being—he's got to understand."

The next day before Oscar came, Dick Rodgers called. He said he had read the script on the train to Boston. His comment was, " . . . and I had a very pleasant trip."

"But did you like the script?"

He repeated, "I told you I had a very pleasant trip."

I wasn't in the mood for understatement, and especially from a man who had had no script whatsoever three weeks ago.

My lawyer was shocked at the intolerable situation. He wanted to talk to Oscar's lawyer, but I told him Oscar was my friend and I would handle it myself.

When our maid announced Oscar the next day, Nedda came over to me and kissed me, and I left the room.

Oscar was in our living room, reading the last pages of the newly typed script. He looked up at me. "What's the matter?"

I said, in a high, tight voice, "What do you mean, what's the matter?"

"You look strange. Are you all right?"

"I'm fine, fine." Then my head swirled. The rug before me seemed to split in two, while the floor below it yawned open, revealing a terrifying chasm fourteen stories deep. I could feel a great wind sucking me down into it, and then it all slowly closed in as I began. "Oscar, I think I should get half credit for the book." The floor trembled a bit, but didn't open this time.

Oscar's face was immobile, but I thought he blushed slightly. After the briefest of pauses, he said, "I wish I'd said it first. I'm sorry you had to." Then he added, "Of course you must have credit. After all, you wrote it as much as I did. We'll work out the exact credits later."

I had a strong urge to run back and kiss Nedda, but I didn't. Oscar and I worked on a bit of polishing for the final draft, and Oscar left, saying he would be back the next day.

At once, I rushed back to Nedda and said, "He said yes!"

She shouted, "Let's open a bottle of champagne!" We had a merry, happy, wonderful evening.

The next day I walked on air—until Oscar appeared in the afternoon.

We sat down, facing each other. Looking painfully stern, he said, "In order to keep me from feeling that I'm being penalized by your demand, I will agree to the following arrangement. You may have equal credit with me for the book."

"That's wonderful, Oscar."

"That's not all. According to our contract, in the credits your name as director was to be in the same type size as mine and Dick's. But now Dick and I must have the top one hundred percent credit with the lead-in 'A Musical Play By Rodgers and Hammerstein'."

"What?"

"*Your* name and *mine* as the book authors" will be below that but with only sixty percent of the Rodgers and Hammerstein credit. And that's still not all. Your director credit must be *diminished* to sixty percent as well."

"Jesus, Oscar," I said, "that's a body blow."

"That's the only possible way we can go on. Of course, it goes without saying that you won't get anything whatsoever of the author's royalties."

"But," I said, in a shocked voice, "if you admit that I'm coauthor on the program, how can you deny it in the royalty distribution? A director's royalties *end* when the original company closes. An author's percentage goes on forever—foreign rights, amateur and stock rights, movie sale. It might mean a great deal to my family, to Nedda—to the children I hope to have."

"Josh," he said, and I could see he was really in pain, "Rodgers and Hammerstein cannot and *will not* share a copyright. It's part of their financial structure. Including you would weaken our position. My partners feel this strongly. It's impossible, Josh."

I couldn't face Nedda, back there in her blissful state.

I said to Oscar, "Oscar, why did you agree yesterday and then hit me so hard today?"

"Because I realized that the public, through previous announcements, was expecting me to write it alone. And so this was penalizing me. Now you're being penalized too."

At that moment, because I cared for him, I felt I could see deep into a suffering Oscar Hammerstein. Obviously, he was speaking lines he had been instructed to say—whether by Dick or their lawyer. I was not listening to a single man, but to a citizens' committee such as those during the French Revolution who decided who should lose their heads to the guillotine.

I also saw by Oscar's expression how hard he must have fought to secure for me as much as he did, and how equally hard it was for him to look me in the eye as he said what he had to say.

Oscar had had great success in his youth, first with Otto Harbach and then on his own with the great Kern on *Show Boat*, and others. His talents had then fallen on barren ground for years. Show after show had failed until Dick Rodgers offered him *Oklahoma!* Whereupon, overnight, he got the backing for *Carmen Jones*, which was another fantastic success for him personally. He was at that time the top man in the theatre and it made him very nervous, so when Christmas came around he took an ad in *Variety* to let the world know how he felt:

HOLIDAY GREETINGS
OSCAR HAMMERSTEIN 2nd

Author of

SUNNY RIVER	Six weeks—St. James Theatre, New York
VERY WARM FOR MAY	Seven weeks—Alvin Theatre, New York
THREE SISTERS	Seven weeks—Drury Lane, London
BALL AT THE SAVOY	Five weeks—Drury Lane, London
FREE FOR ALL	Three weeks—Manhattan Theatre, New York

I'VE DONE IT BEFORE AND
I CAN DO IT AGAIN

But he didn't do it again. In a few short years the names Rodgers and Hammerstein, with *Carousel* and the film *State Fair* had become the strongest in the entertainment world. Oscar's new partner was brilliant, a near genius. I knew that Oscar had forced himself to accept second place to a younger and more successful man. He had to make adjustments, but he did so without complaint to avoid any friction with his new associate. Oscar was safe at last, and he didn't want to "rock the boat," or as we say even more vulgarly, "make waves."

I should have taken a strong, hard line, such as threatening to resign and then suing to stop production if a word of my dialogue was used, but deep in my innards *I wanted to do the show more than anything else in the world.* And I had the greatest respect for Oscar as a man, as a dramatist and as a human being. If Dorothy Hammerstein, whom I adored, could love him, then I could too. My feelings for Dick had suffered a sea change, but I still respected him. Therefore, I accepted the terms without conferring with Nedda or my own lawyer. But made one last request.

"Suppose I switched a part of my director's royalties to the author's. It wouldn't cost the show any more, and then I would at least have some of the future earnings."

He looked pained again. "I'll ask our lawyers about it," he said, weighing each word, "But frankly, it doesn't sound feasible."

While the question of transferring royalties was being fought out in the snake pit by our lawyers, I decided to go ahead with casting. Nedda was most unhappy that I had agreed to such terms, and only acquiesced because I begged her to. She felt I could have forced them to share the copyright, and looking back I suppose I could have, since later, Lindsay and Crouse got them to share one for *The Sound of Music.*

Leland [co-producer Leland Hayward] felt I had brought it on myself by letting them get control of the basic rights. Leland was torn between saying, "Josh, you were robbed," and "You deserve it, you bastard." But what he did say was, "You're at their mercy."

An enormous change had taken place in Dick Rodgers's life that affected our relationship. It came with his gigantic and worldwide success. He became, almost in front of our eyes, a monument. He was so sought after that he had to closet himself in an office and dictate letters daily in order to handle his business affairs and to fend off the many people who wanted to sap his talent. To me, his fun seemed gone—the fun he and I used to have.

And I tried to decide for myself, What is a Richard Rodgers?

It's a brilliant, talented, highly intelligent, theatrically sound, superbrain. It likes to work, it particularly likes to write music, which flows up plentifully from some underground spring. It plays the piano better than most composers. It's not given to smiling too much, and yet when it scowls I've found that does not indicate anything unpleasant; it is simply making a judgment, thinking things over, watching a private preview. It has a strong sense of discipline; it likes to be on time, to deliver work as promised. And when it works with an Oscar Hammerstein, that is accomplished frequently. But when it worked with a Larry Hart, well, that's when the scowl sets in. It pretends to hate business, and yet it is my theory that it is only really happy making contracts, haggling about royalties, salaries or theatre leases. I often believed it was a bit embarrassed about the ease of writing music, as though it were too easy, too soft a thing for a man to do. Therefore, it enjoyed being a hard-bitten businessman.

When I first knew Dick, he and I were cronies, pals, especially on the road when we were away from our families. We'd take out a couple of members of the cast and give them dinner, and have a warm, relaxed time of it until we were ready to rest up for tomorrow's rehearsal. Surely, Dick Rodgers did more for me, more to solidify my career in musical comedy, than any other person. He scowlingly (which means warmly) approved of me initially to direct my first musical, *I Married An Angel*. He liked my work on that in spite of the fact that I didn't. He insisted on having me for his next, *Higher and Higher*, and after I had had my well-publicized nervous breakdown, Dick was the first person to offer me another show, *By Jupiter*. After the war, he offered me *Annie Get Your Gun* while I was still overseas. And show after show till *South Pacific*.

So what happened? What made him change? Was it, as I suspected, stratospheric fame, the pedestal that the whole world put him on? Was it the money? Was it the business side of his life that erased the fun?

When he teamed up with Oscar Hammerstein there were all kinds of remarks that the big one is a nice guy but the little one is a son of a bitch. To me, Dick and Oscar were both tough as nails, and although Oscar was easier for me to get along with by that time because we somehow spoke the same language, Dick still had something for me that I could never shake off.

We went full steam into casting. The leads had been set months ago. Mary Martin was Nellie Forbush. She had agreed on hearing Oscar's first scene. Then Edwin Lester of the Los Angeles Civic Light Opera Company, who had just signed a two-year contract with Ezio Pinza, asked if we would take the contract over—providing Pinza was interested in playing our lead. We jumped at the chance of having such a great singing actor play Emile.

My old Princeton friend, Myron McCormick, was my first choice for Billis, and I cannot remember anyone else's being considered.

Only two roles seemed to give us trouble, Bloody Mary and Cable. But at an audition, Juanita Hall, a marvelous mulatto singer with an Oriental cast of features, took off her shoes and stockings and struck a squatting pose that said, "I am Bloody Mary and don't you dare cast anyone else!"

Young William Tabbert looked somewhat wrong for Cable until he started to sing, and then he looked absolutely right. But in talking to him I learned he was a "health nut" too. I told him that he had to lose about twenty pounds and firm up his body, which he promised to do before rehearsal.

Five days prior to rehearsal, I went to Bill Brown's Health Farm up near Garrison on the Hudson to get in physical shape for the big push.

While I was there, back in New York rival lawyers were still sparring. The dickering that was going on would have chilled my blood and shriveled my soul had I known about it. As it was, my wife and agent handled it all and kept it from me out of fear that I would blow up and jeopardize the entire project.

I would learn of it all later, but as I drove home the day before rehearsals started, my mind was in a whirl with ideas for movement during songs, with wisps of dance, and particularly with the use of music under the dramatic pantomime for changes of thought a la Stanislavsky.

Dick Rodgers had hired Trude Rittman, a superb German-born composer, orchestrator and arranger, to work with me during the staging. This would be my first chance to have a true composer by my side during rehearsals, one who would create passages based on Dick's themes, to illuminate thoughts and feelings.

As my car approached New York it occurred to me that the operatic form I had first thought right for the Michener stories was being achieved.

At nine-thirty the next morning the bare stage of the Majestic Theatre began to fill with people.

The New York opening may be a musical's most exciting moment, but close to it is the first reading of the full score and book. Will it or won't it?

Bill Tabbert came over to me to show his new physique; he had lost two inches from his waist. Betta St. John, our Liat, was so beautiful she made everyone feel good just looking at her.

Mary Martin arrived at five to ten, and shortly afterward Pinza came in with his full coterie of accompanist, lawyer, arranger, wife and several others. Whispers had it he had been waiting in the alley until Mary showed up; the most important must arrive last.

Jo Mielziner showed the model of his settings, and we began to read.

The Spanish-American children, masquerading as Polynesian, Barbara Luna and Michael de Leon, sang "Dites-moi Pourquoi." Then Mary as Nellie and Ezio as Emile began speaking their offstage conversation. The thrill of hearing their voices together was enough for a star.

But the spell got a jolt when Pinza pantomimed a coffee cup and said, "Sooker?" Shades of the Black Pool oasis! I corrected him by saying softly, "Shh. Shoogar." With great effort, he said, "Sh-shoo-ker," and we continued.

Mary Martin sang "A Cockeyed Optimist" with her open charm, and quite soon the two of them began singing Dick Rodgers's insistent, marvelous tune, "Twin Soliloquies"—each using the same melody, but at a distance apart, with Oscar's words of tentative, doubting love. This was the moment when for me the show became great. But the song stopped too quickly; the music had to continue to strengthen the passionate, almost sexual, feeling. Trude provided the thrilling continuation later.

Soon Emile declared himself with "Some Enchanted Evening." When Pinza first sang the word "enchanted," it came out "enshonted"—but he worked hard, and before long his diction was both understandable and attractive. He was unique. His deep, sonorous voice, massive muscular bulk, his magnetic eyes, brought back from the past the matinee idol.

Everyone loved him, especially Mary Martin. Unlike the usual star, she had no jealousy; she wanted Pinza to succeed. She knew that if the audience loved Pinza, they would know why Nellie Forbush did.

The second scene opened with the roughneck Seabees singing "Bloody Mary." Juanita Hall took off her shoes and squatted to read. "Hallo, GI! Grass skirt? Very saxy! Fo' dolla? Send home Chicago. You like? You buy?"

McCormick treasured this part more than he did his Phi Beta Kappa key. He was a perfect opponent for the old girl.

When the men sang "There Is Nothin' Like a Dame," I imagined myself pacing back and forth in rhythm. I was getting excited.

Juanita Hall, with chilling concentration on Bill Tabbert's musculature, sang "Bali Ha'i." I looked at Oscar. How many peaks could a show have?

Yet they continued, song after song, each seeming more apt than the last because of a growing involvement with the story.

During lunch, Dick and Oscar seemed calm and so did Leland Hayward, who had entered that morning gray with nerves. But I was used to that Hayward apprehension.

I began the actual staging, placing the actors in approximate positions and asking them to go through sketchy moves. I threw together a rough draft of the first scene. Rather than perfect it then, I jumped right to the second, which was more complicated. I began blocking out "There Is Nothin' Like a Dame," and I started pacing as I imagined a caged animal would pace. The men followed me, restlessly pacing back and forth— killing time till the end of the war, till the change of seeing women again. Then I asked Trude to repeat the song, and motioned one man to pace in one direction, another to go the other way, breaking the pattern constantly. Within fifteen or twenty minutes I had staged it. It didn't exactly fall into place but it looked as if it had. It was an *acted* musical scene. I thought Stanislavsky would approve.

"There Is Nothin' Like a Dame" joined *Annie*'s "goon look" as one of the things most remembered about my work. The really hard work I did as director was never noticed—and never should be. My best direction was to give approval and encouragement. When an actor was on the right track I would say, "Keep it that way—that way you spontaneously did it. Except do it *again—exactly the same way*, so I know it is fixed in your memory." That's good direction in my book.

In two days the entire show was put roughly on its feet. Dick and Oscar were amazed and a bit frightened at how fast I had gone. I asked Oscar for the second song he planned for Bloody Mary, the one which he called "Happy Talk."

Oscar said, "I decided to chuck it. I couldn't imagine how it could be staged, and I didn't want to give you any more problems."

I felt a surge of good-humored arrogance. "You write it, I'll stage it," I said.

The next morning, Oscar and Dick brought me the song, and as Dick played it the background rhythm for some reason made me think of two birds talking to each other. I imitated the rhythmic motion of their beaks with my thumbs and forefingers. Then I took the actors and Trude Rittman down to the piano in the theatre lounge. Betta St. John was a dancer and loved the finger gestures. While Bloody Mary sang to Cable about how happy life with Liat would be, Liat pantomimed to him a flower, and then at the word "dream" I had her rest her face in her two hands, palms front. We pantomimed the whole song in five or six minutes, and we showed it to Oscar and Dick. They were as delighted as we were.

Of course there were a few changes during rehearsal. Dick and Oscar had a late song for Pinza called "Now Is the Time," to be sung as he decides to go with Cable into enemy territory. But it seemed wrong. If Cable and Emile were going on a mission to save Allied lives, why didn't they get a goddamn move on instead of standing and singing, "Now is the time to act, no other time will do?" The song was quickly eliminated, but it had to be replaced just as quickly, because Pinza was frightened of anything new.

In an emergency meeting, the three of us decided it had to come well before the mission is even suggested. The mission should come out of the song, and of course the song must be a lament of losing Nellie. Dick asked for a title line that he could work on. One of us called out, "This nearly was mine."

"That's it," said Dick. "A big bass waltz." And he disappeared.

Within a day or two Dick and Oscar brought "This Nearly Was Mine." It was so beautiful that in staging it I just let Ezio stand there and sing. I feared that any fancy movement would detract from the effect of Oscar's heartfelt lines and Dick's rich, slow waltz. Pinza loved singing it.

Cable had no song to sing after he had made love to Liat in the hut. Oscar studied the scene again and again. He was fascinated by Liat's waiting for Cable's boat to come around the bend. One day they took me to the lobby and sang one they had just written. It began:

> My friend, my friend
> Is coming around the bend.

I was so let down that I blurted out my first feelings. "That's awful! That's the worst song I ever heard. Good God, that's terrible!"

They looked at me in shock; no one had ever spoken to them like that before, I'm sure. I'll never forget Dick's stricken face. But they were professional enough to go back home and try again. A day later they turned up with another. It was a lilting schottische, the words of which began like this:

> Suddenly lucky,
> Suddenly our arms are lucky
> Suddenly lucky,
> Suddenly our lips have kissed.

When they finished, I was thinking so hard I didn't speak. Oscar said, "Well, have we passed the test this time, Teacher?"

"You're close," I said. "I love the tune, but isn't that song a bit lightweight for a hot, lusty boy to sing right after making love to a girl who will change his life?"

Dick rebelled. He announced uncharmingly that he was not going to go on writing till "this guy" agrees on a tune. He played a song they had dropped from *Allegro*. It was then called "My Wife." The melody was lovely, and I urged them to go ahead. Oscar spent two days writing new lyrics for it and it became the classic and powerful "Younger Than Springtime."

"Suddenly Lucky," too, had a reincarnation, for two years later when I heard Gertrude Lawrence sing "Getting to Know You" in *The King and I*, I knew where I had heard that tune before. . . .

I had been shaken to the marrow by this experience, and although I still have a letter from them offering me full coauthorship and direction of *The King and I*, a project I loved, I politely refused—a decision I will regret for the rest of my life.

But as it turned out, I wasn't out of it completely. During the writing of *The King and I*, Oscar suddenly sent for me, and I hurried to his office. He was shaking with emotion as he spoke. First, he made me read his lyrics to a new song for the show. He said he had started to write a song called "Tom," about the heroine's dead husband, and ended weeks later with a song called "Hello, Young Lovers." I was so moved by the beautiful emotion of the lyric that I figured that's why he asked me to come.

He said, "It's my best lyric, isn't it, Josh?"

I said, "Well, certainly I've never read anything better. But why do you seem so upset? You should be happy."

"I know I should, but I'm not," he said, with mounting emotion. "I finished it after digging away for three weeks. I thought it was my top work. I wanted someone to appreciate it. I sent it by special messenger to Dick and told the boy to wait for an answer, but he never came back. Then I waited for Dick to call me. I waited an hour. Then two hours. Then, to my horror, he didn't call that evening. He didn't call me the next day. It was hard to work while watching the bloody phone all day long.

By that time I had broken out in a sweat. I began to think there was something wrong with the lyric. The third day I waited all day long, unable to work. A lost day. No call—nothing. I was determined not to call him. Besides, I was so frustrated my voice couldn't make a call. Finally, the fourth morning he called me, but it was a business call—Rodgers and Hammerstein office business—I don't know, something about a benefit someone wanted to do next March, or publishing some extra songbook, or allowing an amateur company to put on *Annie Get Your Gun*, or *Carousel* in concert form. I kept saying like an automation, 'Yes, all right by me, yes, okay,' and Dick almost hung up—but just before he did he said, 'Oh, I got that lyric. It works fine.'"

And calm, contained Oscar Hammerstein stood there before me, broken to pieces. "You're the only person I could tell it to," he said. "You're the only person I know who would understand."

I tried to calm him by saying that Dick loves to understate things, and recalled to him how very coolly Dick had reacted to his first reading of our book on *South Pacific*, but nothing seemed to calm Oscar down. He started to pour out all the things he had kept bottled up for years, and then he stopped, abruptly stuck out his hand, saying, "Okay, that's it. You've helped me. Thanks."

I left the room as quickly as I could.

"There's Hope for Everyone"

The Theatre Guild shows created new stars (Alfred Drake, Joan Roberts, Celeste Holm in *Oklahoma!*, John Raitt and Jan Clayton in *Carousel*). *South Pacific* began with stars already in public orbit, Broadway's lustrous Mary Martin (1913–1990) and the famous bass Ezio Pinza (1892–1957) crossing over after several decades of leading roles with the New York Metropolitan Opera and London's Covent Garden. By the time Rodgers and Hammerstein asked Martin to play Nellie Forbush, she had long since made her auspicious supporting debut in Cole Porter's *Leave It to Me* (1938) with the song that would provide her autobiography its title. Several years later, she attained stardom in the title roles in *One Touch of Venus* (1943) and in the first touring company of *Annie Get Your Gun* in 1947 (an Irving Berlin musical produced by Rodgers and Hammerstein the previous year). After playing Ensign Forbush for a little more than two years, Martin would go on to create the title role in Broadway's *Peter Pan* (1954) and Maria von Trapp in R & H's *The Sound of Music* (1959). In yet another claim to fame, Martin was also the mother of Larry Hagman (1931–), known to millions as J. R. Ewing in the long-running television series *Dallas* (1978–1990).

My Heart Belongs captures Martin's excitement at being chosen *South Pacific's* female protagonist, her condition that she and Pinza would not sing a duet "in competition" (a prerequisite that led to the imaginative alternating exchanges in "Twin Soliloquies"), and the first time she sang "A Wonderful Guy," an exuberant rendition that prompted Rodgers to say, "Never sing it any other way."* Martin fans also learn that it was her suggestion to take a real shower onstage that led to "I'm Gonna Wash That Man Right Outa My Hair" and that, at Josh Logan's insistence, her sailor suit in "Honey Bun" kept getting baggier and baggier and her tie longer and longer until it reached comic proportions. Pinza recalls his involvement in *South Pacific* in his *Autobiography* (New York: Holt, Rinehart and Winston, 1958), 229–54. See also the memoirs of James Michener (1907–1997), who wrote the Pulitzer Prize–winning novel *Tales of the South Pacific* (1947), which served as the basis for the Broadway show [*The World Is My Home* (New York: Random House, 1992), 290–95 and 328–29].

MARY MARTIN

South Pacific was one of the most fabulous things that ever happened to me. It was one of those magic shows that comes along once in a decade—maybe once in a lifetime—and stand for their era forever after.

When I think that I almost turned it down, I nearly die. Richard [Martin's husband and manager Richard Halliday] first mentioned it to me in the car one night as we were driving from Los Angeles to San Francisco to open in *Annie*, in early 1948. Dick and Oscar, Josh Logan and Leland Hayward had an idea for a musical, he said. There was a star part for me, as a nurse.

"A what?"

"A nurse."

Me, a nurse? Richard wouldn't allow me in the room if he had a cold, because I'd sail in with a lusty hand pat and a big "How are ya?" If anybody around me was ill he wanted me out of the house as fast as possible. If I even walked into the room it made his head hurt.

"An army nurse," Richard added.

"An *army* nurse?" I repeated. "You mean I'd have to wear a uniform all the time, one of those tacky khaki things?"

Richard discreetly dropped the subject, for the time being. It didn't come up again until after *Annie* closed. The night before we left California to drive home to Connecticut, Dick and Oscar telephoned, all excited.

---

*Although Martin claims otherwise, the agreement not to compete was in fact briefly broken in the harmonized Act II reprise of "A Cockeyed Optimist."

Source: Mary Martin, *My Heart Belongs* (New York: William Morrow, 1976), 157–67.

"It's set," they said. "We're going to do *South Pacific*. We have Josh Logan to direct, we have Ezio Pinza to sing the French planter, Emile de Becque. We would like Mary to play the nurse stationed on his island; she's to be Nellie Forbush from Little Rock, Arkansas."

The very thought of appearing on the same stage with an opera singer terrified me. Besides, my voice had sunk what seemed like several octaves from belting out the *Annie* songs so long. I remember saying to Dick Rodgers on the phone that night, "What on earth do you want, two basses?"

There are different versions of whose idea it was to adapt James Michener's book *Tales of the South Pacific* as a musical. So far as I know, Josh Logan and Leland Hayward may have suggested it to each other. They had just had a huge success with *Mister Roberts*, a straight play about the Navy in the Pacific. Then Michener's book came along. It was a series of lyrical tales about life in the islands during the war. There was a native woman who chewed betel nut and sold souvenirs to the sailors; there was her lovely daughter, Liat, who fell in love with a lieutenant; there was a French planter, a widower with beautiful half-caste children; there were Seabees; and there was Nellie Forbush. Each of Michener's stories was different, but a single thread ran through: the slow growing of tolerance, of understanding, of love as two completely different cultures collided in wartime.

Josh and Leland took the book to Dick and Oscar, asking them not only to do music and lyrics but also to produce it. Oscar and Josh were to do the libretto. At first they thought they would build the show around Liat and her lieutenant, Cable. Then they were caught by the idea of the French planter and the nurse. In the end they decided to have two plots, a central one with Emile and Nellie, a subplot with Liat and Cable. The character of the betel-chewing woman was, of course, the unforgettable Bloody Mary.

If I was frightened at the thought of singing with Ezio Pinza, I was absolutely paralyzed with fear after the first time I heard him. Richard and I went to Brooklyn to one of his concerts and sat way up in the gallery because there never were seats available for a Pinza performance. Oh, that glorious voice! I rushed home from the concert and telephoned Dick Rodgers to say he couldn't, he wouldn't, dare to put us together on the same stage. Dick promised he would never have us sing "in competition," and he never did.

Our only song together was a soliloquy in the first act, a kind of counterpoint called "Wonder How It Feels." Ezio sang his thoughts from his side of the stage; I sang mine from my side. Each of us in our own style; never a duet, never in competition.

I'll never forget the first time I heard our soliloquy. Dick Rodgers, who was our neighbor in Connecticut, called and urged us to come over to hear some of the numbers. We still weren't convinced that I should do the show, but we went over. He played and Oscar sang "Wonder How It Feels."

There were other songs, I've forgotten in what order, and then there was "Some Enchanted Evening." Oh, the impact of that song! They said they had no idea how long it would take to finish the score but they wanted me. They said we should go away and think it over for two or three days.

That night in bed Richard and I talked about the glorious "Some Enchanted Evening." We both were sure that no matter whether the show was a success or not, that would be one of the memorable songs of the musical stage. It wasn't "mine," it was Ezio's, but that didn't matter. It was three o'clock in the morning, but we picked up the phone and asked, "Do we have to wait three days? Can't we say yes right now?"

The marvelous songs kept rolling out . . . "Bloody Mary," "There Is Nothing Like a Dame," "Happy Talk," "I'm Just a Cockeyed Optimist," "Bali Ha'i," and "Younger Than Springtime."

One night Dick called to ask us to go to Josh and Nedda Logan's apartment in New York. He said he and Oscar had a present for me. Richard and I arrived late, driving in from Connecticut, and Dick sat down at the piano to play "I'm in Love with a Wonderful Guy" while Oscar said-sang the words.

"This is your song, Mary," they said.

It went straight to my head, my heart. I had to sing it, right that moment. I sat down on the piano bench next to Dick and began "I'm in love, I'm in love, I'm in love," getting more and more excited, singing full speed ahead, waving my arms around. Finally I got to "with a WONDERFUL GUYYYYYY" and finished it—and *clunk*, fell right off the piano bench onto the floor.

Dick Rodgers turned his head, looked down at me rather solemnly, and said, "Never sing it any other way." My darling Dick Rodgers.

I couldn't stop singing it that night. Before long telephones started ringing like crazy. People in the apartments above, below, on both sides, were complaining, "Stop that terrible noise. We can't sleep."

Josh was so exhilarated that he told them all, "You'll be sorry. Someday it's going to cost you I don't know how much to hear all this."

We often thought of that night later, when scalpers were selling *South Pacific* seats for one hundred dollars each. After "Wonderful Guy" came "I'm Gonna Wash That Man Right Out-a My Hair." I have never written a song in my whole life, but I can take some credit for that one. It all started with a crazy idea of mine. It came to me in my shower one day. Richard was working at his desk and I came tearing out of the shower, dripping wet, without a stitch on, to say, "Richard, always in movies and the theater people say, 'I've just washed my hair and I can't do a thing with it.' But they looked utterly perfect. Now, wouldn't it be great if sometime I washed my hair, right on stage, maybe even singing a song, and then came out all dripping? Wouldn't that be a great scene?"

Richard looked a little bit patient and more than a little bit worried.

"Don't you dare tell that to anyone," he said. "Not a soul. If you do, they'll go for it, and then you'll have to do it onstage eight times a week."

The very first person who telephoned after that conversation was Josh. I heard my equally crazy husband saying to him, quite clearly, "Josh, Mary has a great idea . . ."

"Don't you dare tell Dick and Oscar," said Josh. "You know what will happen."

So, naturally, we all told them both, the very next time we talked. They said I was balmy, but if I was willing to do it they loved the idea. Then they wrote "I'm Gonna Wash That Man." The song really helped the plot along. It established Nellie's reluctance to fall in love with Emile, and it helped set up her collapse, her surrender, in "I'm in Love with a Wonderful Guy."

From the very beginning, *South Pacific* was pure joy. Dick and Oscar, Josh and Leland, Richard and I were all close friends who loved working together, but it was more than that. Josh and Leland had auditioned forever to cast it, so everybody in the show was somebody special. Everyone had a beautiful voice, great talent. We couldn't *wait* to get to rehearsals. No matter how many hours we worked we never wanted to stop. We couldn't wait to get back. It was like the excitement of an operating room, when somebody's life is being saved by the team, or like a delivery room when a new life is coming.

The show kept growing from the first day, getting better, because we were having a ball and everybody was contributing. The idea for the show-within-a-show, when the Seabees and the nurses put on an evening's amateur entertainment for the troops, began with Myron McCormick. Myron was a marvelous actor who had gone to Princeton with Josh. Somewhere, somehow, he had learned to do a belly dance. He was just dying to do it onstage. Josh liked the idea. I announced that I could do a soft-shoe number with some of Sister's waltz clog steps included, of course.

At just about that time an old girl friend sent me a picture somebody had taken of me at Camp Mystic in Kerrville, Texas, about 1925. Like most children, I absolutely adored summer camp; I went as often as I could and stayed as long as I could. In the Camp Mystic picture I was standing in semishade, grinning with delight, wearing a pair of men's shorts with wide stripes, a long shirt, a sailor hat, and a man's necktie. The predominant features of the picture were two rather large round water pitchers which I held in my hands, two round knees, one round nose, and one long neck.

I thought the photo was so funny that I gave it to Oscar Hammerstein. He took one look at that gangly girl and then put the picture by his mirror where he shaved every morning. Under it he wrote, "This proves there is hope for everyone."

When Josh Logan saw the picture, he said, "You've come a long way, honey, but you're still a baggy-pants comedian at heart." Then he dreamed up my costume for the show-within-a-show: I was to wear a sailor hat, baggy pants, and a long black tie. I was to be the baggy-pants comic sailor and Myron, who played the Seabee Luther Billis in the show, was to be my girl friend, done up in a grass skirt and coconut-shell "bazooms."

Then Dick and Oscar wrote our number, "Honey Bun" . . . "A hundred and one pounds of fun, that's my little Honey Bun . . . Get a load of Honey Bun tonight. . . ." I will never forget the half-embarrassed, very pleased look on Oscar's face when he first sang me the lyrics. Never in his life had he written such corny words, but I shrieked with joy. It was my kind of song, my kind of singing. I learned it in nothing flat and we set the routine in one afternoon. This was right down Josh's, Myron's, and my alley.

Then Josh went to work improving it all. Of course the sailor suit had to be a bit large for me because I was supposed to have borrowed it from one of the Seabees. Josh kept making it larger. He kept saying, "Make the pants bigger," "Make the tie longer." The pants got longer and longer in the crotch, the sleeves grew so long that they covered my hands. Then he thought of elastic suspenders being attached to the pants under the over-sized blouse. The elastic made the pants bounce up and down as I moved.

His final piece of business came before one matinee in Boston. Josh came into my dressing room and said, "This afternoon, when you've gotten all the laughs on your dancing, bouncing pants, at the last minute put your leg through the tie. Right up to the crotch, so the tie finally holds up the pants."

I thought this was going too far. We argued for quite a while—we often did, with wild affection. Then we compromised. I wouldn't try it at the matinee, with all those ladies out there, but I would do it at the night show. Josh was right, as usual. That little business brought the house down, and from that moment on you couldn't have taken it away from me on a ten-foot pole. Of all the fun moments Josh staged for me in the theater, dancing and singing "Honey Bun" was the most.

He had the same skill with everybody else in the cast. He was forever asking, "What can you do?" and somebody would jump out and show him. One of the girls could do acrobatic dancing. Somebody else could do a barrel roll. Juanita Hall, who played Bloody Mary, could do every-thing. She sat down on the floor one day with Josh and with beautiful Betta St. John, who played Liat. The three of them worked out all the hand movements for "Happy Talk." I can still see the concentration and hear the stillness as the three of them perfected that beautiful song.

Even now I can hardly believe, though I saw it, the way Josh choreo-graphed the Seabees in the "There Is Nothing Like a Dame" number. All these gorgeous guys, playing Seabees, were up there on the stage and Josh jumped up with them. The music started and he began to pace around, saying "Follow me." He directed some of them forward, others back-ward. He was singing all the time—Josh always knew the words—tramping, gesturing, shouting "Follow me," or "Reverse." Big, massive Josh with all those guys. He knew the whole lingo of the servicemen, their spirit. He was magic that day. The entire ballet of pacing men, directed by Josh, was done on the first day of rehearsal. When it was finished everybody who was watching stood up and screamed, just screamed. "That's it, Josh. Never touch it."

There kept being screaming moments in *South Pacific*. One day just before we went to New Haven for tryouts the cast was asked if we would mind having an audience for one of the rehearsals. Fortunately, we didn't know that they intended to fill the theater with professionals—actors, dancers, singers, composers, directors. We were working with rehearsal props, old benches, and junk. We didn't even have proper lights. When we finished, it was so quiet it was like church. We didn't know what to think, because we couldn't see the audience. Then all of the sudden there was an unbelievable roar. I've never heard anything like it in my life. Our peers approved. Some people say that this rehearsal was the best performance they ever saw in the theater. I have seldom heard such yelling, whistling, applause.

From that exciting day we went to New Haven. In spite of the wealth of music, the richness of every melody and every lyric, there were still a few problems. One was a song worthy of Ezio Pinza's voice for the second act. He had "Some Enchanted Evening" for the first act, but he needed something for the second. Dick and Oscar kept saying, "We'll get one; we'll do it," but Ezio was getting very nervous and upset. They had one called "Will You Marry Me?" which was lovely, but it didn't have the dramatic intensity for the scene. Just the week before we went back to New York they came up with "This Nearly Was Mine." Ezio by this time was so worried that he didn't even think it was good. Then he settled down to learn it, and I was delighted to discover that this great basso didn't read much better than I did. He had to learn it note by note, with his accompanist. The song, of course, was fantastic. All my life I shall hear that great organ of a voice as Ezio sang it.

The Art of Adaptation

From *The Cradle Will Rock* (1937) to *I Can Get It for You Wholesale* (1962) Lehman Engel (1910–1982) occupied a prominent and ubiquitous place as a Broadway conductor. Among his many recordings are the first (nearly) complete studio cast recording of *Porgy and Bess* in 1951 and a studio cast recording of *Pal Joey* in 1950 that is frequently credited as the impetus behind the successful revival two years later. In the 1960s Engel gained new distinction as a leading Broadway historian and developer of new talent in his role as a teacher at New York University, the American Musical and Dramatic Theatre Academy, and as the director of the BMI Musical Theatre Workshop.

In the first edition of *The American Musical Theater* (excerpted here) Engel extols the characteristics and common virtues of twelve musicals from *Pal Joey* to *West Side Story* that depict Broadway "in its most complete and mature state."* Included in Engel's exclusive list are no less than five shows with music by Rodgers: *Pal Joey, Oklahoma!, Carousel, South Pacific,* and *The King and I.* Both in *The American Musical Theater* and later in *Words with Music: The Broadway Musical Libretto* (New York: Schirmer Books, 1972) Engel emphasizes his influential view that "the largest share of the responsibility for a show's success rests on the librettist." While he might agree with Rodgers that the secret to the formula of musical theater success is the knowledge that there is no formula, Engel believes that great musicals consistently exhibit common denominators that can serve as models for future practitioners. In the present passage he explains why he believes that the four canonic Rodgers and Hammerstein musicals "demonstrate some of the principles of successful adaptation."

LEHMAN ENGEL

Some comparisons between source material and corresponding librettos will, I think, demonstrate some of the principles of successful adaptation.

The conversion of *Green Grow the Lilacs* into *Oklahoma!* provides an excellent case in point. This adaptation was in most respects a simple affair, which is to say that the order of the play was adhered to in the musical. (This is not always possible.) The play was in six scenes, and the musical is in two acts or six scenes (three in each act). The scenes, however, do not always parallel one another.

In addition, Hammerstein created a new character of major interest, Will Parker, whom Riggs had given only one offhand mention—in his Scene 3 in the smokehouse:

CURLY: You know Will Parker?
JEETER: Never heard of him.
CURLY: Ole man Parker's boy up here by Claremore? He can shore spin a rope.

---

*By Engel's criteria the only musicals after *West Side Story* to achieve canonic status (in either edition) are *Gypsy* (1959), *Fiddler on the Roof* (1964), *Company* (1970), and *A Little Night Music* (1973).

Source: Lehman Engel, *The American Musical Theater* (New York: Collier, 1967; rev. ed., 1975), 63–69.

Early in Scene I, Hammerstein introduces Will Parker, who has just returned from winning the steer-roping contest in Kansas City. He is full of enthusiasm for his first glimpse of "modern," big-city life, and he has won a prize of $50—the amount Ado Annie's father has insisted he must have to be allowed to marry Ado Annie.

Will becomes an opposite number to Ado Annie and adds to the fun of Ado Annie's relationship to the Peddler. In fact, Will's existence helps to give the character of Ado Annie a new dimension. In the original play, the author describes her: "She is an unattractive, stupid-looking farm girl, with taffy-colored hair pulled back from a freckled face. Her dress is of red gingham, and unbecoming." In the musical, she becomes something far more interesting—in fact beguiling, and a full "comic."

The secondary triangle—Will, Ado Annie, and the Peddler—supply indispensable comedy for *Oklahoma!*, but their shenanigans also form a perfect example of a complete subplot. Their story line is complete in itself and can be told separately, although its function is contrapuntal to the main plot—Laurey, Curly, and Jud, also a triangle.

The idea of having Curly sing a song at the very opening comes from the original, and the lyrics of "The Surrey with the Fringe on Top" are largely indicated in the Riggs play. "Pore Jud Is Dead" is, in essence, to be found in the original smokehouse scene, and in that same scene Curly talks about "the purtiest mornin'," which gives a hint of the song that became the musical's opening.

The Rodgers and Hammerstein changes in the proportions of several scenes are of great import; and the addition of Will, with its chain-effect on everything around him, adds the comedic color so wanting (at least for a musical) in the original.

In his introduction to the play, Riggs wrote: "Two people in a room, agreeing or not agreeing, are to me truly dramatic. The edges of their being can never be in accord; psychically, as well as physically, they are assailed by an opposing radiation." And later on: " . . . I thought of the first three scenes as The Characters, the last three scenes as The Play."

Rodgers and Hammerstein seem to have tried as much as possible to work within Rigg's conception—particularly in the ballet at the end of Act I, which explores Laurey's psyche through her dream and provides some of the motivation for her subsequent behavior. (It is interesting to note that while the original play ended its run without making back its investment, *Oklahoma!* earned profits of historic proportions.)

The following is a chart comparing the progress of the play with that of the musical libretto:

PLAY	MUSICAL
Scene 1 The (Laurey) Williams farm-house (This is a living room interior.)	*Act I, Scene 1* The front of Laurey's farmhouse. (This is out of doors.)
Scene 2 The same, showing Laurey's bedroom. (The material in this scene is included in the musical's first scene.)	*Scene 2* The smokehouse.
Scene 3 The same, showing the smokehouse.	*Scene 3* A grove on Laurey's farm. (This scene is an invention of the adapter. It leads into Laurey's dream ballet, which ends in Jud's awakening her and taking her to the social.)
INTERMISSION	INTERMISSION
	Act II, Scene 1 The Skidmore Ranch. (This is a new scene in which Will Parker is duped into getting back enough money from the all-too-willing Peddler to be able to marry Ado Annie. Also (and more importantly) there is an auction of picnic baskets, and Jud almost outbids Curly, who has had to sell horse and gun in order to win. Bad feeling between them is expressed.)
Scene 4 The porch of Old Man Peck's house. (The party is in full swing. Laurey has her confrontation with Jeeter, discharges him, and decides to marry Curly.)	*Scene 2* Skidmore's kitchen porch. (Jud dances on with Laurey. She has the confrontation scene with him and discharges him. She is eager to marry Curly.)
Scene 5 The hay-field back of the Williams house, a month later.	*Scene 3* Back of Laurey's house. (The setting is the same in both. The wedding of Laurey and Curly is over, and their friends give them a "shivaree"—a customary folk celebra-tion—which is a prankish annoyance to the couple. Here, as in the play, Jud enters, starts an argument and, in a fight with Curly, falls on his own knife. In the musical Aunt Eller amusingly arranges Curly's trial on the spot, and the show ends with the happy couple leaving on their honeymoon.)
Scene 6 The living room of the Williams house three nights later. (Ado Annie and Aunt Eller discuss Curly's trial scheduled for the next day. Laurey is worried. Curly enters, having broken out of jail. He is pursued by a crowd of men who mean to return him to jail. Aunt Eller talks them into letting Curly spend the night with his bride.)	

To recapitulate, in Act I of the musical, the material follows closely the first half of the play but divides itself differently and concludes with a ballet. Act II, Scene 1 of the musical is an invention, and the events of Scene 2 happen in Scene 1 of the play. Act II, Scene 3 of the musical contains the fight, the trial and the happy ending, whereas in the play the fight and the arrest of Curly occur in Scene 5, and the reuniting of Curly and Laurey is in Scene 6—with the trial not as yet having happened but a strong feeling that everything will come out happily.

I would like to mention briefly several other of these conversions to libretto.

South Pacific, based on the stories by James Michener, has a well-integrated plot line. Logan and Hammerstein took three of the nineteen tales: "Our Heroine," the story of Ensign Nellie Forbush and Emile de Becque; "Fo' Dolla," the story of Lieutenant Cable, Liat, and Bloody Mary; and "A Boar's Tooth," which describes Luther Billis. Some of the other tales have contributed extra color, background, or nuances, but the above three supply the principal ingredients. Although the characters in all three tales are in the same location or nearby in the book they are never brought together. The Forbush-de Becque story as told in the musical *South Pacific* is elongated by de Becque's agreeing to go on a dangerous military mission after Nellie's break with him.

The suspense created by de Becque's mission and by the prolongation of the separation between the lovers is a major contribution of the librettists; in the original story, the break and reconciliation occur during the same night. The musical treatment is theatrical, as it needs to be.

Further, the libretto's use of Luther Billis as part of this particular tale (in which he fits admirably), making him Bloody Mary's complement, is brilliant. By being paired with Luther, Bloody Mary becomes more developed, and in addition to her original qualities she also becomes a major comedienne.

The dovetailing of these elements with the poignant story of Liat and Lieutenant Cable completes a model three-couple plot. In addition, there is the marvelous contrast between mature and very young love. And finally, in the libretto it is Lieutenant Cable who accompanies Emile on the dangerous mission. The knowledge of Cable's death is in itself deeply moving, but it also serves to conclude the Liat-Cable plot satisfactorily without Cable's having to refuse to marry her (on racial-social grounds) as he does in the original *Tales*.

Margaret Landon's novel (based on fact), *Anna and the King of Siam*, was the basis of *The King and I*. Each chapter of the novel contains a harrowing episode, complete in itself, and linked to other episodes through the personalities of the King, who is responsible for creating most of the issues, and Anna, who tries to resolve them.

Hammerstein's treatment alters the King's physical presence by making him attractive, not, as according to Miss Landon, "of medium height and excessively thin." The subplot involving Tuptim comes from one of dozens of horrifying tales in the novel and occurs more than three-quarters of the way through it; the man involved with her is a priest who neither has any amorous relationship with Tuptim nor has he ever been previously aware of her. The libretto has altered this story to make the King's two luckless victims lovers even prior to Tuptim's "arranged" marriage to the King, and their subplot extends throughout the musical.

Hammerstein's achievement here is in his selecting, simplifying, and bringing into focus a few of a multitude of characters and situations and in his ability to create one direct, effective main plot line. Almost none of the details of the original is left unchanged, and yet there is in *The King and I* an essentially truthful distillation of the book's intention. Everything has been telescoped so as to become more viable. The death of the King at the end—a radical alteration of the book—presents a far more effective (and conclusive!) piece of dramaturgy. Humor, entirely absent from the novel, is wholly original with Rodgers and Hammerstein and appropriate to their show. It is especially felicitous in the songs such as "A Puzzlement," "Shall We Dance?" and "Shall I Tell You What I Think of You?"

In *Carousel*, the most striking single element in the transformation of Molnár's *Liliom* is the alteration of time and place. *Liliom* is set in Budapest about 1919, and *Carousel*, on the New England coast between 1873 and 1888. Naturally, such a change had a profound influence on the color and style of the musical. The action in the musical has fluency which the original does not have, and the comic characters of Carrie and Mr. Snow soar high above their dour literary alter egos, Marie and Wolf Beifeld. In *Liliom*, after plunging a knife into himself, the title character spends a long scene dying, during which everything that is capsulized in *Carousel* (and *after* Liliom goes to heaven) is argued or spelled out. The play's heavenly scene is much longer, further spelled out, and drab. The dialogue between the heavenly magistrate and the characters in his court sounds like an object lesson for prospective Eagle Scouts. In *Carousel* Billy dies without seven pages of dialogue; he simply says, "Julie!"—following which he exits, then is seen in heaven arguing with charming heavenly people, who instantly communicate the passage of time by telling him that his daughter is fifteen years old.

If we are ever to have excellent original librettos, it will be necessary for playwrights to study the techniques that musical theater peculiarly requires of its librettists. The same is true of songwriters. Regardless of their talents or achievements, men who write songs will not be able to compose a proper musical score without considerable knowledge of theater.

Since the largest share of the responsibility for a show's success rests on the librettist—and since today's exorbitant production costs seriously diminish the beginner's opportunities for learning through doing, it is essential that potential librettists learn everything possible from the growing list of musical-show models—as well as from the formidable catalogue of failures.

Rethinking *Pal Joey*

Critics were by no means immune to the hegemony of the integrated musical as exemplified by Rodgers and Hammerstein. *New York Times* critic Brooks Atkinson's response to Rodgers and Hart revivals in the wake of the Rodgers and Hammerstein era provides a particularly striking example of a marked attitudinal shift. When reviewing the premiere of *On Your Toes* in 1936 Atkinson praised the "sophisticated" book as well as the songs. Eighteen years later, he found the book "labored, mechanical and verbose," and only a few songs and the final fifteen to twenty minutes of the story remained fresh. On the other hand, *Pal Joey*, the musical Atkinson described as a "foul well" when he reviewed the premiere twelve years earlier (reprinted in Part I)— because the show had the courage to depict odious characters and unsavory situations—was now deemed a worthy precursor of the Rodgers and Hammerstein ideal, "a pioneer in the moving back of musical frontiers" with its "integrated story" and "knowing point of view."

BROOKS ATKINSON

As an augury of a Happy New Year, the town has inherited a brilliant production of *Pal Joey*, which opened at the Broadhurst last evening. This is the Rodgers and Hart musical play for which John O'Hara wrote the book in 1940, and strictly speaking, the new production is a revival.

But there is no sign of age in the brisk performance that Robert Alton has expertly staged: and the acting is sharp and original. Vivienne Segal is on hand again to sing "Bewitched, Bothered and Bewildered," which is one of the most eloquent songs Richard Rodgers has written. Again Miss Segal presides over the sordid affairs of an astringent tale with humor, reserve and charm.

It would be hard to improve upon Harold Lang's performance as the heel of Chicago night life. He acts with the cheap guile that Mr. O'Hara

Source: Brooks Atkinson, "At the Theatre," *New York Times* (January 4, 1952), 17.

caught in his pitiless portrait of one of the most revolting characters in current letters—plausible, clever, superficially ingratiating, but constantly odious when the balance is struck. Mr. Lang is pleasant as a singer. As a dancer he is superb; he is light, swift, gay, and inventive. If there was ever any doubt about the genuineness of his talent, Mr. Lang has removed it with this searching and resourceful performance.

The acting is delightful throughout the evening. Helen Gallagher's sleek night club dancer, Elaine Stritch's caricature of a tough columnist, Lionel Stander's unctuously ferocious gangster—are adroit characterizations and they are also hilarious. And the brassy choruses Mr. Alton has directed in a sardonic style are thoroughly enjoyable.

In 1940 *Pal Joey* was regarded by its satellites as the musical that broke the old formula and brought the musical stage to maturity. There was a minority, including this column that was not enchanted. But no one is likely now to be impervious to the tight organization of the production, the terseness of the writing, the liveliness and versatility of the score, and the easy perfection of the lyrics.

Since the days of *Oklahoma!* the musical stage has grown in awareness and artistry. On Forty-fourth Street, where *Pal Joey* is now installed, Mr. Rodgers is represented by the scores of *South Pacific* and *The King and I*, which are musically more ambitious. But it is true that *Pal Joey* was a pioneer in the moving back of musical frontiers, for it tells and integrated story with a knowing point of view.

The Rodgers and Hammerstein musicals are moving toward folk operas. *Pal Joey* does not stray outside the bailiwick of commercial musical comedy, and the dance routines, satiric in accent, are pretty much in the old patterns. But there is something refreshing about the return of musical comedy in an unhackneyed rendering, with Oliver Smith's pungent settings and Miles White's amusing costumes.

Brimming over with good music and fast on its toes, *Pal Joey* renews confidence in the professionalism of the theatre. Mr. O'Hara's night-club tout has begun Broadway's new year auspiciously.

"The American Musical"

Not everyone approved of the Rodgers and Hammerstein model of a modern major musical. One eminent drama critic and theorist, Eric Bentley (1916–), emphatically rejected the lofty ambitions of musical and dramatic integration. For Bentley, "the last scene of *Carousel* is an impertinence" and in *The King and I* it was the king's "duty to stay alive and amuse us." In contrast to Brooks Atkinson's born-again impatience with old-fashioned musicals prior to *Pal Joey*, Bentley laments the loss of the "cocky, satirical, devil-may-care philosophy" of "true musical comedy" he welcomed in the 1954 revival of *On Your Toes*. In Bentley's view "the best musicals at present are not those with the biggest intentions behind them but those with the simple virtues in them of singable tunes and sheer showmanship."

ERIC BENTLEY

The American Musical has become a byword, but a byword for what? At a recent press conference in Paris, a poet from behind the Iron Curtain was asked if there was anything of value in American theatre: he replied that there had been the Federal Theatre and there were still the musicals. His grounds for approving the Federal Theatre being presumably political, musicals were evidently the only kind of American theatre in which he found any artistic merit. The idea was that while the serious drama was monopolized by a decadent and reactionary intelligentsia, in the musicals the vitality of the masses found expression. Not, of course, that the musical was truly progressive; it was largely without content, "formalistic"; but the form was lively and interesting and, if taken over by the right people. . . .

Now the odd thing is that, though most of us disagree with the form of this very argument, we agree to its content. We feel that more could some day be done with the musical than has been done up to now, that the music and the book could both be raised to a higher power.

And yet the best musicals at present are not those which indicate an effort to transform the musical, such as, to take a recent example, *The Golden Apple* by John Latouche and Jerome Moross. I found these men at their best when they stayed well within the convention, as they did in their fooling, and at their worst when they tried to transcend it, as they did in repeated attempts at poetry and social significance.

It is true that the musical does, at some points, break down the barriers between highbrow and lowbrow. A triumphant example was to be found in the scenery of *The Golden Apple* (designed by William and Jean Eckart) which in its spare, Mondrian lines and light, bright (not gaudy) colors was perhaps the loveliest sight of the 1953–54 season. But the idea of calling in the High Artist doesn't always have such happy consequences. When Oliver Smith's sophisticated cleverness adorns a George Abbott show, you tend to say: Oh dear, couldn't they have hired someone with less education?

The best musicals at present are not those with the biggest intentions behind them but those with the simple virtues in them of singable tunes

Source: Eric Bentley, *What Is Theatre?* (New York: Atheneum, 1968), 190–93. Originally published in *The New Republic* (October 1954).

and sheer showmanship. If I had to say what single man could do most to give us a good musical, I would reply: Richard Rodgers. I would place George Abbott second; and third, say, Michael Kidd or Jerome Robbins. A great designer is not an absolute necessity. Nor is a star actor, especially not if we have Mr. Abbott to find new talent for us. But excellent featured players are indispensable. In fact they are the life and soul of the party. During the past two years, I have not seen many first-rate musicals, but to every second—or even tenth—rate musical featured players contributed first-rate items. All I can recall of [Jule Styne's] *Hazel Flagg* is Jack Whiting, with his smart, soft-shoe rhythm, his suave, grave way of speaking his songs, his comical, cockeyed dignity. From *Golden Apple*, I retain Jonathan Lucas woozily dancing "Lazy Afternoon" and Portia Nelson jigging up and down, with voice and body alike, for "Doomed, Doomed"; from *Show Boat*, Helena Bliss leaning against the proscenium arch and dreamily singing till we forgot the time; from [Cole Porter's] *Can-Can*, Gwen Verdon's homey smile, un-homey body and high, high kicks; from *The Threepenny Opera*, Charlotte Rae, savagely grimacing and lewdly hitching her stocking up. . . .

To admit that Rodgers's name leads the rest is not necessarily to approve the direction that the Rodgers-Hammerstein musicals have recently been taking. On the contrary, I think Hammerstein is one of those whose soul is in greatest peril: He, more than anyone, is out to make the-musical-that-is-more-than-a-musical. His success with the public has been enormous, but is this always because his shows are good? Or could it sometimes have been because they fell in with a new trend in public feeling?

James Thurber says that America no longer wants comedy, and he blames this on McCarthyism: We are too scared to laugh. But surely the anti-humorous trend in popular culture began before McCarthy did? And has much broader than political causes? Take the difference between early and late Hitchcock movies. The public ceased to want the spry comicality of *The Lady Vanishes* and was given Ingrid Bergman ravenously chewing Cary Grant's ear. Or compare the Myrna Loy of around 1930 with the same actress in *The Best Years of Our Lives*: she had been rewritten, as it were, by Oscar Hammerstein.

No wonder that *On Your Toes* by Richard Rodgers and Lorenz Hart (revived at the Forty-sixth Street Theatre) strikes the newspapermen as old-fashioned. But anyone *except* a newspaperman will prefer it that way. The breath of a less stuffy generation is in the piece. I agree with Mr. Thurber that something was lost during the forties and early fifties—and here, in this musical of the thirties, it is: namely, a cocky, satirical, devil-may-care philosophy that is certainly very attractive and possibly rather useful. Anyhow, it is good light theatre, whereas, for example, the last scene of *Carousel* is an impertinence: I refuse to be lectured by a musical comedy scriptwriter on the education of children, the nature of the good life, and the contribution of the American small town to the salvation of souls. I regard such a *gaffe* simply as an opportunity to get out of the theatre before the crowd. I deplore the death of the king in *The King and I*; it was definitely his duty to stay alive and amuse us. But *On Your Toes* is true musical comedy, ending in a bracing "Slaughter on Tenth Avenue" in which no one is really slaughtered.

The new show is not beyond reproach. There are some quite loathsome fruity-spangly costumes by Irene Sharaff; and the delicate Vera Zorina is badly miscast as a sort of Tallulah of the dance. But George Abbott cannot only get along without stars; he can get along *with* stars who don't quite fit. *On Your Toes* is not a setting for a leading lady, it is an ensemble show in which the two great motive-forces are Abbott and Balanchine. I sometimes think the classic choreographers do better work for Broadway than for City Center or the Metropolitan. Jerome Robbins, for example, is a much freer spirit when he is frivolous than when he is trying to interpret W. H. Auden. And I intend no slur on Balanchine's past when I say that his presence on Broadway is no anticlimax. How the "serious" theater would come alive if anything ever happened there like that lovely moving pattern of limbs and umbrellas in fading light which is the dance in the rain from *On Your Toes*!

The find of the show (as far as I am concerned: others doubtless found her before) is Elaine Stritch, who combines an assured and taut technique with an enormous and relaxed warmth of personality.

Who is the great exponent of what the American theatre does with most gaiety and zest? It would be hard to name anyone other than Mr. Abbott.

"The Musical Stage"

George Jean Nathan (1882–1958) shared some of Bentley's disdain for musicals that sing songs of social significance, including Rodgers and Hammerstein's message for racial equality in *South Pacific*, "You've Got to Be Carefully Taught." Also like Bentley, but in contrast to Atkinson, Nathan, a *Smart Set* co-editor with H. L. Mencken beginning in 1914 and an early advocate for the serious dramas of Eugene O'Neill and Sean O'Casey, proudly maintained a double standard when it came to the American musical. According to Nathan, the Broadway musical is doomed to fail when it tries to emulate higher artistic realms such as the Metropolitan Opera. As an advocate of "the lighter stage," Nathan vigorously defends Hammerstein's sentimentality and Rodgers's relentless tunefulness and praises the team for "abstaining from an indulgence in the social significance deemed by some of their colleagues as desirable in lending a bit of weight to their shows" ("Carefully Taught," of course, represents a fall from grace). For Nathan, the "lighter stage occupies the same position in music that the cocktail does at the dinner table" since at its best (the songs of Rodgers), it whets "the appetite for the better things to come."*

In the second excerpt, also from *Theatre in the Fifties*, Nathan offers five reasons to explain why the London critics, who loved *Oklahoma!*, "simply did not care for *South Pacific*."** Concerning the fifth reason, Nathan's conjecture that audiences may have been put off by possible borrowings, one wishes that he might have been more specific about the details of "Bali Ha'i's" alleged indebtedness to Camille Saint-Saëns's Piano Concerto No. 2 in G Minor (or for what it's worth, that the opening three notes of Rodgers's tune do, however, duplicate the first three notes of the finale of Dvořák's Symphony No. 7 in D Minor).

GEORGE JEAN NATHAN

Each and every return of the durable *Oklahoma!* to the New York scene has been the occasion for a revival of the complaint that Oscar Hammerstein's lyrics for it and his other shows are in the main so sentimental that they make one feel as if one had swallowed a large bowl of violin strings boiled in sweet cream. In late years there has grown up a school of amateur but confidently assertive realists who regard as truly expressing human emotions only four-letter words and who are distressed that those like moon, love, home and the sort fall indecently into the same numerical category. They are as outraged by sentiment of any kind as they are by the hairless chest of Apollo, and they smile indulgently at the gentler feelings as being the mark of a milksop and a reflection on any writer who wastes his time on them.

Hammerstein, they should appreciate, is not writing lyrics for Strindberg, Wedekind or Kafka but for light, gay musical shows about fellows

---

*For criticism that goes considerably beyond either Bentley or Nathan in its contempt for Rodgers and Hammerstein, one might turn to Martin Gottfried, who faults Rodgers and Hammerstein and their "right wing" musicals for taking themselves seriously and other artistic felonies [*A Theater Divided*: The *Postwar American Stage* (Boston, Little, Brown, 1967), 3–5, 176–81, and 209–11].

**London audiences as well as Broadway audiences favored *Oklahoma!* over *South Pacific* and both of these more than *Carousel*. For more than six years the three shows ran consecutively at London's Drury Lane: *Oklahoma!* (1,548 performances, April 1947 to 1950 at the Drury Lane [and May to October at the Stoll]); *Carousel* (566 performances, June 1950 to October 1951); and *South Pacific* (802 performances, November 1951 to September 1953). See Stanley Green's *Rodgers and Hammerstein Fact Book* for additional details about all the major productions of these shows before 1980.

Source: George Jean Nathan, *The Theatre in the Fifties* (New York: Alfred A. Knopf, 1953), 232–36, 268–70.

in love with girls, the joys of the countryside under clear, blue skies, the fun of clambakes, and similar minor pleasures of human existence. To ask him to interpret them in the disillusioned and bitter manner of a Gian-Carlo Menotti is as absurd as it would be if he actually did it. He writes warmly and simply and very appropriately of warm and simple subjects, and his relevant innocence is his charm. One doesn't go to a musical show in the mood that one goes to a serious drama; if one does, one is dotty. One doesn't demand that the chorus girls look like college students, or that the bass drummer read Kierkegaard while he is walloping the drum, or that the lyrics sound as if they were written by Gorki.

There are, of course, grades of sentiment as there are of realism. Both may be carried too far and become ludicrous, objectionable and tiresome. The lyrics we get in some Broadway shows are as sickening in their treacle content as the realism we get in some novels by the younger bravos is artistically offensive. Both sentiment and realism call upon writers to exercise some critical restraint. Hammerstein, I think, has that restraint. More, he has a healthy humorous sense and a touch of pepsin that spare his lyrics the syrup we so often gag at in those of some of his colleagues. The fundamental truth about him is that he has something of the innards of a poet, whereas many of his competitors are merely commercial rhymesters. If presently he is the victim of the anti-sentiment fanatics, he may take some comfort from the fact that there are other good men in the same boat with him. I will not go into that phase of the matter here further than to mention one, Douglas MacArthur. It seemed to the fanatics that the General ruined what they allowed was otherwise an impressive speech by descending at its conclusion to the sentimental moisture of the old-soldiers-don't-die-but-just-fade-away business, and their sarcasm reached lush proportions. I content myself by asking them just one question. Opposed as they are to all sentiment, have they lately chanced to re-read Lincoln's Gettysburg Address or Washington's Farewell to his troops, both of which they have admired since boyhood? Or, for that matter, the New Testament?

It seems also to be their resentment that Richard Rodgers's music for the shows is strongly given to melody, which they look down on as being fit only for the ears of musical illiterates. This prejudice against anything that is tuneful and does not sound as if the composer had poured a gallon of butyric acid into the piano is an increasing mark of the Newer Criticism and toadies to it. True music, they believe, should not resort to such child's-play as melody but should studiously avoid it as it would the musical saw and other such passions of the moron ear. What they demand is music that does not sound much more like music than Gertrude Stein's prose, for all its rhythms, sounds like literature, or than the political oratory of André Malraux, for all its pulsations, sounds like sense. It does no good to suggest to them that Wagner, scarcely a Philistine, is boozy with melody and that Tin Pan Alley has cribbed ceaselessly and liberally from him—at least two of the best songs in recent musical shows stem directly from numbers in *The Flying Dutchman*; that it was the hardly microcephalic Schubert's hummable songs that made *Blossom Time* the gold-mine it was and is; that there is more melody in scarcely cheap Chopin than in any dozen ambitious Frank Loessers one can name; and that, to give even the musical saw its due—which is certainly stretching things to the limit—Heitor Villa-Lobos, the worthy contemporary Mexican [Brazilian], has gone the saw ten better with the most eccentric lot of instruments this side of a Johns Hopkins surgery or a kitchen utensils factory.

Rodgers, like Hammerstein, is not writing for the Metropolitan but for the lighter stage and if anyone contends that lighter stage is properly accommodated by the kind of music that keeps Olin Downes at his desk until six the next morning trying to think up reasons for admiring it, he is either ready for the psychiatrist or in line for a good job as a music critic. That lighter stage occupies the same position in music that the cocktail does at the dinner table; it whets, or should whet, the appetite for the better things to come; and Rodgers is one of the best cocktails served hereabouts. There is not the slightest deprecation in the analogy, believe me. The lighter stage, after all, has given us the admirable Arthur Sullivan, the estimable Oscar Straus, Kalman, Lehár and various other such worthies. It has brought wit and charm and tears and laughter to audiences the Western world over, and has added immeasurably to our momentary happiness and contentment. It has given us the matchless waltzes of Strauss and the tender songs of Herbert and Kern and the delightful trivialities of the old Gaiety shows, and a lot more besides. And Rodgers, in his way, is singing as best he can in the old tradition.

There is criticism and there is criticism. One doesn't take a Uffizi mind to a tennis match or go to a musical show with a Brahms concerto in one's pocket. One goes casually in the spirit that one goes to a Springtime picnic or to call on one's best girl. And it is in that spirit that Rodgers and Hammerstein faithfully and so very happily serve it. Particularly are they to be commended for abstaining from an indulgence in the social significance deemed by some of their colleagues as desirable in lending a bit of weight to their shows. Only once, and then but briefly, have they succumbed to the temptation in the form of a racial equality song in *South Pacific*, and it was that single song that damaged the otherwise smooth current of their exhibit and irritated not alone their otherwise most partial critics but almost as much so the majority of their audiences. Social significance, or what is regarded as it by those members of an audience who profess to see in a patch on the comedian's pants-seat an analogy to the revolt of the downtrodden against capital is, they appreciate, surely as inappropriate to a song and dance show as an Ibsen plot or a girl with both her legs shot off. It is a dreadful thought, however, that now our social significance dramatists like Clifford Odets, Lillian Hellman and the like have abandoned social significance, it may be taken over by our music show writers. That it has already been taken over by writers of the higher and more serious musical exhibits like Menotti, we know; and no particular complaint in that quarter. But if the time comes when the girls will kick up their indignations instead of their legs, when the tenor instead of going back to Maxim's will go back to Union Square, and when the heroine will start singing about Aneurin Bevan [Ed. British Labor Leader who served in Parliament from 1929 until his death in 1960] instead of about moonlight on the Caribbean—if that time comes, I shall buy myself a tambourine and stay home. . . .

The local indignation over the London critics' castigation of *South Pacific* is as meritless as would be any London indignation over the New York critics' low opinion of some such English exhibit as Roger MacDougall's *To Dorothy, A Son*. The circumstance of the critical prosperity here of the musical play and over there of the comedy has nothing to do with the case, no more, in fact, than the preference of the American for hot dogs as opposed to the Englishman's for kippers; nor, further, has the local view that *South Pacific* is an excellent show and that *To Dorothy, A Son* is an extremely poor one as opposed to the English that the former is not much good and that the latter is very amusing indeed. The theatrical differences in taste have now been in operation for years and will doubtless continue to be for years to come, and not much can be done about it. In many ways there are not two more dissimilar nations on the face of the earth and to argue that one is right and the other wrong is senseless, at least much of the time.

I will not say anything of the promptly collapsed *To Dorothy, A Son* other than to express my personal critical opinion that it was dreadful claptrap dealing with the musty plot about the baby who will inherit a fortune if born within a specified time limit. Why English audiences have relished it, I no more know than why American audiences have relished even more some such local dose of claptrap as [Ronald Alexander's] *Time Out For Ginger*. But, though we esteem *South Pacific* as an admirable show and though the English proportionally disesteem it, it is not hard to deduce the contrary British attitude. In the first place, the theme of acute racial prejudice in the matter of a young American woman's bitter reaction to a Frenchman who once was wed to a dark-skinned South Seas native naturally impresses the English as silly, forasmuch as wide travel and residence in the far corners of the globe, together with an adaptability to *mores* as they find them, have rid them of any such feeling. But even more to the point is their unacquaintance, in this specific case, with such primitive back-reaches of the United States as Arkansas, where the priggish school teacher [nurse] with her antagonism hails from. If, with perhaps a single exception, there is currently a practicing London dramatic critic who ever explored the varied peculiarities of the American scene much farther west than Dinty Moore's or much farther south than Keen's Chop House, I have not heard of him.

In the second place, the brag and bluster of the show's United States

Marines [Seabees] is unquestionably offensive to the English critics, who like to think, however much they may pretend the contrary, that if it were not for their own soldiery, whether on land or sea, or in the air, we would long ago have been speaking German or Japanese as our national language. In the third place, such a key song number as "You've Got To Be Taught To Hate" ["You've Got To Be Carefully Taught"] strikes them as being quite as violative of the show's flow as it struck the New York critics. In the fourth place the appropriation of the *Madame Butterfly* theme in the secondary love story of the young naval lieutenant and the Tonkinese girl occurred to them just as it did to some of our critics. And, in the fifth place, though they liked the Rodgers score, they probably, as the local critics did not, here and there recognized some of its inspirations as, for example in the "Bali Ha'i" song, Saint-Saëns' second concerto in G minor. (Saint-Saëns has surely stood some of our composers in good stead, as witness, among others, Gershwin and his "Rhapsody In Blue.")

It is claimed that the advance build-up of the show, together with an anti-American attitude, operated further to its critical disadvantage. The advance build-up of *Oklahoma!* did not seem to influence the same critics against it, nor did any anti-American attitude. It is perfectly true that the English do not like us, but the dislike has not kept their theatre critics from wholeheartedly endorsing some of our plays and shows and some of our actors and actresses, let alone vaudeville performers, who have played over there. If those critics occasionally do not like one of our products, it no more testifies arbitrarily to any prejudice against us than our own dislike of some of theirs testifies to any conceivable dislike of the English on our part, even though, to be quite honest about it, a lot of Americans not in the White House are not too crazy about them. The London critics simply did not care for *South Pacific*, and that is all there is to it.

"Moving in the Direction of Opera"

The present printed selection from the best-selling *The Joy of Music* concludes what was originally a telecast on the American musical delivered by conductor, composer, pianist, and educator Leonard Bernstein (1918–1990). First seen on the *Omnibus* series, October 7, 1956, the lecture was broadcast only two months before the debut of his own *Candide* (December 1, 1956) and less than a year before *West Side Story* (September 26, 1957). After exploring the continuum of musical theater from the variety show to Wagnerian music drama (with revue, operetta, comic opera, *opera buffa*, *opéra comique*, and grand opera somewhere in between), Bernstein presents the history of the American musical as a period of growth from primitive roots in 1866 to the blossoming of the past fifteen years, i.e., from childhood and "young manhood" to the "prime of life" musicals of the Rodgers and Hammerstein era. He interprets the opening scene between Nellie and Emile de Becque—the program included a performance of "Twin Soliloquies" and "Some Enchanted Evening"—as a move "toward opera but *in our own way*," and as a recent high point in a progressive evolution toward integration of music and other elements. Despite its recent maturity, however, Bernstein sees the genre as ripe for a new Mozart, a genius who can transform a "popular form" into a "work of art." On the eve of *Candide* and *West Side Story* one wonders whether Bernstein nurtured a hope that he himself would be destined to lead the musical to these new heights.

LEONARD BERNSTEIN

Ever since 1936, when Rodgers and Hart came up with *On Your Toes*, dancing has come into its own as a plot-furthering medium. In this show, Rodgers and Hart devised a scenario for a ballet called "Slaughter on Tenth Avenue," which has not only its own ballet plot, but also participates climactically in the plot of the whole show. This scenario calls for Ray Bolger to keep dancing for his very life, even after the ballet story is over, since two gangsters are waiting in box seats to let him have it the moment he stops.

(A passage from "Slaughter on Tenth Avenue" is danced.)

This ballet, choreographed by George Balanchine, broke ground for the building of a whole tradition of plot-dancing, for all the action ballets, love ballets, decision ballets, dream ballets and passage-of-time ballets that we have almost come to expect now, after such shows as *Oklahoma!*, *On the Town*, and *Guys and Dolls*. In other words, choreographers like Agnes de Mille, Jerome Robbins, and Michael Kidd have become almost as important to our form as the authors and composers and directors; and the whole look and sound of musical comedy has been radically changed.

Which brings us neatly up to modern times.

For the last fifteen years we have been enjoying the greatest period our musical theater has ever known. In these last fifteen years we have finished with young manhood and entered the prime of life. Some of our shows of this period are already young classics: *Pal Joey, Annie Get Your Gun, Oklahoma!, South Pacific, Guys and Dolls, Kiss Me, Kate*. Some people say that the reason for this spurt has been our great prosperity; others say that it is due to American know-how, that world-famous quality of ours.

Source: Leonard Bernstein, *The Joy of Music* (New York: Simon and Schuster, 1959), 174–79.

I don't much like either of these theories, because they don't regard the essential root of it all—the creative spirit. And that is the main reason for our success with musical comedies: they are extravagantly creative. Each one is a surprise; nobody ever knows what new twists and treatments and styles will appear next. There seems to be no limit to our creative energy, or to our reservoir of creators. Gershwin and Hart and Kern and Youmans have died but have not remained unsupplanted. Rodgers found a great new partner in Hammerstein; Ira Gershwin found the tremendously gifted Harold Arlen.

Then along came a new great: Frank Loesser. Five minutes later, it seemed, there were two young Loessers named Ross and Adler, who were turning out material in his style. A marvelous show called *Finian's Rainbow* introduced Burton Lane as a remarkable new composer. Arthur Schwartz, Harold Rome and Jule Styne have made charming contributions. The team of Lerner and Loewe, which gave us *Brigadoon*, hit the jackpot with *My Fair Lady*. And Berlin, Porter, and Rodgers are still very much with us. We're swimming in talent.

Talent has changed everything. For instance, talent has enabled Rodgers and Hammerstein to take the best elements of opera, operetta, revue, vaudeville, and all the rest, and blend them into something quite original. Perhaps the best example of this is *South Pacific*, which many people regard as our supreme achievement in musical comedy. It is as though a new strain has been cross-bred out of the past.

When the Seabees are singing "There is Nothing Like a Dame," or when Nellie sings "I'm Gonna Wash That Man Right Out of My Hair," then it is a musical comedy in our best tradition; but when Bloody Mary sings "Bali Ha'i," it is a romantic operetta, in our best tradition. And somehow it all works like a charm, smooth and utterly professional. No more stylistic hash. No more stringing numbers together. No more sticking in of prefabricated songs, whether they suit the action or not.

Just compare the integration of songs as we saw it in [George and Ira Gershwin's] *Oh, Kay!* with the way "Some Enchanted Evening" is introduced in *South Pacific*. The song occurs in the first scene, where Nellie and Emile are falling in love and are uncertain as to whether they ought to. In the process of getting to know each other better, she has just sung him a song revealing her nature— "A Cockeyed Optimist"—and when it is over, she speaks:

Singer-actors:
> NELLIE: *Want to know anything else about me?*
> EMILE: *Yes, you say you are a fugitive. When you joined the Navy, what were you running away from?*

L.B.:
Here the orchestra sneaks in, giving us a hint of her feelings.

Singer-actors:

NELLIE: *Gosh, I don't know. It was more like running to something. I wanted to see what the world was like—outside Little Rock, I mean. And I wanted to meet different kinds of people and find out if I like them better. And I'm finding out.*

EMILE: *Would you like some cognac?*

NELLIE: *I'd love some.*

L.B.:

It is in the poised moment of this brandy-pouring that the miracle happens. Rodgers and Hammerstein take advantage of the lovers's temporary separation to fashion a double soliloquy, in which each of the pair can *sing* his or her thoughts; yet it is neither a song, as such, nor a recitative. And still it performs the functions of both.

Nellie and Emile sing the double soliloquy:

NELLIE: *Wonder how I'd feel,*
  living on a hillside,
  looking on an ocean,
  beautiful and still.

EMILE: *This is what I need,*
  this is what I've longed for,
  someone young and smiling
  climbing up my hill!

NELLIE: *We are not alike;*
  probably I'd bore him.
  He's a cultured Frenchman—
  I'm a little hick.

EMILE: *Younger men than I,*
  officers and doctors,
  probably pursue her—
  she could have her pick.

NELLIE: *Wonder why I feel jittery and jumpy!*
  I am like a schoolgirl waiting for a dance.

EMILE: *Can I ask her now?*
  I am like a schoolboy!
  What will be her answer?
  Do I have a chance?

L.B., as orchestra continues:

We are now standing firmly on operatic ground, since the plot is being furthered by singing, and doing it better than dialogue could in this case. But what is happening now? The lovers are standing, brandy in hand, tense, in love, fighting it. And this is told us, neither by dialogue *nor* by singing, but more eloquently still by the orchestra alone. *(Orchestra plays alone up to climax.)*

L.B., after orchestra diminishes:
> Thus we are made ready for the introduction of the "big song." A few more lines, over music, lead directly to the fulfillment of "Some Enchanted Evening."
> *(Emile sings "Some Enchanted Evening.")*

You see how carefully woven all this is. There is nothing so bald as a cue line and then bang—into song. They have snuck up on it, with elaborate musical preparation. We have been weaving in and out of music, sometimes sung, sometimes underscored, sometimes with orchestra only, so that when the big song finally does appear, there is no sudden jolt from speech to song, as there always used to be. And this was accomplished by none other than our old friend recitative, a new kind of recitative, based on simple American song forms, and resulting in a lovely double soliloquy. Our colloquial American speech does not like recitation; it is far too rhythmic and accentuated a language to be so free-floating. But Rodgers and Hammerstein, by using this new song style of recitative, are now able to further plot by singing without seeming ridiculously operatic. Again, our musical comedy has moved toward opera but *in our own way.*

What does all this add up to? Simply this: that the American musical theater has come a long way, borrowing this from opera, that from revue, the other from operetta, something else from vaudeville—and mixing all the elements into something quite new, but something which has been steadily moving in the direction of opera.

Certain elements may get more emphasis in one show, and other elements in another. For instance, *Oklahoma!* is a Western that leans way over toward operetta, whereas *Annie Get Your Gun* is a Western that is pure musical comedy. The question again is one of the vernacular: *Oklahoma!* uses realistic Western speech, whereas *Annie* uses tough talk that belongs to New York. *Oklahoma!* tries for cowboy music, whereas *Annie* says it with jazz, Indians to the contrary. Similarly, Frank Loesser's hit *The Most Happy Fella* leans heavily on opera; *Guys and Dolls*—by *the very same composer*—is the purest musical comedy. *My Fair Lady*, because of its subject matter, is necessarily closer to operetta, whereas *Damn Yankees* is necessarily further from operetta because of *its* subject matter.

But they all qualify, different as they are, for that term "musical comedy" on the grounds of one great unifying factor: they all belong to an art that arises out of American roots, out of our speech, our tempo, our moral attitudes, our way of moving. Out of all this, a new form has been born. Some people claim it is the forerunner of a new kind of opera; others insist it will never become opera, because it is not art, nor is it meant to be anything but light entertainment. Being a liberal, I can see both sides. We will always have with us the line of gorgeous girls, the star comic, and the razzle-dazzle band in the pit.

But there's more in the wind than that. We are in a historical position now similar to that of the popular musical theater in Germany just before

Mozart came along. In 1750, the big attraction was what they called the *Singspiel*, which was the *Annie Get Your Gun* of its day, star comic and all. This popular form took the leap to a work of art through the genius of Mozart. After all, *The Magic Flute* is a *Singspiel*; only it's by Mozart. [Ed. Bernstein inserts a note here to "compare with related ideas in 'Whatever Happened to That Great American Symphony?,' page 40."]

We are in the same position; all we need is for our Mozart to come along. If and when he does, we surely won't get any *Magic Flute*; what we'll get will be a new form, and perhaps "opera" will be the wrong word for it. There must be a more exciting word for such an exciting event. And this event can happen any second. It's almost as though it is our moment in history, as if there is a historical necessity that gives us such a wealth of creative talent at this precise time.

(The telecast concluded with a performance of "Another Opening [Op'nin'], Another Show," from Cole Porter's Kiss Me, Kate.)

A Few Favorite Things
about Rodgers with Hammerstein

Alec Wilder (1907–1980), the author of the *American Popular Song*, a widely acknowledged classic in the field, was himself a composer of numerous works for stage, orchestra, and chamber music and whose songs were sung by Judy Garland and Frank Sinatra and performed by the Benny Goodman and Jimmy Dorsey bands. In the introduction to the Rodgers chapter in this widely quoted volume (see also his remarks on "My Heart Stood Still" selection in Part I), Wilder puts his critical cards on the table: "Of all the writers whose songs are considered and examined in this book, those of Rodgers show the highest degree of consistent excellence, inventiveness, and sophistication."

Despite his admiration for Rodgers, Wilder admits a strong predilection for Rodgers and Hart over Rodgers and Hammerstein. For this reason he devotes fifty-three pages to Rodgers's songs with Hart and only six pages on Rodgers and Hammerstein, all of which are reprinted in the present excerpt. Read out of context, Wilder's selective praise of a handful of Rodgers and Hammerstein songs may seem faint indeed, especially relative to his delight in so many songs with Hart. Nevertheless, he finds *Oklahoma!*'s "Out of My Dreams" to be "a simply superb waltz" (and "Hello, Young Lovers" from *The King and I* "one of Rodgers's finest waltzes"); he also praises "Boys and Girls Like You and Me," a song deleted from *Oklahoma!* but recycled in the 1965 version of *Cinderella*, as "a song of great gentleness and most endearing turn of phrase." Beyond that, only "odds and ends" of other Rodgers and Hammerstein songs bring him out of his seat. He concedes that *Carousel*'s songs might work in a theatrical context, but considers them less effective "as songs per se," and in perhaps his sharpest departure from conventional taste, he admits that he finds "Some Enchanted Evening" "pale and pompous and bland."

ALEC WILDER

From this point on most of the songs to be mentioned have lyrics by Oscar Hammerstein II. While Rodgers continued to write great songs, and even to top himself, generally speaking I find missing that spark and daring flair which existed in the songs he wrote with Hart.

At first this is not apparent. After all, *Oklahoma!* (1943) was perhaps the most successful show Rodgers ever wrote (unless one wishes to consider the phenomenon of the film of *The Sound Of Music*, which is said to have made more money than *Gone With the Wind*). Certainly no bloom was off the peach in "Out of My Dreams," a simply superb waltz.

This song has no verse, only an interlude which adds nothing to the song as such. Its principal idea is a step-wise ascent and descent followed by wider steps. In the course of its progress it does many lovely things. For example, at the twentieth measure, it introduces a wholly new idea which is immediately imitated, to bring the melody within two chromatic steps of the original statement. The effect of this is magical.

Ex. 1: **"Out of My Dreams"**

The lyric is highly poetic.

"Boys and Girls Like You and Me" is a short song, only sixteen measures, originally slated for *Oklahoma!* and not only unused in that show but existing today only in the full score of *Cinderella* [the 1965 remake], at the stiff price of ten dollars. It is a song of great gentleness

Source: Alec Wilder, *American Popular Song: The Great Innovators—1900–1950* (New York: Oxford University Press, 1972), 217–22.

and most endearing turn of phrase. It attempts to do no more than make a hand-holding, summer-strolling statement of affection. I think it is a shame that it has never been published separately. Any song with such a captivating opening phrase deserves to be.

Ex. 2: "Boys and Girls Like You and Me"

It is said that the melody of "People Will Say We're in Love" originally had an earlier lyric by Hart. The Hammerstein lyric is extremely fine, finer for me by far than the melody which, in spite of its popularity, has never appealed to me, nor does it represent the high level which, at this point, Rodgers had reached.

In 1945, from *Carousel*, there were many highly respected songs. I'm sorry to say that outside the theater, as songs per se, I don't find them as ingratiating as others do. "Mister Snow" I am very touched by in its first half, but find myself thrown completely off by a spoken measure just before the restatement. This, frankly, makes it impossible for me to say more than that these spoken lines probably were very effective in the theater. The more I examine this song, the more I'm certain that it should not be judged out of its theatrical context.

In the film *State Fair* (1945), there was a wonderful song, "It Might As Well Be Spring," unlike any song Rodgers had ever written to this point. It's almost instrumental in its disposition of notes in the third measure.

Ex. 3: "It Might As Well Be Spring"

This kind of measure occurs nowhere else but in the restatement.

The last section is extended from eight to sixteen measures and this extension is most unexpected and effective. The only thing I dislike is the use of two notes for the single syllable "might." For the three notes in that measure suggest the phrase "might as well." I wouldn't mind as much hearing the word "be" sung to the following three notes, if only to avoid the awkwardness of the other.

Ex. 4

Hammerstein's lyric is truly a treasure of sparkling imagery.

"It's a Grand Night for Singing" is a charmingly direct, four-square, old-fashioned back-porch waltz. Nor do I mean any one of those attributes to be taken negatively. It's all very healthy and the dividend of the tag makes it even better. The lyric is fresh and cheery and uncontrived. There is no verse, but an interlude of no import.

"That's for Me" is another good song from the same film, with an excellent lyric and verse. There are two aspects of the chorus worth mentioning in terms of special interest. The first is the unexpectedly long second phrase starting at measure five. The way it builds both musically and lyrically to the high *e* where the strong word "that's" occurs is worthy of illustration.

Ex. 5: "That's for Me"

Also, note the telescoping of the short release with the second phrase of the song and the extension that follows.

Ex. 6

"The Gentleman Is a Dope," from *Allegro* (1947), was, I presume, what they call a "follow-up" to "The Lady Is A Tramp." It's a much, much longer song, with curiously shaped sections. The form is *A-A-B-A1* and the first two *A's* are eighteen measures long, the *B*, sixteen, and the *A1*, twenty-two.

It should be a great song. After the first section, you're sure it is. Then (due to its length, I think), the second A begins to lag. The B section somehow falls flat. It doesn't belong in the song. And by that time, the last A1 lasts too long and disappoints with its *f* sharp in the penultimate measure suggesting a major ending. You're somewhat saved by its turning out to be minor, but I can't find the wit in the *f* sharp. And I must assume that it was intended as such.

None of this is due to Hammerstein's lyric, which is extremely good. But in the event that the melody was written to the lyric, then it is the fault of the latter. Better to have written two sets of lyrics and halved the melody. Then what about that curiously alien release?

I'm sorry to say that the melodies from *South Pacific*, immensely popular though they were, took on a kind of self-consciousness that is akin to the piping on Kern's vest that I mentioned many pages ago. [Ed. On several occasions in his long chapter on Rodgers, Wilder acknowledges Kern's influence. Despite his admiration for both songwriters, Wilder doesn't consider this influence a salutary one. For example, "With a Song in My Heart" from *Spring Is Here* "smacks of the same arty tendency one finds in Jerome Kern."] I almost feel as if I should change into formal garb before I listen to them. Or it may be that I've stopped believing. Something's missing: fire, impact, purity, naturalness, need, friendliness, and, most of all, wit.

No, I don't like "Some Enchanted Evening." I find it pale and pompous and bland. Where, oh where, are all those lovely surprises, those leaps in the dark, those chances? I'm in church and it's the wrong hymnal!

In *The King and I* I find "Hello, Young Lovers" right back on home base. Not so the verse, which tries too hard. But the chorus is enormously touching, beautifully written, harmonically colorful and unintrusive, indeed, one of Rodgers's finest waltzes.

The pedal point fifth (c and g) throughout the first six and all, equivalent measures sets the mood of the melody with a kind of sentimental sense of sound. The unexpected E-flat-major chord in the eleventh measure is an inspiration. Also the extended ending is unusual and marvelously effective in its use of chromatic steps.

But for the, to me, highly inappropriate and unrelated last section, I very much like "Do I Love You Because You're Beautiful" from a television play, *Cinderella*. I can't imagine what went wrong, but I feel as if someone had turned a radio dial just before the end of the song and there I was listening to an opera audition, perhaps. I very much like the last six measures of the release of "A Lovely Night" from *Cinderella*. I'm sorry to be so choosy, but these measures are very engaging and the main strain is not.

Ex. 7: "A Lovely Night"

In *Flower Drum Song* there is a very interesting song unlike anything of Rodgers I know, called "Love, Look Away." The verse is a small cloud moving inexorably toward "Fly Me to the Moon." But the chorus holds up beautifully until its second-to-last measure. It's such a good song I wish I could say otherwise.

"My Favorite Things," from *The Sound of Music*, though a material "list" song, has a very effective, curiously brooding melody which eventually works its way out into the sun.

I've examined, and very carefully, all of Rodgers's songs up to 1970. And since I must be honest, I can find no whole song about which I want to talk, or whose merits I am impelled to praise. It must be clear by now that I am more enthusiastic about the majority of his songs than about the majority of those of any other writers. But from "Hello, Young Lovers" on, as is evident, I can find only odds and ends which bring me out of my seat.

As I said at the beginning of this chapter, Rodgers's songs have, over the years, revealed a higher degree of consistent excellence, inventiveness, and sophistication than those of any other writer I have studied.

"The Nicest Guys in Show Business"

Cleveland Amory's profile of the pair who "not only have written the best musical comedies but have also changed the whole concept of the musical theater," is a worthy representative of the deferential media treatment Rodgers and Hammerstein received in the 1950s.* After quoting Rodgers's defense of "sweetness and light" and Hammerstein's defense of "sentimentalism," Amory revisits such familiar territory as their "slow and painstaking" planning of a show and Rodgers's speed in setting Hammerstein's lyrics. Future journalists and historians would modify Amory's depiction of Rodgers's disposition as "placid" or the assertion that he was a nonsmoker and only an occasional drinker, but the profile nonetheless fairly attempts to address the familiar story of their interconnected careers and their lives in the last year of collaboration. Readers also learn that Hammerstein, to refute the accusation that he was the "nicest guy in the theater," let a press agent know he had stolen a radish from a blind man (at a dinner party) and that Rodgers takes his croquet games more seriously than practically anything else in life outside of the theater.

Amory concludes by discrediting three "outright canards" about the team: 1) "that Rodgers is the businessman, Hammerstein the poet"; 2) that they have made more money than is good for them; and 3) "that they are lucky." To the first two canards Amory notes that neither Rodgers nor Hammerstein sees himself as a businessman and that both men generously donate their time and money to many organizations and good causes and have not allowed their wealth to lead to social or artistic complacency. In responding to the final canard Amory deftly shifts the topic from luck in the theater to personal luck and cites the misfortune of Rodgers's cancer and Hammerstein's gallbladder operations and a son's divorce.

CLEVELAND AMORY

Not long ago Richard Rodgers and Oscar Hammerstein II were being honored at a large banquet. Present, among other dignitaries, was a certain Governor. Suddenly, in a burst of confidence, he turned to Rodgers. "You know what I really love about your shows," he said; "it's that they don't try to say anything."

---

*Two other worthy later interview-profiles of Rodgers not included in this anthology are Samuel Chotzinoff, *A Little Night Music* (New York: Harper & Row, 1964), 99–115 and Max Wilk, *They're Playing Our Song* (New York: Da Capo, 1997), 70–75.

Source: Cleveland Amory, *Holiday* (February 1959), 91–94, 96, 98–99.

Rodgers looked at the Governor in amazement. "But, Governor," he protested, "we do try to say something."

"That's just what I mean," replied the Governor. "But you do it so beautifully that nobody minds it."

On another occasion, shortly after the New Haven opening of *South Pacific*, Rodgers and Hammerstein were sitting in the dining room of the Hotel Taft when a strange young man, the worse for drink, approached them waving an accusing finger. "I saw the show," he said, "and don't think I didn't know what you were saying, because I did. You didn't slip anything over on me. I got it—every bit of it."

This time it was Hammerstein's turn. "Well," he said, "I hoped you liked it."

"Liked it?" said the man indignantly. "I loved it!"

Rodgers and Hammerstein believe that these contrasting stories are both typical reactions to their shows.

Two months ago they opened their eighth show, *Flower Drum Song*, adapted from a novel by Chin Y. Lee, and written as a show together with humorist Joseph Fields. It is the story of second generation (American) vs. first generation (Chinese) in a San Francisco Chinatown family; and thus it concerns once more the familiar East vs. West theme of *South Pacific* and *The King and I*, as well as the basic theme of all Rodgers and Hammerstein musicals—that of people getting along together. Yet already the show is being enjoyed not for what it says but for how it says it, and once more, ironically, the real meaning of Rodgers and Hammerstein has been in a sense obscured by their enormous talent. Obviously they have had, in all their shows, things to say—they have in fact contradicted Moss Hart's famous line "Let Western Union carry the messages"—and yet they have these things so well integrated—to use a particularly appropriate word—that to the public their messages are almost subliminal.

"We don't think of what to say," says Hammerstein, "and then write a show to go with it. We pick our story and then say something."

"And," adds Rodgers, "we don't say everybody has to love each other, we just say that they might give a thought to trying to understand each other."

But Rodgers and Hammerstein can also strike out strongly. Their song "You've Got to be Carefully Taught" from *South Pacific* has become a kind of international anthem for racial tolerance:

> You've got to be taught to hate and to fear.
> You've got to be taught from year to year,
> It's got to be drummed in your dear little ear.
> You've got to be carefully taught.
>
> You've got to be taught to be afraid
> Of people whose eyes are oddly made,
> And people whose skin is a different shade.
> You've got to be carefully taught.

If "Carefully Taught" is Rodgers and Hammerstein's most controversial meaning, it is not by any means their only one. Indeed probably their chief meaning or message is the simple and yet all-embracing one which is often called, much to their rare irritation, "sweetness and light." And yet this message, too, in these days of cynicism, nihilism, satire and humorous escape, is also controversial. Even some of Rodgers and Hammerstein's closest friends are sometimes bothered that they seem to have sold their birthright as New York showmen for a kind of sentimentality which does not seem to square with the fact that they are civilized and sophisticated men.

"What's wrong with 'sweetness and light'?" Rodgers asks. "It's been around quite a while. Even a cliché, you know, has a right to be true. I'm not interested in cracking out at anything and I'm certainly not interested in kicking sentiment around. I love satire but I couldn't write it. I would find it just as impossible to live with a wise-cracking wife as I have found it extremely possible—and extremely agreeable—to live for some twenty-eight years with a lovely, gentle, sweet, quiet, soft-spoken gal who knows what the score is."

And Hammerstein, whose wife describes him as "only funny talking, not when he's writing it down," puts it equally directly. "No, I'm not sophisticated. I'm a sentimentalist. The sophisticate is a man who thinks he can swim better than he can and sometimes drowns himself. In my book there's nothing wrong with sentiment, because the things we're sentimental about are the fundamental things in life, the birth of a child, the death of a child, or anybody falling in love. I couldn't be anything but sentimental about these basic things. To be anything but sentimental about them is being a poseur."

The public has agreed, and the public's hunger for something that it is just possible no one else has dared to do has made Rodgers and Hammerstein what they are. Probably the best example of their daring to be optimistic occurs in *Carousel*, considered by many people, including Rodgers and Hammerstein themselves, to be their best work. They refused to recognize the unmitigated tragedy of Molnár's *Liliom*, on which their show was based. "*Liliom*," explains Rodgers, "was a tragedy about a man who cannot learn to live with other people. The way Molnár wrote it the man ends up hitting his daughter and then having to go back to purgatory, leaving his daughter helpless and hopeless. We couldn't accept that. The way we ended *Carousel* it may be still a tragedy but it's a hopeful one because in the final scene it is clear that the child has at last learned how to express herself and communicate with others. The curious thing is that when Molnár saw our final scene—which was the exact opposite of his—he told us it was the best scene in our play."

One thing is certain. Whether *Flower Drum Song* turns out to be another incredible hit such as *Oklahoma!, Carousel, South Pacific,* or *The King and I* (and if its impact has been gentler, it is already in the same league), it is not likely to change either Rodgers and Hammerstein's place in the theater or their place in posterity. It has often been said that the greatest single contribution this generation has made to the theater has been the musical comedy; it must also be said that Rodgers and Hammerstein not only have written the best musical comedies but have also changed the whole concept of the musical theater. Indeed, and this includes their failures like *Allegro, Me and Juliet,* and *Pipe Dream* as well as their successes, they have created a new art form—the totally integrated (again that unavoidable word) musical play, in which the story is advanced not only by the dialogue and songs but also by the dancing and even the jokes. They have done this so skillfully that the public and even some critics are still unaware of it. (Witness, for example, almost the first joke of *Flower Drum Song,* when the Chinese father says he can't remember the bandit who held him up: "All white men look alike.")

"I like to think," says Rodgers gently, "that we've pushed the walls out a bit." "Musical plays," adds Hammerstein, "are not 'books' written by an author with songs later inserted by a composer and lyric writer. The musician is just as much an author as the librettist. He expresses the story in his medium just as the librettist expresses the story in his. They weld their two crafts and two kinds of talent into a single expression. This is the great secret of the well-integrated musical play."

Rodgers and Hammerstein were well fitted for their task. Aside from their looks and personalities—Rodgers is a small, alert, boyish-looking man with a quick wit and a quizzical manner, while Hammerstein is a big, slow-moving bearlike man with a craggy, philosophical face and a gentle, shy manner—there are so many similarities about the two men that their biographies could almost be written as one. Both came from middle-class families, grew up in the same section of New York (around 125th street) and both even went to the same summer camps. ("We weren't rich," Rodgers says. "On the other hand, we weren't so poor that when we made some money it threw us off balance.") Both had parents and grandparents who had great influence on them ("Don't consult the encyclopedia—ask Grandma" was a saying in the Rodgers family, while Hammerstein's grandfather was, of course, the celebrated opera impresario, Oscar Hammerstein I). Both attended Columbia, and have often given the same reason for choosing Columbia ("Because the Varsity Show played, with a *professional* orchestra, in the Hotel Astor ballroom. What better reason could you have for choosing a college?").

And yet, of course, it was a full quarter of a century before Rodgers and Hammerstein worked together (with the exception of a 1920 song for the Varsity Show entitled, prophetically enough, "There is Always Room for One More"). In the interim, beginning with *The Garrick Gaieties* in 1925, Rodgers worked with the late Lorenz Hart as his lyricist, while Hammerstein had an equally long and distinguished career working with such composers as Rudolph Friml, Jerome Kern and Sigmund Romberg. Then in 1942 Rodgers came to Hammerstein and said he wanted to "get together on *Oklahoma!*"

Today, both Rodgers at fifty-six and Hammerstein at sixty-three have placid dispositions and are thoughtful, unselfish men who are not given to tantrums, outbursts of ego, or even the quirks and idiosyncrasies associated with genius. They lead orderly, well-balanced, disciplined lives. Both live well but by no means ostentatiously in New York, and also have beautiful but by no means flamboyant country houses, Rodgers in Fairfield County, Connecticut, and Hammerstein in Bucks County, Pennsylvania. Their hobbies vary—Rodgers likes to play croquet and entertain, Hammerstein likes to raise Black Angus, play tennis and chess and go to bed early—but they both play their games seriously. I recall seeing Rodgers crosser at croquet than I have ever seen him anywhere else, and even Hammerstein at chess is not above a kind of hummanship—humming other people's tunes—to distract his opponent.

Neither Rodgers nor Hammerstein smokes, drinks more than occasionally, or favors night life, night clubs, all-night parties or even, strangely enough, theater First Nights. Hammerstein, in the words of his wife, is "abnormally normal" and "likes people, hates parties." Rodgers, if more gregarious, is also capable of a disappearing act or "celebrity fade." Both have at social gatherings, incidentally, far more humor than they allow themselves to put into their shows. Rodgers dearly loves an outrageous pun, and Hammerstein cannot help being humorous even when he does not necessarily want to be. Once, weary of being praised as the nicest guy in the theater, Hammerstein backed a press agent into a chair. "Listen," he said, glowering, "if you want to know what kind of man I am, I once stole a radish from a blind man." To this day he claims the story is true. He was seated at a dinner party next to a blind composer who had a radish on his butter plate and did not know it was there. Hammerstein grabbed the radish and ate it—and ever since has felt terrible about it.

Passing from the similarities between the two men to the coincidences in their lives, the joint biography becomes almost eerie. Both had fathers named William, both married girls named Dorothy, to whom they have been married just about the same length of time, and both fell in love not only the same year but also aboard transatlantic liners returning from Europe. Rodgers's wife, the former Dorothy Feiner, is a perfectionist in running her house, and is also an inventor of note, with several patents, as well as parlor games, to her credit. Her counterpart, Hammerstein's wife, the former Dorothy Blanchard, who is Australian by birth is also a perfectionist in her way—which happens to be interior decorating (her latest project being a cottage at Round Hill, Jamaica). Both women were indeed former professional interior decorators, both have keen senses of humor, are almost unbelievably observant and quick and are their husbands' (but not each other's husbands') most unerring critics. "It's as if we were all married," says Dorothy Hammerstein. "No matter what happens we're relatives for life." In both families, too, there are children in the theater. The Rodgerses have two musically talented daughters, Linda and Mary, who are now working professionally, and the Hammersteins' two sons, James and William, are also in show business.

Talk to either Rodgers or Hammerstein and you will find that each is almost as likely to use the other's shop talk as he is his own. Ask Hammerstein about the character of Jud in *Oklahoma!* and he is likely to tell you that "Jud was the bass fiddle that gave body to the orchestration of the story." And Rodgers, who is also no mean user of words, will rise to deny vehemently the age-old cry of the composer that "Nobody whistles the words." "They may not whistle them," he says, "but they think them." He will also talk, as concernedly as his partner, about "open vowels" and "no hard consonants on high notes." And, when they are talking about how they actually work together, they are almost interchangeable speakers. Rodgers is a rapid worker, Oscar a slow one—at least in the finishing process ("I hand him a lyric," says Hammerstein, "and get out of his way"), but in the initial phases of a show they are both slow and painstaking.

"Dick and I," says Oscar, "stay very close together drawing up the blueprint. Before we put a word or a note on paper we have agreed on a definite and complete outline, and we have also decided just how much of the story will be told in dialogue and how much in song. But we use music as much as we can. Most often I write the words first, and yet in nearly all our scores there are at least one or two songs in which Dick wrote the music first. It is not at all unlikely that he will give me valuable lyric ideas, and while I have no melodic gift whatsoever, I have a feeling for the treatment of a score, and I work, with my lyrics, with little dummy tunes of my own—which my wife calls 'miserably melancholic melodies.'"

Rodgers is fond of pointing out that "anybody" could provide the proper tune for a line like "The corn is as high as an elephant's eye," and he talks with deep feeling about "the almost inevitable musical pathway" leading from the words:

> I'm as restless as a willow in a windstorm,
> I'm as jumpy as a puppet on a string—

But in that very song, from the motion picture *State Fair*, Hammerstein got stuck. He wanted to have the girl go to the fair but he also wanted her to have spring fever—and yet he knew (despite his theory that writers can get what he calls "research poisoning") that state fairs are held only in the autumn. "I toyed," he recalls, "with the notion of having her say, in effect, 'It's autumn, but I have spring fever so it might as well be spring,' and rather halfheartedly, I threw the idea at Dick. He

jumped up excitedly and said, 'That's it.' And from then on, that was it."
In recounting the story of how he came to think of his favorite song,
"Oh, What a Beautiful Mornin'" (he shuts off the radio if anyone sings
the final "g"), Hammerstein, with his characteristic modesty, as well as
honesty, credits the stage directions of the original, *Green Grow the
Lilacs*, written by Lynn Riggs, as his inspiration for the song.

Rodgers, when once asked how long it took him to write "Oh, What a
Beautiful Mornin'," replied, "How long does it take to play it?" But he
can also work long and laboriously. One of the songs which was hardest
for him is possibly the simplest song he ever wrote—one which,
combined with Hammerstein's unbelievably simple lyrics, became
perhaps the greatest of all their songs, "You'll Never Walk Alone," from
Carousel:

> When you walk through a storm hold your head up high
> And don't be afraid of the dark.
> At the end of the storm is a golden sky
> And the sweet, silver song of a lark.

Not the least remarkable thing about Rodgers and Hammerstein is
that they are as remarkable as people as they are as successes—which
demands, of course, an ability to handle failure as well as success.

"I wrote a play once about success," Hammerstein says wryly, "and it
failed. It was called *Allegro*. Many of the critics completely misunderstood what I was saying. They seemed to find in my play an indictment
of the city doctor as opposed to the country doctor. This was not my
intent at all. The fault was not theirs, but mine. If a writer's aim is
misread, it can only be because he has not written clearly enough. My
play was about the discovery that after you're successful, whether you be
a doctor or a lawyer or a librettist, there is a conspiracy that goes on, in
which you join, a conspiracy of the world to render you less effective by
bestowing honors on you and taking you away from the job of curing
people, or of pleading causes, or writing libretti."

In the case of Rodgers and Hammerstein this conspiracy has been an
enormous one. "People," says Rodgers, "have made a production of us,
and we can't live down the casting." The conspiracy contains a number
of outright canards. The first canard is a personal one—that Rodgers is
the businessman, Hammerstein the poet. "People have to have you
pigeonholed," says Rodgers. "Actually Oscar is far more practical than I
am, but the business for both of us is done by businessmen we pay to do
it. Look at our office. We may be big but we're not U.S. Steel. I don't
recall ever writing anything in my life for money. The money has always
come as the result of wanting to write something."

The second canard declares that Rodgers and Hammerstein have made
too much money, not only too much from the point of view of other
people but also too much to be good for themselves. Admittedly Rodgers

and Hammerstein have made a great deal of money. A tribute in his regard came two years ago in a biography of Rodgers by musicologist David Ewen. In it he made the statement that the profits from *South Pacific* alone—and not even including the motion-picture revenue—had, as of 1957, reached five billion dollars. Actually the figure was a typographical error—it should have been five *million*, but so great is the awe of R & H high finance that for a whole year not a single person, outside [of] the Rodgers and Hammerstein office (and, they hope, the Bureau of Internal Revenue), questioned it, let alone challenged it.

It is true that Rodgers and Hammerstein were able to finance their last two shows with no outside investors at all, but from the point of view of taxes, they chose the poorest time in history to be so successful. Even today, since no one has yet figured out any way of making capital gains of royalties, they are by no means as well off in spending money as commonly supposed. Nevertheless, almost alone of people in their bracket, they have never once complained of having to pay high taxes or allowed their political views to be influenced by them. And neither of them has ever been found wanting where deserving charity is concerned, although the demands are literally endless. Rodgers makes constant trips to all parts of the country to conduct symphony concerts for the benefit of orchestras in the red, and Hammerstein gives unstintingly, in money and time, to such endeavors as United World Federalists, the Dramatists' Guild of the Authors League, of which he is president, and Welcome House, which takes care of children of half-American, half-Asian parentage and of which he is chairman of the board of directors.

Both men take pains not to duck controversy, and, on the Mike Wallace [TV] program, when Hammerstein was asked what he thought of Paul Robeson, he answered the question head on. "Well," he said, "Paul Robeson was in *Show Boat* and sang "Ol' Man River," and I knew Paul very well and I used to admire him. It troubles me to sit as a judge upon Paul, because I think of myself and wonder how I would feel if I were the son of a minister—if I had been a Phi Beta Kappa man at Rutgers, an all-American tackle, a tall, handsome man, singer and actor and athlete, and could not live in the same hotel with the other members of my theatrical troupe. I would be good and sore and I don't know what I might do." ("I watched the broadcast from the house," says Mrs. Hammerstein, "and I just forgot I was married to him. I felt like getting up and applauding.")

The third and final canard in the great Rodgers and Hammerstein conspiracy is that they are lucky—that they hit the musical field when the time was ripe for the kind of change their shows represented and have not had trouble since. The answer to this canard is the easiest of all. The last few years have been a time of trouble for both men. Three years ago, at fifty-three, Rodgers received perhaps as staggering a blow as can befall a human being. He was told by a doctor that he had cancer, that "We didn't get this thing too early but I don't think it's too late."

"It happened on a Friday," Rodgers recalls. "I was to be operated on on Wednesday and *Pipe Dream* was about to go into rehearsal, so I went to work. First, though, I had lunch with my wife. 'I'm going to lick this thing,' I told her." Then, between that Friday and Wednesday, when he had part of his left jaw and the lymph nodes in his neck removed, he wrote one brand-new song and three, as he calls them, "manuscripts."

Today Rodgers is a complete recovery, and indeed considers himself "lucky"—but hardly in the sense that the canard has it. This year curiously enough, just before their current show went into rehearsal, Hammerstein was stricken ill. He underwent a serious gall-bladder operation. A second operation was needed and, when he was recuperating from this, he received word that his only brother, with whom he was very close, had died. As if this weren't enough, he also learned that his son and his son's wife, parents of his only grandchild, had separated. And yet, eight lyrics behind for the show and only five weeks to rehearsal time, he, too, started to work, and he wrote, among other things, the wonderfully touching song sung by Miyoshi Umeki as a sad little mail-order bride:

> My father says
> The sun will keep rising
> Over the eastern hill—
>
> My father says
> He doesn't know why
> But somehow or other it will.

These became the opening lines of "A Hundred Million Miracles," which is one of the loveliest songs of *Flower Drum Song*. And if as the song so beautifully says "a hundred million miracles are happening every day," then surely, "those who say they do not agree" are indeed, as Rodgers and Hammerstein so eloquently prove, "those who do not hear to see."

"Introduction" to *Richard Rodgers*

According to *Baker's Biographical Dictionary of Musicians* (8th ed., 1991), David Ewen (1907–1985) has "published more books on music and edited more reference publications than anyone else in the 20th century (some 85 in all)." His many American musical theater subjects include the dated but still useful *New Complete Book of the American Musical* (Holt, Rinehart and Winston, 1970) and books on Irving Berlin (1950), Jerome Kern (1953), George Gershwin (1956; rev. 1970), Leonard Bernstein (1960), and Cole Porter (1965). In his introduction to the first published biography of Rodgers, the first edition of which was completed after *Cinderella* but before *Flower Drum Song, The Sound of Music,* and the five post-Hammerstein musicals, Ewen emphasizes Rodgers's innovation, achievement, popular acclaim ("success of such magnitude finds few parallels, if any, in American music"), and historical influence. Ewen goes so far as to place Rodgers at the historical center of his field, asserting that "more than any other single composer of our era he has helped to change the destiny of our musical theater."

DAVID EWEN

Since 1925 with his first Broadway success, *The Garrick Gaieties,* and his first song hit, "Manhattan," Richard Rodgers has dominated the American musical theater. He has written the scores for thirty-four stage productions—thirty-five, if we include the television musical, *Cinderella.* Sixteen were major successes, two of them establishing box-office records which to this day remain unequaled by any other musical production. First with Lorenz Hart and Herbert Fields, then with Hart (occasionally supplemented by George Abbott), finally with Oscar Hammerstein II, Rodgers has written plays which are surely the proudest achievements of the musical theater of our generation: *Dearest Enemy, A Connecticut Yankee, Peggy-Ann, On Your Toes, I Married an Angel, Babes in Arms, The Boys from Syracuse, Pal Joey, By Jupiter, Oklahoma!, Carousel, Allegro, South Pacific, The King and I.* Plays like these led Ira Gershwin to say, "I am certain that musicologists, present and future, will have to agree that Rodgers is not only one of our most successful composers of theater music but also one of exquisite taste and resourcefulness; and as a composer-showman, one of integrity and courage."

For this long string of plays, Rodgers has written over one thousand songs. At least two hundred have been substantial hits, and about a hundred have become classics in the popular-music repertory. "Here in My Arms," "Where or When?," "My Heart Stood Still," "With a Song in My Heart," "Oh, What a Beautiful Mornin'," "You'll Never Walk Alone," "A Fellow Needs a Girl," "What's the Use of Wond'rin'"—the man who wrote such songs, and many others like them, is a musical creator without peer. "He is, perhaps, the most imitated songwriter of our time," writes Leonard Bernstein. "He has established new levels of taste, distinction, simplicity in the best sense, and inventiveness." Today it can be said that nobody in the past forty years has written as many good songs for the stage over such a sustained period as he; nobody writing music for the popular theater has been heard and loved by so many people in so many different parts of the civilized world.

Source: David Ewen, *Richard Rodgers* (New York: Henry Holt, 1957), 17–22.

For his achievements Rodgers has been bountifully compensated by material rewards as well as public acclaim. He gained both fame and fortune when he was comparatively young, only twenty-three. From then on his success has continued to mount, with only negligible lapses, up to the present-day peak, where he sits atop the world of music and the theater, at the height of both his prosperity and creative power. He is now not only a world-composer, a master in his field, but also, with Hammerstein, the head of a theatrical empire that includes a Broadway and London producing firm, a publishing house, and a motion-picture company. Success at such magnitude finds few parallels, if any, in American music.

Such a record of achievement is remarkable enough. Yet Rodgers's importance transcends even such formidable accomplishments. No less important than the consistently high standard of his musical writing through the years—and the measure of success he has gained through his writing—is the influence he has exerted upon an entire generation. The fact is that the history of the American musical stage since 1925 is also the history of Richard Rodgers. Its evolution from the now-dated musical comedy of the early 1920s to the vital and vibrant musical play of the 1950s can be traced step by step in the successive stages of Rodgers's career.

In the early Rodgers musicals, in which he collaborated with Hart and Fields, there was a conscious attempt to be freed from stereotyped boy-meets-girl themes. Such early plays as *Dearest Enemy* (1925) and *A Connecticut Yankee* (1927) went for their texts to American history on the one hand and Mark Twain on the other. Soon the iconoclasm grew bolder. *Peggy-Ann* (1927) not only was created from the then exotic fabric of dream psychology but even dispensed with some of the ritual which the musical comedy had followed so religiously for so long a time, such as an opening and closing chorus. In *Chee-Chee* (1928) music became integral to the stage action through the introduction of all kinds of incidental musical episodes.

Then in later Rodgers and Hart musicals a new concept of musical comedy was realized; indeed, the term "musical comedy" was discarded in favor of "musical play." These later plays included *Babes in Arms, On Your Toes, I Married an Angel, The Boys from Syracuse, Pal Joey*, and *By Jupiter*. Songs, dances, and humor (and at moments even tragedy) arose naturally from the situation of the play; each musical number now became a "plot number." Music, no longer an obstruction to the stage action as it so often had been in the past, became a contributing force to carry that action onward. It was no longer a decorative ornament to the play but an essential element to emphasize emotion and atmosphere and dramatic conflict. The chorus also now became basic to the plot; the dances not only acquired validity within the text but also achieved some of the artistic amplitude of ballet. And so the climate was prepared for the wonderful musical plays of Rodgers and Hammerstein which followed immediately—

plays in which the musical comedy finally became a native art form: *Oklahoma!, Carousel, Allegro, South Pacific*, and *The King and I*.

Some have said that the American musical comedy at its best is perhaps the greatest single contribution we have made to the theater of the world. Others have written that when great American operas are finally written they will resemble more closely musical plays like *South Pacific, Carousel*, and *The King and I* than the stylized productions American composers have been presenting at the Metropolitan Opera. In any event, the artistic importance of the American musical play is now an established fact, both in this country and abroad. And it is Richard Rodgers, above all others, who established this fact. More than any other single composer of our era he has helped to change the destiny of our musical theater.

That he should have always been willing to work with the unusual texts and techniques which his collaborators frequently provided him in their plays is remarkable in itself. For Broadway composers have been notoriously reluctant to associate themselves with any kind of play or stage method that does not cling to the tried and accepted formulas, particularly in the 1920s. But more remarkable still is the fact that Rodgers did not merely submit to such new procedures. In those conferences in which these fresh ideas were first projected, he was often the one to introduce them. Then in writing his music he continually kept pace with the ever-increasing demands made upon him by his texts—growing all the time musically even as his plays were becoming more mature and adult, continually broadening his musical canvas, enlarging his artistic horizon, giving his music ever greater scope, freedom of movement, articulateness.

Within the past quarter of a century most writers of popular songs and music for the stage have been influenced by him. But his influence has reached beyond the practitioners of music to embrace even the public. Since no living composer has had a larger audience for his music than Rodgers, and since in his writing he has adhered to a high level of musical and dramatic aesthetics, he has succeeded in elevating the prevailing taste for popular music in general, and music for the theater in particular. The ready acceptance that musical plays with extended and often complex and subtle scores find today with so many people everywhere has surely been made possible by the indoctrination that these people have received through the years from Rodgers's musicals.

In a professional career that spans almost forty years, Rodgers has worked intimately with only two writers, Lorenz Hart and Oscar Hammerstein II. It is neither accident nor coincidence that in selecting writing partners Rodgers should turn to collaborators who are not only adept at creating lyrics for songs but who also are keen and trenchant intellects of the theater, who know the theater in all its facets, and who have had the will and the talent to write for it with fresh and independent thought. For Rodgers is a man of the theater. His musical talent has its roots in the theater. He can work fruitfully only with those collaborators to whom the theater is as much a vital and ever-growing and ever-changing art as it is to him. And his creative strength is drawn for the most part from the theater: he finds abstract musical composition difficult. Without the stimulation of a play, or a situation, text, or character, his artistic inspiration is slow in coming. Most composers get thematic ideas which they jot down in a notebook for future use. Rodgers does not have such a notebook—a handy reservoir of musical materials—because ideas simply do not leap into his mind when he does not have a specific assignment to complete. "Songs never come to me," he confesses. "I have to go after them."

Given a play that arouses his imagination, Rodgers becomes singularly fertile. He then produces music quickly and easily, turning on his inspiration as if it came from a faucet. The more artistically ambitious a play is, the greater become the dimension and depth of Rodgers's musical writing. It is for this reason that Rodgers's talent was able to blossom so fruitfully and quickly in such early musicals as *Dearest Enemy, Peggy-Ann*, and *A Connecticut Yankee*, with their provocative texts and often novel procedures. And it is the reason why, associated with the beauty and poetry of Oscar Hammerstein's plays, he has so often touched musical greatness.

The productive years that lie ahead of Richard Rodgers can only strengthen the position he has acquired in our musical theater. They cannot undermine it or basically change it. Whatever else he may yet do, he is already a creative figure of first importance both in the American theater and in American music—with few if any rivals.

III
Rodgers after Hammerstein,
1960–1979

Richard Rodgers and Stephen Sondheim (1965)

"You Can't Force It"

In 1938 Winthrop Sargeant (1903–1986) published one of the first serious book-length treatments of jazz: *Jazz: Hot and Hybrid* (third ed., Da Capo, 1975). The remarkable Rodgers profile that follows appeared midway through Sargeant's tenure as music critic of *The New Yorker* (1947–72). He begins by crediting Rodgers as "a continuous and restless innovator" at the rebellious forefront of revolutionary changes in the modern American musical. In addition to descriptions of Rodgers's physical presence, personality, lifestyle, and a survey of his career from childhood to a pending creative union with librettist-lyricist Alan Jay Lerner, Sargeant ruminates seriously on the nature, uniqueness, and significance of Rodgers as a composer of original, distinctive, and memorable melody "designed to fit a given dramatic situation."

In Sargeant's view, Rodgers's melodic variety "is probably greater than that of any other Broadway composer." Without denigrating the classical tradition, he also thoughtfully defends Rodgers's inherent gifts and the creation of tunes, "fully as beautiful as any melody in 'classical' music." For Sargeant, "it is yet to be proved that melody is not the most inspired and the most fundamental ingredient of all music worthy of the name." And if musical comedy is "not as lofty an art as opera," "writing for it demands great talent—a talent that sometimes surpasses that of the operatic composer."

WINTHROP SARGEANT

In the Broadway musical theatre, Richard Rodgers occupies a unique place, not only because of his great success and the sheer number of musical shows he has turned out over a period of more than forty years but also because of the immense influence he has had on the form, content, and tone of the art of musical comedy—an art that many people, with considerable reason, believe to be America's most characteristic and vital contribution (aside, perhaps, from jazz) to music. He has survived two of the most skillful lyric-writers of the Broadway stage, Lorenz Hart and Oscar Hammerstein II. In collaboration with them, he has produced an astonishing succession of shows, some of which have altered the traditions of the musical stage, bringing to it new elements of musical and dramatic cohesion and sophistication, and developing the ancient art of

Source: Winthrop Sargeant, "Richard Rodgers: You Can't Force It," *The New Yorker* (November 18, 1961), 58–60, 62, 65–66, 68, 70–72, 75, 77–78, 80–82, 85, 87–88, 90–92, 95.

comic opera into the distinctly American form it has today. He has not been the form's sole developer, of course. His art goes back a long way to European prototypes—to a string of lighthearted masterpieces by Offenbach, Johann Strauss, Gilbert and Sullivan, and Lehár, and by their Irish-American follower Victor Herbert, whose operettas were in some ways more European than American. In its career on this side of the Atlantic, musical comedy has been strongly influenced by such relatively immortal popular composers as Jerome Kern, Vincent Youmans, George Gershwin, and Cole Porter, some of whom, considered purely as melodists, may have been superior to Rodgers, and some of whose scores—Kern's *Show Boat* and Porter's *Kiss Me, Kate*, for example—stand out as masterpieces of the genre. But Rodgers's position in the art is a special one. He has been a continuous and restless innovator. He has never conformed to a pattern, either in his choice of dramatic subjects or in the melodies he has written to ornament them, His output of shows and show tunes has been greater than that of any of his contemporaries. (The tunes have been estimated to number as many as two thousand, and though Rodgers himself thinks that a thousand or so is probably more accurate, even he is not sure just how many there are.)

This incredible melodic fertility, which is comparable to that of such great classical melodists as Mozart, Verdi, and Tchaikovsky, would alone make him a startling phenomenon in contemporary music, particularly since it has been accompanied by a full-fledged revolution in the concept of the musical theatre—a revolution in which he has been one of the leading rebels. The old-fashioned operetta, which is exemplified by the works of Herbert, Friml, and Romberg, and which leaned heavily on historical fantasy interspersed with sentimental song, has long since ceased to exist, and so has the old-fashioned revue, with its voluptuous, static showgirls and its reliance on gags and comedy routines. The modern American musical show takes its drama seriously, and its drama is, for the most part, a reflection of modern life. It frequently utilizes the skills of ballet in place of the old high-kicking chorus line. Both its tunes and its lyrics show greater wit, and its music is generally better integrated into the total theatrical conception.

Rodgers's contribution to this new art has been enormous, and in the long list of his shows quite a number have broken entirely new ground. As historians of the subject have pointed out, *On Your Toes* (1936) was the first Broadway musical to make extended use of ballet in the plot, and also the first to include a sustained section of purely instrumental music (in the famous "Slaughter on Tenth Avenue" scene). *Babes in Arms* (1937) introduced the now familiar element of informal youthful exuberance, laying to rest once and for all the old-time parade of the standard musical-comedy chorus. *I Married an Angel* (1938) carried ballet—and Broadway ballet music—a step farther. *Pal Joey* (1940), considered by many people to be Rodgers's finest work, flouted tradition by presenting a full-fledged knave as its hero, and by making him a dancer instead of a singer. *Oklahoma!* (1943) had a carefully worked-out dramatic theme that was regarded at the time by some people as too highbrow for popular musical treatment. *Carousel* (1945) had an even stronger dramatic theme (and one with tragic overtones, something that had almost never appeared in the popular musical theatre before), along with a score that approached opera in the continuity of its music and in the variety of its declamation. (Rodgers himself is inclined to consider it his best work.) And even the less successful Rodgers shows—the experiments, the ones that had slightly flawed books or patches of uninspired music—have always contained at least a few numbers that have left a lasting mark on popular music. To this remarkable outpouring of Broadway scores—reaching in an unbroken span from *The Garrick Gaieties* of 1925 down to the current *The Sound of Music*—plus some fifteen scores for Hollywood movies, he has added two large and highly effective pieces of instrumental background music for television serials. These were the wartime documentary *Victory at Sea* and the recent series on Winston Churchill, and the score for the former, as Deems Taylor pointed out some time ago, encompassed an expanse of music as long as *Tristan, Die Meistersinger*, and *Parsifal* combined. In the process, Rodgers has, of course, become a millionaire and acquired whole shelves of citations, prizes, and medals. But affluence and honors have in no way diminished either his devotion to the musical theatre or the steady flow of his scores. He continues to turn out songs and musical ideas as prolifically and as professionally as a cabinetmaker turns out furniture, and at fifty-nine he is as busy as ever, or busier.

Physically, Rodgers is a comparatively short, stocky, gray-haired man who conveys an impression of roundness and unquenchable geniality. His round body, usually encased in a conservative gray or pin-striped blue suit, gives him, as quite a few people have noted, the appearance of a prosperous banker—a resemblance intensified by an air of authority common to successful businessmen and by a degree of social aplomb that enables him to meet almost any situation with outward tranquility and good nature. His round face rarely betrays worry or anger, being generally suffused with a smile that seems to extend all over its surface. Nothing about him suggests pompousness or self-conscious wit, on the one hand, or bohemianism, introversion, or sarcastic dishevelment, on the other hand. He talks the language of show business—a direct, earthy idiom containing occasional four-letter words and punctuated with exclamations like "Pow!" and "Wham!"—and if he happens to use an abstract or slightly pretentious word, he usually follows it with an apology. He is often gently ribald in his conversation, and never arch or sententious. He loves to talk to people, and is very sensitive to their reactions—a sensitivity undoubtedly nurtured by his long experience in gauging and encouraging the personalities of actors, musicians, directors, and producers. He is, in fact, extremely gregarious, and though he hates night clubs and the formality of Broadway opening nights (he attends them only for professional reasons), he is an inveterate giver of parties and a joyous basker in the company of others.

Rodgers's offices, at 488 Madison Avenue, which he visits three or four days a week, look like the headquarters of an industrial firm, which, in fact, they are. Rodgers & Hammerstein is the center of a wide range of activities, among them the booking of his Broadway and out-of-town productions, the rental of scores and scripts to schools and stock companies, and all the complicated transactions involving contracts, promotion, and publicity that are the concern of big theatrical booking offices everywhere. The place contains a large library of scores, a secretary, nine or ten office workers, a grand piano, and a reception room for the constant stream of visitors who want to see the great man for one reason or another. The walls are entirely free of the disorderly array of posters and autographed photographs that decorate the classic theatrical offices; instead, there are neatly framed eighteenth-century engravings of Shakespearean performances. The furniture, except in the purely functional offices of the administrative help, is formal and elegant. "The fact is," Rodgers has said, "the place makes me feel like a nose-and-throat specialist." On the days when he is holding court, the visitors—actors, singers, conductors, publicity men, gossip columnists, and so on—sit patiently in the reception room, happily discussing theatre news (sometimes for an hour at a stretch) until Rodgers is free to see them. The spectacle is a little like a levee held in the palace of some old-time European aristocrat. Rodgers complains a good deal about the demands that the office imposes on his time. "Who makes all the decisions around here?" he exclaimed recently. "Me! I wish to God that just once somebody would turn up who wanted to do something for me, instead of wanting me to do something for him. The trouble with this place is like the trouble with old automobiles. It's in the clutch, and I'm it. I have to take charge of the changing speeds. I couldn't compose here. There's too much going on." Still, there is no doubt that he hugely enjoys the human contacts provided by the turmoil. When Rodgers is not in his office, he is very apt to be haunting various theatres where his shows are being auditioned for or rehearsed. He attends all these rehearsals—even the numerous ones necessary to get a road company into shape—supervising the work of his singers and directors, making slight changes, complaining about diction, exulting over the beauty and personal charm of his leading ladies, chuckling at lines or stage situations that he already knows by heart, and generally helping to mold the production to his own high specifications. The sight of a bare stage full of uncostumed actors and cluttered with disused flats and lighting equipment is enough to set his mind racing. "It's the most exciting thing in the world to see that drab background and to know that when the curtain rises on opening night, it will all be transformed into something with meaning," he once said.

It is, indeed, almost impossible to detach Rodgers's contemplative life as a creator of tunes from his highly extroverted life as a theatrical man of action. The two seem to run concurrently, without the slightest conflict; tunes occur to him while he is supervising dramatic situations, and dramatic situations are always present in his mind when he is composing tunes. And both lives are smoothly geared to an existence that involves him in no end of outside activities, some of them related to his stature as a public figure—he is a member of the board of directors of the New York Philharmonic, a trustee of Barnard College, and a member of the New York State Council on the Arts—and others to his responsibilities as a devoted family man. He is without eccentricities of any sort. "When you reach a certain position—that's a horrible word, isn't it?—you have to be responsible for a lot of things besides feeding your face," he remarked not long ago. He feels a special obligation toward the promotion of music that is more highbrow than his own, and he has commissioned many works by symphonic and operatic composers, even though the results have not always conformed to his personal tastes. "I believe those boys should be encouraged," he maintained recently, and added, a little wistfully, "I've always hoped that something might come of it."

Rodgers's more private life is led in a rather imposing fourteen-room cooperative apartment that occupies two floors of a Park Avenue building in the Seventies, and on a country estate near Southport, Connecticut, where he spends his weekends and a good part of his summers. Both establishments are fairly conventional habitats for a man of means. (He is a bit apologetic about the size of the apartment, explaining that he bought it about twenty years ago, when he was the father of two young daughters, and that even though the daughters have grown up and married, he has simply not been able to bring himself to move to smaller quarters.) Both are resided over by his wife, a tall, handsome woman with the social ease of a diplomat, the feminine solicitude of a dedicated housewife, and the cultivated taste of a great lady. Rodgers claims that he first met her when she was two months old (his father, who was a physician, was treating her older brother for typhoid), and that he fell in love with her on a steamship trip from Europe when she was seventeen and he a hopeful young songwriter of twenty-four. In the matrimonially unstable world of the Broadway theatre, their marriage is widely regarded as a model of serenity. Mrs. Rodgers was originally a sculptress, under her maiden name of Dorothy Feiner, but she abandoned that career without regret to marry him ("The world lost absolutely nothing when I gave up sculpting," she has said), and, now that their two daughters have left home, she busies herself with various charitable undertakings and some successful household inventions—a cleaning mop and a material for making dress patterns among them. One important remnant of Mrs. Rodgers's early artistic training persists, however. She is a fervent collector of modern painting, and the New York apartment is decorated with a fine display of canvases by French Impressionists and Post-Impressionists and American, French, and Italian Abstract Expressionists. Her enthusiasm for modern art long ago infected her husband, and today the two of them are in the habit of buying each other paintings for Christmas and birthday presents. "It has solved a problem," she told a friend recently. "I can't buy Dick clothes—he cares nothing about them—but he is crazy about pictures. We don't just amass them, as some collectors do. We buy only things that we think would look good in a certain space on the wall, and after they're hung we get to love them." The collection fills most rooms of the apartment, the principal exceptions being Rodgers's small private study, which is decorated with theatrical scenic designs, the majority by Jo Mielziner, and Mrs. Rodgers's bedroom, which is quietly antique, with a canopied fourposter bed and an air of old-fashioned reserve. Elsewhere, the place glows with color, and among the explosive abstractions and more subdued Impressionist works are a number of very distinguished items, notably a superb Toulouse-Lautrec of a woman seated in a box at the theatre and a rare Vlaminck still-life from his early Fauve period, which hangs over the grand piano in the living room. Another striking feature of the apartment's décor is the abundance of flowers—either potted or assembled into lavish bouquets. Flowers are one of Mrs. Rodgers's passions, and fresh ones are sent along every few days by the gardener of their Connecticut estate, who maintains a garden in summer and a hothouse in winter. Mrs. Rodgers herself does no gardening in the country. "I haven't the patience to plant seeds and wait for them to grow," she explains. "I'm better at things where I can get quick results—cooking, for example. I'm really quite a good cook, and I love to fix things for small dinner parties." There are apparently many such parties, and often they include the Rodgers's daughters and their families. One daughter, Mary, is now a musical-comedy composer in her own right, having created the tunes for the musical comedy *Once Upon a Mattress* and the recent television show *Feathertop*. The other, Linda, is a talented pianist and the wife of an American Broadcasting Company executive. Altogether, there are four grandchildren.

When the Rodgerses are at their Connecticut place, sociability is somewhat less intense, and Rodgers devotes his remarkable energies to taking long walks and playing croquet. He is, however, a man of distinctly urban tastes, and he cannot bring himself to stay away from Broadway for any length of time—from the endless round of garrulous meetings with his theatrical colleagues, from the lunches and dinners at midtown restaurants that range all the way from Le Pavillon ("You can hardly get away from there for less than twenty dollars a head") to the Canton Village ("That's a place on West Forty-ninth—near the theatre that shows those sexy movies—where you get a whole meal for a dollar and a half"), with Sardi's and Lindy's in between. His strenuous participation in the hurly-burly of Manhattan life might make one wonder when he finds time for composing. The answer is that composing takes up about two per cent of Rodgers's time, and even less of his energies. He has been quoted as saying, "It's easier to write a tune than to bend over and tie your shoelaces," and in his case the statement seems only slightly exaggerated.

The speed and ease with which Rodgers turns out successful show tunes has become one of Broadway's persistent legends. The melody for "Bali Ha'i," from *South Pacific*, is supposed to have been jotted down in five minutes while he was having after-lunch coffee, and it is undoubtedly true that he seldom spends more than an hour on the first draft of any of his tunes. Oscar Hammerstein often expressed astonishment, combined with a little envy, over Rodgers's ability to instantly set to music a lyric that it had taken him a week or so to perfect. Rodgers's gift in this respect does indeed approach genius. The performance is not, however, quite as incredible as it might seem. Popular tunes—and, for that matter, tunes in general—usually occur to their creators in sudden flashes of inspiration. There have been composers—Beethoven is an example—who were noted for their tireless revising and reshaping of melodic material, but in the long history of music they stand out as exceptions, and as a rule they are to be found among composers who devote themselves to the intricate craft of symphonic architecture, where tunes are often mere cells that combine into large organisms. The pure melodist—a classification that includes such masters as Tchaikovsky, Bellini, Chopin, Verdi, and Rossini as well as the composer of popular songs—is nearly always a fast worker once the melodic inspiration hits him, and his melodies usually well up as full entities from some unconscious source. For the popular tunesmith who depends on professional arrangers for the details of orchestration and extended musical development, the writing down of a melody—plus a few basic harmonic ideas and perhaps an indication here and there of a notion for appropriate orchestration—is a process that can be accomplished in a few minutes. The melodic gift must be present, though, and, as Igor Stravinsky has recently pointed out, it is a really mysterious and unanalyzable phenomenon. Some people have it; others don't. You can't teach it, you can't reduce it to a science, and you can't subject its products to any very rigid intellectual criticism. More than any other aspect of music, it is a matter of pure talent. Rodgers has it, and appears able to turn it on and off with an ease that few of his contemporaries possess. The remarkable thing about his creative ability is not the speed with which he jots down his melodic ideas but the dependability of his source of inspiration—the inexhaustible fecundity of his melodic thought, and the originality and catchiness of its products. But even Rodgers's talent has its limitations, for although he can think up a fresh tune in record time, he admits that he would be hard put to it to think up two or three tunes in one day; apparently, the unconscious reservoir of inspiration requires some time to renew itself. "After all," he has remarked, "I do need to take time off for lunch, or for a night's sleep. When you're doing this kind of thing, you can't force it."

Except for the comparatively rare occasions when he turns out a tune during the actual rehearsals of a show, Rodgers does nearly all his composing in Connecticut or at the grand piano under the Vlaminck still-life in New York. In the old days with Lorenz Hart, he usually wrote the tunes first, and Hart fitted lyrics to them; with Oscar Hammerstein, the lyrics were apt to come first, and Rodgers did the fitting. The two methods appear to be equally congenial to him; evidently a lyric can suggest a tune as readily as a tune suggests itself. In either case, however, Rodgers's work is designed to fit a given dramatic situation. The situation is very important. Only a few times in his life has he written a tune out of the blue, in the manner of Irving Berlin, and presented it as a separate, self-contained piece of work. Almost all his melodies are conceived to fill a specific dramatic need in a specific show. They are what the trade calls "plot numbers"—songs or instrumental episodes that are an integral part of the story line—and they result, according to Rodgers, from his contemplation of the emotions of a particular character at a particular point in the drama. Since these emotions are apt to be few and relatively simple in musical comedy—awakening love of one sort or another, loneliness, nostalgia, pride, irresolution, joy, sheer animal spirits, and so on—they lend themselves very well to the sort of uncomplicated melodic treatment that he gives them. His mind is never very far from the exigencies of the actual stage production, and he often writes with the personality and technical abilities of a particular singer in mind. As he sets down a song, he puts himself in the role of the character, evoking the mood that is called for, and the melody seems to grow naturally out of the mood. This, of course, involves him in fantasies of one sort or another as he plays all the roles in his mind, imagining himself as, successively, a virile hero, a villain, and a young girl in love. "What's that fancy word?" he asked recently, while discussing this technique. "'Dichotomy'—that's it. You cut yourself in half. Half of you is you, and the other half is the girl." When he completes his final draft, containing the melody and a few chords indicating the harmony and rhythm, written in a neat hand on music paper, the creative part of the act is nearly finished. Later, Rodgers, who is a fair pianist and a trained musician, gets down to the much less congenial task of writing out a full piano score. This takes more time, and generally fills him with a certain amount of impatience. After that, the tune goes to an arranger—often the very skillful Robert Russell Bennett, who has orchestrated, either alone or with a group of assistants, a great many of the musical shows that have appeared on Broadway. Bennett turns out the finished product, adding a touch of musical figuration here and there, deciding (after consultation with Rodgers) what instruments should be used for certain passages, and creating the substructure of the number as it is eventually performed in the theatre. This division of labor, in which one man furnishes the ideas and another the orchestral clothing for them, is, of course, standard practice on Broadway, and it is the main reason that symphonic composers, who do all this arduous work themselves, tend to regard the Broadway tunesmith as an amateur technician. There is perhaps some justification for this view. But the tunesmiths have a case, too. They point out, quite correctly, that very few arrangers—and nowadays very few highbrow composers—are much good at writing tunes, and that honest arrangers like Bennett are the first to admit it. The ability to create successful tunes is a special talent, often lacking among the most learned and technically accomplished musicians and sometimes found, paradoxically, among men of the most rudimentary musical knowledge. As it happens, Rodgers's musical knowledge is far more than rudimentary. He has studied harmony and composition at the Institute of Musical Art (now the Juilliard School), and he knows a great deal more about these subjects than the one-finger pianists who, as legend has it, write the bulk of American popular music. But tunes are his specialty, and he is content to let others do the main part of the paperwork. In such mammoth undertakings as the background music for *Victory at Sea* and the Churchill series, the musical arrangement was the work of orchestrators. The first was done by Robert Russell Bennett and Eddie Sauter; Rodgers's contribution was simply a succession of tunes and other musical ideas devised, like Wagnerian leitmotivs, to fit various dramatic emotions. Having analyzed the dramatic material into a group of recurrent emotional themes—for example, "Churchill worried," "Churchill strong and dauntless," "England bloody but unbowed," "Nazis cocky," "Nazis sinister, expert, and evil," and "England triumphant"—Rodgers wrote a motif for each. His job was then done. The arranging of these compositions into a complete score was accomplished in many days of painstaking toil by [Hershy] Kay and Sauter.

Rodgers admits that he has occasionally felt an ambition to score his own work and produce a total composition of which every note, like the work of a grand-opera composer, would be entirely his own. He has, however, firmly resisted it. "I suppose that I could learn to orchestrate—study up on the range of the oboe and all that kind of thing," he observed not long ago. "But what's the use? Robert Russell Bennett orchestrates much better than I could, and often, in the process of putting together a show, there isn't the time for me to figure out all those details. Besides, what would I be doing if I composed the whole score by myself? It would be nothing but ego on my part—I would be writing something for people to admire. I don't want to write things for people to *admire*; I want to make them *feel* something." And what makes people "feel something" is, of course, the lilting quality of the melodies themselves. These are all his own. They may eventually be orchestrated in various ways, or strung together in symphonic arrangements or dance-band medleys, or sung, hummed, or whistled by people of unusual ability or no ability at all. The only really important thing about them is their melodic form and the peculiar crystallization of a mood that they convey, and this is an element that survives whether their dress is complex or simple. "All I really want to do," Rodgers once said, with an air of self-disparagement, "is to provide a hard-worked man in the blouse business with a method of expressing himself. If he likes a tune, he can whistle it, and it will make his life happier."

*   *   *

To anyone looking over the enormous number of tunes that Rodgers has created, several characteristics are immediately noticeable. One is the virtual absence of the jazz and ragtime idioms that are such a pervasive ingredient of the melodies of, say, Gershwin. In his early days, Rodgers did turn out a few moderately jazzy ditties that could be easily converted into dance music. One of them was "Manhattan," from *The Garrick Gaieties*, and it was promptly picked up by dance bands like Paul Whiteman's and played to death all over the country. Rodgers describes it as schottische—a rather quaint German term that is used by Rodgers to designate a tune played in four-four time with four beats accentuated. But if he has turned his hand now and then to a melody of the schottische type, most of his tunes are songs that do not lend themselves very well to dance-music treatment. It is possible that the decline of the big dance band has influenced his style in this respect. Nowadays, American popular music is propagated by radio, television, and the recording industry, and Americans in the mass have taken to listening instead of dancing. "There's been a displacement in popular music," Rodgers explained recently. "There's society dance music, done by bands like Meyer Davis's, but the big, famous dance band is extinct. Nowadays, the place for tunes is the radio, television, Muzak, and records. For instance, the album of *The Sound of Music* grossed far more than the Broadway show did during the first year. It sold eight hundred and seventy-five thousand copies and took in something like five million dollars." But Rodgers's style has also been influenced by his personal taste, and his personal taste rebels at the confinement of the routine pattern of four-four time and the thirty-two-bar phrase. Most of his melodies break out of these conventional molds, and a great many of them have a quality of musical sophistication that seems to reflect the play of conscious intellect rather than purely unconscious inspiration. Rodgers disclaims any deliberate intellectual approach to his work but admits that he may be influenced by something he refers to as "the conscious unconscious." Whatever this "conscious unconscious" may be, it produces a striking departure from the norms of Tin Pan Alley—a sort of unexpected twist. Many of his tunes are rapid waltzes or scherzos ("I'm in Love with a Wonderful Guy" and the waltz from *Carousel*, for example); others are polkas ("The Lonely Goatherd," from *The Sound of Music*); and still others ("If I Loved You," from *Carousel*) are so far from the conventions of dance music of any kind, and so meditative in character, that they seem more closely related to the operatic aria than to what is commonly thought of as the American popular idiom. Many attempts have been made to pin down the characteristics of the Rodgers style. It has been said, for instance, that he is addicted to melodies built on major and minor scales. This particular mannerism, typical of the melodies of Tchaikovsky, is, however, by no means universal in Rodgers's work. There are certainly scales to be found here and there, but there are also plenty of tunes built out of leaping arpeggios, such as "Oh, What a Beautiful Mornin'," whose lingering over the notes of both tonic and dominant chords recalls a number of old folk songs. Rodgers does occasionally play, teasingly, with the tonic and the leading tone just below it, especially in tunes of a highly emotional character. ("Bewitched, Bothered, and Bewildered," "If I Loved You," and the final repetitions of "I'm in love" in "I'm in Love with a Wonderful Guy" are striking examples of this.) But any attempt to reduce his style to a formula is doomed. He is always doing the unexpected, and the variety of his melodic invention, though it is now and then expressed in a traditional category, is probably greater than that of any other Broadway composer. If anything can be said to characterize his output as a whole, it is a certain smartness—a remarkable absence of cliché and a restless tendency to break away from standardized methods. Other Broadway composers—Kern, Porter, Gershwin, and so on—have sometimes written more haunting melodies, but their melodies have, in general, followed well-established prototypes. Rodgers almost never follows a prototype, and when he does, it is chosen with a very eclectic ear. The most extraordinary feature of the thousand-odd tunes he has written is the immense variety of their structure, and this variety extends to their harmonies as well as to their melodic lines. True, he is famous for discarding the thirty-two-bar phrase that is typical of nearly all popular music, or else extending and altering it in various ways. But a more impressive and more subtle distinction lies in the way he alters the standard harmonies that make up this phrase, substituting progressions that the average tunesmith would never think of. Time and time again, you think you can guess what Rodgers is going to do next, only to find him doing something else entirely.

There are lovers of serious music who dismiss all popular tunes as trash, and there is, of course, a large public that loves popular music and takes no interest whatever in symphonies and operas. The former group argues that the art of music consists of complex masterpieces that express noble sentiments and demand exquisite craftsmanship from both their creators and their performers. To these people, popular tunes are trivial, childishly simple in structure, tiresome, and comparatively vulgar. Actually, however, they listen to a great deal of melody that is just as simple and sometimes—as in most Liszt symphonic poems—just as vulgar as the most commonplace American popular music, and though one may have a special affection for Tchaikovsky's ballet melodies or Rossini's rather standardized operatic melodies, they are not intrinsically any more profound than the work of the gifted Broadway tunesmith. What it all comes down to, no doubt, is the nature and function of melodies in general. They are to all music, including symphonic music, what ideas are to literature, and it can hardly be denied that every composer of any stature whatever is a melodist of distinction. But from here on the thesis gets more complicated, for there are many kinds of melodies, suited to many kinds of music, and melodies that are right for one kind are not necessarily right for another. Among the supreme masters of German musical architecture—Bach, Beethoven, Wagner, and so on—a melody is apt to have the same status that an idea has in philosophy; that is, a germinal notion capable of development into a large edifice of musical thought. Such melodies may be beautiful in themselves, but their main function is to serve as themes for extended discourse, and what one admires about them is not so much their intrinsic beauty as their suitability as building blocks. The opening theme of Beethoven's Fifth Symphony is perhaps the perfect example—a four-note idea of no particular charm that becomes significant because of what Beethoven does with it. And there are countless other examples, ranging from the fugal motifs of Bach to the main theme of the Schumann Piano Concerto and the Hunding leitmotiv in *Die Walküre*. These are, in general, knotty melodies of strong physiognomy, created for a special purpose. They are not, however, the only kind of melody created by the great German architects (they wrote singable and charming melodies, too), and when one descends from the austere and rather specialized realm that the knotty kind occupies, one comes across a vast amount of music in which melody, as the average man recognizes it, is predominant—music of the kind that one hears in most opera; in Mozart, Chopin, and Tchaikovsky; in all the great Italian masters; in much of Beethoven and Wagner; and in all the lighter composers. But even here there are distinctions, a great many of them arising from the differing functions of the music. Chopin did the bulk of his writing for the piano, and his melodies exploit the subtleties of the instrument to such an extent that an audience will still hang on the slightest nuances drawn from them by master pianists. They are pretty tunes in the abstract, and one can whistle most of them, but to take them out of their frame as piano pieces is to lose a great part of their significance. Similarly, Bellini and Verdi—and, for that matter, Mozart in his operas—wrote for voices of unusual caliber. Again, the tunes are pretty, and some of them can be whistled, but in order to exert their full spell they demand the extraordinary technical capacities and dramatic insights found only among great vocal artists. Descending another rung or two to the comparatively "popular" melodists, one arrives at the kind of melody that the average man can be sure of singing or whistling with considerable success. Even here, though, there are peculiarities of the original score that make singing or whistling something less than totally adequate. Tchaikovsky—most of whose tunes are eminently whistlable—was a master of orchestration, and only an orchestra can give his works their full due. Offenbach's orchestration was inimitably sprightly, and often superior in verve and inspiration to his tunes. Johann Strauss was basically a composer of nineteenth-century dance music, utilizing an orchestra in which the violin was dominant. His tunes are works of genius, but one need only hear them miserably moaned by saxophones in modern dance-band arrangements to realize how closely wedded they are to their original instrumentation.

It is true that the Broadway tune lacks a challenge to unusual performing ability; it is conceived along such simple lines that almost anybody can sing it. Nobody who seeks the peculiar thrill that comes from listening to Joan Sutherland sing "Qui la voce," from Bellini's *I Puritani*, or hearing Artur Rubinstein play a Chopin nocturne is going to be enormously impressed by "Some Enchanted Evening" sung by a personally charming but relatively untrained Broadway matinée idol, and when a highly trained and extraordinary operatic voice like that of the late Ezio Pinza undertakes the task, the average opera enthusiast is apt to feel that its great resources are being wasted. But this is hardly proof that "Some Enchanted Evening" is less a work of art than a comparable "classical" tune. It is certainly proof that "Some Enchanted Evening" is less difficult to sing, and that it does not offer scope for the sort of polished artistry one expects in the opera house and the concert hall. On the other hand, of course, that is not its function. Its function is to be immediately intelligible to and easily memorizable by the large theatrical and radio audience that takes its music as casual entertainment. This is not to say, however, that it lacks musical appeal and distinction. Its very simplicity is a virtue at a time when melodic simplicity is shunned by nearly all highbrow composers. It contains the attributes of charm and mood that are the minimal requirements of all important music. It is, indeed, a work of art. In common with the "classical" tune, the Broadway tune has the peculiar adhesive quality of all good melody. It is a musical idea that sticks in the memory—that leads one to hum it imperfectly at first and then to discover, with some satisfaction, how it really goes. Its adhesive quality may even become lightly annoying; one may try to get rid of it, only to find that it has temporarily got an iron grip on one's unconscious. It is what Hungarians refer to as *"fülbemászó,"* or "ear-creeping." It also tends to attach itself to episodes in one's life—to recall, in a somewhat haphazard manner, situations, people, and sensations that one encountered when first hearing it. All these attributes show that it has the hypnotic power over the fantasy-building side of the psyche that distinguishes genuine music of all kinds. It may not be as intellectually elaborate or as profound as a fugue or a symphony, but, simply as a tune, it is often fully as beautiful as any melody in "classical" music. And it is simply as a tune that one must judge it. It has no further function, except that of embellishing or underlining the dramatic situation on the stage.

People who seek an aesthetic pigeonhole in which to place musical comedy are often inclined to view it as a lesser form than opera; the words "operetta" and "comic opera" hint at this idea, and it is true that the musical show is something like opera in that it offers its audience a play ornamented with music. But the comparison is a little misleading, and not at all fair to the art of musical comedy, which has its own structural laws and its own goals. Because of the relative simplicity of these goals, a tune in a musical comedy is a self-contained number that stands or falls on its own merits and must make its effect without the vast machinery of climax and development that goes into most operas. Musical comedy is, of course, not as lofty an art as opera. But writing for it demands great talent—a talent that sometimes surpasses that of the operatic composer. There is, for example, an enormous gap between the work of Wagner and Richard Strauss, on the one hand, and that of Johann Strauss, on the other. The first two were great opera composers, and nobody would compare *Die Fledermaus* with *Die Walküre* or *Der Rosenkavalier* as a monumental contribution to the musical theatre. Still, almost anyone who examines the music of these widely disparate works will agree that while Wagner and Richard Strauss were operatic composers of tremendous stature, Johann Strauss was superior to either of them as a tunesmith. The main distinction seems to be that while the opera composer is a greater master of musical and psychological characterization and dramatic continuity, the tunesmith is frequently a more skillful creator of self-contained melodies that have meaning both within and outside the context of the drama for which they are written. A Rodgers tune, for example, leads a life of its own, independent of the show for which it was created, and in order to do so it must have qualities of succinctness and catchiness that guarantee its accessibility to people unaware of its specific dramatic connotations in the show. Rodgers practices his art with due regard for this factor. His tunes must be capable of giving momentary pleasure all by themselves, whether they are hummed by a taxi-driver or played on a jukebox. In them, it is the momentary crystallization of a mood and emotion that counts; large-scale continuity is irrelevant to their purpose. Indeed, the more usual machinery of operatic continuity is highly uncongenial to Rodgers's habits of thought. "I hate recitativos," he declared some time ago. "If singing is called for, I give my characters a tune to sing. If they want to talk, I let them talk. There is nothing so dreary as trying to set a line like 'I'm going downtown to buy a bunch of bananas' to music. You need lyrics. Just setting talk to music is inartistic. Nobody likes it. The difference between a tune and a recitativo is the difference between captivating your audience and losing it. The Italians use recitativos, and in Italian opera they sound fine, but in an American musical show they are just a bore. Even in my most freewheeling passages—the soliloquy in *Carousel*, for example—you'll find that the lyrics are poetry, not prose."

Rodgers also dislikes the rather formal and self-conscious type of singing that is demanded of professional operatic artists, and though he occasionally uses such artists in his productions, he does so sparingly. They are apt to destroy the intimacy, naturalness, and realism that he is after by calling attention to themselves as singers—something he tries hard to avoid in his shows, on the ground that it demolishes the stage illusion. He is constantly on the lookout for voices that are trained but give the effect of being natural and untrained. Such voices are exceedingly difficult to find, and when he does find them—and if they are accompanied by physical beauty and acting ability as well—he is beside himself with enthusiasm. One such recent discovery of his, Florence Henderson—who has grown from a bit part in *Wish You Were Here* to playing Laurey in a road company of *Oklahoma!* to the starring role in *Fanny* and in the road company of *The Sound of Music*—strikes him as being the ideal vehicle for his kind of music. Miss Henderson is pretty and full of extroverted spirits. She studies like a Trojan. The Metropolitan Opera would not be interested in her voice, which is deliciously naïve for all the training it has undergone and, though highly expressive, has not been forced into the operatic mold. For musical comedy she is perfect. She gives the impression of being a natural, if unusually talented and attractive, American girl both in her singing and in her acting. As for the Metropolitan's vocal standards, Rodgers is entirely uninterested in them. "I think Mr. Bing does a good job with what he has," he remarked recently, "but I think we are more appealing physically. We are not opera, we are theatre."

Most people who argue that Rodgers is not entitled to be called a composer in the grand sense base their argument on three points: that he does not toil and suffer enough to rate a place in what is certainly a toilsome profession; that the music he writes is so easily grasped that it makes no demands on the cultivated listener; and that its very popularity sets it outside the domain of art and within the domain of "mass culture"—a phenomenon that the intellectual élite instinctively distrusts, and not without reason. In answer to the first argument, one might note that there is, in reality, no necessary correlation between the quality of a composition and the amount of toil and suffering that has gone into it. Even classical music is full of composers who tossed off melodies as easily as they tied their shoelaces. There is a famous anecdote about Rossini— too lazy to get out of bed to retrieve the manuscript of an aria that had fallen to the floor, he wrote an entirely new aria instead. And the world has always had its quota of toiling composers who have never succeeded in writing anything really worth listening to. It is true that in Rodgers's case much of the toil is done by his orchestrators, and that he undergoes no perceptible suffering at all. But whatever view one takes of the peculiar processes involved in show-tune composition, Rodgers is without any doubt an artist using a God-given talent to the full. In answer to the second argument, one can point out that not all classical music is intellectually demanding, and that a great deal of contemporary highbrow music makes a fetish of its intellectual demands while leaving the emotions untouched—something that Rodgers's music is never guilty of. In answer to the third, one must remark, first of all, that no music of any validity is totally incomprehensible to the audience for which it is written, and that nearly all the great masters of the past were popular with large sections of the public of their time. Moreover, though "mass culture" may, in our era, have certain rather horrifying features, it is not necessarily altogether bad. Sometimes—as in the comic strip, the detective story, and the popular tune—it reaches a degree of sophistication and emotional charge, and even shows a degree of skill, that is equal or superior to what is officially, and often rather preciously, designated as "serious" art. Rodgers's talent expresses itself in a musical vernacular of well-established and well-understood meanings. "I have always doubted the importance of any composer whose mother was frightened by a good, simple tonic chord," he said not long ago. His gift is simply for melody. He is very good at melody. And it is yet to be proved that melody is not the most inspired and the most fundamental ingredient of all music worthy of the name.

Aside from his music, Rodgers's life—like that of many composers—has been comparatively uneventful and unspectacular. It refutes completely the persistent—and nowadays quite untrue—rags-to-riches myth, according to which popular tunesmiths are supposed to be the offspring of immigrants on the Lower East Side and make their way to success, without any musical education, by picking out tunes on the piano with one finger. There have been, it is true, a few such instances, but Rodgers is not one of them. (Neither was Jerome Kern, nor is Cole Porter.) "I know that it would all be much more interesting if I had once been a waiter at Lindy's," Rodgers has often been quoted as saying. The fact is that he is the product of a prosperous, cultivated, bourgeois background. His father, a respected physician named William Abraham Rodgers, who was an amateur musician and a man of rather Germanic appearance, came to New York not from Minsk but from Missouri. Richard Rodgers has an older brother who has followed his father's profession and is now Director of Obstetrics and Gynecology at Lenox Hill Hospital. Both his parents (his mother was a musician and an admirer of the theatre) encouraged his early musical ambitions, which, from the age of fourteen, expressed themselves in the writing of songs and in a deep love of the light music of Sir Arthur Sullivan, Victor Herbert, and Jerome Kern. He was sent to the opera, and to the concerts of the old New York Philharmonic (under Josef Stransky) and the old New York Symphony (under Walter Damrosch), and at a very early age he developed the profound respect for serious music that he still has. But he never felt impelled to write serious music; he had a shrewd sense of his own talents and limitations from the very beginning, and though he listened with enormous admiration to Bizet's *Carmen* and to Wagner ("There was a time when I knew all those leitmotivs by heart," he said recently), as well as to the symphonic masterpieces of Beethoven, Brahms, and Tchaikovsky, he devoted his own energies exclusively to writing tunes of a type suited to the Broadway musical stage. He attended Columbia University briefly, having entered it mainly in the hope of writing its varsity show—which he did twice, in 1920 and 1921. His collaborator in both shows was Lorenz Hart, who had left Columbia a couple of years earlier but who returned to work with Rodgers because he was an old friend. (Rodgers's collaborator on one song in the 1920 show was Oscar Hammerstein, class of '16.) Following the varsity shows, the close association of

Rodgers and Hart, which was to last for twenty-four years, sputtered along with various semi-amateur productions for camps and clubs and charity benefits, plus one moderate Broadway success, *Poor Little Ritz Girl*, on which the team collaborated with Sigmund Romberg. Shortly afterward, in an attempt to improve his musical technique, Rodgers entered the Institute of Musical Art, where he studied harmony and composition for two years with the eminent teachers George Wedge and Percy Goetschius. These studies did indeed give him an increased mastery of the composer's tools (he has always thought very highly of technical accomplishment, and as late as 1937, when he was already a big success, he devoted a great deal of time to perfecting his piano playing), but even while he was pursuing his academic training, he was busy writing shows with Hart. The first of them to achieve large Broadway acclaim was, of course, *The Garrick Gaieties*, in 1925, with the hit tune "Manhattan" (which was lifted out of an earlier, unproduced show called *Winkle Town*). *The Garrick Gaieties*, presented by the Theatre Guild, put Rodgers and Hart on the map. Still, it was merely a collection of skits—a revue—and though it was a success, Rodgers and Hart were still obsessed with the idea of creating a more closely integrated combination of music and drama. If show business in general is a lowbrow affair, Rodgers and Hart were its highbrows. They were men of taste. Hart, a descendant of the poet Heinrich Heine, was always striving for literary quality and technical adroitness in his lyrics, and Rodgers, though he wrote simply, was by no means unaware of the standards by which fine music is judged. Their next shows, including *Dearest Enemy, The Girl Friend, Peggy-Ann, A Connecticut Yankee, Present Arms*, and *Chee-Chee*, nearly all worked in the direction of their ideal, and *Chee-Chee*, though it had a rather unpleasant book, was, from a technical standpoint, something of a milestone in their development. All were studded with delightful songs, but they also had the sort of dramatic continuity that allied them with true comic opera. Quite naturally, success led the collaborators to contracts in Hollywood, where they did the scores for several movies, but both of them chafed under the conditions of movie production, and they soon returned to Broadway for good, making their reëntry with the music and lyrics for Billy Rose's extravaganza *Jumbo*. After that, they got down to the series of bright and highly original Broadway musicals for which they are chiefly remembered—*On Your Toes, Babes in Arms, I'd Rather Be Right, I Married an Angel, The Boys from Syracuse*, and, finally, *Pal Joey*.

In style and sophistication, these shows were something new on Broadway. They had visual beauty and youthful freshness. (The great choreographer George Balanchine had a hand in several of them.) They contained no end of unconventional music by Rodgers, and they inspired Hart's peculiar talent to its most tricky and ingenious endeavors. But Hart was one of those unhappy geniuses who are more apt to be found in the loftier forms of art. He was a rather grotesque-looking, gnome-like man of disorderly, bohemian habits. He was a heavy drinker, a half-mad visionary, and a man to whom financial success and the cautiousness of bourgeois life meant very little. He had the gift of fantasy and satire that characterizes people for whom the world is somehow unreal and unsatisfying. For a long time, he had seemed destined for the tragic fate of men like van Gogh and Toulouse-Lautrec, and on November 22, 1943, he died, officially of pneumonia but actually of a combination of troubles, of which malnutrition, alcoholism, and acute mental disturbance were a few.

There are those who claim that Hart was Rodgers's finest librettist, and that none of the lyrics Rodgers has subsequently set to music have had quite the urbanity and satirical bite of Hart's. In any case, Rodgers's next collaborator, Oscar Hammerstein, was Hart's diametric opposite—an unabashed sentimentalist, a believer in optimism, religion, noble causes, and wholesome emotions, and a devotee of upright and highly respectable living. Hammerstein, a large man of affectionate disposition who was a much respected figure in the theatrical and literary worlds, had little or no gift for satire. He lacked the bitterness of the true satirist, and he found life a wonderful thing. But he was a very skillful lyric-writer as his previous collaborations with people like Rudolf Friml and Jerome Kern (*Show Boat*) had demonstrated. It was inevitable that he should give the Rodgers musical show a new atmosphere—one in which the accent was on romantic love, political idealism, and serious, if sometimes rather obvious dramatic ideas. The new touch was evident in their first Broadway collaboration, *Oklahoma!*, in which the hero was all heroic virility and the villain a man with a suggestion of abnormality about him—a character whom Hart would probably have painted more subtly. But *Oklahoma!* had its points. It bubbled over with enthusiasm. Its stage spectacle, to which Agnes de Mille contributed lovely choreography, was wholly engaging, and, of course, it was a hit of historic proportions. Furthermore, it is interesting to note that although Hammerstein brought a more conventional moral tone and more obvious sentimentality to his side of the collaboration, Rodgers continued to expand the daring and freshness of his musical approach. Their other hit shows—*Carousel, Allegro, South Pacific, The King and I, Me and Juliet, Flower Drum Song,* and *The Sound of Music*—were all remarkable for the dash, gaiety, and unconventionality of their music. Hammerstein's death left Rodgers crushed for the moment. He has experimented—successfully, he says—with writing his own lyrics for five new songs for the film *State Fair* [the 1962 remake] and for a forthcoming show, *No Strings*; more recently he has entered upon a new collaboration, which most Broadway show people consider not only a happy but an almost inevitable one, with Alan Jay Lerner, the lyricist of such hits as *Brigadoon, My Fair Lady,* and *Camelot.* [Ed. See the introductory remarks to "Rodgers Without Hammerstein" by Arthur and Barbara Gelb, which follows.]

What personal touches Lerner will bring to the Rodgers musical show remain to be seen, but there can be little doubt that Rodgers himself will go on writing tune after tune with his dependable fecundity and his eternal search for melodic novelty and catchiness. "I want to get humanity into my music," he has been quoted as saying. "That's all that really counts. I like to feel the direct reactions of an audience. I don't like abstract music. Nowadays, they claim that Haydn was abstract, but I wonder if Haydn was abstract to Haydn." And though he often forestalls his highbrow critics by saying deprecatingly, "I'm just a commercial-theatre kid—I don't write for posterity," he actually takes his craft very seriously. His attitude toward his work is, in fact, anything but purely commercial. Nevertheless, like practically all composers of any importance, he never discounts the tastes of his public. "I suspect," he once said to his biographer, David Ewen, "that the limitations of any art form are set by its creators and not by the public, and I can think of no field in which the viewpoint can be better substantiated than in the musical theatre. Too often I have heard the producer say, in all his expansive smugness, 'If I don't understand it, neither will the public.' What he doesn't understand is that the public is a lot smarter than he is, or I am, for that matter. Its taste is enormously catholic, and in its choice of entertainment it is precise and knowing. To the public, *Parsifal* is good, and so is *My Fair Lady*. The range is large, and the entertainment need only be good of its kind to attract hordes of people. The public is not only willing but anxious to go along with us in the theatre in search for better things, if we continue that search with honesty." The search seems to be the main impulse behind Rodgers's boundless versatility and his tendency to experiment within the framework of popular music. "I composed very serious music for the Churchill series," he told an acquaintance recently. "It was altogether different from my musical-show numbers. One of the things that have kept me alive all these years has been my unwillingness to settle for a prescribed formula. I like to think that I can write about the U.S. Navy, as I did in *Victory at Sea*, and also do boy-and-girl songs like 'You Are Sixteen,' and turn from that to the religious chorales in *The Sound of Music*. There are great possibilities in the musical theatre. All you have to do is find them."

"Rodgers Without Hammerstein"

For nearly eighteen years Rodgers and Hammerstein enjoyed perhaps the most fruitful collaboration in the history of the American musical, and Hammerstein's death in 1960 was an incalculable personal and professional loss. Five years earlier Rodgers himself endured an operation in which cancerous portions of his jaw, tongue, and lymph nodes were removed (see Rodgers's "Cancer? I've Had It!" in Part IV), but at fifty-eight he remained in relatively good health and clearly possessed the will and need to keep working. Along with other journalists, Arthur and Barbara Gelb announced a possible collaboration with Alan Jay Lerner, the distinguished librettist and lyricist, who in recent years had written *My Fair Lady, Camelot*, and the Academy Award–winning film *Gigi*. They could not foresee, however, that Rodgers would dismiss Lerner's idea for a musical based on the life of Coco Chanel in favor of a musical about extra-sensory perception, or that the collaboration with the slow working and dilatory lyricist would prove unworkable. Eventually Lerner was able to transform both ideas into musicals with other composers, *On a Clear Day You Can See Forever* with Burton Lane in 1965 and *Coco* with André Previn in 1970.

The Gelbs also note Rodgers's evolution as a lyricist, a process that began when new lyrics were needed for Rodgers and Hart revivals—in future interviews Rodgers would acknowledge that he wrote uncredited lyrics while Hart was still alive—and for various new film songs after Hammerstein's death. Although their chronology is somewhat confused (for example, Rodgers didn't begin working with Lerner until after successfully completing a musical on his own), the Gelbs may have been correct to characterize the projected union with Lerner as "a kind of cushion, in case things don't work out for Rodgers as a lyricist." One year after this *Esquire* piece, *No Strings*, the first show with lyrics as well as music by Rodgers appeared. It turned out to be the composer's last unequivocal artistic as well as commercial Broadway success.

ARTHUR AND BARBARA GELB

At fifty-nine, Richard Rodgers—the lone survivor of Broadway's two most famous teams of collaborators, Rodgers and Hart, and Rodgers and Hammerstein—has teamed up again. Not only with My Fair Lady's *Alan Jay Lerner, but also with himself. In the future, you may want tickets for the latest Rodgers and Lerner, playing right across the street from the latest Rodgers and Rodgers. [Ed. This is a note from the Esquire editor.]*

Losing a collaborator by death in the course of a successful theatrical career is comparable to being widowed at the height of a happy marriage. Even the most transient alliances in the theatre are apt to be charged with emotionalism, and a show-business partnership solidly based on achievement can reach a state of mutual adoration.

It is therefore not surprising that Richard Rodgers, who had already lost one collaborator, Lorenz Hart, in 1943, was thrown into something of a panic by the death from cancer of Oscar Hammerstein II in the Summer of 1960. In the first shock of grief, Rodgers decided, so to speak, not to re-marry, but to try what he called a "great experiment." After

Source: Arthur and Barbara Gelb, "Rodgers Without Hammerstein," *Esquire* (September 1961), 97–98.

forty-two years as Broadway's most highly regarded composer, he would now attempt to create his own lyrics.

Within four months, he had completed the words as well as the music for half-a-dozen new songs. Three were a remake for the movie, *State Fair*, one for the movie version of *Flower Drum Song*, and the rest were exercises. He had been assured by numerous professional friends that the songs were wonderful, and was talking excitedly about attempting the lyrics for a new Broadway musical. "If my experiment doesn't work," he said at the time, "I suppose I'll have to find a new collaborator for Broadway shows, but there isn't any one person I can see myself working with on a steady basis."

The passion for matchmaking dies hard, though, and suggestions of a new alliance with one or another of the established lyricists were repeatedly made by Rodgers's friends. In addition, hundreds of offers of collaboration from would-be poets—many of them containing sample rhymes—poured (and continue to pour) into his Madison Avenue office.

Early this year, rumors were heard along Broadway that the second-most-celebrated composer-lyricist team was splitting up. Frederick Loewe, composer of *My Fair Lady* and *Camelot*, had been ill with a heart ailment and wanted to take a prolonged rest; that left Alan Jay Lerner, who had inherited Hammerstein's position as Broadway's top lyricist, without a partner. But because of Rodgers's professed determination to be his own collaborator, it startled the theatre world when he announced, in April, that he and Lerner would write a musical together this winter for production in the Fall of 1962.

Nevertheless, his association with Lerner is in the nature of a trial marriage. He is hopeful that it will work and that he and Lerner will continue to write other shows, but he is leery of committing himself to a permanent collaboration. A man gets cautious—and nervous—after losing two partners.

As for Lerner, he is delighted with the arrangement and eager for Rodgers to have all the freedom he wants. "I'm pretty sure Dick will continue writing lyrics on his own from time to time and I feel that he should, to get it out of his system," Lerner says. "I'm just as anxious as he is for him to do things alone. Who knows? I may want to do something alone, too. I may want to write a straight play, for instance."

For Lerner, who is only forty-two, a switch in partners and outlook holds no terror. But Rodgers is somewhat past the age for making professional changes without apprehensiveness. He is not, however, the doddering octogenarian some people, aware that his career has spanned more than four decades, imagine him to be. Rodgers will be sixty years old next June.

Hammerstein, who was sixty-five when he learned he had only a few weeks to live, had the remarkable sensitivity and selflessness to be concerned about Rodgers's future. During a bedside conference at his farm in Doylestown, Pennsylvania, he suggested that Rodgers team up with someone young and enthusiastic, someone who would introduce fresh ideas and a new point of view. Rodgers would profit from such an arrangement. Hammerstein said, and a younger man would gain from the composer's long experience.

But when Hammerstein died on August 23, Rodgers could not bring himself to consider a replacement. Though he had known for eleven months that the man whose lyrics he had been setting to music for eighteen years was going to die, he simply could not grasp the concept "of Oscar's not being there."

Now that Rodgers *has* teamed up, even if it is only tentatively, with the young, enthusiastic lyricist Hammerstein prescribed, he finds himself embarked on a two-pronged career. The projected collaboration with Lerner, still several months off, is a kind of cushion, in case things don't work out for Rodgers as a lyricist. But proving that he can write his own words for his own tunes is what he would really like to do. And, though a full musical may prove to be more than he can cope with (even though he will not attempt to write the book), writing lyrics, so far, has turned out to be almost frighteningly easy.

"I've been working forty-two years with other people's words," he says, somewhat defensively. "I think something must have rubbed off by this time."

Although none of the new Rodgers and Rodgers songs have been released yet, the three for *State Fair* have been approved by the producers, and appear to demonstrate the truth of Rodgers's contention. Friends who have heard them and the others he wrote more or less for practice are ecstatic. The consensus is that the lyric style falls somewhere between that of Hart and Hammerstein—a little less tricky, brittle and sophisticated than Hart's, but a little more worldly and subtle than Hammerstein's. According to his daughter Mary, who is also a composer, the lyrics have "a quality that neither Larry's nor Oscar's had: a kind of Jewishness—a tough sweetness."

Rodgers soon discovered that he could write his lyrics with the same facility he brings to composing. The speed and intensity with which he has always lived and worked has long been a source of awe to his associates.

"He tries to cram in as much work as possible," his secretary, Lillian Leff, who has been with him for seventeen years, points out. "He does everything in a hurry because of his acute consciousness of death. His attitude is: 'I'm lucky so far, but I don't know what tomorrow will bring.'" (Rodgers underwent an operation for cancer five years ago.)

"I kept thinking about the songs all the time," Rodgers says. "I didn't let go for a minute; while changing my clothes, for example. The first two songs were written in three or four days, the third one after an interval of a week."

The first song turned out to be a romantic ballad entitled "Willing and Eager," the second a comedy-love song called "The Little Things in Texas" (the remake of the picture having switched its locale from Iowa to the larger state), and the third is a comic-situation number, "More Than Just A Friend."

In the face of his nimbleness with lyrics, Rodgers feels conscience-bound to explain that his reputation for speed as a composer is, in a way, based on a false premise.

"The stories about how I wrote the music for 'Oh, What a Beautiful Mornin'' and 'Bali Ha'i' in the time it took to sing the words are really pure myth," he says. "Though I got the tunes quickly, and seemingly without any effort, I had been thinking about them for months. I didn't need the actual words for that. Oscar and I had thoroughly discussed what kind of songs they would be and what they would try to say. All the time I was waiting for him to give me the lyrics, the music was working inside me."

With his own lyrics, Rodgers has come closer to the kind of inspirational flash commonly attributed to the creative artist. "This Isn't Heaven," for the *Flower Drum Song* movie [Ed. the *State Fair* remake], for instance, came to him in a barber chair at the Plaza Hotel.

"I got the idea for the lyrics and the opening bars of music simultaneously," he explains. "That was at three in the afternoon. I went straight home and finished the song before dinner."

It was a somewhat jolting experience. "I've never had a spontaneous melodic idea in my life," Rodgers says. "A tune has never awakened me in the middle of the night, so that I've had to grab a pencil. Up to now, and idea has only come when I've reached for it while sitting at the piano, concentrating on something specific. I've had my hair cut at the Plaza for years without ever having gotten an inspiration there before. But now that I've become excited about writing lyrics, I find myself jotting down ideas at odd times."

Rodgers likes to point out that he has actually written lyrics before.

"This is the first time I've admitted it," he says. "Up to now, I've done lyrics under the table (except for a couple of amateur shows I wrote with members of my family when I was fifteen). I've updated lyrics for the revivals of shows I wrote with Larry Hart—*Babes in Arms, Pal Joey*, and *On Your Toes*. And I've altered some of Larry's lyrics for movies and television. Also, when I worked with Larry in his last years, during which he was ill a great deal of the time, I helped out a little. I don't claim I supplied the actual words; I performed an editing job."

For all practical purposes, the Rodgers-Hart partnership ended a year or so before Hart died. Hart had been drinking heavily for years. *By Jupiter*, the final Rodgers-Hart collaboration, produced in 1942, was written largely in Doctors Hospital. Hart was being dried out, and Rodgers checked himself and a piano into a guest room. After the opening, Hart told his partner he was going to Mexico City for a rest. Rodgers felt sure he was going for a protracted binge.

Anxious to have Hart collaborate with him on a new Theatre Guild project that ultimately turned out to be *Oklahoma!*, Rodgers offered to check into a sanitarium with Hart and write the show there. Hart refused.

"I told him I'd have to do the show with Oscar Hammerstein, to whom I'd already explained my predicament sometime earlier. Larry said he didn't like the project anyway. He realized at this point that he couldn't write, and being a very decent person, he wanted me to work with Oscar. He went to Mexico City.

"Larry was carried off the train on a stretcher when he got back from Mexico City. But he was well enough to come to the opening of *Oklahoma!* on March 31, 1943. He was there with his mother. He came up to me later in Sardi's. He was wildly enthusiastic. He said, 'You've got at least another *Blossom Time*'."

Eight months later, the 1927 Rodgers and Hart hit, *A Connecticut Yankee*, was revived on Broadway. Hart vanished after the *première* and was not seen for two days. When he turned up, he had an advanced case of pneumonia. He died in the hospital a few days later, with Rodgers weeping at his bedside.

In his long career on Broadway, Rodgers has composed thirty-nine musicals—thirty of them with Hart, nine with Hammerstein—and hundreds of songs. With each partner he took different strides forward (and an occasional stride backward); with Hart he helped set the course of the American musical toward adulthood; with Hammerstein he helped to bring it to full maturity. The direction he will take alone is anyone's guess and where he will go with Lerner is a puzzle that beguiles no one more than it does Lerner himself.

"I'm so damn curious to see what our style together will be," Lerner said recently. "I do a great deal of thinking about how we're going to work together. I don't have a clue where my lyrics will go at the moment."

It is possible that the Rodgers-Lerner musical will be based on the life of the French *couturière*, Coco Chanel. But whatever their subject, both have made it clear that there will be no lack of artistic accord and amity.

"When our lawyers brought us together early last March to discuss the possibility of collaborating," Lerner said, "we discovered that we talked the same language. We hit it off right away. The thoughts he began, I'd finish, and vice versa. We realized we had the same attitudes toward the theatre, the same ideas about casting, management and breaking old theatre molds.

"It was like 'Where or When'," he added, referring to the well-known Rodgers-Hart number from *Babes in Arms*:

> Some things that happen for the first time
> Seem to be happening again.
> And so it seems that we have met before. . . .
> But who knows where or when?

"Richard Rodgers Is Calling"

Before Rodgers selected her to star as the African American in Paris in *No Strings* (1962), Diahann Carroll (1935–) had made her Broadway and Hollywood debuts at the age of nineteen in Harold Arlen's *House of Flowers* and the film version of Hammerstein's *Carmen Jones*. Her work in *No Strings* led to the first Tony (American Theatre Wing Prize) awarded to a black actress in a leading role (shared with Anna Maria Alberghetti for *Carnival*) and her pathbreaking title role in *Julia* (1968–71), the first television series to star an African American. Younger television viewers may recall her stint as a wickedly beautiful villainess in the popular soap opera *Dynasty* (1984).

In *Diahann*, Carroll makes several serious accusations against Rodgers. She quotes him in a homophobic slur against his first lyricist, she recalls his callous acceptance of a patron's racism and attendance at a theater party from which, as a black woman, Carroll was excluded, and blames Rodgers for at least tacitly agreeing to the selection of a nonblack actress to play the lead of a projected *No Strings* film (the film was never made). By the time Carroll's memoir appeared, Rodgers was no longer alive to defend himself. The following decade, his biographer, William Hyland, while acknowledging Rodgers's reticence and perhaps discomfort at fully confronting Hart's homosexuality, considered Rodgers's alleged disparaging remark "highly implausible."

As recently as the *American Masters* PBS profile on Rodgers, "The Sweetest Sounds" (2001), Carroll has publicly denied a sexual affair. Biographer Meryle Secrest, however, presents evidence from photographs and interviews to suggest that Rodgers was at the very least emotionally involved with his leading lady during the development and rehearsals of *No Strings* [Secrest, *Somewhere for Me: A Biography of Richard Rodgers* (New York: ALfred A. Knopf, 2001)].

Rodgers may have been circumspect in print and recorded interviews about Hart's sexual preferences, but he was unequivocally clear about his feelings for his difficult, lovable collaborator. The only time Rodgers ever acknowledged breaking down emotionally was when he realized that Hart could not be helped and that their partnership was doomed (see *Musical Stages*, pp. 216–17). Hart may have been a "blight" and "a permanent source of irritation" (see Rodgers's self interview in Part IV), but for twenty-five years he was also Rodgers's "best friend," loved for himself as well as for his magnificent talent and accomplishment.

DIAHANN CARROLL

The morning after one of my appearances on the *Tonight Show* with Jack Paar (I had by then become a sort of regular, appearing almost once a week, along with Eydie Gormé and Steve Lawrence—and I loved it!), the phone rang and a voice announced, "Miss Carroll, Richard Rodgers is calling."

"Of course he is," I answered. "And this is Greta Garbo."

I had met Richard Rodgers briefly, but that was four years earlier, in 1957, shortly after I finished *House of Flowers*. He was then casting *Flower Drum Song*, his new musical set in San Francisco's Chinatown, and asked if I would allow Eddie Senz to do a special makeup job for me to see if I might be able to play an oriental. It really didn't work. By the time Eddie Senz was through, the powder and paint were so thick I could barely open my mouth. Rodgers dropped the idea but promised there would be another show some other time. That's something you hear very often in my business, and as the months and years went by I completely forgot about it.

"Who is it really?" I asked, certain it was one of my friends playing a practical joke. But to my astonishment, it actually was Richard Rodgers, and he wanted to talk with me again.

We met for lunch at Gallagher's, the actors' hangout in the theater district. I decided the look would be Givenchy from head to toe—a pale pink wool dress with a matching simple clean-lined pink coat and one of those wonderful little pillbox hats that were popular at the time.

"You look marvelous," he said as I sat down. "That's exactly the way I would like to see you on stage. . . . Have you ever done any modeling?"

I told him I had, that I started modeling for Johnson Publications when I was fifteen and continued until I left college to go to work as a professional singer. That seemed to please him. Obviously he had something in mind.

He asked why I hadn't returned to the Broadway theater, and I explained that I hadn't been offered anything that really interested me. I had been asked to do several plays about ingenues in the West Indies or Haiti who run around in their bare feet, but I felt I had already explored that character in *House of Flowers* and wanted to move on to something a little more sophisticated. I also thought there was a certain danger in being typecast as an eternal ingenue.

Rodgers agreed, and returned to the subject of modeling. Almost thinking out loud, he began to talk about how interesting it would be to do the first musical about a successful black fashion model, someone very much at home in the world of haute couture, who operates at the top of her profession. "Of course it wouldn't be possible for a black model to achieve that kind of success in this country," he went on. (He was perfectly right.

Source: Diahann Carroll, with Ross Firestone, *Diahann: An Autobiography* (Boston: Little, Brown, 1986), 107–10, 112–17.

This was still 1961.) "But that does happen in Europe. Maybe the story could take place abroad." He seemed very excited about the idea, and asked if I had any thoughts about how it might be developed. It struck me that the main problem would be finding a writer familiar with black people, someone who would be able to write convincingly about the struggles of a young woman who has made her way through the fashion world. When I ventured that opinion, he remained noncommittal.

It was time for the meeting to end. Rodgers assured me he was going to pursue the idea, but since he was on his way to Europe, he would call me as soon as he returned. I told him how very much I looked forward to that, and then put it out of my mind. It was, of course, terribly exciting to meet with a man who was a living legend, then to hear him praise my work and say he would like to write a show for me. But I had been in the business long enough to know that you must never ever let yourself become emotionally involved in the germ of an idea. Not that it couldn't become a reality, but the possibility was equally as great that I would never hear from Mr. Rodgers again.

Less than two weeks later he called from London. Sounding even more enthusiastic than before, he said he was working on the idea with the playwright Sam Taylor and had developed it to the point where he felt certain he had a show. The plot would deal with the romance between an American model living in Paris and an expatriate American writer who is knocking around Europe with the jet set. Sam Taylor had written a number of successful Broadway shows, but what really excited me was that he was also responsible for the screenplay for *The Moon Is Blue*, one of my favorite films. Rodgers went on to say that Taylor was returning to New York to meet me, and they planned to approach Richard Kiley about playing the male lead. Suddenly, the project began to seem deliciously real.

Everything came together very quickly. Rodgers called and asked which arranger and conductor I had worked with and respected. I suggested Peter Matz (arranger, producer, conductor—Peter could do anything!). A month or so later I found myself sitting with Peter in Rodgers's office on Madison Avenue listening to him play his new score for me. I was entranced! The melodies were so beautiful, so appealing. Like practically everything else he wrote, they had a certain something that catches the ear and makes you want to hear them again. When he said, "This is your love song," and played a few bars from "The Sweetest Sounds," it was more than I could bear. Trying to keep both feet on the ground, I kept telling myself, "Come on, concentrate, concentrate. This is the music you're going to have to perform. Pay attention, Diahann." But it was almost impossible. I was floating.

Not until the very end of the afternoon was there any indication that Richard Rodgers was not the epitome of tact and sensitivity. Before *No Strings* Rodgers had always collaborated with a lyricist—first Larry Hart, and then, after Hart died, Oscar Hammerstein. Now for the first time he had composed the words as well as the music, and he was extremely pleased with himself.

"You just can't imagine how wonderful it feels," he told me as we were saying goodbye, "to have written this score and not have to search all over the globe for that drunken little fag."

I was stunned. The unexpected cruelty of the remark shook me to my very being. I hoped I was mistaken, but as he went on there was absolutely no question that he was talking about Larry Hart. All my life Rodgers and Hart epitomized the very best of American popular music. Their partnership produced some of the most glorious songs ever written. I had heard the gossip about Larry Hart's self-destructiveness, and I'm sure he must have caused Rodgers great anguish over the more than twenty years they had worked together. However, it was inconceivable to me that a man the stature of Richard Rodgers could be so lacking in kindness and generosity of spirit. Rodgers had been blessed with an extraordinary gift and been lavishly rewarded for it. Everything in his elegantly appointed office, from the paintings on the walls to the exquisitely beautiful piano, reeked of quiet money and long-time success. If he could be that mean-spirited about Larry Hart, he could be that way about anyone. My respect for his genius was undiminished, but I was so disappointed by the character of the man that, from that moment on, I never quite trusted him. . . .

Another problem was communicating with Richard Rodgers. Rodgers wasn't exactly intimidating, but there was never any of that easy give and take and sense of camaraderie between composer and company I had experienced with Harold Arlen. Arlen was a wonderfully warm human being, and everyone in the cast of *House of Flowers* adored him. Rodgers was much more formal. As time passed, I came to the conclusion that he was really incapable of hearing someone else's point of view without regarding that person as a potential adversary, and his frequent insensitivity was appalling.

I will never be able to forget the smile on his face when he informed me that there would be no opening night party for the cast in Detroit because the hostess had refused to invite me. It seems that this local socialite was afraid to have a black person who wasn't a servant around her children, and unless Rodgers could assure her that he had created me himself—trained me to speak and walk and dress properly—she would not allow me to set foot in her home.

Rodgers found the whole episode vastly amusing. He didn't seem terribly bothered by his friend's racism. It only confirmed that he accomplished what he set out to accomplish, which was to present this glamorous, very desirable black woman in a vehicle that would startle the white community. This woman gave a party for Rodgers—and he went. I held my own party for the cast in the restaurant across the street from the theater.

Other problems weren't solved quite so simply. When I first saw the script, I was much too excited even to begin to evaluate it. The author's note stated on the front page that the play never once mentioned the female lead's color, but I didn't allow myself to ask why. I wanted to do it. I wanted to star on Broadway. As we moved into rehearsal, Sam Taylor openly acknowledged that he and Rodgers had quite consciously arrived at that decision and there was nothing more to discuss. "It's a love story," he said, "a beautiful love story with beautiful songs and beautiful clothes, and the fact that she happens to be black and he happens to be white is not going to be discussed. It's just going to be there." But then as time went on, it became increasingly clear that this ridiculous evasion was going to catch up with us, and it finally did. The ending of the show simply didn't work. The plot spent an hour and forty-five minutes getting these two people together. It established that they love each other. Now suddenly, without any explanation, they are made to part. Kiley's character decides to return to the United States so he can resume writing his novel. My character thinks that's a wonderful idea and tells him goodbye. End of story.

"But why can't they go home together?" Kiley and I kept asking. "If they love each other so much and are so well suited, why do they have to separate?"

Sam Taylor insisted that we were being totally unrealistic, and informed us that the subject was not open for discussion. I guess he felt that it was perfectly feasible for a white man to have a brief affair with a black woman in the fantasy world of Paris, but that was as far as it would go.

"Well, they have to," was the explanation. "You know, they just have to."

The problem of the ending was finally resolved when someone came up with the idea of reproducing the opening scene of the show detail for detail. Kiley and I are on stage together but haven't yet met, aren't even aware of each other's presence. Both of us are singing "The Sweetest Sounds," that beautiful song I had heard that first day, full of yearning about wanting to fall in love. When the song ends, the lights begin to dim and, still not seeing each other, we cross and move off separately into the opposite wings. It was an absolutely brilliant solution, making everything that came in between a fantasy, a love story that may or may not have actually happened.

We opened in New York on March 15, 1962. There were enough rave reviews to make us a solid hit.

Two months later I received my second nomination for a Tony Award—this time for best female performance in a musical. And this time it was a "big to-do" in my life. I was ecstatic that my peers thought so highly of my work. But, in truth, I became a little too full of myself. It was all so much so soon! I had never dreamed that by the age of twenty-five I would have had a Broadway show written especially for me by

Richard Rodgers, and then to top it off, a Tony Award nomination. It was a lot for me to handle (and to handle *gracefully*) because I didn't have any experience with this kind of attention.

My friends were wonderful! Everyone called and sent flowers in congratulations. My parents were in heaven, and Sidney [the actor Sidney Poitier] was happy for me, too. Almost immediately Donald Brooks and Geraldine Stutz began trying to solve the big question: what *would* I wear? After much discussion we agreed on a white jersey gown that was spectacular because it was so simple. And the day of the awards my old friend and furrier, Abe Rein, sent over a gorgeous fox coat for the occasion. Our friendship had begun when Lou Walters [the owner of the New York nightclub the Latin Quarter and father of television news reporter and interviewer Barbara Walters] sent me to Abe's showroom when I was eighteen, and Abe custom-made a black diamond mink coat for a mere fifty-dollar deposit, reassuring his partners that I was to be trusted (and our relationship has lasted thirty years!).

And that evening I sat in the theater in a trance. When they announced the nominees—Anna Maria Alberghetti for *Carnival*, Molly Picon for *Milk and Honey*, Elaine Stritch for *Sail Away*, and Diahann Carroll for *No Strings*—my heart pounded so hard I began to shake. It sounds trite—but it is true. I was so certain I wouldn't win against such competition that I never prepared a proper acceptance speech. When they announced my name, saying I had tied with Anna Maria Alberghetti, it wasn't until I saw the audience turning to smile at me that I knew I had heard correctly and allowed myself to move to the stage.

When I reached the podium, I was overwhelmed! I wanted to thank Richard Rodgers, but instead I was so overcome with emotion I became incoherent and rather theatrical. "Isn't it incredible?" I proclaimed. "*He* knocked on *my* door. *He* called *me*." I'm sure everyone was delighted when I finally finished speaking and returned to my seat.

Receiving that kind of recognition is a glorious feeling, and I was on top of the world for days. But nothing lasts forever, and life is so full of surprises you never can tell what's going to happen next. One day you win the Tony Award and are performing the lead in a Broadway musical Richard Rodgers wrote for you. The next day you pick up the morning paper and read that an actress named Nancy Kwan has just been hired to play your role in the film version.

I was furious. I was hurt. I felt betrayed. And, hearing the news that way was a terrible shock. I assumed that Richard Rodgers would have had, if not at least compassion, then the common courtesy to tell me himself. I understood that he had no legal obligation to do so, but this was not a legal question. There had been rumors about the possibility of a movie sale to Ray Stark at Warners-Seven Arts, and the implication, I thought, was clear that I would be part of the package. But now that the negotiations had been completed, I was suddenly out of the picture, and no one seemed to feel I should be told the bad tidings before the announcement hit the papers.

I would like to believe that when Richard Rodgers stopped by my dressing room that evening of the announcement, he was trying to soften the blow.

"Of course you realize," he told me, "that I had nothing to do with casting the film."

"Well, no, I didn't realize that."

"Not that I have to explain this to you, but I sold the rights to Warners-Seven Arts, and they're free to do as they please."

I found it hard to believe that Richard Rodgers would sell a property outright without retaining some power over the project. But there was nothing more to say. I wished him every success, and he left. It was a very uncomfortable meeting for the both of us.

Earl Wilson called the next day to ask if I would come to his office to discuss my feelings. I threw caution to the wind and said that I would. I met him at his office and he immediately got to the point. He wanted to know if I was disappointed by the news. I told him that of course I was. At the risk of sounding presumptuous and naïve, I felt that *No Strings* was my baby. But I made it clear that I was also disappointed about something else. If Warner Brothers didn't think I was right for the part— fine; that was their prerogative. I would have to live with that. But the fact that they didn't select a black actress (Nancy Kwan was Eurasian, a minority, but she was *not* black) told the story. It was explained to me that a black actress was not box office.

I had no idea what a furor Wilson's column would cause when it appeared in the papers the next morning. Almost every show business journalist in the country had something to say. Some of the writers cheered me on. Others accused me of sour grapes. Didn't I realize, they asked, that this sort of thing happens all the time when Broadway shows are made into films? Julie Andrews played *My Fair Lady* on Broadway, but Audrey Hepburn took over her role on the screen version. That was perfectly true, but they seemed to miss my point. Audrey Hepburn and Julie Andrews are both white. And since *No Strings* was written for a black woman, a black woman—if not me, someone else—ought to be given a chance to play the part.

Earlier that month Adam Clayton Powell had held a series of congressional hearings about racial discrimination in the entertainment industry. I had testified about the limited opportunities afforded black performers, and now, two weeks later, here was a perfect example of what I meant. The NAACP sent a petition to Warners-Seven Arts demanding to know how many black people were employed by the company. Several other groups started discussions about boycotting the film. That may or may not have been the deciding factor, but the studio eventually decided to shelve the project.

The experience was more than disappointing. For a long time it marred my work. Whenever I walked onstage I had this terrible feeling that everyone in the audience thought I was good enough to perform in the theater but not good enough for the film. Even though I understood the racism of what happened, and tried to remember my mom's words ("It's their problem, Diahann, not yours"), I felt an overpowering sense of failure that I couldn't shake.

This was hardly the first time I had come up against the reality that parts for black performers were not in abundance. For example, while a Broadway star is in a successful play, he or she often receives many scripts to read for his or her next project. For black performers, this is not the case. Parts have always been few and far between.

I thought I was prepared for the blows, but one never really is. The studio—the entire industry—seemed to be telling me, "We're not doing this movie with a black female lead." And that was something "they" wanted me to accept. But I couldn't. I walk around in this skin all the time. So it wasn't just this one movie that was at stake. It was my very life.

"The Less Said, the Better"

In the penultimate pages of his entertaining and insightful survey, *Rodgers & Hammerstein* (New York: Harry N. Abrams, 1992), Ethan Mordden (see "The Age of Rodgers and Hart" in Part I and "The Work that Changed the Form" in Part II) delivers an epiphany about the fruit of Rodgers's unhappy collaboration with Stephen Sondheim and Arthur Laurents. Mordden writes: "He [Rodgers] was in form for *No Strings* and at his best in *Do I Hear a Waltz?*, a box-office failure disdained by its creators but—take it from me—a wonderful show with a really lovely score" (p. 214; see also Ken Mandelbaum's positive assessment of this show in "Anatomy of a Flop" to follow). Craig Zadan's assemblage of quoted recollections—mainly Sondheim, Laurents, and original choreographer Wakefield Poole—records how a promising collaboration went sour and led to the creator's rejection of their own work. In passing remarks George Oppenheimer, a drama critic for *Newsday* and a longtime friend of Sondheim, asserts that Rodgers "*hates* homosexuality" without offering any corroborative details, and Poole accuses director John Dexter of misogyny.

Readers of *Sondheim & Co.* meet a reluctant lyricist who was persuaded to undertake a project against his better judgment. Two close friends, Mary Rodgers, the elder daughter of the composer, and Laurents, Sondheim's librettist on *West Side Story, Gypsy*, and *Anyone Can Whistle*, and the author of the play upon which *Waltz* is based, asked Sondheim to work on Rodgers's new show. Shortly before he died, Hammerstein, Sondheim's neighbor and mentor, had also encouraged a Rodgers-Sondheim partnership. After reading Sondheim's famous insult in *Newsweek* (describing Rodgers as a man of infinite talent and limited soul, the reverse of Hammerstein), Rodgers decided that "the less said, the better" and said nothing else. In brief and restrained remarks in *Musical Stages* several years later, Rodgers alluded to the escalating estrangement with Sondheim and Laurents and concluded that *Do I Hear a Waltz?* "was not a satisfying experience" (p. 319). Perhaps he overheard his fellow creators one of the times they said, "Here comes Godzilla," as he entered the theater.

In stating his critical judgment that audiences would be unable to accept the unsympathetic heroine they had created, Rodgers blames Laurents and Sondheim for colluding to override his objection to the scene when Leona Samish "gets drunk and tells a young wife that her husband has had a dalliance with the owner of their *pensione*." In *Original Story by Arthur Laurents: A Memoir of Broadway and Hollywood* (New York: Alfred A Knopf, 2000) the original playwright and librettist explains why it was dramatically imperative to make the central character unlikable. For more on the personal and artistic disagreements between Rodgers and his collaborators see Geoffrey Block, *Yale Broadway Masters: Richard Rodgers* (New Haven: Yale University Press, forthcoming).

CRAIG ZADAN

"The original intention," suggested Burt Shevelove, "was to do something that would make a lot of money. If I were to list all of Steve's work, I would never list *Do I Hear a Waltz?* Although there are some very good lyrics, as far as I'm concerned, it was streetwalking."

Immediately after the dissolution of *Anyone Can Whistle*, Arthur Laurents set out to have his 1952 play, *The Time of the Cuckoo*, the story of a middle-aged single woman finding love for the first time in Venice, musicalized by Richard Rodgers. (The play, which starred Shirley Booth, was later, in 1955, turned into a film called *Summertime* starring Katharine Hepburn.) Actually, Laurents had always wanted to do the play as a musical and during the writing of *West Side Story* had even brought the project to Oscar Hammerstein II, who liked the idea but suggested that Laurents wait a few years since the movie had been done too recently. Then, unfortunately, Hammerstein died.

"Dick Rodgers had previously asked me to write songs with him," Sondheim says, "and although I didn't want to write just lyrics ever again, I told Dick I'd be honored to write with him if a project came up

---

Source: Craig Zadan, *Sondheim & Co.* (New York: Harper & Row, 1990), 99–107.

that excited me—and I hoped against hope that nothing would. Somehow, Arthur and Mary Rodgers (Richard's daughter), after a great deal of pressure, convinced me to write lyrics for Dick's music for *Do I Hear a Waltz?*"

"The thing I objected to the most," Flora Roberts [Sondheim's agent] says, "was not the Rodgers situation, which was another matter altogether. It had to do with making somebody, through friendship, do something that he artistically did not want to do."

"My first mistake," Laurents readily admits, "and a mistake that was most important to me personally, was talking Steve into working on the show. Rodgers was foul to him. I remember when we got a new song one day out of town, Rodgers looked at the lyric sheet and in front of the whole company said, 'This is shit!' Well, needless to say, the lyric was a great deal better than the tune."

"I never thought the play should be a musical," Sondheim says. "The reason, and I still think I'm right, is that it's about a lady who, metaphorically, can't sing. How can you do it as a musical? One way is to do it as a chamber opera or another way is to have a musical in which everyone sings the whole time with the exception of the main character, which I think would have been very interesting—if she wouldn't be able to sing until the climax of the piece, then breaks open in anger and is able to sing."

Although Laurents now agrees that the project should not have been done, he strongly opposes the idea that the lady could not sing. In a piece written by Laurents in the *World-Telegram and The Sun* prior to the show's opening, he wrote: "An attractive lady has been libeled. For over ten years now, she has been called a virgin and worse, and I would like to clear her record. . . . My theory is that the actresses who played her were too old for the part. . . . The story of an aging woman who could not give herself physically is something small and rather dirty. What *I* wrote is the story of a woman who could not give herself emotionally, a woman *young* enough to have a chance at a future. Leona, the original Leona, the Leona I wrote, does sing."

So the casting of *Do I Hear a Waltz?* began with a search for a younger actress to play Leona, the lady who goes to Venice looking for love. Dorothy Kilgallen reported in her column that Anne Bancroft was up for the role. Arthur Laurents relates that Mary Martin wanted to do the part but Rodgers said she was too old. Finally chosen was actress Elizabeth Allen. Her costar was Sergio Franchi.

Brought in to direct the show, making his Broadway musical debut, was John Dexter, at that time assistant director of London's National Theatre (even though *Variety* first reported that William Ball, of the Stratford Shakespeare Festival, would stage the show).

"The whole thing was a mistake all the way around," Laurents further admits. "I don't think anybody's work was any good. What we got was a lot of songs sort of stuck into my book that might have been better if someone else did the adaptation. John Dexter, who had done great things in London, was a deadly error as director. We also made the mistake of deciding that we didn't want any dances in the show originally. It was all supposed to be this great songfest, which it never was."

Hired to stage the musical numbers (sans dancing) was choreographer Wakefield Poole, who eventually became used as a go-between, leveling the steadily opposing factions.

"Rodgers was a strange man," Poole has said. "I did three shows with him and I think I was brought into *Waltz* to be on his side. Arthur Laurents wanted John Dexter as director and Rodgers wanted Joe Layton. But none of them wanted any choreography, which was ridiculous. They gave me a musical number in which the entire company strolls. And I said, 'This is a twelve-minute number. What do you want me to do, twelve minutes of walking patterns?' But Dexter never allowed me into creative meetings. He's an opportunist and I think that because of his insecurities I wasn't allowed to express any opinions."

Although trouble was apparent very early in rehearsals, the bomb exploded at the run-through of the show in New York prior to its New Haven opening.

Poole: "Even though the split in interpretation began as soon as the show got off paper, the real trouble started when Liz Allen had not been told that there would be a run-through and that three or four casts from other shows would be coming. Suddenly, that Sunday morning, we were informed that at two in the afternoon we would be having a gypsy run-through and that our cast could invite anyone they wanted. Liz was furious and said, 'I'm not ready to perform this in front of an audience. I need some preparation. Look at me, I'm a mess!' Her insecurities came through and the pressures of the role were building in her. She felt John pulling her one way and Arthur pulling her the other. And John had an outburst and yelled, 'Fuck you, you pig!' and it turned into one of those screaming nasty fights in front of the whole cast. That afternoon she performed the show with the fevered pitch of Ethel Merman in *Gypsy*, rather than as the vulnerable lady the character was meant to be. From that point on, I served as the intermediary because Liz didn't speak to Dexter until a week before we opened in New York."

Laurents: "Steve will tell you that I behaved quite badly also. After that first run-through I just stomped out. I saw it was a disaster and I went out and bought a coat.

"You can talk concept until you are blue in the face . . . but it's the doing that counts. That's absolutely a primary rule in the theater. Everybody talks and thinks they agree and it turns out they are either talking about two different things or they approach it in then different ways. What you had on the stage in the case of *Waltz* is best characterized as bland. It had no style. No concept. It had characters and it should have had emotion. You *can* have a good musical with a bad book, but I certainly don't think you can have a good musical with a bad score. There was a song in *Waltz* called 'Stay' that always sounded to me like a lament from the Russian steppes. The first *note* bored me. There were new songs put in but Dick seemed to be afraid of Steve. I think he was afraid of his own talent not being what it was. I think there also was great resentment that we had to *convince* Steve to do the show—Dick took it as a great insult. He was very hard to move and very insulting to Steve. He kept calling me over and making remarks about 'my friend' and 'how dare he.' He had known Steve since he was a child and I suppose that made it very difficult for him. I wasn't exactly enamored of Jerry [Jerome Robbins] when we did *Gypsy*, but when you do a show with somebody, you really must put aside personal feelings. And then, you see, Rodgers was the producer on *Waltz* as well as the composer, so if there were any objections, it didn't matter. It was what *he* wanted. Even after the show opened, when I wanted to go in and make some changes since Dexter was gone and the thing was in a shambles, Rodgers wouldn't allow me in the theater."

Jerome Whyte, the late executive of the Richard Rodgers organization and production supervisor of *Do I Hear a Waltz?*, described the administration of the show quite differently. "The working relationship was pretty good compared with many other shows I've worked on. There was a difference of opinion and of course it was all put to a vote. The majority won. There was, I think, one moment of unpleasantness in New Haven where Steve became upset and Dick was momentarily upset, too." (Although Rodgers had agreed to discuss his experiences on *Do I Hear a Waltz?* for inclusion in this book, following the Stephen Sondheim *Newsweek* cover story of April 23, 1973, he changed his mind. In *Newsweek*, Sondheim referred to Oscar Hammerstein as a man who had limited talent and infinite soul, and described Richard Rodgers as a man of infinite talent and limited soul. Rodgers offered little explanation for his reluctance to talk about Sondheim but succinctly noted, "The less said, the better.")

"I had a kind of feeling that Dick was terribly unhappy with the group," George Oppenheimer related. "Dick wouldn't talk to me, my being the critic for *Newsday*, even though we were very, very close. I'd known Dick for fifteen years and I wasn't aware, until much later, that he was a very strange man. For instance, he *hates* homosexuality, cliques, groups as such, but blinds himself when he wants to."

In the *World-Telegram and The Sun*, Rodgers and Sondheim were interviewed early in their collaboration about their working relationship—and it was all safely respectful.

"Working with Steve," Rodgers said, "is much closer to working with Oscar than with Larry Hart—Larry was not as dependable. Steve has a curious way of making people sing as if they were talking."

"Working with Dick is very different," Sondheim commented in the same article. "I write the lyrics myself—and he composes by himself. Then we get together to work it over. With Lenny [Leonard Bernstein, composer of *West Side Story*] and Jule [Jule Styne, composer of *Gypsy*] we did more talking first."

Do I Hear a Waltz? opened in New Haven to generally mixed reviews, but there was unanimous criticism about the lack of choreography. Soon a decision was reached and John Dexter offered a statement to the press: "We made one initial miscalculation—Dick, Arthur, Steve, and myself—that there should be no dancing in the show. We found the dancing was transparently necessary."

A call went out for help and Herbert Ross arrived in New Haven, supplying some inspiration to the generally insipid show. With Wakefield Poole assisting him, Ross first had to break through the personality factions that were openly waging battle.

Ross: "There was a total conflict of opinion as to how the roles should be played. Steve and Arthur wanted a dry and tough interpretation and Rodgers wanted a sentimental one; therefore the show lacked any positive quality. I restaged the musical numbers, but there wasn't much that could be done. The show was in terrifically good taste but was passionless. Elizabeth Allen was good, but she wasn't right. The show needed someone who would break your heart. She just wasn't vulnerable enough."

Poole: "Sergio was very sterile. He worked hard, though, and if we had told him to stand on his head, he would have—or at least he would have tried. There was much less pressure with Liz after Herb came in because he is so good at handling people. There was one point where we had a discussion of replacing Liz when we got to Boston, and I even remember Gwen Verdon's name being brought up, but they decided to stick it out with Liz. Dexter remained difficult. Throughout the show, Dexter did things that made a lot of people very angry. For instance, he called all the boys by their first names. The women's names he didn't bother to know. He would stage the show and say, 'Hey, you over there,' or 'Miss, you go there,' which alienated every woman in the show. Though his track record is fabulous, I think that any director who can't communicate with actors is a failure."

Although a great deal was happening in restaging, the visual aspect of the production was faltering as much as the stolidly written material. "The whole concept of the show," Poole says, "was Venice remembered rather than Venice realistically. It went all the way, even to the costumes which were filmy and chiffony, but they didn't work because on the stage they looked cheap."

There also still existed the terrible unpleasantness among the creative people. "When Rodgers would come into the theater," Poole remembers, "everyone would say, 'Here comes Godzilla'—that was his nickname.

And I looked around and the whole thing completely freaked me out. Here was Richard Rodgers, one of the most renowned composers in the theater, Steve Sondheim, the most brilliant lyricist, Arthur Laurents, a great playwright, and John Dexter, the fair-haired boy who directed all those things at the Royal Court—and no one is talking. Those brilliant minds and there wasn't an ounce of communication. It was most exasperating."

"The show," Sondheim explains, "most simply was what Mary Rodgers calls a 'Why?' musical. And the theater is full of them. You take a successful property, add songs to it, and put it on the stage. And to adapt such properties is like the dinosaur eating its own tail. Although they never intended it, Rodgers and Hammerstein are partly responsible for this. But what people don't understand is that *Oklahoma!* is very different from *Green Grow the Lilacs*, on which it is based. *Lilacs* is a dark play, but they saw something past it and *Oklahoma!* has its own tone, spirit, and style—it's got its own vitality. The same way that *Carousel* does not depend on *Liliom* for its strength—it's a wholly different piece of goods.

"The reason *Waltz* flopped was that it had no real energy—no excitement whatsoever. That's because it need not have been done. When you see *Hello, Dolly!*, no matter what you think of it, there's a feeling that the people who put it on really loved it a lot. You never got that feeling with *Waltz*. It was a workmanlike, professional show. Period. And it deserved to fail."

Do I Hear a Waltz? ran for half a year, regaining part of its $450,000 investment due to the lineup of theater parties pre-booked for Broadway's "new Rodgers musical."

Saturday Review began its critical evaluation of the show with a headline that read "Dearth in Venice," and *Newsweek*'s review was equally discouraging: "To make a musical comedy without comedy is possible, but to make one without music is, it would seem, unthinkable. Yet this is what Richard Rodgers and Arthur Laurents have unaccountably tried to do in *Do I Hear a Waltz?* Rodgers has written songs, all right, but they add up to the flattest score the old master has produced in years." Perhaps fortunate this time around, Sondheim received no mention. But ironically, after being totally overlooked for his work on *West Side Story*, *Gypsy*, and *Forum*, he received his very first Tony nomination for his work in the musical theater for *Do I Hear a Waltz?* (though all the awards that season went to *Fiddler on the Roof*).

In an interview in the *New York Times* before the opening of *Do I Hear a Waltz?*, Richard Rodgers somewhat jokingly described his relationship with Stephen Sondheim: "The first time I saw him was when I was working on *Oklahoma!* in 1942. . . . I watched him grow from an attractive little boy to a monster."

The less said, the better.

"The Plot Against Musicals"

Increasingly, as Rodgers continued his work without Hammerstein, audiences had the opportunity to see and compare multiple eras in the career of a living legend. The selection that follows contains three parts: 1) a review of a successful Off-Broadway 1963 revival of Rodgers and Hart's 1938 classic, *The Boys from Syracuse*; 2) a comparison between Rodgers and Hammerstein's *Oklahoma!*—in 1968 on the eve of a single concert performance in Philharmonic Hall at Lincoln Center to commemorate its 25th anniversary—and a pretentious new musical, *Here's Where I Belong* ("burdened with substance and shackled to seriousness"), based on John Steinbeck's *East of Eden*, another production destined to last one night (but in this case an unplanned one-night stand); and 3) a review of the first performance of Rodgers's new musical *Do I Hear a Waltz?* All three pieces are by Walter Kerr (1913–1996), widely considered one of the most distinguished theater critics of his generation, first with the *New York Herald Tribune* (1951–66) and then with the *New York Times* until his retirement in 1983.

In the first review Kerr offers effusive praise for Hart's sophisticated lyrics and Rodgers's "inappropriately perfect" and invariably "unexpected modulations" in songs like "The Shortest Day of the Year." After extolling the virtues of the perennially fresh *Oklahoma!* at the expense of the short-lived and still-born Steinbeck adaptation, Kerr's final review rejects the cognitive dramatic dissonance of *Do I Hear a Waltz?*, a show in which Rodgers's excellent musical-comedy songs must be made to "carry the evening when the evening isn't a musical comedy."

WALTER KERR

A Line I'd Call Pretty

Having been rash enough to write a piece deploring the prevailing custom of basing all musical comedies on old movies or old plays, I now want to modify my position. In fact, I want to admit I was wrong. Wrong.

My confession comes not as a result of certain angry letters from composers and librettists who continue to display an exemplary loyalty to the movies they saw when they were in college. Loyalty is a quality I like in a man, but it is not what has persuaded me. Neither can I claim to have retired to my study prepared to rethink my position, retracing the progress of my error step by step. Thought had nothing to do with it.

I just happened to see a revival of *The Boys from Syracuse*. Reviewers

Source: Walter Kerr, *Thirty Plays Hath November: Pain and Pleasure in the Contemporary Theater* (New York: Simon and Schuster, 1969), 192–95, 184–92.

rarely "just happen" to see things; mostly they go to the theater because dictatorial newspaper managements expect them to. But one or another conflict of obligations kept me from reviewing *The Boys from Syracuse* in the first case (I was probably off seeing some play that failed to communicate our failure to communicate), and I came to it carelessly and carefree, as well as late.

It was like the gentle rain from heaven, that show. All you had to do was sit there and let the lyrics kick their syllables. "I am sinless," sang the condemned old man who is also father to those identical Antipholi, "I am twinless" and you sank back in your seat in ecstatic relief that someone had remembered—some kind, kind soul had remembered—the pleasures to be wrought from compactness, from comic aptness, from the deft and daffy mating of the dead pan and the impertinent mind.

As we've said, most lyrics nowadays perform the functions of slave labor. They are always pushing something—the plot, or character, or whatever else the authors have not been able to get into the dialogue. Almost never do we hear a lyric with a leap in its heart, with a slyness in its condescension to the music, or even with an unlikely rhyme.

"This is a terrible city," began the jaunty-voiced hero of the Rodgers and Hart word-game as he contemplated manfully, and metrically, the unfriendly landscape he'd landed in. He wasn't being significant, mind you. There was nothing wrong with the city. He wasn't doing exposition, either, or recitative, in the manner of imitation Menotti. The tune was not a wail, the phrase was neither broken nor heartbroken. He was really getting ready for an impishly transplanted parody of all those hometown songs that used to keep people steadily moving into the big cities (here, it was called "Dear Old Syracuse") and he was being blunt, brassy, and right on beat about it:

> This is a terrible city,
> The people are cattle and swine,
> There isn't a girl I'd call pretty
> Nor a friend that I'd call mine. . . .

If your ear just happened to be pleased by the conversational suddenness of "a girl I'd call pretty," you were going to be pleased again later, even in the ballads, where the mockery was kept—oh, three or four millimeters away:

> It rained the day before we met,
> Then came three days that I forget. . . .

And if the jubilantly composed performers in the off-Broadway revival all seemed to be taking a special, most precise delight in making certain that you heard each pleasant, pointedly spaced word, it was no doubt because the lyricist's attitude of mind—cool but secretly confiding, ironic in the presence of poetry but not unaware that the poetry was there—was a comfort to them, too. The women of the house, busy at their sewing because their men gave them nothing else to be busy about, seemed truly content so long as they could sing:

> I weave with brightly colored strings
> To keep my mind off other things,
> So, ladies, let your fingers dance
> And keep your hands out of romance.
> Lovely witches, let the stitches
> Keep your fingers under control.
> Cut the thread, but
> Leave the whole heart whole.

The lyrics that were still so effortless in Ephesus were, of course, Larry Hart's, and Mr. Hart has been sufficiently praised since he left us. One of the troubles with posthumous praise, though, is that it tends to assume that the kind of thing a man did died with him and can never be recaptured, dare never be tried again. I think somebody should try. They might not get the hang of it right off, and people might say that though the lyrics were in Larry Hart's vein they weren't as good as Larry Hart's, but how about if they came out *half* as good? I mean half as crisp, half as witty in stealing a note from what ought to be the next line. I'd settle.

No need here to dwell on Richard Rodgers, either, the Richard Rodgers who is so adaptable that, after having buttoned his tunes so snugly to Mr. Hart's fit, he was able to unbutton them without thrashing and write just as good music for an altogether different kind of lyricist. When I say "just as good music," I hear a wrinkling of noses. Surely, everyone will say, "better" is the word for what came out of *Oklahoma!* and *Carousel* and *South Pacific*. And perhaps it is. But I'm not going to commit myself. I don't know that anyone has written more melodic surprise into what was meant to be a conventional musical-comedy than Mr. Rodgers did for *The Boys from Syracuse*, and to hear the unexpected modulations of "The Shortest Day of the Year" or "You Have Cast Your Shadow on the Sea" is, today as twenty-five years ago, a shocker. Mr. Rodgers never did live along Tin Pan Alley; he was lost at sea as a boy and, when rescued, kept hearing inappropriate sounds. They remain inappropriately perfect. I've decided that I never *will* expect the modulations in "The Shortest Day of the Year," and I'm not going to try.

But what I started out to say was that *The Boys From Syracuse* is, as everyone has always known, based on a play, on two plays, perhaps on three or four plays. Its plot is borrowed, with due credit and a certain pride of race, from Shakespeare's *The Comedy of Errors*, which was borrowed from the *Menaechmi* of Plautus, which in turn may have been borrowed from a couple of oldies by Menander. And it does make hash of my earlier, querulous remarks.

It may not seem quite as sober and plodding and sentimental and earnest as so many of the musicals we now borrow from Loew's, Inc., or from *The Best Plays of 1947*. It may even seem somewhat slapdash, cocky, improvised, and unrestrained. But we must mind our manners and remember our sources with respect. A play is a play is a play, and a play by Shakespeare is a play like anything. I am using the phrase "like anything" in the sense in which Gertrude Stein used it:

> I am Rose, and when I, sing
> I am Rose like anything.

Perhaps it is too bad that Miss Stein did not devote more of her time to the musical theater. Anyway, the situation now calls for an apology, and a revised attitude, on my part, and I do oblige. I wish to revise my earlier statement and say that it is perfectly all right for musicals to borrow their stories from plays that are between four hundred and three thousand years old.

The Night the Dancing Stopped

Oklahoma! is now more than twenty-five years old. That's strange. Most of our new musicals are still children of *Oklahoma!* and most of our new musicals look fifty.

Something's backwards here. Since when do the sprigs feel older than the grandfather oak? Why should the second generation get the backache? Oh, we all know about impulses running dry, and styles going stale, and composers who don't happen to turn up when you need them. That would account for imitativeness. But that doesn't account for the ague.

And this is the time of the ague, the time in which musicals can scarcely bring themselves off the drawing board, scarcely drag themselves in from out of town, scarcely survive the rude winter of Broadway when they do come. Snail-slow and gasping, they shuffle through the city, obviously elderly but without old-age insurance, newborn and born tired. Indeed a recent venture which lasted exactly one night in New York and was clearly intended to mine the *Oklahoma!* tradition had a stroke right on stage.

It wasn't the show that had the stroke, to be sure. It was an actor named Paul Rogers, stumping about the woodland stage on a handy crooked cane, pursuing a plot based on John Steinbeck's *East of Eden* as fast as his failing legs could carry him. Mr. Rogers was, at the time, either fretting about carloads of frozen lettuce that might never reach their destination, or about how many soldier boys would be lost in World War I, or about his own wild son Caleb who had probably gone where the whores are. Whatever pressure may have been uppermost in his weary mind, there was a sudden tremor, a startling slackness in his good right hand, and then the cane he was leaning on slipped out of control. Face ashen, he cried out, "What's happening to me?" And I thought on the spot it might have been *Oklahoma!* crying out.

For the last thing *Oklahoma!* would ever recognize is the revolution it began, or the backache it's come to. We do still date our current musical-comedy form from the arrival of that Rodgers-Hammerstein-Mamoulian-de Mille inspiration, from the sunny surprising night the book made sense, the songs fitted in, the dances expressed emotional states instead of Rockette mathematics, and Pore Jud in the smokehouse began to worry about being Daid. *Oklahoma!* was based on a substantial play, it had real characters, it developed its story logically, it had a flash of menace instead of comedy routines, it held its head high as an elephant's eye over all that had been corn before. It had a coherent structure. It could be taken seriously. And now we are so burdened with substance and shackled to seriousness that we groan as we move, prematurely gray.

I don't think we can quite understand what's happened—or at least one important thing that's happened—unless we look back at *Oklahoma!* itself. Look at the show as it was, not at the smash it turned out to be. *Oklahoma!* ballooned very rapidly. From a modest opening, and what might be called friendly reviews, it expanded in no time at all into the success of the century, not only the hottest ticket in town but the biggest deal. Its success determined its proportions in our mind's eye; thinking back, trying hard to remember, we're still conditioned by our own excitement. That wonderful show we finally got into had the size of the Hippodrome and the impact of a howitzer, didn't it?

No, of course it didn't. Nothing like it. The one thing we should never let ourselves forget about *Oklahoma!* is that it was an extraordinarily simple evening in the theater. That was its impact. The curtain went up on a wide-open backdrop and a fellow came in and leaned on a fence and after a while started to sing a song. He stayed there until he'd finished it, while a lady churning butter rocked in a rocking chair and listened to him. A girl who couldn't say no walked over toward the side of a shanty—left stage, slightly up, not very near the audience at all—and went right through her song without budging an inch. I suppose something busy did happen. A buggy was pushed out on stage and various cowhands who had no work to do sang fondly about its decor, beginning at a whisper.

Oklahoma! had a plot. It had to do with whether a boy would succeed in taking a girl to a picnic lunch. At the end of the first half this great issue was still unresolved, so unresolved that its emotional implications had to be danced out at great length in what remains the most exhilarating dancing—and, for that matter, the sexiest—ever devised for the American musical-comedy stage. Girl and boy did manage to settle things up between them by eleven o'clock.

If *Oklahoma!* was a straw in the wind, it was light as a straw. The wind lifted it into the air nightly. No canes, no arthritis, no crawling off to bed for a death scene. The show could lift because it had freedom, and it had freedom because it was simple. The plot left room to breathe. Room for the choreographer to invent and play and skip and not fuss about mighty issues, room for the composer to say what a nice day it was, room for the designer to splash paint—very sunny paint—over an uncrowded sky. The horizon was open. Not the Oklahoma horizon, the musical-comedy horizon. The so-called "substantial" story was no more than a couple of telephone poles leaning lazily in the distance. And, with so little hard work to do, a show could get on with its natural, buoyant business of exploring melody and movement, raising its face to the breeze. What was there to stop it, or cramp its joints?

But, next year, then the year after that, the problem. How do you top *Oklahoma!?* You can get a bigger success only by building up a bigger show. Bigger in what way? Not musically, for heaven's sake: you can't hope to have more songs, or better songs, than *Oklahoma!* had. Not choreographically, either: within a year or two everyone was saying there was too much dancing around, and by the time Rodgers and Hammerstein got to *South Pacific* they'd dropped the dancing altogether. But if you can't expand on song or dance, and you still want to be bigger than ever before, there's only one place to go: to more and more Story with more and more Substance.

The reach was upward, toward the library shelf, and after a while nothing but a Modern Library Giant would do. Slender volumes were obviously lightweight: no significant advance there. What everyone was really after was *Gone With the Wind*, and if that wasn't available then *How Green Was My Valley* would have to make do. Rodgers and Hammerstein themselves escalated quickly: *Carousel* was bigger than *Oklahoma!* and *South Pacific* was bigger than both of them. For a while the inflation was exhilarating: the steam was still up, the extended arm confident, the bubble of melody uncompromised.

But all the time there was an obstruction in the making. Like the ever-swelling corpse of Ionesco's *Amédée,* one musical-comedy ingredient was overwhelming the house, filling up all the living spaces. Multiplot was pushing its way into every nook and cranny, and doing more than eat away dance time. If, for instance, an actor has to sing "The times were restless then, You'd work a place awhile and then hop a train," he has clearly stopped thinking about what a beautiful morning it is and begun punching a time clock. The necessary narrative is getting rammed into the lyrics, all right; but the lyrics are no longer very lyrical.

Melody is robbed, too, surreptitiously. If the source material is so complex that a good actor must be hired to act it out, that actor probably won't sing as well as a singer. A composer may still write melodically; but he may never hear what he wrote.

With dance, lyrics, and melody all backed breathless against the wall, center stage is promptly choked with double-decked scenery: there must be three or four flights of windows for the subplots to look out of. *War and Peace* is a pretty busy novel; we may be ready for it.

If we weren't ready for *East of Eden* when it came (under the new title of *Here's Where I Belong*), the evening was still, for us, a typical failure. Its long arm went out to span the histories of a defeated father (now on the rise, now on the downgrade, then rise and downgrade all over again), a mother who'd wandered off seventeen years earlier ("You couldn't keep away, could you?" she said to her husband when he knocked on her door for the first time in seventeen years), a wild son, a bookish son, World War I, the development of refrigeration in the Salinas Valley, the morals of profiteering, the horrors of prostitution, a double love story and a father-son relationship complex enough to have gobbled up *I Never Sang for My Father* for breakfast. Small wonder that father Paul Rogers—a sturdy actor and sort-of-singing member of the Royal Shakespeare Company—began to feel poorly rather early in Act Two. It would have been less work playing *Macbeth*.

Miraculously, choreographer Tony Mordente did manage to make space for one sinuously staged dance. But do you know *what* was being danced? The problem of getting crates of lettuce into boxcars before the lettuce wilted.

All powers wilt under the burdens we assume in the interests of ever richer substance. Yet that isn't the sort of substance *Oklahoma!* first invited us to toy with. Nor, if anyone cares to count, is it the sort of substance the most resoundingly successful musicals since *Oklahoma!* have staked their lives on. *Guys and Dolls* was a short story, *Hello, Dolly!* a lovely, spindly farce. *How to Succeed* was a joke, *The Music Man* took up the staggering problem of whether the children of River City would ever learn to play musical instruments, and *My Fair Lady* was about teaching a girl to pronounce words. A few of the smashes have been massive, yes: *South Pacific*, *West Side Story*. Most have found something to sing about in relative lightness and slightness; they were girls of slender means.

If there's a handy rule to be concocted here, it might be this: when materials must be contracted into music, they're probably going to crowd the music, maybe cramp it; when they can be expanded into music, the dance is on.

Sobriety in Venice

Everyone who has ever been to Venice knows that no matter when you arrive you have always just missed the concert in the courtyard of the Doge's Palace. It took place last night, while you were packing your bags somewhere else. Now you can go watch the bandstand being dismantled and the chairs stacked away, wondering wistfully just what it was you were late for.

That happened to Leona Samish, the doomed-to-be-frustrated heroine of *Do I Hear a Waltz?*, and it may have been the truest thing that did happen in a musical determined to be true. True to itself, that is—rigid in its adherence to the Spartan outlines of Arthur Laurents's source play, *The Time of the Cuckoo*, firm in its resistance to all the ordinary bland-ishments of color, dance, and massed choral voices with which most musicals struggle to make themselves ample and merry and by means of which some musicals betray themselves. There was to be no betrayal here. Mr. Laurents meant to look head on at the unlovely inhibitions Americans of Puritan stock take with them when they go abroad and he intended to sentimentalize nothing. Leona was going to miss more than the band concert. She was going to miss going to Harry's Bar because no one really wanted her along. Attractive as she was, there was something clammy about her rectitude. She was going to miss having so much as coffee with a shopkeeper who took a fancy to her. She could not conceive of coffee without a long-range commitment first. And she was going to miss whatever pleasure she might have taken in her long-delayed and reluctant surrender to the shopkeeper. Afterwards she would ask so many questions and make so many emotional demands—and she would do these things so publicly—that humiliation awaited her admirer and embarrassment her "friends" at the *pensione*. She would go home a shade wiser, but without much in the way of happiness stored up. Thus the narrative.

The production was wholly commiteed to Mr. Laurents's astringent vision. Even the color blue had been banished from Venice. In a series of very strict washes, designer Beni Montresor had bronzed the lagoons and the latticework, the bridges and domes, until they were uniformly autum-nal, spinster-dry. "Look, they even painted the damn sky!" cried Leona in her first burst of exuberance. But they had painted it the color of her locked-up heart, as a warning.

Choreographer Herbert Ross was not asked to display abandon where there could be none. In his few moments of dance he convinced himself, chastely, to the invitations a few boys extended to the few girls who would link arms with them, or to the reshuffling of couples who weren't certain they were properly mated or ever would be. Richard Rodgers's songs, careful to preserve the quality of fundamental reserve, were offered singly to principals who were forced to keep their distance from one another or to groups of four or five who might wish to compare travel notes. No orchestrated ensemble disturbed the lonely night.

Admirable? In intention, yes. Mr. Rodgers in particular was to be congratulated upon his restiveness, his continued unwillingness to redo the last show that had succeeded, his voluntary surrender of the devices traditionally used to wake customers up—though he may have been plac-ing too great a burden upon his own gift for melody in demanding that it walk alone. Lyricist Stephen Sondheim had here and there given him some pleasantly compressed rhymes, if no very touching ones.

But an intention pursued as severely as this one must be prepared to offer its own compensations. What reward might we look for, with color and dances and the hurly-burly gone? Why, the rewards of seriousness, I suppose: character complexity, emotional involvement of however disturbing a kind, weight, wisdom, a piercing of once-showy surfaces.

Mr. Laurents could not or did not give us these things. His libretto, necessarily no doubt, was thinner again than the play on which it had been based. Leona and her tourist acquaintances had to be sketched in swiftly if there was to be time left for songs. Sketchiness, however, was very hard upon all of them. Because they were frigid or frustrated or otherwise dissatisfied people—causing the Italians they met to become distressed or disgruntled people—economy of line made them come out all the colder. We felt very little for figures whose inadequacies were reduced to flat statements, whose obtuse and fumbling gestures were recorded in two dimensions. When the Italian shopkeeper announced to Leona that he was sufficiently drawn to her to entertain the thought of an affair, we didn't feel that we had been caught up in an intricate contest between temperaments and cultures; we only felt that a standard musical-comedy leading man was being oddly blunt about matters. We hadn't noticed, while he was singing a song in praise of Venetian glass, that he was that much attracted to Leona. And when Leona was making so much fuss about whether she would or wouldn't accept a first casual invitation to coffee, she did not seem unduly virginal; she seemed merely to have a thing about coffee.

The problem of the straight-faced musical and its "purity" of execution went deeper still in this instance. For, after having shorn away from the surrounding production every last trace of gaudiness, Mr. Laurents had not kept his own sober text "pure." In a pinch, he was as ready to write sentimentally as the next man. "You make many jokes," the shopkeeper said to the flustered girl who was evading him, "but—inside—I think you cry." That is a line that would normally be accompanied by a throb of violins from the pit, if not a flight of choral voices from the wings. To attend to it seriously, and without its usual blanket of appurtenances, was like listening to *Blossom Time* raw. The narrative was newly sober and ascetic; but the lines were often like last week's, or last year's.

Nor in his dismissal of the kind of open comedy that helps most musicals become infectious had Mr. Laurents been consistent. Trying to persuade Leona to come lie with him, the shopkeeper reminded her that "Your friends would have done the same things in Kansas City." "Not in a gondola," she quipped. The quip may perhaps have been offered as one more example of Leona's foolish evasiveness; it came out as a routine musical-comedy snapback, and a lame one. The texture of the language was decidedly variable, and it was often at variance with the analytical earnestness of the master plan.

In the end, there was only one conclusion to be reached: if a musical is going to be as serious as *Do I Hear a Waltz?* it has got to be more serious than *Do I Hear a Waltz?*—still richer in its insights, still more uncompromising in its way with words. Conceivably this applies to the score as well. The songs here were musical-comedy songs, generally of a high order. But will musical-comedy songs carry the evening when the evening isn't a musical comedy? The materials in this instance might have been abrasive even for light opera—certainly they did not seem to suggest such treatment.

What, then? I don't know the answer, short of intimate opera itself. But there is a great yearning in the playhouse for the entertainment to turn one way or another, to dress itself more charmingly or to stir up a stronger fire. Half measures taken toward sobriety tend to leave us all halfhearted, torn between an elusive passion on the one hand and a lost playfulness on the other.

The Perils of Producing Rex

Despite his independent artistic achievements, Richard Adler (1921–) remains best known as the co-composer-lyricist, who along with Jerry Ross (1926–1955), created a double-header of hits in the mid-1950s, *The Pajama Game* (1954) and *Damn Yankees* (1955). Twenty years later, he produced a Rodgers musical based on King Henry VIII (*Rex*) that lasted only forty-eight performances. The excerpt below chronicles this failed attempt (see also Mandelbaum's remarks that follow).

With disarming honesty Adler tells his readers what went wrong and what he learned. Perhaps the major mistake in retrospect was the decision not to accept the financial terms of director-choreographer Michael Bennett, who would soon be developing and directing the phenomenally successful *A Chorus Line*. Adler also relates how "collaboration with a legend [Rodgers] had a negative effect upon Sheldon Harnick," the lyricist of *Fiorello!*, *She Loves Me*, and *Fiddler on the Roof*, when he tried to emulate Hammerstein rather than be himself. Another problem was the deleterious offstage behavior of the brilliant Nicol Williamson, who played the title role. As with most failures, "major book problems" proved insurmountable. All things considered, Adler concedes that he should have closed the show in Wilmington. He also realized, "in hindsight, that Elizabeth was *the* fascinating person about whom the musical should have been written in the first place."

RICHARD ADLER

One morning, during the winter of 1975, Eddie Colton, who'd been my attorney on and off since before *The Pajama Game*, called me.

"Dick," he said, "I want to have lunch with you. I have something important I want to discuss with you."

Source: Richard Adler, *You Gotta Have Heart: An Autobiography* (New York: Donald I. Fine, 1990), 266–69.

We had lunch, and partway through, Eddie leaned forward and lowered his voice. "Dick, I'm going to let you in on a little secret," he said. "I think it might be helpful to you, and somebody else as well." He paused. Eddie was given to dramatic pauses. "That somebody is Richard Rodgers. He hasn't anything to do, and he's itching for a project. Do you think you might have something for him?"

Richard Rodgers! He was seventy-two now, and in frail health, but he was one of the remaining giants of the theatre. It was a golden opportunity.

I didn't have to think twice. "I'll have something tomorrow," I told Eddie.

Actually, an idea I'd already begun to research had been in the back of my mind for some time, as a possible project for myself. King Henry VIII was one of the most colorful figures of English history. Alexander Korda had made a wonderful film, *The Private Life of Henry VIII*: Charles Laughton had had an enormous amount of fun with this multifaceted character, who was, I found from my reading, tender, emotional, insanely jealous, ruthless, and gifted. It was he who had supposedly written the song "Greensleeves," and it was he who had definitely written some of the most beautiful love letters ever set to paper.

He was also a son of a bitch and a murderer, and no musical had yet been written with a son of a bitch and a murderer as its central character. But that important piece of knowledge somehow slipped past not only me but all of the people with whom I would become involved, in yet another doomed musical venture.

I was confident in 1974 that I could pull this one off, if I didn't overextend myself. Producing and writing the music and the lyrics had been a backbreaking and perhaps fatal overload in *A Mother's Kisses*.

So I decided to just produce this show, which would also leave me free to begin work on the music and lyrics for another musical that Mr. Abbott proposed to me at the same time, *Music Is*, based upon Shakespeare's *Twelfth Night*.

The next day, I phoned Eddie Colton, and asked him to set up a luncheon meeting with Richard Rodgers, whom I had already met a few times. We discussed the project, and he agreed to write the music, and a lovely friendship began.

For his collaborator, I suggested Sheldon Harnick—the lyricist of *Fiorello!, She Loves Me, Fiddler on the Roof,* and *The Apple Tree.* Sheldon had also contributed to my first Broadway venture, *John Murray Anderson's Almanac* those many years ago. And he was, besides being brilliant, a really likable man. He still is.

For librettists, I picked Jerome Lawrence and Robert E. Lee, who, with *Inherit the Wind*, had proved that they were marvels at bringing history to life onstage. But that would be a non-productive choice. They were fine in the context of straight plays, but at sea in a musical. Sherman Yellen, who'd worked with Sheldon on the unsuccessful but well-conceived historical musical *The Rothschilds*, replaced them.

That fall I'd met Roger Berlind, an investment banker who'd been ripped to pieces by a shattering personal tragedy from which he was trying to recover. He'd gone to La Guardia Airport to meet his wife and two daughters, who were flying in from a vacation. As the plane approached the runway, it was hit by wind shear, and went down, exploding on impact. Everyone aboard was killed instantly.

Roger had told me that, as an undergraduate at Princeton, he'd been involved in the Triangle Club productions. So, I proposed, as therapy, that he come in as co-producer, with financial wizard Ed Downe. He accepted the offer, and he's been producing successes on Broadway ever since.

Next, I went to the Shuberts, to ask them to invest in *Rex*, as the show was now called. We'd already received $100,000 from RCA, who would record the cast album. The Shuberts were willing to invest $150,000 and bring it into a Shubert theatre, *if* I could get Michael Bennett to direct it.

I tried. But his price was far too steep. I tried Hal Prince, but he was committed to Steve Sondheim's *Pacific Overtures*, and Jerry Robbins, who'd retired from Broadway and gone back to ballet. I made the rounds of other directors with solid experience in staging musicals, and they were all unavailable. So, I finally hired Ed Sherin, who had little musical experience, but who'd staged *The Great White Hope*, which had the same kaleidoscopic qualities we saw for *Rex*.

The decision cost me $150,000 of backing and a Shubert theatre, and, I think, the good will of the Shuberts. It was a considered decision that had to be made, and it turned out to be a costly one. In retrospect, I now see that I made a big mistake in not hiring Michael Bennett—at *any* price.

For a star, I had only one actor in mind: Nicol Williamson. I was told that he sang very well, and I'd seen him do several roles, including a smashing *Uncle Vanya*, under Mike Nichols's direction that year. For my money, he was one of the greatest actors in the world, and I was determined to cast him in the show.

I discovered that he was presently living near Stratford, right next to a castle that had once been occupied by none other than Henry VIII. Perhaps serendipity was on my side, I thought as I flew to London, rented a car, and drove out to Stratford, to keep a luncheon invitation offered to me by Williamson and his wife.

The home was a comfortable, British country retreat. I was let in by a butler and shown to the study, which had a full view of a sumptuous staircase. Five minutes passed, and there was a stirring at the top of the stairs. I looked up, and there, descending the staircase, was Henry VIII— redheaded, virile, reining in regal energy and fire. It was as if the character I'd envisioned had suddenly, precisely come to life.

We had a convivial, relaxed lunch. Nicol and his wife couldn't have been more charming. And to make it all perfect, as dessert neared, they both launched into melody, singing the songs from *Kwamina*.

Before I left, he'd agreed to do the part.

He was magnificent as Henry; few could have done it better.

But, unfortunately for us, and unknown to me at the time, he was a load of trouble—incredible antics fueled by copious amounts of wine mixed with brandy. It made for tumultuous times, in rehearsal, on the road, and in New York.

Rex's problems, however, didn't all originate or center upon Nicol Williamson's sometimes bizarre behavior. It was a show with a load of trouble, right from the start. If I'd had the same clear vision I'd had with *A Mother's Kisses*, I might have closed it in Wilmington, where we opened. But I reasoned that the show was in the hands of true professionals, with a freight train load of experience among them. I hoped we could pull it out.

Ned Sherin's direction was solid; Dania Krupska's dances were appealing, and the genius of Dick Rodgers, while not at its peak, was still in plentiful evidence. He wrote incessantly and easily. If a song didn't work, he wrote another one, without complaint. If that didn't work, he wrote another.

But unfortunately, collaboration with a legend had a negative effect upon Sheldon Harnick. Sheldon is a genius in his own right, but he was intimidated by Richard Rodgers. "It's a little like collaborating with God," he confessed to me onc night, and when Marilyn Stasio caught up with us in Boston, and interviewed him for a lengthy article in *Cue*, he told her, "I'm consciously trying to avoid flashiness, the cleverness of the intricate rhyme. I'm trying to get more direct, more emotionally naked; to find fresh images to communicate genuine feeling. That's why I respond to Mr. Rodgers's music. It has such feeling."

Sheldon's evaluation was wrong, and Martin Gottlieb [Ed. Gottfried] picked it up in his review in the *Post* when we opened in New York, when he said, that "Sheldon Harnick's lyrics . . . don't sound like Harnick. They sound like Hammerstein."

Still, that in itself wasn't enough to produce a bad show. Back in Wilmington, despite good reviews, it was apparent that we had major book problems. Henry VIII was just too nasty to exist as the central character in a musical. So, he was toned down, and by the time we'd gotten to the Opera House at the Kennedy Center in Washington, he was almost Mister Nice Guy.

Queen Katherine underwent a sea change, too. In fact, the only character that seemed to weather it all was Elizabeth, played beautifully by Penny Fuller. I know now, in hindsight, that Elizabeth was *the* fascinating person about whom the musical should have been written in the first place.

After we opened in Washington, I sent an SOS to Hal Prince in New York. I asked him to come down and see the show. And Hal came, and, as agreed, went back to New York without commenting.

Anatomy of a Flop:
Pipe Dream, *Do I Hear a Waltz?*, *Rex*, and *I Remember Mama*

A lthough today mainly remembered for their rich song legacies rather than as integral dramatic works, remarkably few among Rodgers's twenty-nine staged shows with Hart were unsuccessful in their day. True, not even Irving Berlin's interpolated hit, "Blue Skies," could extend *Betsy* (1926), Florenz Ziegfeld's star vehicle for Belle Baker, beyond thirty-nine performances, and the "castration" musical *Chee-Chee* quickly closed after thirty-one performances in 1928 (see the readings on *Chee-Chee* in Part I). After *Jumbo* (1935), however, which lost money for Billy Rose and Jock Whitney, only one of Rodgers and Hart's final ten shows, *Higher and Higher*, was less than a critical and financial winner.

Even taking into account relatively disappointing runs for their "original" musicals, *Allegro* and *Me and Juliet*, Rodgers and Hammerstein musicals had an even higher batting average. In fact, only one show with Hammerstein, *Pipe Dream*, an adaptation of John Steinbeck's *Sweet Thursday*, lost money and is usually regarded, including by the composer, as a lesser effort artistically. After Hammerstein's death Rodgers would enjoy one hit with himself as lyricist, *No Strings*, before enduring a "missed opportunity" with Stephen Sondheim, *Do I Hear a Waltz?*, and a modest commercial success aided by the star power of Danny Kaye, *Two By Two*. Sadly, Rodgers closed his long and brilliant career with two commercial and critical failures, *Rex* and *I Remember Mama*.

Ken Mandelbaum offers a thoughtful assessment of the reasons behind Rodgers's uncharacteristic flops from *Pipe Dream* to *I Remember Mama*. In each case he asks the telling questions that address fundamental problems such as, RE: *Rex*, "How does one make sympathetic a man like Henry VIII who kills his wives because they give birth to daughters rather than sons?" In contrast to many theater historians and critics who dismiss much of Rodgers's work after *No Strings*, including *Do I Hear a Waltz?*, in only once instance, *I Remember Mama*, does Mandelbaum blame the *music* for the failure of a Rodgers show. In fact, he characterizes the score of *Pipe Dream* as "generally fascinating," *Rex* as "very attractive," and *Do I Hear a Waltz?* as "excellent, with Rodgers in generally fine form and Sondheim in altogether superb form."

KEN MANDELBAUM

By the 1950s, Richard Rodgers and his partner, Oscar Hammerstein II, had not only revolutionized musical theatre in terms of the integration of book, score, and dance but had also created expectations for each new project they announced that were not easy to live up to. If the controversial *Allegro* (1947) and the disappointing *Me and Juliet* (1953) were not as universally satisfying as *Oklahoma!*, *Carousel, South Pacific,* and *The King and I,* Rodgers and Hammerstein had never had a show that didn't run over three hundred performances, show a profit, and tour after Broadway. Not until 1955, that is, and **Pipe Dream** (Shubert, November 30, 1955, 246 [performances]).

It began when Feuer and Martin purchased the musical rights to John Steinbeck's 1945 novel, *Cannery Row,* and asked Steinbeck to write the book, Frank Loesser to write the score, and Henry Fonda and Julie Andrews to star. As Steinbeck struggled with the libretto, he worked on a new novel, eventually called *Sweet Thursday,* using the same characters and setting as *Cannery Row.* Changing their minds, Feuer and Martin decided to use the new book as the basis for their musical, but after a year, they turned the whole thing over to Rodgers and Hammerstein, who had decided to adapt *Sweet Thursday* and produce the show themselves. Rodgers and Hammerstein supplied the entire $250,000 cost, and Feuer and Martin were promised twenty percent of the ultimately nonexistent profits. Russell Nype and then David Wayne were announced for the role of Doc, who experiments in his biological lab in Monterey, California, without benefit of an MD certificate, but the part went to William Johnson, playing Alfred Drake's *Kismet* role on Broadway at the time of his hiring. For the part of the tough, insecure drifter, Suzy, to whom Doc is drawn, Rodgers and Hammerstein chose Judy Tyler, best known as Princess Summer-Fall-Winter-Spring on the "Howdy Doody" television show. And as Metropolitan Opera star Ezio Pinza had done wonders for *South Pacific,* Rodgers & Hammerstein hired Helen Traubel, the Wagnerian diva who had left the Met for television, films, and nightclubs, to play Fauna, the owner of the local bordello. Harold Clurman, who had never staged a musical before, took on the direction. While working on *Pipe Dream,* Rodgers was operated on for cancer, and he was still in discomfort throughout the tryout and Broadway run.

The reviews in Boston were favorable if subdued. Two songs, "The Happiest House on the Block" and "How Long?," were written on the road. When Clurman faltered, Hammerstein stepped in, and Joshua Logan did some doctoring as well. *Pipe Dream* arrived in New York with the largest advance sale in Broadway history, $1.2 million. Perhaps indicating some doubts about their new show, Rodgers and Hammerstein

Source: Ken Mandelbaum, *Not Since Carrie: 40 Years of Broadway Musical Flops* (New York: St. Martin's Press, 1991), 96–104, 254–56.

had lifted their ban, in effect since 1946, on theatre parties, and *Pipe Dream* opened with more than seventy performances sold to groups. The New York critics were more divided than those in Boston, with Brooks Atkinson in the *Times* and two others moderately favorable, and Walter Kerr in the *Herald Tribune* and three others negative. Steinbeck predicted the show would become one of Rodgers and Hammerstein's "two-year flops," and the show underwent revision in late March, with several numbers shifted. Traubel missed a number of shows and withdrew when her contract expired three weeks before the show closed (she was succeeded by Nancy Andrews). *Pipe Dream* was nominated for the Best Musical Tony (it lost to the only other nominee, *Damn Yankees*) and eight other Tonys. But its run was the shortest of any Rodgers and Hammerstein show, it sustained a small loss on its investment, and there was no post-Broadway tour. An announcement that *Pipe Dream* would go into the Drury Lane Theatre in London (where *Oklahoma!*, *Carousel*, *South Pacific*, and *The King and I* had played) in the fall appeared to be wishful thinking. Two strange postscripts to the *Pipe Dream* saga: within a year of its closing, William Johnson died of a heart attack, and Judy Tyler was killed in an automobile accident, and many years later, a film version was proposed, then shelved—it was to have starred the Muppets.

Pipe Dream contains a generally fascinating score. There's a gorgeous ballad of yearning for Suzy, "Everybody's Got a Home but Me"; Doc's opening statement of the show's theme, "All Kinds of People"; the flat-out hit ballad "All at Once You Love Her"; a rueful duet for the no-longer-dewy-eyed lovers, "The Next Time It Happens"; the unconventionally structured "Suzy Is a Good Thing," "A Lopsided Bus," and "Bum's Opera"; and other good songs like "The Man I Used to Be" for Doc and "Sweet Thursday" for Fauna.

The show's problem was clearly not its score. So what were the problems? First, there was the matter of audience expectation. *Pipe Dream* was a quiet, relatively uneventful show by a team from which the public had come to expect the serious, the monumental, the deeply moving. Then, there was the question of sex: Steinbeck believed that one of the show's problems was that the character of Suzy was cleaned up and no longer specifically a prostitute before her arrival on Cannery Row and at Fauna's Bear Flag Cafe. Rodgers and Hammerstein may have been uncomfortable with handling sex openly; it's never made clear whether Suzy is a hooker or not, and the other denizens of the neighborhood have also been sanitized. For once in their careers, the celebrated team may have been playing it safe.

But the biggest problem with the show was not the character of Suzy, or even Traubel, whom many, including Rodgers, blamed for its failure. Rodgers and Hammerstein were aware that the characters of this story were unlike those they had dealt with in their recent shows. In a Sunday advance piece they wrote for the *Herald Tribune*, they said of the show's characters: "They stimulate us because we haven't met them before in our work. Their problems are simple. . . . We find pleasure that their worries, this time, are not concerned with the future of a kingdom or with miscegenation. . . . Just like other beasts, we need desperately to have change in our lives." But the team was best when they had something to say, as in *The King and I, South Pacific*, and *Carousel*, except for the idea that "It takes all kinds of people to make up a world," *Pipe Dream* had little substance. While the characters had charm, they were never especially interesting, and the story was devoid of conflict and suspense. Layabouts—people who don't really do anything—are not the stuff of drama, it would seem. *Pipe Dream*'s failure can be attributed to the choice of material itself compounded by an overly tasteful treatment of potentially raffish characters.

After Hammerstein's death, Rodgers wrote the music for five more Broadway musicals. One, with his own lyrics, was a distinctive success (*No Strings*), one ran mainly because of its star (*Two by Two*), and the other three were flops. The most inexplicable was **Rex** (Lunt-Fontanne, April 25, 1976, 49 [performances]), which was coproducer Richard Adler's idea. The book originally to have been by Jerome Lawrence and Robert E. Lee, was instead written by Sherman Yellen, who wrote a much better one for the earlier *The Rothschilds*. For his lyricist, Rodgers chose one of the best, Sheldon Harnick. Edwin Sherin, whose principal musical-theatre credit was being fired from *Seesaw*, was hired to direct. Tempestuous British actor Nicol Williamson was cast as Henry VIII, Penny Fuller was to play both Anne Boleyn and Anne's daughter, Elizabeth, and an as yet unknown Glenn Close was chosen for Princess Mary.

During the show's second tryout engagement in Boston, Harold Prince, who had produced Adler's two hit musicals, *The Pajama Game* and *Damn Yankees*, and four of Harnick's shows, agreed to take over the direction, although Sherin stayed on and Prince was not credited. *Rex* opened to a unanimously negative New York press, and its run of six weeks was the shortest of Rodgers's career. *Rex* was momentarily awakened on May 13 when during curtain calls, Williamson—who had not endeared himself to either the cast or the creative team—slapped dancer Jim Litten in front of a shocked audience. Litten had said, "That's a wrap" during the bows, but Williamson seems to have heard it as "That was crap."

Rex raised a question that was never answered: what made Adler, Rodgers, and Harnick think Henry VIII a good subject for a musical? While Henry was indeed a fascinating figure, how does one make sympathetic a man who kills his wives because they give birth to daughters rather than sons? Henry's reason for insisting on a son for the throne (a woman there would provoke chaos and civil war) was not made believable, and his sexism was particularly unpleasant for a seventies audience well into the women's movement. While the material would have benefited from a darker treatment than it received, it is doubtful that it could ever have worked: Henry, who by that time had been amply covered on stage, screen, and public television, should have been left alone.

Rex had other problems in addition to its fundamental one. First, it was of necessity episodic: one wife replaced another—Henry went through two during the intermission—and there was no way to develop each one. Second, the book was literate but heavy, the only humor being the unfunny bawdy jokes given to the court jester. And third, it only caught dramatic fire in the second-act confrontation between Henry and Elizabeth.

Again, Rodgers provided very attractive music. "No Song More Pleasing" (the last of many great Rodgers waltzes) and "Elizabeth" for court minstrel Smeton, "Away from You" for Henry, "As Once I Loved You" for Catherine, and "Time" for Elizabeth were all strong, with Harnick contributing simpler lyrics than was his wont.

When the disastrous movie-musical *Lost Horizon* was released, Bette Midler told a reporter that she intended to see it anyway, quipping, "I never miss a Liv Ullmann musical." Midler couldn't have known then that six years later the solemn film star would be starring in her very own Broadway musical, a show that would be Rodgers's last. Rodgers and Hammerstein had produced John Van Druten's play *I Remember Mama*, based on stories by Kathryn Forbes, on Broadway in 1944. It told of the Hansens, struggling Norwegian immigrants in San Francisco in the early twentieth century, and in particular of Mama—who pretends to her children that she has a bank account to give them a sense of security—and her eldest daughter, Katrin, an aspiring writer. *Mama* worked beautifully on stage, on film in 1946, and as a TV series from 1949 to 1956. In 1956 Rodgers and Hammerstein contemplated turning the play into a musical, to star Charlotte Greenwood and Shirley Jones, but stopped because of the property's recent exposure. (It did become a musical, called *Mama*, at the Studio Arena Theatre in Buffalo in 1972, written by John Clifton and Neal Du Brock and with Celeste Holm in the title role.)

But by 1979, Rodgers, seventy-six and seriously ill, responded when Martin Charnin suggested *I Remember Mama* to him again. By this time, Charnin had had his one big hit, *Annie*, so producer Alexander H. Cohen put *Annie*'s book writer (Thomas Meehan), director-lyricist (Charnin), and set designer (David Mitchell) together with Rodgers and Ullmann, who had worked for Cohen in a revival of *Anna Christie*. It took 323 investors to come up with the necessary $1.25 million, half of which was supplied by Universal Pictures, which had recently dropped $700,000 when the musical *Alice* closed in Philadelphia the year before.

In contrast to *Rex*, **I Remember Mama** (Majestic, May 31, 1979, 108 [performances]) had one of the stormiest tryout/New York preview periods ever. The day after poor reviews appeared in Philadelphia, Charnin was fired; Cy Feuer assumed control within a week. After his dismissal, Charnin sent a telegram to his three Annie companies, stating, "As you may or may not know, artistic differences have been responsible for my stepping aside as director of *I Remember Mama*. Ms. Ullmann and I do not see 'I to I' about how musicals are made. To make a long and ugly story short, there's no longer a fjord in my future." Charnin later added that he was let go because of his desire to replace Ullmann: "Singing frightened her, and she couldn't memorize her lines. . . . It was my idea to ask Liv Ullmann. However, where I had thought of it as an ensemble piece, she thought of it as a vehicle for her." There were also rumors of a romance between Ullmann and Charnin.

Many musical-theatre fans are capable of coming up with the first six names in the answer to the trivia question, "Who were Richard Rodgers's seven lyricists?": Lorenz Hart, Oscar Hammerstein II, Rodgers himself, Stephen Sondheim, Martin Charnin, and Sheldon Harnick. They may be pardoned for stumbling over the last name: Raymond Jessel. As Charnin was fired as director, he was obviously not going to be around to write new lyrics, so Jessel, whose only other credit was producer Cohen's earlier musical *Baker Street*, was brought in to write the lyrics for five new songs. In Philadelphia, there were two Katrin[e]s: an older one looking back and narrating (Kate Dezina) and a younger one appearing in the scenes (Kristin Vigard). Dezina was dismissed, the two roles were combined for Maureen Silliman, and a new part was created for Vigard. Justine Johnston, who was playing authoress Florence Dana Moorhead, was replaced by Myvanwy Jenn, now playing authoress Dame Sybil Fitzgibbons.

The Shuberts pushed Michael Bennett's *Ballroom* to an early death to bring the ailing *I Remember Mama* into the Majestic Theatre. The show played forty previews, postponing its opening twice. In New York, Graciela Daniele was succeeded as choreographer by Danny Daniels, one more child was replaced, the role of Mama's boarder, Mr. Hyde, was cut, and more songs came and went. *Mama* opened to only one good review (Clive Barnes in the *New York Post*) but stayed open, at a loss, until Labor Day. Although the show's postponements had rendered it ineligible for the 1979 Tony Awards, Cohen, then producer of the Tony telecast, managed to get a number from *Mama* on the show by presenting Rodgers with a special award. An unintentionally comic television commercial, in which Ullmann told viewers that as a child in Norway she had fallen in love with the music of Rodgers and was now fulfilling her dream of singing his music on Broadway, ran frequently. When Charnin suffered a severe heart attack in June and attributed it to his *Mama* firing, Ullmann fired back with, "I hope that Martin Charnin will start doing something more constructive than blaming his failures and illnesses on other people." The show lost $1.5 million and was not recorded until five years later, with only George Hearn and George S. Irving of the original cast appearing on the album.

The idea of a musical *Mama* seemed like a sound one, but a closer examination of the original play proves otherwise. The play was episodic, with several plots but no overall dramatic through-line. In order to provide one, Meehan made the musical's plot hinge on Papa's inability to find work and his decision, at the end of the first act, to leave the family and take up a shipyard job in Norway. A severe mistake, this served to make the kindly father into a villain and slighted the relationship between Mama and Katrin[e], the play's most touching aspect.

Ullmann was also a problem. She had lovely moments but was not fully at ease as a musical leading lady, coming to life only in the "Fair Trade" number with Dame Sybil where mama offers her prized recipes in exchange for the authoress's opinion of Katrin[e]'s stories. *Mama* might have worked better in the sixties with Mary Martin or Inga Swenson heading the cast, and Florence Henderson was briefly considered as a replacement for Ullmann.

Rodgers's score contained only traces of the musical theatre's greatest melodist: best were "A Writer Writes at Night," Papa's expression of love for his wife, "You Couldn't Please Me More," and "When?," the latter cut on the road but restored on the recording and in the acting edition. As Uncle Chris, George S. Irving once again had his usual "I am in a flop" numbers—even the song *about* him was a dud—and David Mitchell's lovely sets were the biggest asset. Rodgers lived only four months after *Mama*'s closing. . . .

In 1958, Arthur Laurents approached Rodgers and Hammerstein about musicalizing his 1952 play *The Time of the Cuckoo*, which had already been made into the 1955 film *Summertime*. The team felt that the play was too recent to musicalize, but Rodgers, seven years later and after Hammerstein's death, became the composer and producer of a musical version of *Cuckoo* called **Do I Hear a Waltz?** (46th Street; March 18, 1965, 220 [performances]), with Laurents writing the libretto and Stephen Sondheim the lyrics. (Sondheim and Laurents had already collaborated on *West Side Story, Gypsy, Invitation to a March*, and *Anyone Can Whistle.*) It was interesting that after writing both music and lyrics for *A Funny Thing Happened on the Way to the Forum*, and *Whistle*, Sondheim was willing to write just lyrics, as he had for his first two Broadway shows. But Sondheim was the protégé of Hammerstein, so it was probably inevitable that he would eventually work with Rodgers— and Laurents and Mary Rodgers talked him into it.

Do I Hear a Waltz? followed Laurents's original play very closely. It was again the story of secretary Leona Samish, in her late thirties, who arrives in Venice and is charmed by antique seller Renato Di Rossi. Leona discovers that Di Rossi is married, and when she sees him taking a commission on the necklace he bought her, she believes he never wanted her, only her money. But the biggest obstacle to the relationship is Leona's own distrustful nature: Di Rossi loses his passion for Leona because of her suspicions, and they bid each other farewell, Leona having perhaps learned not to make the same mistakes again. The only significant changes Laurents made in his original were making the Yeagers, fellow guests at Leona's *pensione*, and their problems more contemporary, and altering the original plot device wherein the currency Di Rossi obtained for Leona turned out to be counterfeit.

The original play took place entirely in the garden of the Pensione Fioria, while the musical also took in Di Rossi's shop and the Piazza San Marco. But the musical had the same number of principals as the original play, adding only a small ensemble for a few numbers. Director John Dexter, then associate director of the National Theatre of Great Britain, who had directed the musical *Half a Sixpence* in London but not on Broadway, conceived *Do I Hear a Waltz?* without dancing, but during the New Haven tryout, Herbert Ross was brought in to add choreography (Ross's production of *Kelly* opened and closed on a Saturday, and he joined *Waltz* that Monday). Florence Henderson and Anne Bancroft were sought to play Leona, but the part went to Elizabeth Allen, with Sergio Franchi opposite her as Di Rossi.

The New York reviews were very mixed, and [as] business fell badly in the summer, the show closed after about seven months. There were Tony nominations for Allen and the score, but *Waltz* was Rodgers's shortest run in over two decades, although shorter ones were to come with *Rex* and *I Remember Mama*.

Do I Hear a Waltz?, because its creators had such a bad time collaborating on it, is now viewed by them as a failure best forgotten. No one seemed to get along: Rodgers was nasty to Sondheim, Laurents refused to listen to Rodgers's suggestions, Allen wouldn't speak to Dexter after he insulted her, etc. Because of all this, those involved may not ever be able to acknowledge that *Waltz* was actually a very well done show. The score was excellent, with Rodgers in generally fine form and Sondheim in altogether superb form. Leona's opening song, "Someone Woke Up," her plaintive reflection alone at a cafe, "Here We Are Again," "Moon in My Window" for the three principal ladies; the final duet for Leona and Di Rossi, "Thank You So Much"; and the title song have never really received the recognition they deserve. Beni Montresor's sets were lovely, and the cast was excellent. Allen and Franchi were extremely good but also problematic: Franchi, a natural actor, was a bit too young, and Allen, while more conventionally attractive than Shirley Booth on stage or Katharine Hepburn on film, actually played the role as written, without the overlay of warmth and vulnerability Booth and Hepburn added. As a result, Leona became less likable, and Allen's honest performance pointed up Leona's unpleasant qualities, which had been somewhat whitewashed by her predecessors in the part. Rodgers tried to persuade Laurents to alter Leona's most unpleasant scene from the original in which she gets drunk and reveals Yeager's infidelity to his wife, but Laurents correctly retained the scene.

Sondheim later maintained that *Cuckoo* should not have been made into a musical as it was about a lady who, metaphorically, couldn't sing (he had already done a musical about a lady who couldn't whistle, however). If *Cuckoo* was not a play that cried out to be musicalized, *Waltz* was an excellent adaptation of the enjoyably sentimental original, nicely staged and performed, and with a score of a very high order. And it didn't make the mistake committed by such straight-play adaptations of the sixties as *Hot September* of blowing up the original with big ensemble numbers in which locals kicked up their heels. The creators of *Waltz* worked with integrity and were careful to keep the show a chamber musical; the result was small-scale but classy and ultraprofessional. *Waltz* is eminently playable and revivable, although it will perhaps always have more appeal to ladies' matinee audiences than to others.

"Overture" to *Richard Rodgers*

William G. Hyland's *Richard Rodgers* is the first major biography of the composer since David Ewen's (introduced in Part III), and the first biography that surveys the last twenty years of Rodgers's long career.* Like earlier biographers, Hyland notes the durability of the songs with Hart and the shows with Hammerstein. He also reinforces such ubiquitous themes as Rodgers's facility, productivity, and inextinguishable passion for the theater. In contrast to earlier biographers, Hyland takes Mary Rodgers's cue (in the reading that follows) in introducing such previously undisclosed topics as Rodgers's depression, a period of excessive drinking, and even "a mental breakdown."**

WILLIAM G. HYLAND

Richard Rodgers was a musical genius. He proved it time and again during his sixty-year career as a composer for the American stage. His first professional song was performed on Broadway when he was only seventeen, his last in a Broadway show six decades later, shortly before he died. In the intervening years he wrote well over a thousand songs and the musical scores for more than forty shows. When he began his career,

---

*The second is Meryle Secrest's *Somewhere for Me: A Biography of Richard Rodgers* (New York: Alfred A. Knopf, 2001).

**Hyland also devotes three chapters to Rodgers in *The Song Is Ended: Songwriters and American Music, 1900–1950* (New York: Oxford University Press, 1995), 64–76, 235–49, and 275–91.

Source: William G. Hyland, *Richard Rodgers* (New Haven and London: Yale University Press, 1998), ix–xii.

he joined the ranks of such luminaries as George Gershwin, Jerome Kern, Vincent Youmans, Sigmund Romberg, Cole Porter, and Irving Berlin. When he wrote his last notes, in 1979, all these colleagues were dead or had retired. He had become an icon—and a relic.

But his career was not just an endurance test. Even if he had retired much earlier, the melodies he wrote to Lorenz Hart's words would earn him a niche in the history of American popular music. By 1942, when their partnership ended, Rodgers and Hart had created a cornucopia of songs that would forever qualify as standards, songs that would be played and enjoyed even into the 1990s.

In Rodgers and Hart's first great hit, "Manhattan," the lyrics proclaimed, "We'll have Manhattan, the Bronx and Staten Island too." And of course they did take Manhattan. Their shows—*A Connecticut Yankee in King Arthur's Court, Simple Simon, Jumbo, On Your Toes, Babes in Arms, The Boys from Syracuse*—were fun, if not so well remembered. But the songs are memorable, though only a few aficionados can recall who sang what in which show or under what circumstances. In *Babes in Arms* the diminutive Mitzi Green—playing a character named Billie who wants to prove that she is one of the gang—introduced "The Lady Is a Tramp." Now the song is better recalled in performances by, say, Frank Sinatra or Lena Horne.

His later shows were a different story. As the partner of Oscar Hammerstein, Richard Rodgers became more than a fine songwriter. R&H, as they became known, created a new art form: the musical play. Not a play with music added, but an integration of music, lyrics, dialogue, characters, and plot in an originally conceived entity. The form began during World War II with *Oklahoma!*

With some obvious exceptions, most Broadway shows, even those created by the great songwriters, have faded. But this has not been true for Rodgers's shows: *Oklahoma!, Carousel, South Pacific,* and *The King and I* are still magical names. They are revived periodically, recorded by each new generation of singers, and seen regularly on television.

It would be romantic if the life story of such a major force in American musical history had been a rags-to-riches tale of a determined young man banging out tunes for Tin Pan Alley on a beat-up old upright piano until he was discovered. Rodgers's life was anything but that. He often said that his career might have prospered earlier if, like Irving Berlin, he had been a singing waiter around Union Square in lower Manhattan.

In fact, Richard Rodgers was born into an affluent Jewish family and grew up in Manhattan. Music came easily to him; both of his parents were musically inclined, and he may well have inherited their talent. His daughters, Mary and Linda, were also talented; Mary continued the tradition of writing for Broadway (*Once Upon a Mattress*), as did his grandson, Adam Guettel (*Floyd Collins*).

Rodgers's music studies were sporadic. His talents were so ingrained— he had a perfect ear for music—that he chafed at instruction, studying only enough to navigate through the theatrical world. As far back as he could remember, he had wanted to write for the theater. Rodgers loved everything about it, from the tumult of out-of-town tryouts to the incandescence of a Broadway opening night.

Richard Rodgers enjoyed three careers. The first was with Lorenz Hart, and the second with Oscar Hammerstein. When Hammerstein died, Richard Rodgers, then in his late fifties, could have retired with numerous laurels. But those who knew him best could not conceive of Richard Rodgers outside the theater. He began his third and final career by writing the lyrics to his own music, to prove that he could do it—and he succeeded. Then he found himself collaborating with a new generation: Stephen Sondheim, Sheldon Harnick, and Martin Charnin. Although his talents were still very much in evidence, he was frequently ill. Nevertheless, at the age of seventy-six he embarked on a new show, *I Remember Mama*. Unfortunately, it was not a success. A few months later, however, just before he died, the lights of Broadway proudly hailed yet another revival of *Oklahoma!*—a fitting coda.

Like many men and women of great creative ability, Rodgers was not easy to understand. In the theater he could be intimidating, but he was also a source of reassurance and stability during the taxing weeks of rehearsals and out-of-town tryouts. He was humorous and quick with a quip. His coworkers respected him but inevitably regarded him with a certain awe. He became extraordinarily successful in his work, enjoyed a privileged life, and shared two Pulitzer Prizes. He was also unhappy and depressed much of the time.

Of modest height, with a trim figure, he was attractive to women. In 1930, Rodgers married the charming Dorothy Feiner. They were married for almost fifty years, even though he was "tough to live with," had a tendency to hypochondria, and for a period drank to excess. In the 1950s he suffered a mental breakdown, and in the next two decades he endured devastating illnesses.

Nothing seemed to affect his creativity, however. He was confident of his abilities and therefore not particularly competitive or envious of the success of his fellow songwriters. Stories of his musical feats—such as writing a hit song in five minutes—grew to the point that he was embarrassed, prompting rather long-winded explanations of how he was able to compose so quickly. His sure touch could even irritate his collaborators, who sometimes worked over lyrics for days and weeks.

Rodgers's monument is the theater on 46th Street in Manhattan that bears his name. A fitting epitaph came from an unusual source. Late in his career Rodgers wrote background music for a television series about the wartime career of Winston Churchill. Perhaps with that great British statesman in mind the essayist and social critic Lionel Trilling said of Richard Rodgers, "Few men have given so much pleasure to so many people."

"Introduction" to *Musical Stages*

Mary Rodgers (1931–) is the composer of the perennially performed musical *Once Upon a Mattress* (1959) and several works of popular fiction designed for younger readers, most notably *Freaky Friday*, both the original 1972 novel and the screenplay to a successful Disney film with Jodie Foster in 1977. At the time of her father's death, his elder daughter informed well-wishers that her personal loss was no greater than theirs, since her father's single-minded devotion to the theater precluded all else, including his presence as a warm and loving daddy.

Introducing the 1995 reprinted edition of *Musical Stages* fifteen years later, Mary Rodgers discusses, perhaps for the first time in print, her father's unhappiness and chemical depression. She also writes of Rodgers's love of collaboration and his successful partnership with two contrasting geniuses, Larry Hart and Oscar Hammerstein. At the end of this touchingly honest remembrance, written, according to Rodgers and Hammerstein Organization President Ted Chapin, after she had rejected his offer to provide an introduction, Mary Rodgers publicly expresses feelings privately denied fifteen years earlier: "Granted, he was hardly your run-of-the-mill father, but *of course* I loved him. A lot. So there!"

MARY RODGERS GUETTEL

My father wrote in our living room with the door wide open. He would request that we, my sister and I, not sing or whistle or otherwise distract him, but aside from that, it was a rather public happening. A morning person, an enviably quick study, and cheerfully businesslike about his work, he'd go to the piano at nine and was usually through by nine-thirty.

There's a kind of marvelous, rich, emotional quality to what my father wrote that didn't often manifest itself in his personality. He could be quite sharp-tongued with my sister and me, and sometimes quite frightening when mad. He could also be very affectionate, but after he finished giving you a squeeze, the implication was, "Now, go do what your mother says and don't bug me."

When he died, I got letters from people saying, "It's terrible for the world to have lost this wonderful man, but how much more terrible for

Source: Mary Rodgers Guettel, "Introduction," in Richard Rodgers, *Musical Stages: An Autobiography* (New York: Random House, 1975; repr. by Da Capo, 1995), vii–ix.

you to have lost your father." It seemed singularly ungracious to write back, "I didn't lose any more than you did, folks, because basically what I loved about him was only what you loved—his music," but in fact, it was true.

When you come right down to it, my father was an extremely complicated man and deeply unhappy much of the time. (Chemically depressed is what we'd call it now; then, we didn't know what to call it, except tough to live with.) He had no hobbies. An occasional game of croquet with my mother and friends—heavy English mallets, elaborate rules, and chess-like strategy—amused him on country weekends. At times he enjoyed going to museums and galleries. But basically, he only wanted to play theatre.

He wasn't interested in writing music in the abstract—the closest he ever came to that were a couple of ballets. He was interested in *stories*—that's what made him want to compose—a good, juicy, romantic, and yes, sentimental story enhanced by good lyrics. Theatre, and theatre only, turned him on and cheered him up—all aspects of it, not just the writing. He loved auditions (pretty girls), rehearsals, and out-of-town tryouts especially.

New Haven, with its miserable Taft Hotel (lumpy beds, lousy room service) and Kasey's (a greasy-spoon theatrical hangout across the street from the Shubert Theatre, where the food was so terrible I got sick once just from eating the pickles) was, to Daddy, a joyful excursion.

Boston, with its serenely elegant Ritz Carlton (perfumed elevators!) and Locke-Ober's for gourmet dining, was a different kind of excursion: four-star bliss instead of "a four-day bellyache."

Then, at last, New York. The final orchestra reading. Opening night. The deliciously agonizing wait for reviews—sometimes great, sometimes not, but hey! it was all part of that grand and glorious adventure called theatre that he loved so much.

After Oscar Hammerstein died, my father wrote one musical with his own lyrics, *No Strings*, which fared well. He evidently didn't like the experience because he never tried it again. He never exactly said why, but he probably found it lonely working with only himself for a sounding board. Collaboration, after all, is the essence of musical theatre; you have to get along with your partner. You *want* to get along with your partner, and when you do, it's a sublime accomplishment. For that brief period when you are co-creating, you enjoy a unique, precious camaraderie you obviously cannot experience alone.

The camaraderie between my father and Larry Hart was unique, too, and God knows productive, but the working relationship was rather less tranquil. Oscar was disciplined, rational, and centered; Larry, that adorable, witty, wistful, sweet, generous (he never arrived on the doorstep without presents for us all), cigar-smoking, booze-consuming, troubled genius was not an easy companion. The best and sometimes the only way to get a lyric out of him was to lock him in a room and play a tune over and over until he came up with the words. Unless the music came first, no song got written; proximity was an obligatory factor.

Not so with Oscar. He and my father collaborated long-distance— from Pennsylvania to New York. Lyrics (which always came first in this partnership) arrived by phone or by mail. But before the actual lyric-writing process began, they met together often and intensively. They would locate the dramatic crest of each scene; that's where the song would go. They established its emotional content, its rhythm, its mood, its intention. They discussed everything you could possibly discuss about that song, short of actually writing it. Then Oscar would go off to his farmhouse in Bucks County, where he had a standing desk in the study, and struggle all morning. Time out for lunch. More struggling in the afternoon. Sometimes for as long as three weeks, until the damn thing was finally finished. Once having received it, my father would sit down at the piano and set it in no time flat; then Oscar would come into town to hear him demonstrate what he'd written. Daddy never sang—he hated singing. He much preferred whistling the tune and playing accompaniment.

Collaboration is also very like a marriage. The way you don't say to your husband, "What's that terrible thing you're wearing!"—you don't say to your partner, "Look, that's a terrible tune/lyric." Oscar, at one point, figured out something brilliant: In "Love, Look Away" from *Flower Drum Song*, the original verse was quite long (and good—I've seen it). Evidently, Oscar didn't think the music was good, or appropriate or whatever, but rather than say, "Hey, Dick, that tune's all wrong," he simply went home and rewrote the verse. It's now only two lines long. As hard as it must have been for him to rethink the whole thing (words being more difficult to write than music), it was easier for Oscar, at least *psychologically*, than to admit he didn't like what he heard—which might have led to a confrontation or awkwardness.

As for how my father handled the situation when he didn't like something of Oscar's, the world will never know. Gently and tactfully, I suppose, because this rich, rare collaboration endured until Oscar's death in 1960. My father never again found a compatible partner although he doggedly continued to grind out musicals (flawed and lack-lustre work, for the most part) until his own death in 1979.

If my father were alive today, I know he'd be pleased and perhaps a little astonished at how popular his music still is. I also know, even at the ripe old age of 91, he would somehow have managed to get himself over to the rehearsals of *Carousel* at Lincoln Center Theater last spring. He would have eased himself into a seat in the tenth row or so, watched the stage with an inscrutable look on his face, delivered a few tersely-worded pronouncements about this tempo and that rhythm—and generally intimidated everyone around him.

But then on opening night, after observing with pride a whole new generation of people laughing and crying at his most favorite musical of all, he would have beamed from ear to ear.

I said earlier, he had no hobbies. I retract that: Theatre was his hobby. And his life.

I also said that what I'd loved about him was no more than what the public had loved—his music. Well, that was fifteen years ago. I retract that now, too. Granted, he was hardly your run-of-the-mill father, but *of course* I loved him. A lot. So there!

New York City
September 1994

IV
The Composer Speaks, 1939–1971

Richard Rodgers (1950)

"How to Write Music in No Easy Lessons:

A Self Interview"

In Rodgers's "Self Interview," the "alleged" composer responds to frequently posed questions, including the inevitable "Which comes first—the words or the music?" As he would for nearly the next forty years, Rodgers emphasizes that he is inspired only by specific dramatic situations and that his usual compositional procedure with Hart was to create the tune or title first. He also explains why he leaves the orchestration of his "complicated" scores to someone else, espouses the importance of making sure that each song in a show "bear[s] a family resemblance to the other material," and praises critics for their eminent fairness and appreciation of novelty, despite their lack of musical knowledge. It is also in this early "self interview" that Rodgers, after briefly describing his historic first meeting, at the age of sixteen, with Hart, then twenty-three, first quipped that he "left Hart's house having acquired in one afternoon a career, a partner, a best friend, and a source of permanent irritation." After this selection appeared in *Theatre Arts*, Rodgers may have felt he had answered enough questions for a while. In any event, readers would not hear much from Rodgers either as a writer or interviewee for more than a decade.

As an alleged composer I am asked certain questions with regularity. It appears that the average person considers musical composition either one of the darkest of the black arts or the result of heaven-sent compulsion. There is never any between ground. Resorting to analogy for answers doesn't help much, but I try it. I say: "Look, you have to write a letter to your Aunt Tessie, a rich old gal who will eventually die. You'd like the letter to be a good one. You have certain equipment at your disposal, such as pen, ink, paper and, most important of all, your knowledge of the language. You're on your own, and the quality of your letter will depend largely on how well you are able to use your equipment. My problem is the same, only related into terms of music. Aunt Tessie is the public or, frequently, my own satisfaction. My equipment consists of paper, pencil, piano, the ability to hum, whistle or sing (horribly) and a knowledge of musical language acquired in the theatres, on the streets and in serious study." I lean back with a glow of self-admiration, having

Source: Richard Rodgers, "How to Write Music in No Easy Lessons: *A Self Interview*," *Theatre Arts* (October 1939), 741–46.

drawn what I consider a pretty clear analogy. Then the next question comes: "But, Mr. Rodgers, where do you get your inspiration?" So I take a drink.

Another time-consumer is, "Which comes first—the words or the music?" The worst part about this query is that it makes sense. It is logical and it demands a logical answer. Actually, there is no set procedure whatsoever. My favorite blight and partner, Mr. Lorenz Hart, often hands me a completed lyric to be set to music. More often I have a tune ready for him to work on, the tune being what it is because it seems to fit a given situation in a musical play and not because the composer was the victim of a rush of hot inspiration, brought on by a beautiful girl or a breath-taking sunset. (I guess you can see I'm pretty sensitive about inspiration.) Sometimes we sit in a room and hate each other until we get a title; then I throw Larry out of the house and fool around until I get a satisfactory melody, inspired entirely by the title and not by nostalgia for Venice in the spring.

"Don't you and Hart ever fight?" And how! Though I must explain that the fighting is all on a theoretical basis. It is difficult to prove this, but in over twenty years of coping with each other we have never had a disagreement over policy or credit or money or, for that matter, any of the things that cause partners to part.

"How did you happen to meet?" That is a bad question because the answer is just what it ought to be. When I was sixteen and still in high school a friend of mine, Phil Leavitt, told me he would like to introduce me to a fellow called Hart. It appeared that this Hart knew something about lyric writing but had no composer. I knew something about composing (Leavitt speaking) but had no lyricist. We ought to get together. On a Sunday afternoon I was taken to Larry's house. Larry came to the door himself, dressed in his Tuxedo trousers, an undershirt and house slippers. He was shy, as he still is, and I don't believe the ice was broken until a disreputable cat ambled into the room. "That's Bridget," said Mr. Hart. "She's an old fence-walker!" He chortled with glee at the joke and rubbed his hands furiously together, a nervous habit of his. There was a sudden crashing "BONG" that lifted me out of my chair. Hart told me not to be frightened. It was his mother's clock and it just did that. Bridget has long since gone to her cat-heaven where fences are brought to her, but that clock still bongs and I still jump.

Well, we sat around and talked theatre and song-writing. I played some tunes for him, about which he was highly agreeable, and he told me his ideas about lyric writing. He was violent on the subject of rhyming in his songs, feeling that the public was capable of understanding better things than the current monosyllabic juxtaposition of "slush" and "mush." It made great good sense and I was enchanted by this little man and his ideas. Neither of us mentioned it, but we evidently knew we'd work together, and I left Hart's house having acquired in one afternoon a career, a partner, a best friend and a source of permanent irritation.

"What do you feel like on opening nights?" That's a cinch. Like death! Larry is more fortunate than I am on these occasions since he is able to work off the nervous tension by walking up and down in back of the audience, cursing softly if a joke fails to get a laugh and rubbing his hands vehemently if a song goes over well. I seem compelled to take it sitting down. I cringe in the last row where I can run to the nearest exit in case of mis-fire. The awful thing about an opening night is that you can't trust anyone or anything to supply you with an accurate indication as to the success or failure of the show. It is madness to listen to people since they are invariably the victims of wish-fulfillment, wanting the piece to be good or bad, depending entirely on their personal attitude toward you. After hearing ultimate failures cheered passionately on an opening night and seeing great successes received with complete coldness you can't even trust the evidence of your own ears. I was badly confused the night *I Married an Angel* opened. I was sure the audience didn't like it and I said so. It took great reviews in the papers and weeks of capacity business to convince me.

"Do tunes come to you in the middle of the night?" NO! No tunes have ever come to me anywhere. I've had to go to them. I've heard about the boys who get swell ideas in taxis, bathtubs and my-baby's-arms, but not me. I have to beat myself into submission by picturing the boy and girl on the stage and imagining what they are singing to the accompaniment of a full orchestra in the pit and a full audience in the house. Then I am ready to start searching for a melody that will conform to a number of arbitrary conditions. To begin with, I write scores and not isolated song numbers; therefore the particular song in question must bear a family resemblance to the other musical material in the piece. However, since changing of pace is almost the first rule of showmanship, I must see to it that this number is in sharp contrast with the one preceding it and the one to follow. These conditioning elements have obviously narrowed the scope of choice, but that is not the end. Who is to sing the song? If our soprano has sound vocal ability she may be given something with range, otherwise it is best to confine the melody to the conventional octave. The size and instrumentation of the orchestra have their bearing, since this is to be a composition for voice and orchestra.

There was a time, in Victor Herbert's day, when scores were orchestrated by their composers. A successful operetta would run for a year or two or three. Thus the composer had time for the laborious business of orchestration. All that has changed. Shows do not run as long, and sheet music stops selling after a few months at best. That means more shows, if a living is to be made, and no time for orchestration. Fortunately there are fine musicians available whose work it is to orchestrate for the theatre, and it is this process which I must bear in mind as I write. With the aid of the piano I can readily hear the orchestra. I make a rather complicated manuscript of the song, indicating orchestral figures, and I confer at length with the orchestrator. All that insures the absence of nasty surprises at the first orchestra rehearsal.

If all these problems appear to be obstacles, let me assure you that that is not the case. They are a definite aid in the sense that they provide sign-posts, speed-indicators, warnings and helpful hints along the otherwise nebulous road of composition. They also must make it obvious why "tunes do not come to you in the middle of the night." As for my sparkling collaborator, not once in all these years has he called me on the phone to say, "Hey, I got a great idea for a song!," so I guess it goes for him too.

"Do you think the critics are fair?" Eminently so. I do think, however, that many of them approach a new musical comedy with certain handi-caps. Most of them fall into the "I don't know anything about music but I know what I like" category. It's true that the majority of the audience also belongs in that class but, considering the fact that music is less capa-ble of appreciation on first hearing, it would be helpful if the boys had a somewhat sharper musical perception which would enable them to tell the public what to expect from a score. On the other hand the critics are enormously appreciative of novelty, whether in a scenic device or a little twist in a lyric. The obvious value of this attitude is that by encouraging the writer to experiment it prevents the theatre becoming a static and inevitably moribund medium.

"Do you get a kick out of hearing your songs played?" Only a liar would say he didn't. There are few experiences so soothing to the ego as that of turning on a radio and hearing something you've written come jumping out at you. This pleasure is sometimes sharply balanced by pain when some maniacal "arranger" goes to town and orchestrates your work out of existence. There has in the past few years been a curious development in the dance-orchestra business which has apparently made it imperative for each band to have its particular personality. Because one saxophone player sounds relatively like another on the radio, the only way in which this personality stamp can be acquired is through orches-tration. Turn your dial and get "Gus Gump and His Gurgling Goofs." Gus has decided that he wants his band to be recognized by the fact that his music gurgles, therefore both "Jeepers-Creepers" and "Smoke Gets in Your Eyes," though dissimilar in intent, sound like soup being drawn through Jo Davidson's beard. One bright lad [Ed. perhaps Guy Lom-bardo] has found it useful to make his saxophones play flat as a means of identification! I cannot believe that this is not deliberate as nobody could play as flat as that by accident. This sourness combined with an over-warm vibrato produces the same effect as herring with chocolate sauce, but the man is famous. Consider, also, the exhibitionist who is convinced that his harmony is better than yours. Over your signature he endows your melody with harmonization that is generally in bad taste if not downright unsound. It is as though the editors of this periodical took this article and invested it with incorrect spelling, bad grammar and more vulgarisms than it already possesses. (Note to Ed. Please check grammar and spelling.) To offset the damaging influence of such relations, there are many times when a mediocre composition is lifted into importance by a brilliant orchestration and a loving performance.

All in all, writing musical shows is a fine way to earn a living. There are many complaints about union unfairness but nobody mentions the fact that the quality of theatre musicians is extraordinarily high, and that stage-hands are invariably capable. There are letters to the *Times* mentioning only the lack of politeness in box-office treasurers but nobody realizes that they are patient, good-natured people for the most part, who go to work behind the grille of a hit show at eight-thirty in the morning and leave for home after midnight. With the lurid tales about chorus girls's activities nobody seems willing to believe that they are the kindest, most loyal group of people in the world. Out of something like thirty shows only once has a producer tried to cheat me. You would be amazed if I told you his name [Ed. probably Florenz Ziegfeld].

Yes, it's a fine way to earn a living, even if you do have to answer a lot of questions.

"Introduction" to
The Rodgers and Hart Song Book

Although in the previous "self interview" Rodgers described Hart as his "favorite blight and partner"—as well as "a source of permanent irritation"—in his Introduction to the first edition of *The Rodgers and Hart Song Book* he writes that in twenty-five years the two "never had a single personal argument with each other" (Rodgers does, however, acknowledge "furious, blasphemous, and frequent" battles "over words"). From the beginning of their partnership Rodgers learned that his collaborator had a pyrotechnical grasp of interior rhymes, so-called feminine rhymes, triple rhymes, and false rhymes. Despite this early demonstration of "pin-wheel brilliance," Rodgers believes that Hart did his best work in the increasingly emotional, philosophical, tender, and deeper lyrics of the later years. Rodgers also demonstrates his pride that as early as 1920 (in the precociously Freudian "You Can't Fool Your Dreams") he and Hart were prepared to continuously tackle new subjects, both in their individual songs and in the shows themselves.

In regard to Larry Hart's words I am perhaps the greatest living expert. Larry and I worked together for over twenty-four years, from the time I was sixteen and he was twenty-three until his death in 1943 when I was forty and he was forty-seven. This was possibly the oldest partnership in the history of the theatre, with the exception of the Shuberts who have been united by blood as well as predilection. I have no fear that my devotion to these lyrics is solely emotional. It was necessary, during all those years, to examine these words and work with them not only in the stage of composition but in the stage of projection (the process of getting actors to sing the words intelligibly and to see that no distractions in the way of bad lighting or loud orchestra interfered). Mr. Hart's composer would have to be highly aware of the phonetic subtleties and semantic overtones in these lyrics, and I believe I have always been very much alive to them.

In a larger sense there is something I should like this book to be. I think Mr. Hart deserves a memorial. It is true that his songs are sung many thousands of times a day, in theatres, on records, on radios, and on people's tongues, but this book will put them in people's hands.

Larry had only one pride that I was ever able to discover. That was his work. He didn't care about the way he looked or where he lived. He wasn't concerned with the social or financial status of his friends or what row he sat in at an opening. He did care tremendously, however, about the turn of a phrase and the mathematical exactness of an interior rhyme. This book has many such phrases and rhymes, and so I think it would have pleased him as it pleases me.

Before Hart, only P. G. Wodehouse had made any real assault on the intelligence of the song-listening public and even his attempts were comparatively tentative and not particularly courageous. Larry, right from the beginning, took the bull by the horns and threw it over the proscenium arch. His lyrics knew, for instance, that love was not especially devised for boy and girl idiots of fourteen and he expressed himself to that extent.

In 1925 he was able to proclaim right out in public, and no one objected, that the "Freudian" subconscious motivated a great deal of our acting and thinking. For a song writer this would be considered radical even today, but Mr. Hart didn't scare easily. By way of proof there is a song (not included in this collection) we wrote in 1920 called "You Can't Fool Your Dreams." This was a great many years before any of us had heard of psychoanalysis, and I mention it here, not to show that our thinking was particularly advanced, but to demonstrate our willingness to employ subject matter hitherto ignored by the songwriting profession. This desire to explore did not stop with the individual songs. It extended to the shows themselves. Looking at the table of contents of this book,

Source: Richard Rodgers, "Introduction," in The Rodgers and Hart Song Book (New York: Simon and Schuster, 1951), 1–4.

it is clear that there must have been an almost continual search for diversification of subject matter. These range from a little revue through romantic fantasy and a musical circus, to political satire.

The reader may be curious about the work methods we employed in writing these songs and shows. Our work habits were almost as diversified as the subject matter. We always had a distaste for artistic self-pampering, as I still have today, and only rarely did we ever take one of those hide-out trips so popular with writers. It was when we were preparing *On Your Toes* for rehearsals. Our writing had been interrupted by extracurricular pressures so often that we took a suite at the Ritz in Atlantic City for a weekend in the hope that we could finish one of three important songs that remained to be done. We returned to New York on Monday with all three completed, and I remember that we felt happy and rested.

Only one thing remained constant in Larry's approach to his job. He hated doing it and loved it when it was done. There was the never-ceasing routine of trying to find him, locking him up in a room, and hoping to fire his imagination so that actual words would get down on paper. It wasn't wise to leave him alone for a moment because he would simply disappear and have to be found all over again. His pencil would fly over the paper and soon the most difficult part of all would begin: the material had to be edited and he loathed changing any word once it was written down. When the immovable object of his unwillingness to change came up against the irresistible force of my own drive for perfection, the noise could be heard all over the city. Our fights over words were furious, blasphemous, and frequent, but even in their hottest moments we both knew that we were arguing academically and not personally. I think I am quite safe in saying that Larry and I never had a single personal argument with each other.

Larry and I were brought together in 1918 by a mutual friend who knew that each of us needed a collaborator. It shocks me to realize that this happened thirty-three years ago, but it excites me to think of the technical content of the discussion that went on that Sunday afternoon. I heard for the first time from the master (he was twenty-three, and seven years my senior) of interior rhymes, feminine rhymes, triple rhymes, and false rhymes. I listened with astonishment as he launched a diatribe against song writers who had small intellectual equipment and less courage, the boys who failed to take advantage of every opportunity to inch a little further into territory hitherto unexplored in lyric writing. "If you wanted to write about New York, you didn't have to be as naïve as 'East Side—West Side'." A couple of years later he said,

> We'll have Manhattan
> The Bronx and Staten
> Island, too.

and Rodgers and Hart had written their first hit, although we weren't to find it out for several years.

Heywood Broun in reviewing our first show, *Poor Little Ritz Girl*, in 1920 said that it was obvious that the lyric writer "had his ear to the ground and not to the nearest stage door." He might have said that again in 1943 had he been able to review the revival of *Connecticut Yankee*. If the reader will examine the words of "To Keep My Love Alive," written nearly twenty-five years after Heywood Broun's review, he will find the same inability on Larry's part to succumb to a cliché or to rhyme any way but brilliantly.

It seems to me that Larry's later lyrics were of higher degree of excellence than his early ones and that they achieved this through a growing maturity of their own. Later on he seemed almost to substitute warmth for wit, and while he really didn't know how not to be clever, he began to show off less and to be more concerned with emotion. "Where or When," for instance, had much of the philosophical in it and I can think of no lyric more touched with tenderness than "Funny Valentine." In the face of the pin-wheel brilliance of some of Larry's work, one is inclined to forget the deeper phases of his writing.

Larry and I met artistically like two volatile chemicals in a retort and the explosion resulted in a series of songs, nearly all of which are now forgotten. [Ed. Rodgers is referring to the songs that preceded *The Garrick Gaieties*, 1925.] This same mutual friend who had introduced us felt that we should meet Lew Fields—what our friend had in mind here was that this team of young writers should form a contact with a successful producer. At that time, Lew Fields had a musical show called *A Lonely Romeo* playing at the Casino Theatre. One Sunday afternoon at his home in Far Rockaway I played at least a dozen of these songs for Mr. Fields. (One of his sons was present at the time. This was Herbert, who subsequently wrote the book for many of our musical shows.) Mr. Fields liked particularly a song called "Any Old Place with You" and a few weeks later interpolated it in the score of *A Lonely Romeo*. It was sung by Eve Lynn and Alan Hale. I suppose it will seem pretty sophomoric, but perhaps this can be excused on the grounds that I wasn't to be a sophomore for another three years. As it was the first song Larry and I had done professionally, perhaps it deserves a place at the beginning of the collection.

"Jerome Kern: A Tribute"

For composers such as Rodgers and Gershwin who wanted Broadway to adopt a more vernacular musical language, Jerome Kern (1885–1945), "the first man to break with European theatre tradition," was a model and an inspiration. In the tribute that follows, Rodgers recalls with love and "a feeling of real gratitude" seeing *Very Good Eddie* (1915), a Princess Theater show, "at least a dozen times in one season," when he was about thirteen. Three years later, it was a recording of the song "Babes in the Wood" from this show that Hart played on the day he and Rodgers met, and it was their mutual appreciation of Kern that helped forge a deep and lasting bond between the new collaborators.

The immediate occasion of this *New York Times* piece was a revival, directed by Rodgers's present collaborator, Hammerstein, of Kern and Hammerstein's *Music in the Air* (1932), Hammerstein's last successful show until *Oklahoma!* eleven years later. Despite Rodgers's endorsement that the show represented "Kern at his best" with songs like "The Song Is You," which manages to combine "a deeply romantic mood with a highly comic one," the revival lasted a disappointing fifty-six performances. Six years earlier, in their role as producers, Rodgers and Hammerstein had asked Kern to compose the score for their new property, *Annie Get Your Gun*, a commission that Rodgers's idol and Hammerstein's composer on *Sunny, Show Boat, Sweet Adeline*, and *Very Warm for May* was unable to fulfill. Kern died suddenly on November 11, 1945, two months before the first major revival of *Show Boat* (January 5, 1946) and six months before Berlin's *Annie Get Your Gun* (May 16, 1946).

Composer of the scores for such hits as Oklahoma!, South Pacific *and* The King and I. [Tag line by *Times* editor.]

It is an unfortunate but perfectly human failing we have in this country of wanting to put everything in its proper numerical order. We must have a number one movie of the year. We must have a number one magazine. It is not necessarily the one with any particular standard of content, but the one with the largest circulation. In light music, of course, the top of the hit parade is comparable only to knighthood or the coveted small red ribbon in a buttonhole.

The fight to name America's number one composer has been going on since the turn of the century and the returns are still not in, nor are they likely to be. It would be futile to ever try to name him here but let us consider Jerome Kern, whose *Music in the Air* [1932] will be revived tomorrow night at the Ziegfeld. Possibly, only possibly, he was not America's number one popular composer, but certainly he was America's first one. This is a chronological position usually assigned to Victor Herbert, but it must be apparent to music students that this German-

Source: Richard Rodgers, "Jerome Kern: A Tribute," *New York Times* (October 7, 1951), section II, 1, 3.

Irishman never wrote a bar of music in his life that was native to this country.

His music was middle European in its concept and its execution. He was the maker of lush, beautiful tunes, but no American soil ever got between the keys of his piano. (For the sake of semantic clarity, it might be wise to point out that to a great many of us the term "composer" usually indicates the creator of a sustained musical composition such as a symphony, an opera, or an operetta, as opposed to the songwriter who deals in a short form and whose efforts are not connected with each other to form an integrated whole. It is for this reason, and this reason alone, that Stephen Foster is not being discussed here, beautiful as his works were and noble as his contribution was to American music.)

Typified Our Maturity

Kern was typical of what was, and still is, good in our general maturity in this country in that he had his musical roots in the fertile middle European and English school of operetta writing and amalgamated it with everything that was fresh in the American scene to give us something wonderfully new and clear in music writing in the world. Actually he was a giant with one foot in Europe and the other in America. Before he died, he picked up the European foot and planted it squarely alongside the American one.

It is possible, of course, that as this country grows older its various art forms will lose their traces of continental origin and perhaps this is as it should be, but the first man to break with European tradition in theatre music was Jerome Kern in much the same sense that Beethoven was the last of the classicists and the first of the romanticists.

If we were to look for one example at each extreme of his geographical range, we might find "Look for the Silver Lining," with its almost beer-hall simplicity, at one end and discover "Ol' Man River," with its deep turmoil and strong native inflection, at the other. Both are fine music and both are Kern.

Great Influence

I have never felt that enough has been said about Kern's contribution to American music through his influence on subsequent writers of music in this country. To begin with, he was the composer of a fabulous theatre combination that contributed a form known as "The Princess Theatre Shows." I use the word "form" because it was a creation separate and distinct from other theatrical ventures. It employed no chorus, it rarely changed sets, but it did impart to a small audience the feeling that the whole composition of the evening had been created for the two ears of the single listener. The orchestra was tiny, as were the voices as a rule, but in this particular theatrical scheme of things the effect was one of intimacy and warmth and something quite rare and memorable.

Kern was almost entirely a composer for the theatre, anyway. His infrequent sorties into fields outside the theatre (the symphony hall) were no more successful than were those of most of us who tried it, and he always came running back to the orchestra pit and the proscenium arch for protection. I think he was happiest there because that was where he made people happiest.

At His Best

Music in the Air may not be Kern at his most typically American but it is Kern at his best. And best of all, it is Kern enjoying himself in the theatre. There is a little bird call at the beginning of the piece that eventually is developed into "I've Told Every Little Star." This is almost childlike in the simplicity of its fantasy, but through its prettiness tells so much about this naïve family with whom we are to spend the evening.

The finale of the first act is "musical scene" writing at its most ingenious and most exciting. It has Kern and his partner, Oscar Hammerstein II, romping all over the stage walloping the daylights out of a dramatic situation. But, perhaps, the best of all, from the viewpoint of theatre writing, occurs late in the second act with "The Song Is You." One of the most difficult feats in all theatre is to combine a deeply romantic mood with a highly comic one at the same time. It is exciting to see how well it was accomplished here.

Along with my love of Jerome Kern's music there is a feeling of real gratitude. This was a man whose *Very Good Eddie* [1915] I saw at least a dozen times in one season at the Standard Theatre on upper Broadway, near where we lived at that time. The influence of such a hero on such a hero worshipper is not easy to calculate but it was a deep and lasting one. His less successful musical comedies were no less important to a listener of 13 or 14. I know that for a large part of one winter most of my allowance was spent in the balcony of the Maxine Elliott Theatre listening to the score of *Love of Mike* [1917].

Debt to Kern

Perhaps the greatest gratification ever allowed anyone in his life is to be able to take a large gathering of people under one roof and through the medium of words and music make them feel something deeply and strongly within themselves. This was Kern's privilege and his mission. He accepted the privilege gracefully and accomplished the mission beautifully. You who read this, and I who write it, stand in his debt.

"*Pal Joey*: History of a 'Heel'"

Rodgers's retrospective on *Pal Joey* appeared a few days before its Broadway revival. Hart's favorite, *Pal Joey* was only the second Rodgers and Hart show to receive this treatment (the first was the considerably revised 1943 return of *A Connecticut Yankee* [1927]). The *Pal Joey* revival would earn further distinction as one of the first revivals to surpass its original run. While some prefer the score-rich *Babes in Arms*, the ballet-rich *On Your Toes*, or the endlessly clever Shakespeare adaptation, *The Boys from Syracuse*, *Pal Joey* has at least since Atkinson's "retraction" (reprinted in Part II) received high marks for its treatment of adult themes, including a "disreputable character" in the title role. Rodgers also discusses the recent history of the belated hit song, "Bewitched," the successful studio album, and the summer stock performances, all of which created interest in a new production. Rodgers, who remained unshakably certain forty years later that at the age of fifteen he was wearing long pants upon meeting Hammerstein (see Hammerstein's Introduction to the *Rodgers and Hart Song Book* in Part I and "Hammerstein: Words by Rodgers" below), concludes with equal conviction that *Pal Joey* was the musical that "forced the entire musical comedy theatre to wear long pants for the first time."

The writer is the composer of the score for Pal Joey, *which will be revived this week. Lorenz Hart wrote the lyrics, and John O'Hara, the book.* [Tag line by Times *editor.*]

Lorenz Hart has been dead for over eight years, but by the time January rolls around he will have had two representations in New York within two months. The first is the publication by Simon & Schuster of the *Rodgers and Hart Song Book*; the second is the new production of *Pal Joey* which will open at the Broadhurst Theatre on Thursday. I have been asking myself which of these two projects would have pleased him more, and I haven't gotten anywhere with an answer.

The book would have pleased him deeply—not only because it is handsome and is selling beautifully—but because it is composed of his best lyrics for each separate period in his career. On the other hand, few things ever gave Larry as much pleasure in his entire life as the original production of *Pal Joey*, and its revival would have been deeply gratifying to him.

Source: Richard Rodgers, " 'Pal Joey': History of a 'Heel'," *New York Times* (December 30, 1951), section II, 1, 3.

Analyzing Joey

Larry loved *Pal Joey* not only because it was successful and people said good things about his work in it, but because of Joey himself. Joey is a disreputable character, and Larry understood and liked disreputable characters. He knew what John O'Hara knew—that Joey was not disreputable because he was mean, but because he had too much imagination to behave himself, and because he was a little weak. If you don't understand this about Joey, you'll probably find him hard to take. If you do understand it, you'll be able to chuckle at him and understand him in more than a superficial sense.

Joey as a person met with a great deal of resistance in 1940, when he was first presented to the American public, but I have an idea that this was due largely to the fact that nobody like Joey had ever been on the musical comedy stage before. In the conventional sense, his characteristics were those of a villain, and so long as there was an orchestra in the pit, the villain was supposed to wear a black mustache and be nasty all the way. Since that time, however, characters in musical plays have become more human, and the attitude of the public toward these characters has become more human, too. It's very possible that Joey will have more friends today than he did eleven years ago.

Looking Backward

It is customary, in this sort of Sunday piece, to review the alumni of the original production and tell of the meteoric rise to fame of various members of the cast. We had two of them. One of them first came to work for us in *Too Many Girls*. I have just looked him up in the program of that show, and this is the way it reads:

> Sue. . . . . .Leila Ernst
> Student. . . . .Van Johnson
> Co-Ed. . . . .Libby Bennett

In *Pal Joey* Van Johnson fared a great deal better—he had a real name, Victor, and a whole chorus of a song to sing all by himself. People, especially female people, had been noticing Van as far back as *Too Many Girls*, and when he sang his one chorus in *PJ*, it wasn't very long before Hollywood took him and kept him.

Gene Kelly, of course, had a small but sensational bit in *The Time of Your Life*, but *Pal Joey* did the trick for him, too.

So far as the people and their lives are concerned, one other stands out in my memory, a little dancer named Tessie. Tessie had very blue eyes and she laughed a great deal. One day they took her to the hospital with a collapsed lung and she died a little while later.

Rebirth of Score

Nineteen forty was the year that ASCAP had its troubles with the broadcasters, and popular music on radio was reduced to a couple of squeaks. The *Pal Joey* score wasn't heard at all until it was too late, and as a result the score was practically unknown except to a few very special fans—unknown, that is, until about a year and a half ago, when something happened to a song called "Bewitched, Bothered, and Bewildered." It climbed to the top of the "Hit Parade" and stayed there a long time, ten years after its original production. The broadcast version of the lyric is somewhat euphemistic, but I'm happy to say the melody is the same. Then, last winter, the Columbia Recording Company put out an album of the score itself, and that too, I believe, has done very well. Most heartening of all, however, was the reception that *Pal Joey* got in summer stock this past season. It seems still to be a vital and valid piece of theatre work.

It is also customary in this sort of piece to go back over the original newspaper reviews and prove what idiots all the critics were. It makes very funny reading and very permanent enemies among the critics. I'm afraid, however, that it won't be possible to do anything of the kind in this space. The reviews were not only fantastically accurate in their approach to the intrinsic values of the piece, but gave a very fine diagnosis as to its commercial possibilities. It's true that one out-of-town lady reviewer panned the show, but ran for cover in her very first sentence by saying that it would be pretty embarrassing if, a hundred years from now, the play turned out to be a great success.

Musical Milestone

Having just finished a long rehearsal period with this *Pal Joey* material, it's possible to form certain conclusions. One of them is that the dialogue is just as rich and impertinent today as it was originally. One other conclusion seems more or less inescapable. While Joey himself may have been fairly adolescent in his thinking and his morality, the show bearing his name certainly wore long pants, and in many respects forced the entire musical comedy theatre to wear long pants for the first time. We were all pretty proud of this fact ten years ago, and I can only hope that we will be again.

"The Right to Revive" (or "Revive and Let Live")

R odgers's "The Right to Revive" offers a spirited defense of a practice that continues to be viewed as a symptom of theatrical decline rather than health. In doing so, Rodgers addresses future critics who disparage the recently added, vigorously competitive, Tony Award category of Best Musical Revival. Among the recent winners in this category are revivals of Rodgers and Hammerstein's *Carousel* in 1994 and *The King and I* in 1996. Rodgers notes that stock and amateur companies were contractually prohibited from performing works during their initial Broadway runs—it remains common today for shows in Broadway revivals to prohibit regional and collegiate productions—and considers it another vital sign that 340 stock and amateur performances of *Oklahoma!* appeared the previous year. In contrast to most critics then and now, Rodgers argues that new productions of earlier shows (such as *On Your Toes*, which was to open the next day) "might even encourage a beginner to stay in the theatre," since their return would assure new talent that the best shows do not necessarily vanish.

Composer of the score and co-author of the book for On Your Toes, *which opens tomorrow at the Forty-sixth Street Theatre.* [Tagline by *Times* editor].

All lasting works of an art nature are continually in a state of revival. This is true of Gainsborough's *Blue Boy, The Man with the Hoe*, Brahms's First Symphony, *Falstaff*, and "The Stars and Stripes Forever." The ceiling of the Sistine Chapel is revived by the persons who travel in vast numbers to see it every year. Musical comedy is entitled no less to be revived from time to time, simply because it is considered a lesser art, provided that what is being revived is a good example of that art. Actually, being more easily understood by a greater number of people than the more serious works, it might be entitled to more frequent revivals.

Onstage, tastes change, mores are different, so that where language is understood, as opposed to grand opera, the life-revival span is usually limited; but *The Merry Widow*, a fine fantasy-romance with a lovely score, was greeted happily once more only a few years ago.

Source: Richard Rodgers, "The Right to Revive," *New York Times* (October 10, 1954), section H, 1, 3.

Vital Past

A number of interested people say, disparagingly, that the weakness of the American theatre can be gauged by the number of revivals. I should like to oppose this view. It's true that any type of creative field may find itself occasionally in a comparatively unproductive mood. Any field is entitled to a hiatus. Is it not wonderful, then, that we have a theatrical past so vital and attractive that the public can be drawn to see works that pleased them before? The fact that new productions of old pieces occur so frequently might even encourage a beginner to stay in the theatre. He might see the possibility of a continuing livelihood. The whole field might die otherwise.

Stock Offerings

I cannot stress too strongly my interest in the "interim" nature of revivals or the part they play in the total attitude of the country at large toward the living theatre. It becomes quite easy to neglect the matter of "stock" presentations and to fail to recognize that these performances are also revivals. As a matter of fact, they can be nothing else, by contract, as it is not permitted to do a stock presentation of a play before the major run is completed.

In the past year there have been approximately 340 stock and amateur performances of *Oklahoma!* This somewhat staggering figure only indicates the vitality of the American musical theatre and the interest of the public in works with which it is already familiar. As a composer who is currently involved in the composition of a new score for the theatre, I can only say that I would be bitterly unhappy over the prospect of the disappearance of the custom of reviving old works. This could only indicate to me that the old were bad works.

I am well aware that stock and amateur performances of old pieces take place because brand-new works are not available to stock and amateur organizations. However, there are two pleasant thoughts in connection with this situation: One is the vast national stimulation of interest in the theatre aroused by these performances (to say nothing of the enormous employment afforded by these presentations), and the other is that once in a great while a revival finds its way to our metropolitan theatre centers.

Nothing to Fear

Any season that produces the sort of theatre represented by *The Teahouse of the August Moon* and *The Pajama Game* need fear nothing from the revival of *On Your Toes.*

Specifically, and for the moment, I am interested in the musical, *On Your Toes,* a piece that George Abbott, Larry Hart and I did for Dwight

Wiman to produce in 1936. George Abbott is presenting this new production. Is anyone near-sighted enough to suggest that George is doing this only because he cannot find anything new and merely would like to stay in business? I would like to point out that his last two efforts were *Wonderful Town* and *Pajama Game*, a couple of brand-new, joyfully successful pieces. I would also like to point out that George already was doing mighty well in 1935 when we met professionally for the first time, and he's still eating well. Perhaps he's interested in this *On Your Toes* because he likes it and because he has a nose for nostalgia.

This word "nostalgia" is, of course, the basic clue to the successful revival. *Carousel* was done again last spring at the City Center, at the comparatively young age of 9. Never, anywhere, was the response to it so heartwarming and enthusiastic. An engagement of eleven days eventually was extended to ten weeks, but what was most gratifying was the reaction in the theatre from the fine and uninhibited audience the City Center always attracts.

Emotional Stimulus

It isn't difficult, if one has respect for the power of nostalgia, to understand what happened. Simply, Aunt Nettie, singing "You'll Never Walk Alone" over the body of Julie's husband, was being heard by people, young and old, who had had some sort of personal and emotional experience connected with the song itself. To watch it on the stage and hear it again lent a deep dramatic impact to the theatre to be stimulated emotionally, the revival succeeded. This was equally true of many of the other songs and the situations developing the play itself.

On Your Toes will have the same assistance from its material, though for comedy and not for tragedy. I understand that many a happy honeymoon has been embarked upon to the strain of "There's a Small Hotel": "Slaughter on Tenth Avenue" hasn't been precisely forgotten either. Then there's always the chance that one of you will suddenly say during the evening, "That song? I didn't know it was from *On Your Toes*." Ah, well, revive and let live.

"Cancer? I've Had It!"

In "Cancer? I've Had It!" Rodgers encourages millions of *This Week* readers that detection can often lead to a full cure. Rodgers relates how a pain in his jaw led to tests and the removal of a portion of one jaw and numerous lymph nodes, and how with mild medication he was able to appear on television, rehearse and write additional material for a new show (*Pipe Dream*), fly to California to attend "a lot of very fine parties," and visit his daughter Linda in Dallas. Rodgers concludes his personal story by expressing the wish that those "who have signs of this kind of trouble will go for early help—not through terror but through hope."A supplement to the article provides five questions to test reader concern about cancer and a message from Dr. David A. Wood, president of the Cancer Society, who vouches for the medical reliability of Rodgers's article, citing 800,000 Americans "alive today who have been saved from cancer" and another 700,000 recent patients who "will live to be added to this list."

Three years later, Rodgers watched Hammerstein die of cancer. Then in 1974 Rodgers was forced to face the illness personally for a second time. A successful operation removed his larynx and Rodgers struggled valiantly to learn esophageal speech.

Broadway's famous composer-producer was recently afflicted with our most dread disease. Here is his candid—and reassuring—story of the harrowing experience. [Tag line by *This Week* editor.]

They led me from the examining room to the consultation room. The array of people there was more disconcerting than the examination itself. My brother, the doctor who had taken me to the surgeon, sat there white-faced. Opposite me were the surgeon and his associate. And next to me was my wife.

The surgeon rolled his chair out from behind his desk and spoke. "This should come out right away." Then I knew for certain that I had cancer. "It isn't too early by any means, but it isn't too late. If you give us the green light on Monday (this was Friday), we'll admit you on Tuesday and operate on Wednesday."

He wanted to know if I had any prejudice against New York's Memorial Hospital because of the fact that it was a cancer hospital. I told him that I did indeed. But when he explained that Memorial and its staff were so well equipped physically and technically to deal with this sort of difficulty, I agreed to go there.

"I Was In Trouble"

It all started quite casually a few months before with a pain in my jaw which I naturally thought was caused by a tooth. My dentist was reassuring but cautious. He said there was some tissue he wanted to watch and asked me to come in for periodic checkups. One Thursday he looked at my mouth and told me I was in trouble. Five minutes later I was in my doctor's office and that evening he and my brother decided on the surgeon for me to see in the morning.

Source: Richard Rodgers, "Cancer? I've Had It!," *This Week* (March 17, 1957), 8–9.

I should like to explain now why I am writing this article. I have no desire to display my wounds and emotional crises in a national magazine, but I feel that the emphasis on fear of cancer has been carried out to the fullest, if, indeed, it has not gone too far.

I am afraid that terror has overcome a great many people and vast numbers of them are simply too frightened to go and find out if a suspicious symptom has any real significance. Often they go too late. Perhaps if they knew the less grim and more optimistic side of the picture they might be encouraged to help themselves sooner.

In the light of my own experience, I should like to present this side of the picture to *This Week*'s millions of readers.

Between Friday, the day of the diagnosis, and Tuesday, the day I entered the hospital, I was a very busy man. A large musical show for which I had composed the score and which I was co-producing with Oscar Hammerstein was to go into rehearsal on the exact morning I was to go into the hospital. I still had a song to write and three piano manuscripts to put on paper.

I did the work on Saturday and Sunday. The rest of Friday and all of Monday were taken up with X rays, the dentist and the medical man. My wife saw me through all this, but, in the decent tradition of wives, was more panic-stricken than I.

No Sense Of Gloom

I received a special dispensation and was allowed to go to the first rehearsal Tuesday morning. I wanted greatly to see the cast in action just once and I wanted them to see me. I took my wife to lunch and she took me to the hospital. Again I was a busy man, this time with medical and surgical technicians. It was all rather good-natured without any sense of gloom or tension, and one pill gave me quite a decent night's sleep.

There were a couple of hypodermic injections in the morning and shortly after noon I was wheeled upstairs for the big job. There was one more shot, this time Pentothal Sodium. What a miracle that is! I never knew the sensation of falling asleep or even blacking-out. The next thing I knew I was conscious again in the "recovery room," minus one malignant growth, a part of one jaw and numerous lymph nodes. Early in the morning they trundled me back to my own quarters where I promptly walked to the bathroom on my own two good feet. Apparently the policy at Memorial is not to press you but to allow you to do what you're able to do.

They gave me no dope whatsoever because the after-effects of this particular kind of surgery are not unbearably painful. I had nothing stronger than an aspirin derivative and at night one fairly mild capsule. I spent nights in a chair—it was more comfortable than lying down.

I won't distress you, or perhaps bore you, with the surgical and medical procedures of my hospital experience. They weren't very pleasant but neither were they very bad. What stays in my mind is the infinite patience and gentleness of the surgeon and his giant, laughing-kind associate, and the pervasive atmosphere of good nature and optimism in an institution where terror is supposed to be its first commodity.

On the eighth day following the operation I went for a ride in the park with my wife. I hated it. On the ninth she took me to a movie. I bore it. On the tenth, still living at the hospital, I went to rehearsal. I loved it.

I left the hospital for home on the twelfth day, but the show was my real convalescence. Had I been forced to sit on the porch at some resort and think about myself, I could never have recovered so quickly. This way, surrounded by health and youth and their passion to succeed, my own determination had to match theirs.

I had handicaps, yes, but no visible scars. I couldn't eat properly nor speak well because my tongue hadn't learned to behave, but I went to New Haven for the try-out and from there to Boston to watch the show for a month. My wife was all I had in the way of a nurse, but she was a kind and wise one.

To make a valid point for this piece, I must point out to you some of the things I was able to do during the first six months following the operation:

- Appear on television at the opening of the film *Oklahoma!* less than three weeks after leaving the hospital.
- Rehearse and go out of town with a new show—and write additional music for it.
- Fly to California; go to a lot of very fine parties; drive to the desert (me at the wheel).
- Fly to Dallas to see my younger daughter and her husband, and fly from there back to New York.

During that time I did six appearances on television and made a few radio tape recordings for charitable causes. I am on several organization boards and have managed to get to as many meetings as I did before I was ill. I even made a speech before a crowded ballroom at the Waldorf-Astoria Hotel and the worst that happened to me was that I was nervous before the event and quite comfortable during it. Most important to my feeling of well-being and usefulness was the happy completion of a full score for a television musical play.

I am continuing to live a full and rewarding life. My left arm had been somewhat handicapped following surgery and for some time I was unable to do any conducting. However, 16 months to the day following the operation I rehearsed and conducted a full concert of my own work with the Philadelphia Symphony Orchastra for the benefit of its Pension Fund. The concert itself came off well, which was gratifying enough but I had no physical difficulties to overcome in doing a job for which a much younger man should have gone into training; nor were there any after-effects except a feeling of great exhilaration and accomplishment.

Though we recognize our attitude is illogical, many of us are reluctant to admit that we have had cancer, even if there has been a complete cure. Most of us seem to feel that there is some sort of stigma attached to the disorder, almost as though it were a so-called social disease. Why this should be, no one seems to know and the doctors themselves seem baffled by what can only be called a phenomenon of unreason.

Reason or no, the net result is that we hear very little from the patient or his family about the cure and only learn of the disaster. The "net-net" result is more fear and less chance of cure. Frankness on a social level could be enormously helpful, and publications, such as this one, could aid greatly by demonstrating that the opposite side of the coin need not always be black.

I am not fatuous enough to believe that everyone who develops cancer can be as fortunate as I have been, but it cannot be denied that my experience stands for what it is—far from happy but far from terrible.

I went to a small party this Sunday. Four people there had been successfully treated for cancer.

I shall feel deeply rewarded if, having read this, some of you who have signs of this kind of trouble will go for early help—not through terror but through hope.

"Introduction" (with Oscar Hammerstein) to *The Rodgers and Hammerstein Song Book*

In a fittingly collaborative "Introduction" to their *Song Book* Rodgers and Hammerstein characterize the musical theater as "not much less complex than war." To make their case, they offer four solutions to "the problem involved in trying to make the semantic expression and the musical thought meet, each one valid by itself and both satisfactory and complete in combination." The musical examples, illustrated in Rodgers's hand, include "It Might as Well Be Spring" from *State Fair* (also singled out in *Musical Stages* to demonstrate how music can match a text, in this case a state of restlessness), "The Surrey with the Fringe on Top" from *Oklahoma!*, and two from *South Pacific*, "A Wonderful Guy" and "Younger Than Springtime."

To collaborate means to work together. The man wielding a sledge hammer and the laborer holding the spike for him are obviously collaborating. At the far end of the scale, though they are not likely to meet, the general of the armies and the shavetail at Fort Sill are also collaborating in the complex mechanism of war. Not much less complex than war is the musical theatre, and its complexities are compounded by the fact that the relationships among its components are not defined and absolute as they are in the army, but subtle, tenuous, and usually emotional.

Some years ago a Southern lady wrote a successful novel. Her next effort, a play for the New York theatre, was a failure. The lady promptly packed up and went back to the South and her novels, declaring that she was abandoning the theatre because she could not bear "the hot breath of the director" on her neck. We agreed with her wholeheartedly. We felt that if she couldn't take the director's hot breath on her, indeed if she didn't pay for it, she had no business in the live theatre and belonged properly at her objective but non-objecting typewriter.

A quick glance at the theatre program for any musical show reveals a staggering number of separate elements. These must complement each other and become fused if the total effort is to stand as a valid artistic representation. The orchestration must be related to the plot elements, the costumes to the choreography. Even the facial contours of the ingenue must be considered by the lighting expert.

None of these relationships, however, is so basic and complex as the relationship between lyric writer and composer. For example, the choice of the proper words to express and emotion is an extremely delicate one. If the composer were to try to explain the emotion in musical terms independent of words, he would find it difficult enough. Imagine then the problem involved in trying to make the semantic expression and the musical thought meet, each one valid by itself and both satisfactory and complete in combination. The hoped-for result is a dramatic musical expression in which one component is ideally enhanced by the other and total result has far greater meaning in the final communication with the listener and viewer.

A song in the motion picture *State Fair* tells of a young girl's need to love and be loved. The piece is called "It Might as Well Be Spring," and the lyrics describe the girl's restlessness and uncertainty. In the second line of the lyrics she says:

> I'm as jumpy as a puppet on a string.

Later on she tells us she is

> Like a nightingale without a song to sing

Source: Richard Rodgers, "Introduction" (with Oscar Hammerstein) to *The Rodgers and Hammerstein Song Book* (New York: Simon and Schuster, 1958), 6–9.

and,

        I'm as giddy as a baby on a swing.

    The music written for these three separated lines is the same. It is nervous and insecure and ends up, not with the positive statement of an F-sharp, but with a tentative slightly worried F-natural:

Ex. 1: **"It Might As Well Be Spring"**

    It is interesting that the graphic contours of music so often describe, as we look at them on paper, the dramatic content of the words. Examine, for example, the fluctuation of the black notes above and then compare them with the monotony and insistence of those below from "The Surrey with the Fringe on Top" in *Oklahoma!* The melody is flat and straight like a road, with a sharp upward flick as the fowl scurry:

Ex. 2: **"The Surrey with the Fringe on Top"**

    The song "A Wonderful Guy" is a series of exciting problems for a composer. Nellie Forbush, in *South Pacific,* is an uncomplicated, unsophisticated girl, suddenly bowled over by a new emotion. Her melody would be all over the scale, as indeed it is, and a simple, fairly rapid waltz would be appropriate to her Midwestern background. She is sure of herself and her feeling, so at the end of the lyrics she repeats "I'm in love" five times running. The melody at that point is equally insistent, hitting strongly at the two highest notes of its range, while the harmony mounts to a climax:

Ex. 3: **"A Wonderful Guy"**

Occasionally words are written to match an already created melody, but even here the music must be appropriate to the content and intent of the situation. Some years ago this composer sat one evening improvising at the piano. A tune came to him which one of his daughters liked. He made a note of it and eventually played it for this lyric writer. He remembered it. Then came the time when we were writing the score of *South Pacific* and had difficulty creating a song that satisfied us for the situation in which Joe Cable, the marine lieutenant, makes love to the young native girl. Any hint of sophistication would have been vulgar and inappropriate. But the lyric writer remembered the little tune the composer had played for him, and the words he wrote were as innocent and unspoiled as the two charming people who sang them:

Ex. 4: "Younger Than Springtime"

It's an untroubled, free musical thought, naïve and straightforward, and to find a good example of collaborative effort on the part of the lyric writer it is only necessary to realize that these words were written for a previously committed situation and a previously committed melody.

The examples above, indeed all the songs in this collection, are individual case histories of words and music illustrating and amplifying one another. However, it should be pointed out that the benefits each of us has derived from association with the other would not be possible without certain intuitive qualities inherent in both of us, even before we began to work together—notably, a high regard for the nature and problems of the other's medium; a happy willingness to bend before the demands of the other's working needs; and finally, a genuine appreciation of the emotion behind the expression.

"Hammerstein: Words by Rodgers"

The *New York Times Magazine* published Rodgers's panegyric two days before Hammerstein's sixty-fifth birthday, one month before his death. On this poignant occasion Rodgers publicly shed his characteristic reserve and expressed his appreciation for the man with whom he shared close to eighteen productive and joyous years. Among the highlights of this tribute is Rodgers's description, upon first hearing *Show Boat*, of being "shaken both by the beauty of Jerome Kern's score and by the emotional and intellectual depth of Oscar's words" and his recollection of the historic meeting with Hammerstein, when Rodgers knew that Hart would be unable to continue working. A deep and long-lasting respect for Hammerstein becomes especially clear when Rodgers recounts how at the age of fifteen (presumably in long pants) he first met his future creative partner—then about twenty-two—the author and "chief comedian" of a Columbia Varsity Show: "I looked up at him in awe and I have to tell you that I still do."

The composer takes a plunge into prose to wish his partner well on his birthday. [Tagline by *New York Times Magazine* editor.]

Oscar and I have been working together for over eighteen years consistently and continuously. In all that time I think I can say with complete safety we have had only one unresolved argument and that was over a matter of short pants versus long ones. He claims that at the time of our original meeting I wore short pants and I claim, and still do, that I was mature enough to wear long ones.

The place of this meeting was the Hotel Astor ballroom and the time was approximately 1917. The occasion was a Saturday matinee performance on the stage of the ballroom of a Columbia Varsity Show. For the sake of the few readers who believe that off-Broadway is a modern invention, it might be well to explain that Columbia University used to put on a student musical each year. It was called the Varsity Show, as it still is. I was taken to see this by my older brother who was then probably a sophomore at Columbia and after the performance I was introduced to a tall man who had not only worked on the book and the lyrics but was also the chief comedian. This, of course, was Oscar Hammerstein II. I looked up at him in awe and I have to tell you that I still do.

Immediately my primary ambition in life became to write the music for a Columbia Varsity Show and I bent every effort to get into Columbia as quickly as possible. I managed to do this three years later and became the first freshman in the history of the school to write the music for this annual affair. Lorenz Hart wrote the lyrics but the entire piece had to be submitted to a graduate committee for consideration. At this time the committee consisted of Richard Conried, Ray Perkins and, of all people, Oscar Hammerstein II. The piece was accepted immediately, which came as no great surprise to any of us as it was the only piece submitted.

It is generally accepted that Oscar and I worked together for the first time in the writing of *Oklahoma!* This is not true. At the time of this Varsity Show Oscar had a lyric in his desk, the title of which was "There's

Source: Richard Rodgers, "Hammerstein: Words by Rodgers," *New York Times Magazine* (July 10, 1960), 26, 54.

Always Room for One More." He showed me the words and, following the custom we still observe today, I wrote the music for it. The song was put in the Varsity Show where it failed to create any commotion whatsoever.

Some years later Herbert Fields, Lorenz Hart and I, working together, had written book, lyrics and music for a musical called *Winkle Town*. We discovered that not only couldn't we sell it but we couldn't get anybody to listen to it and naturally the blame for this was placed on the book (a custom that is still observed religiously today). Oscar was friendly to all of us and it was easy enough to call on him to try to help. He tried all right but he didn't get anywhere at all.

The one noteworthy thing about this effort is the fact that the score contained one song which, a number of years later, turned out to be the first song hit that Larry Hart and I ever had. It was called "Manhattan." From there on Oscar's path and mine seemed to separate completely. Larry and I made our first big success with a little revue called *The Garrick Gaieties* and Oscar produced gigantic hits such as *Rose Marie, The Desert Song*, and *New Moon*.

My next contact with Oscar was not personal in nature at all. I went to a Saturday matinee of *Show Boat* and found myself shaken both by the beauty of Jerome Kern's score and by the emotional and intellectual depth of Oscar's words. We saw each other occasionally on a social level following the production of *Show Boat* but I think it was the deep impression that this piece made on me that sent me to him years later with the suggestion that we might find it advisable to work together in the near future.

I'd like to tell the rest of this story at this point because I think it is typical of Oscar's viewpoint toward ethics and social procedure and behavior in relationship to his friends and even, perhaps, life in general. It had become more apparent all the time that Larry was quickly reaching a point where he would be unable to work. I was worried about him and frightened for him but there was nothing I could do to help him.

On the other hand, I was too young to abandon my career, I had a wife and two children, and even myself, to worry about. Staying with Larry was something I could only do up to the point that Larry was able to stay with me and it was clearly evident that he could not lead a useful life for very much longer. I called on Oscar at his farm in Doylestown and told him that Larry and I were about to embark on a musical version of a Ludwig Bemelmans novel [Ed. Stories about the Hotel Splendide that had appeared recently in *The New Yorker*], but I was terribly afraid that Larry would never be able to finish it.

Oscar said to me, "I think the solution is quite clear. Start to work with Larry and if he is able to finish the job, all well and good. If he isn't even able to start, I'll do it with you. If he starts it and is unable to finish it, I'll finish it and naturally I would never think of asking to have my name put on it. I don't even want to discuss any financial consideration whatsoever."

I know now that that afternoon on his farm in Pennsylvania was the beginning of our understanding as working partners and as friends. Nothing has ever changed any of that.

Now we come to a milestone in Oscar's life. Tuesday will be his sixty-fifth birthday. Obviously, he acquired maturity many years ago, maturity in his philosophy toward life, his feelings about love, his ideas about the field in which he works, which is the theatre. One of the things I find most inspiring about him is that, while these theories and feelings have become deeper and stronger, they are not set in concrete but stand as a sort of working proof that the ideas and ideals of a young man were valid then and still do quite well.

Like most fully grown people he is a curious study in contrasts. As anyone who knows him will tell you, he is extraordinarily gentle and yet I've seen him rise to horrendous heights of fury. These furies, however, are almost always directed in one way against injustice.

He is a passionately loving man and yet any overt expression of this love I've never seen anywhere except in his work. I know, for instance, beyond any question, that he is fond of me—very fond, I think—as a man, and yet he has never even hinted vaguely at this. On the other hand, he's gone before the entire country on television and told everybody what a great person I was.

He's a meticulously hard worker and yet he'll roam the grass of his farm for hours and sometimes even days before he can bring himself to put a word on paper. In anyone else this would be called laziness and yet you could never say that Oscar was a lazy man.

In the past few years it's become chic on the part of quite a few members of the press to regard "love" as somewhat of a dirty word. Oscar has always been an exponent of quite the opposite theory and, fortunately for a great many of us, he hasn't changed. Most of us still feel that nature can have attractive manifestations, that children aren't necessarily monsters and that deep affection between two people is nothing to be ashamed of. I feel that way rather strongly myself or obviously it would not be possible for me to write the music that goes with Oscar's words.

Happily the chic, usually effete, press has had no influence on Oscar. What I point out here has nothing to do with the business of making money but it is curious that the play running in New York this season to the greatest number of people and to the largest amount of money, *The Sound of Music*, is concerned with a young Catholic about to become a nun and her friends. Somebody down here likes us.

* * *

It has long been recognized that a writing collaboration consists of the closest possible meeting of mind and spirit. Indeed it is often impossible to recall who advanced which idea or even when. I can remember, however, at least one instance where the lyric writer contributed strongly to the music. It occurred in the case of "I'm in Love with a Wonderful Guy."

Oscar had written the lyric and turned it over to me with the simple finish, "I'm in love with a wonderful guy." When I played him the music I had written for his words, he jumped out of his chair and said, "Why don't you repeat 'I'm in love, I'm in love, I'm in love' as often as you think you can with increasing intensity? It might give the feeling of exultation and express the girl's great joy over her love for this new man."

The result, in the theatre, was that Mary Martin reached a peak of near-hysteria at the end of the song and brought the house down at every performance. This lyric is a perfect example of Oscar's phenomenal talent for construction.

Oscar and I have been noticing an interesting phenomenon of late. When we are interviewed for a newspaper or a magazine, the writer so often wants to know what we "fight" about. We both detect a sense of disappointment when we say that we don't fight. Now I don't believe that it can be said that we're a couple of idiots living in a complete and blissful state of euphoria, and it's perfectly true that we can and do disagree over an idea, a rhyme or certain technical usages. But I've always felt the fact that we get on so well together is due essentially to the circumstance that our basic philosophies are so much alike.

On the odd occasion when we don't agree, we resort to the old "Alphonse and Gaston" technique. One of us is always saying to the other, "Let's try it your way first and if it doesn't work then we'll try mine." This, incidentally, is not a bad way for two people to stay married to each other and it seems quite obvious that a writing collaboration differs very little from a marital one except, of course, in the obvious sense.

It is pretty well established that by the age of 65 the ingrained habits of a lifetime, in the sense of personality traits particularly, tend to become more exaggerated. The man who was very careful about his money at the age of 35 tends to become downright stingy when he gets into his sixties, the introvert becomes a hermit, the grouch becomes a terror.

Oscar's characteristics, just like everybody else's, have also become exaggerated. Luckily, it isn't too difficult to bear up under them. I think he's a little more gentle, if possible, than he used to be. Where he was slow to anger, he now has to be goaded into it. Today we can take a look at a man who has been very successful in his work, who has had a fantastically happy home life and who has been singing very clearly for all these years about everything that's good and decent and enjoyable in this country.

He's never been accused of being rude or dishonest or intolerant. His mind and his heart have given enormous pleasure and comfort to millions of people. There remains only one more thing to point out on Oscar's sixty-fifth birthday and that is that for the last sixty-five years he's been having an absolutely wonderful time himself. I congratulate him.

Richard Rodgers has written eight Broadway musical plays with Oscar Hammerstein II since their first—and memorable—success, Oklahoma! *was produced in 1943.* [Tagline by *New York Times Magazine* editor]

"Opera and Broadway"

In this article, targeted to opera-loving *Opera News* readers, Rodgers anticipates Lehman Engel's thesis (see "The Art of Adaptation" in Part II) when he writes that "musical comedies of our Broadway theater might be called, without apology or self-consciousness, American opera." Without disparaging European traditions or the mature song-writing craftsmanship of earlier musicals, Rodgers's view of history favors the evolution toward "perfectly integrated," "unmistakably American," and innovative musicals like *Oklahoma!* in which "songs and dances flowed naturally out of the story while remaining natural to the personalities of our characters." In advocating a musical theater that rejects "pat formula" and welcomes "new subjects and ideas," Rodgers demonstrates an awareness of "serious" composers who have explored American themes (e.g., Marc Blitzstein's *Regina*, Carlisle Floyd's *Susannah*, Douglas Moore's *The Ballad of Baby Doe*, and Aaron Copland's *The Tender Land*, an opera that Rodgers himself generously funded). According to Rodgers, these works, though "operatic in concept" are "completely American in their working out" and "would be as much at home in the theater as in the opera house, as would many of our Broadway musicals."

Over the past two or three decades, it has become increasingly difficult to pigeonhole the works of our musical theater into the convenient categories of opera, music drama, "play with music," or even "musical" and musical comedy. The line between them has grown increasingly elastic; there has been a healthy interchange of devices, ideas and themes among them. The one major difference seems to lie in where they are produced: opera house or theater.

Source: Richard Rodgers, "Opera and Broadway," *Opera News* (February 25, 1961), 9–11.

Opera, states the *Harvard Dictionary of Music*, is "a drama, either tragic or comic, sung throughout, with appropriate scenery and acting, to the accompaniment of an orchestra." According to this flexible and useful definition, it is thus a play in which all the lines are sung rather than spoken. Dialogue interspersed with song was introduced with the development of comic opera, but such composers as Mozart and Beethoven used spoken dialogue even in serious operas. They made it legal, so to speak, for an opera to remain an opera even when not "sung throughout." In opera, then, all the arts combine: music, both vocal and instrumental, poetry, acting, design—and dancing. All of these are joined into a perfectly integrated (that is the popular word these days) whole. To the extent that the pieces mesh and match, so will the work be popular and successful. But what is even more important is that our latter-day definition of opera could serve equally well for *Carmen*—or *Show Boat, Porgy and Bess* and *Carousel*. Obviously none of these falls into the category of the traditional idea of an opera. As the form has developed and changed over the years, however, and as the musicals of the American theater have developed over an even shorter period, it has become clear that the "plays with music" or musical comedies of our Broadway theater might be called, without apology or self-consciousness, American opera.

During the twenties, when jazz permeated the American imagination and art, lively and serious, there was a good deal of talk about the "American jazz opera." While such an opera never actually materialized, the talk itself was important; it focused attention on musical works in the American idiom—American in terms of the music and the language of the lyrics. The musical comedies of the twenties, with few exceptions, were devoted purely and simply to entertainment; their "books" were not designed to pose any problems, nor did they attempt to solve any. They were in fact constructed according to a time-tested formula that determined the point where the fast "rhythm" number was to be introduced—or the ballad, or the comedian, or (even more important) the girls. The typical musical of the twenties was hardly expected to deal with a mature subject—it practically always had a simply boy-meets-girl plot—but it was delightful on its own terms, and in many ways important. Because the songs were composed, mainly, by a new generation of song-writers—by composers who often had a solid musical education, and lyricists who had proved themselves masters of light verse in their college publications—the music and the lyrics of the twenties songs reached new levels of quality. What the books lacked in maturity was made up by the maturity of craftsmanship that went into the song-writing.

There was a break, too, with the traditions of Europe: French *opéra-comique*, English ballad opera and Viennese operetta. All were wonderful, but they did not naturally fit the American scene. The very shape of our melodies, the crackle of our rhythms and the language (which, in turn, had its effect on melody and rhythm) were completely

American. The result was that during the twenties we younger composers and lyricists—Irving Berlin, Jerome Kern, Oscar Hammerstein II, George and Ira Gershwin, Vincent Youmans, Lorenz Hart and I—were breaking ground for a native American musical theater. We drew on everyday life for our themes, our musical ideas, our language. We did this unconsciously, for we were more concerned with doing our work as well as we could. Making history was incidental.

A musical play completely in the American mold, with an American story, sung in American English to music characteristically American, was inevitably on its way. *Show Boat* (1927) is an outstanding example that gracefully eludes any cut-and-dried label; it is unmistakably American in every way. There were many other shows of which this could be said—the neglected but revolutionary *Rainbow*, with music by Vincent Youmans and lyrics by Oscar Hammerstein; the Gershwins' *Of Thee I Sing; Music in the Air* (Jerome Kern and Otto Harbach [Oscar Hammerstein]), *On Your Toes* (Lorenz Hart and me)—and all of them contributed in some way to the growth of a form of musical theater distinctively our own.

I have emphasized nationalism, however subconscious in practice, because the works that have proved meaningful and viable with the passage of time are those composed by men who wrote in the accents of their native music and language. This applies equally to symphonies, operas or musical shows; it is as if a composer manages to be most universal only when he is most completely himself. The operettas of Gilbert and Sullivan are thoroughly English, yet universally understood and loved. I can think of no music more typically German than Bach's.

Of course, we were not trying to be American Bachs, or even American Gilberts and Sullivans, but their example of being completely themselves was valuable to us. In following their example we could have tradition on our side, even when we were being most untraditional; for example, we could absorb the folk devices of jazz—could, that is, if we wished. Lyricists could use slang expressions, even words of more than two syllables. We could take contemporary American stories as a base for our musicals. We were, in short, establishing our own traditions. The popularity of American musicals, both at home and abroad, attests to the rightness of our instincts.

Broadway and Tin Pan Alley have hardly been acknowledged as spawners of art—not, at least, until fairly recently. Part of the problem may have been our inability to recognize our own art when it was presented to us. But like jazz, another purely American contribution, the musicals of Broadway, for all their commercial success, are just that. Aside from the songs, the developing maturity of the books has contributed to this artistic status, and so has the close integration (opera-like in its way) of songs, dances and story. The attention given to the book of a musical led not only to the telling of stories that made sense, but to the choice of more varied and adult subjects. Some important musicals have already been mentioned. Others during the thirties and early forties exemplify the unusual themes that were used: the Depression (Irving Berlin's *Face the Music*), the Presidency (Hart's and my *I'd Rather Be Right*, with Kaufman and Hart), the history of early New York (Kurt Weill's and Maxwell Anderson's *Knickerbocker Holiday*), psychiatry (Weill's and Ira Gershwin's *Lady in the Dark*) and that hard look at the world of the night-club, *Pal Joey*.

In *Oklahoma!* (1943) the songs and dances flowed naturally out of the story while remaining natural to the personalities of our characters. Had it failed, *Oklahoma!* would possibly have been dismissed as too experimental, but since it succeeded it is called innovational instead. The very elements that contributed to its simple charm were those that brought objections from Those Who Know. For example, who would open a Broadway musical with a slow song instead of a lively number with lots of girls? But we used the gentle "Oh, What a Beautiful Mornin'" to open *Oklahoma!*, and we used dances by Agnes de Mille that were related to the story clearly expressing the state of mind of the characters. Some felt that one of the songs, "Lonely Room," at once grim and poignant, did not belong in a light musical. It was too serious, they claimed; but it did present an insight into the character of Jud and made him an understandable, less hateful villain.

Carousel (1945), our next production, posed other problems. Not only did it lack a real villain, but its hero died long before the end of the show. Since it was based on Ferenc Molnár's *Liliom*, we had the further complication of a European setting; we struggled with that for a long time until one day the happy thought came to me to set it in New England. All the collaborators agreed, and we were able to go on with our adaptation. With some changes in the book, authorized by Molnár, we could adapt his universal theme to our American scene.

We went even farther in *Allegro* (1947): the setting is contemporary and completely American. For *Allegro*, Oscar Hammerstein supplied the first original book of our partnership—and it was a book that meant a great deal to both of us personally. In fact, he admitted that in *Allegro* he came the closest he had ever come to autobiography. The main character was a doctor. *Allegro* was not, however, a medical musical, but rather a modern morality play exploring the problem of personal integrity in today's fast-moving, success-oriented society.

To tell this story we departed from the conventional practices of the musical play. We employed a modern-day equivalent of the Greek chorus, commenting on the action in speech and song. Using the audience to represent the child growing up had never been done before. Costumes were modern, of course. Sets were reduced to minimum, the props were the simplest. Dramatic effects were achieved in song, heightened by the use of color in the lighting; dancing was so important to the telling of the story that Agnes de Mille not only choreographed the dances but staged the musical numbers.

Though "innovational," especially in its stagecraft, and generally well received, *Allegro* did not enjoy the success of *Oklahoma!* or *Carousel*. Hammerstein frequently spoke of revising it and trying again, for he was as fond of it as I. The comments we made on the compromises demanded by success, as well as some of the satiric side issues—hypochondria, the empty cocktail party—still hold, it seems to me.

The American musical theater has produced other successes—*Bloomer Girl, Annie Get Your Gun, Kiss Me, Kate, South Pacific, Guys and Dolls, The King and I, Gypsy, The Sound of Music, Fiorello!*—all proving the value of the mature story set to music. The rejection of pat formula exemplifies a reaching out for new subjects and ideas that is the very keynote of our growing lyric theater. *West Side Story* is a perfect example of this, and so is *My Fair Lady*. Composers of more serious music, too, have pursued American themes; Copland's *Tender Land*, Moore's *Ballad of Baby Doe*, Floyd's *Susannah* and Blitzstein's *Regina* are among the more recent works operatic in concept yet completely American in their working out. They would be as much at home in the theater as in the opera house, as would many of our Broadway musicals.

The distinctive form that has developed in our musical theater is not, of course, grand opera in the traditional sense. It is rather a musico-dramatic expression particularly native to us; to borrow a term from the industry, it is the product of American know-how. This implies a marriage, not only of the arts but also of the technical aspects of modern stage-craft. When all these elements blend into a gratifying evening in the musical theater, we can take pride in it and enjoy it. The labels don't matter at all.

Mr. Rodgers has composed some of America's most memorable scores from his undergraduate days at Columbia, when he first collaborated with Lorenz Hart, to his historic partnership with Oscar Hammerstein II, who died August 22. [Tagline by *Opera News* editor.]

"Now the Musical Theater Is Enshrined"

In his role as president and producing director of the Music Theater of Lincoln Center, Rodgers served himself as well as audiences by successfully programming *The King and I* and *The Merry Widow* in 1964, its inaugural year, *Carousel* the following year, and a revival of Berlin's *Annie Get Your Gun*, originally produced by Rodgers and Hammerstein, two years after that. While some critics may lament the "museum" mentality of a Broadway that prefers past accomplishments to new work, Rodgers argues that "the need to preserve and recreate the great works of our musical theater is of equal importance to preserving and recreating the masterpieces of the concert hall and the opera house." Rodgers uses this opportunity to review familiar themes, for example, the need for innovation and risk-taking, the importance of expressing convictions without "sermonizing," and his conviction that musical theater is "possibly the most imaginative form of non-objective theater we have."

Rodgers also addresses "one of the oddest paradoxes about musicals." He notes that some critics denigrate musicals as "escapist" works that should be "dismissed as unworthy of serious critical study" (see, for example, Nathan's "The Musical Stage" in Part II). For others, musicals, including those by Rodgers and Hammerstein, deserve censure for making the genre "too serious" (e.g., Bentley's opinion that in *The King and I* it was the King's "duty to stay alive and amuse us," also in Part II).

For the first time a hall has been built in recognition that it, too can be an art. [Tag line by *New York Times Magazine* editor.]

In two weeks, the Music Theater of Lincoln Center will inaugurate its first season with a new production of *The King and I*. After a five-week run, it will be followed by Franz Lehár's *The Merry Widow*, which will run five weeks and then tour for about three months.

As these plays are intended to be part of a permanent home for the musical theater, their selection was not easily made. In each case, the decision was dictated by the same consideration that would motivate the choice of works to be included in symphony, ballet, drama, and opera repertories. That is, we plan to offer musicals that have won both critical and popular acceptance, and that posses certain timeless qualities we feel will continue to attract audiences. This does not necessarily mean that all of our future productions will be limited to successful musicals of the past; we sincerely hope that the Music Theater, as a representative and responsible artistic company, will offer works that, quite possibly, will be created specifically for our use.

I feel that it is no landscaping accident that the building in which our company will be housed—the New York State Theater—forms a triangle with Philharmonic [now Avery Fisher] Hall and the new home of the Metropolitan Opera company. For the need to preserve and recreate the great works of our musical theater is of equal importance to preserving and recreating the masterpieces of the concert hall and the opera house. Although many of the plays we shall present have enjoyed revivals at the New York City Center and at summer theaters and colleges, this

---

Source: Richard Rodgers, "Now the Musical Theater Is Enshrined," *New York Times Magazine* (June 21, 1964), 20–23.

will mark the first time that a theater will act as a repository for this form of entertainment. Moreover, the exceptional facilities of the New York State Theater will contribute immeasurably to productions that, hopefully, will not only keep alive the cherished traditions of the musical theater but will also set new artistic standards.

Even though I have been associated with the musical theater almost all my life, I am constantly amazed at its vitality and undiminished hold on the public. What is the reason for this enormous appeal? Why does it have such a special appeal? Why does it have such a special magic? My deep conviction is that musicals will always attract large audiences because music gives the art of the theater a new dimension and a greater depth. It adds something that people can feel emotionally and intellectually, and that cannot be experienced in any other form of dramatic presentation.

Of course, I am well aware of the music of the spoken word. There is music in the dialogue of Shakespeare's plays as well as in others, such as the works of Sean O'Casey and J. M. Synge. But plays of this type are seldom being written today. For the most part, the realistic, representational theater only occasionally reaches the emotional heights that are achieved in a play told through music. Whether it is called opera, operetta, or musical, it is really all the same thing. For when a dramatic story is enhanced by music, it has a far greater impact on its audience than is possible in almost any other type of play.

Let me give you an example. *Funny Girl* is a musical that goes back to the time-tested device of the backstage story. Yet even when Barbra Streisand as Fanny Brice is supposed to be performing in a Ziegfeld show, the Jule Styne music and the Bob Merrill lyrics are building and developing the character. And when Miss Streisand sings her heart out about the man she loves, an audience cannot help but respond in a way that far transcends anything that could be achieved through the spoken word.

Whenever a solo performer in a musical expresses a deep emotion through song, it is, in effect, a soliloquy. We have long since passed the day in our nonmusical theater when this form of self-revelation was a familiar device, yet it is an ever important part of our musical theater. It is the kind of unreal technique that we not only accept but believe in.

It is in the matter of belief that the musical theater has always been in a rather strange position. Musicals are not realistic depictions of life. No boy ever stops a girl on a street in real life and, after some preliminary conversation, bursts into a newly created song. No group of ranchers, or cabaret waiters, or whatever they are, suddenly are able to perform spontaneous and intricate dance steps. The musical theater is a stylized world but with its own logic and believability. Everything about it contributes to this atmosphere—from the dimly seen musicians in the pit orchestra to the gaily painted scenery. Take away the illusion of unreality and the musical is no longer believable. That is one reason why the essentially realistic medium of the movies has always posed so many problems for musicals adapted to the screen.

One of the oddest paradoxes about musicals is that they have been attacked from two opposite camps. There are those who feel that because they are generally a light, frequently escapist form of theatrical art, they should be dismissed as unworthy of serious critical study. On the other hand, I recall a time not too long ago when my late partner, Oscar Hammerstein, and I were taken to task for helping to make the musical theater too serious. Neither attitude is valid, of course. The musical stage today can be almost anything it wants to be, and can deal with almost any theme. The degrees of lightness or of heaviness depend entirely on the proper mood and spirit of the work being offered. Indeed, a lighter form of musical entertainment can frequently be more effective as social commentary than a more serious form. *How to Succeed in Business Without Really Trying* is a recent example, and there are many others. On the other hand, the modern theater also has room for *West Side Story* and *Gypsy*, neither of which could be mistaken for simple escapist entertainment.

I have frequently heard it said that the musical theater is a distinctly American art form. This is true up to a point. The point is that we have borrowed much of the form from the European theater. France had its opera bouffe. Vienna its operetta, and England its comic opera long before Americans were creating works of comparable merit.

The Merry Widow, the most famous importation of them all, told a bubbly tale that utilized music perfectly to enhance its mood and to help its plot development. It is still considered a well-integrated score today, over 50 years after it was written. But this is a unique work chiefly because the librettists took the trouble to make their characters understandable human beings. Unfortunately, the plethora of European operettas that followed *The Merry Widow* to our shores turned out to be exaggerated romances with pasteboard lovers, weighted down by massed choruses and cumbersome settings.

What has made the musical theater distinctly American is what we have done with the form. Although George M. Cohan and Irving Berlin were expressing themselves in a truly indigenous manner early in this century, the real birth of the American musical comedy were the shows written in the mid-1910s by P. G. Wodehouse, Guy Bolton and Jerome Kern for the tiny Princess Theater. These musicals—*Very Good Eddie, Oh, Boy!* and *Oh, Lady! Lady!*—were intimate and believable, and there was a genuine attempt to make the music and lyrics flow smoothly as part of the stories. They were far from being realistic, but they made sense both musically and dramatically.

* * *

It is odd, however, that while these productions were popular, they had little immediate effect on the kind of musicals that were produced at the larger Broadway houses. Well-integrated musicals seemed less important than vehicles in which to feature comedians and dancers. But what did influence those of us just beginning to write for the musical theater was the music of Jerome Kern. In addition to myself, I know that George Gershwin, and Vincent Youmans, to name just two, were greatly influenced by Kern's lead to break away from conventional musical ideas and to express themselves with a freshness that reflected the exciting times in which we all worked.

But it remained for Kern himself—this time in partnership with Oscar Hammerstein—to take the lead again by creating the score for the immortal *Show Boat*. When this masterpiece came along in 1927, it was the first truly modern American musical *play*, as opposed to musical *comedy*. It told a romantic but serious story strong enough to stand on its own, but its use of music and lyrics to reveal character and heighten emotion was what has given it its great durability. Also, by facing up to deep-rooted problems in our society, *Show Boat* was the forerunner of such musicals as *Porgy and Bess, South Pacific*, and *West Side Story*.

The musical theater has also, of course, been a great medium for satire. When in 1932, Gershwin's *Of Thee I Sing* became the first musical ever to win the Pulitzer Prize for drama, it helped bring about a new attitude toward the musical stage. Not only did it take aim at some of our most cherished national institutions, it did it with an almost total reliance on music, very much in the manner of Gilbert and Sullivan comic opera.

To a certain extent, *Of Thee I Sing* was a product of the Depression years, as were many other musicals produced during the thirties. The country's economy and the rise of Nazi Germany had a profound effect on the development of our musical theater, with such shows as *Face the Music, Pins and Needles, I'd Rather Be Right*, and *Knickerbocker Holiday* dealing with many subjects of vital concern at the time.

As writers of musical comedies began treating audiences with greater respect, the actual form of the musical began to change. Songs and stories were now being more carefully integrated, and dances were given greater importance. In 1936, Larry Hart and I worked on a show, *On Your Toes*, in which, for the first time, a ballet sequence was used as a vital part of a climactic scene in the play itself.

Not many years after *On Your Toes*, two remarkably adult works appeared on Broadway within a few months of each other: *Pal Joey*, which dared to have an unsavory character in the central role, and *Lady in the Dark*, whose musical sequences were devoted to depicting the dreams of a woman undergoing psychoanalysis.

It would seem by the time Oscar Hammerstein and I wrote *Oklahoma!* that the public would be ready for almost anything. However, there were many who warned us that it broke too many rules and was doomed to failure. But it did succeed, despite such innovations as an opening number without chorus girls, a psychopathic villain, and dream ballets expressing the fears and desires of the leading characters.

I should like to think that the success of a musical as unconventional as *Oklahoma!* did much to encourage other writers to attempt new and challenging themes. Certainly the history of the musical theater during the past 20 years shows that the public is receptive to a wide range of subjects and treatments. *Finian's Rainbow* and *Bloomer Girl* were pioneering works in setting the struggle of civil rights to music. Though they were quite different, *South Pacific, The King and I*, and *West Side Story* all had something to say about the need for greater understanding between peoples of different backgrounds. *Fiorello!* dealt with important issues in local politics. *The Pajama Game* was about a threatened strike in a pajama factory. Both *Allegro* and *No Strings* concerned themselves with the problem of individual integrity in today's fast-moving, pleasure-loving society. The corroding effects of personal ambition were exposed in *Gypsy*, while *How to Succeed in Business without Really Trying* gave a thorough going-over to corporate mores and morals.

These shows have had impact not alone because of the maturity of their themes but because their writers were aware that the surest way of getting across their convictions was to keep their musicals free from sermonizing. Most musicals, of course, do not have this problem, since the area of works created as pure entertainment is certainly the larger one. It includes such classics of the commercial Broadway theater as *Annie Get Your Gun, Kiss Me, Kate*, and *Guys and Dolls*. It finds room for the musical farce with its emphasis on speed and exaggerated comedy, as exemplified by *A Funny Thing Happened on the Way to the Forum* and *Hello, Dolly!* It also takes in such plays as *The Music Man, The Sound of Music*, and *She Loves Me*, which are unashamed of expressing themes of honest sentiment.

With regard to sentiment in the theater, I should like to point out that Oscar Hammerstein and I deliberately added an optimistic note to the ending when we adapted *Liliom* into *Carousel*, and that Lerner and Loewe did much the same thing in transforming *Pygmalion* into *My Fair Lady*. Since both of those works have done pretty well, I must conclude that those who consider sentiment a dirty word are in a minority.

My Fair Lady, of course, occupies a unique place in the development of the American musical theater. Not only did Lerner and Loewe create a work of enduring appeal, they also managed to retain the essence of Shaw's biting wit in both the dialogue and the songs. Theirs was a formidable achievement and one that set new standards for our musical stage.

Because theater music usually has a life of its own via records and dance bands and the like, the well-being of the American musical stage has become of vital concern to many people not directly engaged in it. But those of us who work in this field must have only one responsibility—to ourselves. I feel that one of the truly imperishable rules of the musical theater is never to have a rule. The only way that a writer can produce anything of lasting value is to do exactly what he feels is right, without worrying whether or not the public will approve. If it is good, the public will flock to see it. In fact, if there is any danger lurking in our musical theater today, it is the feeling in some quarters that there is a magic formula that can be turned on to insure both critical approbation and lengthy queues at the box office.

The question, "Where is our musical theater heading?" has been put to me many times. I don't mean to be flippant, but my honest answer is that I can't tell where it's heading until it gets there. Suddenly, a new show opens and it has left tradition far behind. It may be about national politics, or the Oklahoma Territory, or leprechauns, or juvenile delinquency in New York. But once it's done, it's done. Its effect may be seen indirectly within the larger canvas of our musical theater, but it starts no trends nor is it the result of a trend. It is simply the result of one or two or three people kicking around an idea and developing it in an original manner.

I firmly believe that the musical theater—possibly the most imaginative form of non-objective theater we have—can have a long and prosperous life if it continues to express the honest thoughts of creative men and women who are unafraid of taking a chance on new ideas, and have the ability to translate these ideas into meaningful theatrical terms. Playing it safe has never produced a masterpiece and it seldom has produced any audiences, either.

Time and again, the theater-going public has shown itself hungry for adventurous, inventive productions both in content and in technique. It is the job of the creative people in the musical theater to satisfy that hunger but not necessarily be motivated by it.

"A Composer Looks at His Lyricists"

Early in this retrospective on his two durable creative partnerships, Rodgers writes that, despite their enormous differences on many personal and artistic levels, "each was a genius at his craft, and each during our association, was the closest friend I had." Rodgers succinctly recalls his meeting with Hammerstein (and then Hart) and early collaborations with each, compares their contrasting work methods, and addresses their idiosyncratic creative strengths. Rodgers's appreciation of Hart's simplicity and "rueful quality" as well has his technical virtuosity has appeared before in these readings (see, for example, Rodgers's "Introduction" to *The Rodgers and Hart Song Book* earlier in this section).

In recalling Hammerstein, Rodgers writes that his second partner "was as meticulous a craftsman as Larry," "extremely versatile," "more positive, more optimistic," and "a man willing to do battle for whatever causes he believed in." Rodgers found it "truly remarkable" (and cites specific examples) of Hammerstein's inexhaustible "ability to find new ways of revealing how he felt about three interrelated themes—nature, music and love"—as well as "the wonders to be found in the simple pleasures of life." Rodgers also mentions disadvantages and advantages to writing his own lyrics and the "strange conflict" between feelings of "loneliness" and "fulfillment" generated by this independence, and credits his two great lyricists with giving him the training and talent "to go it alone."

In many ways a song-writing partnership is like a marriage. Apart form just liking each other, a lyricist and a composer should be able to spend long periods of time together—around the clock if need be—without getting on each other's nerves. Their goals, outlooks and basic philosophies should be similar. They should have strong convictions, but no man should ever insist that his way alone is the right way. A member of a team should even be so in tune with his partner's work habits that he must be almost able to anticipate the other's next move. In short, the men should work together in such close harmony that the song they create is accepted as spontaneous emotional expression emanating from a single source, with both words and music mutually dependent in achieving the desired effect.

I've been lucky. During most of my career I've had only two partners. Lorenz Hart and I worked together for 25 years; Oscar Hammerstein II and I were partners for over 18. Each man was totally different in appearance, work habits, personality, and practically anything else you can think of. Yet each was a genius at his craft, and each, during our association, was the closest friend I had.

I met Oscar before I met Larry. I was 12 and he was 19 when my older brother, Mortimer, a fraternity brother of Oscar's, took me backstage to meet him after a performance of a Columbia Varsity Show. Oscar played the comic lead in the production, and meeting this worldly college junior was pretty heady stuff for a stagestruck kid.

Source: Richard Rodgers, "A Composer Looks at His Lyricists," *Dramatists Guild Quarterly* (1967); repr. in *Playwrights, Lyricists, Composers On Theatre*, O. L. Guernsey, Jr., ed. (New York: Dodd, Mead, 1974), 98–102.

I met Larry about four years later. I was still in high school at the time, but I had already begun writing songs for amateur shows, and I was determined even then to make composing my life's work. Although I had written the words to some of my songs, I was anxious to team up with a full-fledged lyricist. A mutual friend, Philip Leavitt, was the matchmaker who introduced us one Sunday afternoon at Larry's house. I liked what Larry had written, and apparently he liked my music. But most important, we found in each other the kind of person we had been looking for in a partner—our ideas and aims were so much alike that we just sensed that this was it. From that day until I wrote *Oklahoma!* with Oscar, the team of Rodgers and Hart was an almost exclusive partnership.

I say "almost exclusive" because Oscar also figured in my early career. We had collaborated on a couple of songs (if you must know, they were called "Can It" and "Weaknesses") for an amateur show, *Up Stage and Down*, for which I had written most of the lyrics and all of the music. Oddly enough, when we rewrote the show and gave it a new title, *Twinkling Eyes*, Larry Hart came in as director. The following year, a Rodgers and Hart score for the Columbia Varsity Show also contained an interpolated Rodgers and Hammerstein effort, "Room for One More." Oscar, incidentally, had been on the panel of judges that had selected our musical, *Fly with Me*, as the Varsity Show. A few years later he even collaborated on the book for a musical, *Winkle Town*, with a score by Larry and me, but we never could sell it. The show, however, did have a song in it, "Manhattan," that later became our first hit.

Larry Hart, as almost everyone will agree, was a genius at lyric construction, at rhyming, at finding the offbeat way of expressing himself. He had a somewhat sardonic view of the world that can be found occasionally in his love songs and in his satirical numbers. But Larry was also a kind, gentle, generous little guy, and these traits too may be found in some of his most memorable lyrics. Working with him, however, did present problems since he had to be literally trapped into putting pen to paper—and then only after hearing a melody that stimulated him.

The great thing about Larry was that he was always growing— creatively if not physically. He was fascinated by the various techniques of rhyming, such as polysyllabic rhymes, interior rhymes, and masculine and feminine rhymes, the trick of rhyming one word with only part of another. Who else could have come up with the line, "Beans could get no keener re-/Ception in a beanery," as he did in "Mountain Greenery" or "Hear me holler/I choose a /Sweet Lolla-/Paloosa/In thee," in "Thou Swell"? Or "I'm wild again/Beguiled again/A whimpering simpering child again," in "Bewitched"?

Yet Larry could also write simply and poetically. "My Heart Stood Still," for example expressed so movingly the power of "that unfelt clasp of hand," and did it in a refrain consisting almost entirely of monosyllables. Larry was intrigued by almost every facet of human emotion. In

"Where or When," he dared take up the psychic phenomenon of a person convinced that he has known someone before, even though the two people are meeting for the first time. As the years went on, there was an increasingly rueful quality in some of Larry's lyrics that gave them a very personal connotation. I am referring to such plaints as "Nobody's Heart," with its feigned indifference to love, and "Spring Is Here," a confession of one whose attitude about the season is colored by his feeling of being unloved.

Oscar Hammerstein's view of life was more positive, more optimistic. He had a wonderful family. He was a joiner, a leader, a man willing to do battle for whatever causes he believed in. He was not naïve. He knew full well that man is not all good and that nature is not all good; yet it was his sincere belief that someone had to keep reminding people of the vast amount of good things that there are in the world. He was as meticulous a craftsman as Larry, and he was extremely versatile. As a partner he was completely dependable; about 70 per cent of the time I wrote the music only after Oscar handed me a lyric.

As far as his work with me was concerned, Oscar always wrote about the things that affected him deeply. What was truly remarkable was his never-ending ability to find new ways of revealing how he felt about three interrelated themes—nature, music, and love. In "Oh, What a Beautiful Mornin'," the first song we wrote together for *Oklahoma!*, Oscar described an idyllic summer day on a farm. In "It's a Grand Night for Singing," he revealed that the things most likely to induce people to sing are a warm, moonlit, starry night and the first thrill of falling in love. In "You Are Never Away," he compared a girl to a song, a rainbow, a spring morning. In our last collaboration, *The Sound of Music*, just about everything Oscar felt about nature and music and love was summed up in the title song.

Oscar believed that all too often people overlooked the wonders to be found in the simple pleasures of life. We even wrote two songs together, "A Hundred Million Miracles" and "My Favorite Things," in which Oscar enumerated some of them. To him there was no greater contentment than two people in love being close together as the day ends—a feeling that is found in, among other songs, "Oklahoma," "A Fellow Needs a Girl" and "An Ordinary Couple." It should not be overlooked, however, that Larry Hart was also attracted to the simple life. Remember his paean to rustic charms in "There's a Small Hotel." Or his attitude in "My Romance," in which he dismissed as unnecessary all the conventional romantic props when two people find themselves really in love.

After Oscar's death in 1960, I was faced with the dilemma of finding a new lyric-writing partner. I knew that I was not ready at that time to cope with another personality after having had so rich and close a working relationship. I had already had some experience updating a few of Larry's lyrics for revivals of our musicals, and I felt confident that I had assimilated the techniques of writing lyrics through my long association with two of the giants in the field. So I decided to go to it alone, to write the words as well as the music for my next stage production, *No Strings*. I also did double duty for additional songs written for the remake of the film *State Fair*, and the movie version of *The Sound of Music*, and I have also written music and lyrics for a TV *Androcles and the Lion*.

Creating my own lyrics has given me a new perspective on the problems of song-writing collaboration. It is, I well know, more difficult to write words than to compose the melodies. In musical composition, I work in wide, broad strokes. Lyrics are more like little pieces in a puzzle that must be carefully put together. But creating both words and music does have certain advantages. Geographically, it couldn't be better; I'm always there whenever I want to meet me. As far as personal satisfaction is concerned, I find that there is nothing more exhilarating than to work on a complete song when I want to, and nothing matches the satisfaction of taking full responsibility for the complete product. There is a strange conflict—part loneliness, part fulfillment—that I feel in becoming my own partner. If I am successful at it, I know full well that it's because some of the talents of Larry Hart and Oscar Hammerstein must have rubbed off on me.

Reminiscences of Richard Rodgers

The longest selection in the *Reader* is excerpted from an extended interview with Kenneth Leish, arranged in twelve parts (392 double-spaced pages of typescript and a two-page index of names). Although only the first four parts include dates, It is clear from references to current productions at places like the Music Theater at Lincoln Center that the final portions of the interview did not extend much beyond Summer and Fall 1968.*

In a portion of the *Reminiscences* not reprinted here readers learn that the press suppressed Hart's excessive drinking as well as his homosexuality, not because Rodgers threatened the publisher of a scandal rag when confronted with questions about Hart's sexuality, but "because the newspaper people were all crazy about him" (p. 200). Also in this section Rodgers discloses that

---

*For the archivally curious this footnote offers topics, dates (when provided in the interviews), and page numbers for each section : (1) Rodgers's current activities (December 14, 1967), 1–39; (2) Background (December 19, 1967), 40–84; (3) Producing *Avanti* and *The Garrick Gaieties* through *A Connecticut Yankee* (February 21, 1968), 85–118; (4) 1927–1932 (March 1, 1968), 119–43; (5) 1932–1936, 144–67; (6) Working with Hart, 168–203 [marked on the title page "closed during lifetime"]; (7) *Pal Joey* and *Oklahoma!*, 204–46; (8) *State Fair* and *Carousel*, 247–78; (9) *Allegro* and *South Pacific*, 279–307; (10) *The King and I*, *Victory at Sea*, and *Me and Juliet*, 308–36; (11) *Pipe Dream* and *The Sound of Music*, 337–62; (12) After Hammerstein, 363–92.

he usually knew where Hart was during one of his increasingly frequent and incapacitating disappearances (in *Musical Stages* he said he didn't know). In an interesting section on another secret, the rise of amplification, we learn that *Carousel* was the last Rodgers and Hammerstein show to be performed without microphones.

The selection that follows focuses generously on Rodgers's remarks on selected shows that first appeared between 1940 and 1965 (sections 7, 9, 11, and 12): *Pal Joey, Allegro,* the Rodgers and Hart film biography *Words and Music, South Pacific, Pipe Dream, The Sound of Music, No Strings,* and *Do I Hear a Waltz?* It also includes a brief section on the last months with Hart and first months with Hammerstein. Some of this material is new, but many of the stories, ideas, and opinions in the *Reminiscences* were subsequently refined for *Musical Stages.* In any event, the excerpts that follow, published for the first time in *The Richard Rodgers Reader,* arguably present Rodgers more directly and candidly than the more felicitous edited prose of the autobiography. The leisurely format also captures Rodgers's informal speaking style characterized by the repetition of short phrases for special emphasis. Rodgers's ideas on what worked and what didn't in his own shows are especially clear and unflinchingly refreshing. Finally, the *Reminiscences* demonstrate that Rodgers did not need the services of a ghostwriter to articulate his memories and well-considered views on musical theater.

Pal Joey

Q: It was a fantastic period for you—*Babes in Arms, I'd Rather Be Right, I Married an Angel, Boys from Syracuse* I think was your sixth smash hit in a three-year period. You really were riding high, and of course many of your shows were tremendous breaks for a lot of young performers. On *I Married an Angel* you worked for the first time with Joshua Logan—that was the first time you worked with him?

RODGERS: Yes. That's right. That was his first musical, too.

Q: You had a flop with *Higher and Higher.*

RODGERS: Right.

Q: Then came *Pal Joey,* which was quite a significant show in the history of the musical theatre. Is it correct that John O'Hara wrote to you suggesting that his stories be turned into a musical?

RODGERS: Yes, he did. Larry and I were in Boston with one of the shows,

Source: Reminiscences of Richard Rodgers (Oral History Collection of Columbia University, 1969), 211–21, 279–84, 291–305, 337–40, 348–53, 363–75.

I forget which it was, and I got a letter up there from John, who was on the Coast. He was in California doing a picture, I think, and he wrote to me asking me what I thought of the idea of turning the *Pal Joey* character into a musical? Well, the *Pal Joey* character is the signer of a series of letter that O'Hara composed about a nightclub hoofer. I'd read them all in *The New Yorker*, and I didn't write back to John. I sent him a wire, and said, "Come East as soon as you can. The idea is wonderful."

And he did come East, and eventually the show turned into *Pal Joey*.

Q: Was Larry Hart enthusiastic about the idea?

RODGERS: Oh, yes. He loved it. Loved it.

Q: It was such a departure for you. So many of the characters would be called disreputable.

RODGERS: They certainly were.

Q: Were you advised by friends or supposed experts in the theatre not to do it?

RODGERS: No. We weren't. The curious thing is that George Abbott, who directed it and produced it, was the least enthusiastic of all the people who were connected with it. He was afraid of it. But, like so many people, I think he was afraid to let it go, too. That was why he went through with it. No, there was one other person who was afraid of it. There was a dance director by the name of Robert Alton who was very popular and very successful, and George Abbott engaged him, because we all wanted him to stage the dances. We had our first rehearsal, which was a read-through one morning at a theatre, and at the end of the rehearsal Alton came to me and said, "I have to quit this. I can't go with it."

I asked him why. He said because there was nothing for him to do. I took him to lunch and talked him into staying with it. Of course, he did a brilliant job. There was plenty for him to do—things like "Happy Hunting Horn," the old "Flower Garden of My Heart"—you know, a lot of burlesque numbers, supposed to be bad Chicago nightclub productions and so on. But otherwise I don't recall anybody being pessimistic about it.

Q: How did you happen to cast Gene Kelly as Joey?

RODGERS: Well, we had seen Gene. I say "we," I'm sure other people had seen him, but I know I had seen him in *The Time of Your Life*, Saroyan, yes. He had a small part and did a little dance, and—oh, you had to look carefully to see him, he didn't have much to do, but I must have been looking carefully, because I thought he was wonderful. And we sent for him, and he ended up with the part. He was simply wonderful in it.

Q: Did the show go out of town?

RODGERS: Yes.

Q: How were the reviews and how was the reaction to it out of town, do you recall?

RODGERS: I don't remember. I don't think that they were wildly enthusiastic. It was a little avant-garde, you know, using characters like that, because as you say they were disreputable, with one exception, and that was the ingenue. She was stupid. This is not customary procedure in the theatre at all.

Q: The thing that surprises me, looking at some of the reviews that the show got, Atkinson of course on the *Times* who, I gather, then as later was the most influential of critics at the time—

RODGERS:—and because of himself, too—

Q: He found the show unpleasant, but many or most of the other excerpts seem to have been favorable. There's a myth today, most people think. Most if not all of the critics said at that time that it was too unpleasant.

RODGERS: Oh, I don't think so. I think it got pretty good reviews generally—not wildly enthusiastic ones, but good enough to give us a run. It must have hit a nerve in Brooks Atkinson, because he was very strong about it. He said it was scabrous and he ended his review saying, "But of course you can't get sweet water from a foul well."

And then, of course, when the revival was done ten years later, he was wonderful about it. He said that he couldn't understand what had been wrong about it. The thing is that he didn't understand the show, didn't appreciate it. He gave it a great review, and of course, as you probably know, this is the only case on record of a show doing better in revival than it did originally. A tremendous success.

Q: The first had broken the ground.

RODGERS: That's right.

Q: It probably is the most popular Rodgers and Hart score today.

RODGERS: No, I don't know. I don't think it's as popular. It certainly hasn't as many popular songs as *Babes in Arms*.

Q: No, but isn't *Pal Joey* probably the Rodgers and Hart show that is done most often today in various circuits?

RODGERS: Yes, I think so.

Endings and Beginnings

Q: It's certainly a fantastic score. We talked a little bit last time too about *By Jupiter*. We mentioned that part of it had been written in the hospital, which was probably your most difficult time with Larry Hart. Is it true that you asked Oscar Hammerstein sort of vaguely if he would be interested in collaborating with you in the future?

RODGERS: Yes.

Q: Earlier than the time when you were specifically concerned with *Oklahoma!*

RODGERS: Yes. George Abbott and I produced a show together called

Best Foot Forward, and we played in Philadelphia, and one day at lunch we were talking about Larry. He didn't write the score for *Best Foot Forward*. Martin and Blaine did. And George and I were talking about Larry, and sort of crystallized my own worries about him, my own fear, and I knew then that Larry was skidding, and this wasn't going to last very long.

I had known Oscar for many, many years, of course, and I hired a car in Philadelphia and drove down to Doylestown, where Oscar had a farm, about three-quarters of an hour away and had a long talk with Oscar. I told him I was worried about Larry and I thought that Larry was about to be through, and I asked him to think about the advisability of our working together. He was immediately agreeable to this idea, liked it, liked to work with me, and this was sort of an early commitment. And Oscar said he would jump in if Larry couldn't finish the job that we were thinking of doing, that we never did do—said he would come in and finish it, with or without credit, he didn't care, and if Larry couldn't do it at all, he'd be happy to do it. But in the meanwhile he thought that I should stay with Larry as long as I could, which of course I did, up to the point where it was just impossible.

Q: You mentioned that you asked Larry Hart to work on *Green Grow the Lilacs* with you and he didn't want to do it and you called Hammerstein.

RODGERS: Well, it wasn't as simple as that. The thing revolved—the split-up revolved around the fact that I wanted Larry to hospitalize himself, and not go to Mexico, which he was about to do. I knew that would be the end, if he did go, and I said—or have I done this before about the hospital?

Q: About his death?

RODGERS: No. No, when I wanted him to go to a hospital, and I offered to go with him.

Q: Yes, we did talk about that.

RODGERS: And he refused and insisted on going to Mexico. And it was finished, as I knew it would be. He came back completely wrecked. I had told him that if he insisted on going to Mexico I was going to Oscar, and he said, "Well, I think you should do that. I don't think *Green Grow the Lilacs* is going to make a good musical, but I think you should work with Oscar," which I did.

Q: Before we get into *Oklahoma!*, after that opened, you did the revival of *Connecticut Yankee*.

RODGERS: That's right.

Q: And then Mr. Hart died, after that.

RODGERS: That's right. During the period we worked on *Connecticut Yankee*—I don't remember whether I've said this before or not—he was in absolutely wonderful shape. Wrote some of the best lyrics he ever wrote. Easy to work with. He used to come out to the country and work with me. And everything was fine, until the opening night in Philadelphia of *Connecticut Yankee*. And he fell apart and never came together again.

Words and Music

Q: Several years after that and several years after *Oklahoma!* opened, five years I guess, there was a Hollywood biography called *Words and Music*, which was a Rodgers and Hart biography. It might be of interest to know how this came about. One assumes of course that the studio, MGM in this case, came to you and said, "We want to do a movie based on Rodgers and Hart, is this OK with you?" But I wonder how much control if any you had over the script? Of the picture?

RODGERS: I had no control over it. I never wanted the picture made. No. But I was the executor, one of the two executors of Larry's will. Larry had died by that time. And I was told by my lawyer that I could not refuse to have the picture made because I would be denying the estate a great deal of money. Well, that's pretty clear and understandable. And I had to agree to the making of the picture. It was made on the Coast. I wasn't there while it was being made. They had a story written that at times impinged on the truth, but not very often.

Q: But you were not able to approve the script?

RODGERS: No. No, I never saw it. What they did, you see, really, was skeletonize Larry and me in story, and what they really wanted was the use of the music and lyrics. They got a pretty good collection of songs out of it, and not a very good story.

Q: But don't they have to get the permission of people that are portrayed? For instance, wouldn't they have to come to your wife and say is it all right if they portray you? I mean, if they're calling a woman Dorothy Rodgers they must have her approval.

RODGERS: Oh, yes.

Q: All she could do was say yes or no, but neither of you could demand any kind of script approval of any sort?

RODGERS: No. As a matter of fact, that was one area—that and Mickey Rooney playing Larry—these were the two areas where they cast very well, where they did very well. Janet Leigh played my wife. Tom Drake played me, and there wasn't much resemblance there, but there was a curious, almost scary thing, that Janet at the time the picture was made looked exactly the way my wife did when she was the age of Janet. They were very much alike. And of course I always felt that Mickey was wonderful as Larry, all the mannerisms, very very good. It wasn't a very good picture. These biographies of song writers never turn out well.

Q: But it's a good excuse to get out the stars singing all these great songs.

RODGERS: That's right. That's right.

Q: How did you feel about watching Tom Drake up on the screen being called Richard Rodgers? Was it almost like watching a regular movie that bears no relation to yourself? Was it that distorted?

RODGERS: Oh, no. I thought it bore a relationship, not a very happy one. I wasn't very pleased about him.

Q: Only in Hollywood, I suppose, could you have. . . . It was amusing too to see the ads of it, with the names of thirty-two stars above the title, and underneath, "with Tom Drake," the one who was playing the leading character.

RODGERS: Sure.

Q: Has anybody ever approached you with the idea of doing a more realistic biography of Larry Hart?

RODGERS: No. It's never come up and I hope it doesn't.

Allegro

Q: Mr. Rodgers, can we talk a little bit about *Allegro*? Was the concept of this show Mr. Hammerstein's idea? Was it something he wanted to do?

RODGERS: Yes, it originated with Oscar, and I think came out of his friendship and discussions with his own doctor. They were very good friends, and I think the concept of the clinic in a rural area came out of their discussions. That was the mechanical basis of the show.

Q: Did you like the vague idea when he broached it to you?

RODGERS: Yes, I did, and after we accepted the idea, we went into techniques and thought that more or less Greek chorus would work well for the show. Actually it did, very effectively. They talked to the audience, sang to the audience, commented on the action. They talked to the actors and told the actors what to do. And what not to do. It was very effective. We had a lot of them, and the singing was fine, and the talking was very good. We got a woman up from Washington whose name I don't recall now, unfortunately, to coach them. She was fine.

Q: When was the decision made to let Agnes de Mille direct the whole show, rather than just choreography?

RODGERS: Very early. Very early, and it was a mistake. She wasn't particularly proficient at directing dialogue. But the work was too much for her, to do choreography and direct the book as well, and Agnes is not particularly equipped to do the vocal parts of the songs, let people just sing. She is essentially a choreographer and a very fine one. So it ended up with Oscar taking over the direction of the book, and I did quite a lot of work on the songs, and Agnes ended up doing the job that she'd always done.

Q: But did she get director credit on the show?

RODGERS: Oh, sure. We didn't change anything.

Q: Do you think there was too much dancing in it, or more dancing than there would have been if there had been a director to say to her, "This ballet is too long"?

RODGERS: No, I don't think so. My impression is not that the ballets, if there were more than one, were too long. The dancing was quite good, as a matter of fact.

Q: When the show opened, Richard Watts in his review said that Richard Rodgers in his interest in the pure idiom of his music has been a little afraid of getting a really tuneful song into his skillful score. What do you think he meant?

RODGERS: Well, I know what he meant by it, but his definition of a "tuneful score" could be a little subjective. There were a lot of tunes in the show, and I was no more interested in not having tunes than I would be in any score I might do or ever did. Watts also said something that annoyed me tremendously.

Q: What was that?

RODGERS: Everybody connected with the show wanted me to do something that I didn't want to do.

Q: What was that?

RODGERS: There was a scene in the school gymnasium, and at the time for the play—it was about 1925, '26—and they all wanted me to use as dance music a song from the Second *Garrick Gaieties* of 1926 called "Mountain Greenery," which was a big hit then and still is played to a certain extent, and I dislike the idea of quoting myself. I thought if you're going to quote a period piece, 1926, it ought to be Gershwin or Berlin, somebody who was around writing at the time. But I bowed to the weight of their opinion and let them use the thing.

Watts in reviewing the show said that the best I could do in the way of a tune was dig up one from the 1926 *Gaieties*. It's the only quarrel I've ever had with anything Dick Watts has ever written, I think. Oh, I think this was just a matter of hurt feelings more than anything else. It didn't matter so far as the show was concerned. But I felt that he should know better than that.

Q: Some of the critics felt that the show was—came across as being a bit pretentious.

RODGERS: I think it was.

Q: I was going to ask you how you would appraise the show now in retrospect?

RODGERS: No, I think it was too preachy, which was the one fault that Oscar had, if any. He tended to moralize a great idea, and this came across in *Allegro* more than in anything he ever did, to such an extent that in looking at the show the newspapers particularly went overboard and saw things that weren't there. They thought that the show tried to say that city life was no good and country life was all beautiful and fine, which was not the idea, wasn't even in the show. But it came off that way, because the city people that the boy, the leading man, did run up against weren't particularly admirable, and a lot of the country folk were. But I myself thought it moralized too much.

Q: You said I believe last time when we were talking about some musical that turned out to be less than successful, you said, "Assuming that there are people of talent involved in it, the main moment when a show is made or broken is the moment when people say how about making a musical out of such and such"—

RODGERS:—Yes—

Q:—Do you think in retrospect that you should not have tried to make a musical out of the idea of the doctor's life?

RODGERS: I'm not sure that it couldn't be done well. I think it was a very sticky idea, [a] very difficult one, and I don't think that from the viewpoint of story it was handled any too well. Of course, even now there are people who remember the show with a great deal of pleasure, and periodically there seems to be a drive launched to get a revival done, in the hope that it might do well now where it didn't when it was done originally. Times have changed, and possibly it was a little ahead of its time. As a matter of fact, some work is being done now on the book by a friend of mine, really, and if it comes off well we might try it. It did have very good things in it. But it had its drawbacks, and I'd like to remove the drawbacks and keep the good things, possibly add a few things.

South Pacific

Q: Shall we talk now about *South Pacific*? The idea of making a musical show inspired by the James Michener stories was Joshua Logan's originally, is that true?

RODGERS: Logan and (Leland) Hayward. I think it was suggested by Ken McKenna, who was then story editor at MGM, and there's a cute story about that. I met Josh at a party one night, and he told me about *Tales of the South Pacific,* the Michener book, and said, "Read a story in it about Fo' Dolla'," which was the way Bloody Mary talked, and I took out my little black notebook that I always carry and still carry, and just wrote the words "Fo' Dolla' " in it. And the next day I looked at my book, and the words meant nothing to me. I couldn't remember what it was, where it came from, and weeks later, I remembered that Josh had talked to me about a book, and got Josh on the phone and he told me again that is was *Tales of the South Pacific,* and he thought that the story "Fo' Dolla' " would make a wonderful musical.

I got the book, and I was laid up with a bad back. I was in bed for about a week. And I read "Fo' Dolla' " which I thought was fine, and because I was in bed and "Fo' Dolla' " was fine I read the rest of the book. And I thought it was wonderful. I called Josh, and said,

"Look, instead of buying the one short story, why don't we buy the whole book? It won't cost very much more, I'm sure, and we'll have other characters, other story possibilities."

He thought that was fine and he called Leland, and we bought the whole book, which was a very lucky thing, because the story of "Fo' Dolla'" concerns Bloody Mary's little daughter, a sixteen-year-old girl, and her affair with the Navy lieutenant, and when you summed the whole thing up, it was *Madame Butterfly*, and Oscar and I were discussing this one day in California, sitting alongside the pool at the Bel Air Hotel, and we started to worry about the Fo' Dolla' thing not being substantial enough, not being new enough, and wondered what other stories there were in the book that could be used either instead or with the story about the native girl and the Navy [Ed. Marine] lieutenant. We thought about the one about the young girl from Arkansas, and the middle-aged French planter on the island in the South Pacific, which was a much more mature story, novel, and we thought much more rewarding, and we realized that the two stories, one about the planter and the Navy nurse and the one about the lieutenant and the Native girl, could run parallel to each other. They'd answer each other. And that was how we arrived at the basic idea for the show *South Pacific*. Then we took characters from other stories, like the character of Billis, who was the big dealer. He always had a gimmick for everything, which made a very amusing character for the show. And we had access to all that material, all of which was very good. That was the genesis of the show.

Q: Was the idea of speaking out in this way against race prejudice an important factor in the appeal that the story idea had to you and to Mr. Hammerstein?

RODGERS: Oh, I don't think that there's any question that it played a part in this, but I don't think that this was central in our choice. They were very good stories, very amusing, very touching, and I think the racial intolerance in the case of, in the case of *The King and I*, was simply evidence of the way we both felt.

Q: I've read references to the fact that there was some pressure to get you to drop the "Carefully Taught" number from the show before it came to New York. Is there any truth at all to that?

RODGERS: Yes. There was some. Some people felt that—oh, I'm not sure how they felt, they were just uncomfortable about it.

Q: It wasn't that they didn't work—did they feel it was too serious?

RODGERS: No, I think the objections came from people who were basically intolerant themselves, and were upset, possibly unconsciously, by the song and the situation. But outweighing it by far were the vast numbers of people who thought it was fine, thought it should be said and thought it was said well. This is true even today all these years later. We get requests for it from ministers who want to use it as a text for a sermon. It's used in schools a great deal. And I think it was wise to keep it in. You never know how much good a thing like that does, if any, but I think you have to express yourself.

Q: I gather that Pinza was cast before anybody else.

RODGERS: Pinza was the first one. That happened at the Bel Air Hotel too. Yes, Ed Lester, who's a very good producer on the Coast, produces in Los Angeles and San Francisco, and whom we'd known for many years, called me up one evening and he said, "I'd like to bring up a subject and see if you can help. I have Ezio Pinza under contract for a show for next year, and I have a penalty clause in the contract. If I don't come up with an idea, not only do I lose Pinza but I have to pay him $25,000." I said, "I think your troubles are over, but let me talk to Oscar."

Q: Had you had any idea of casting that part before?

RODGERS: No. Hadn't even discussed it, as I recall. I talked to Oscar, and he called Ed Lester back, and told him we both liked the idea of using Pinza in a new musical we were just discussing.

   We arranged then to meet Pinza in New York. We were going back to New York and Pinza would be there shortly. And we had lunch, the three of us, in the Oak Room of the Plaza Hotel, and told him the idea, and he loved it, wanted to do it, saw that it was time for him to leave the Met, he'd been there too long, and wanted to do a Broadway show. We thought we could write one that he could appear in. And that was how Pinza got into it.

Q: How was he to work with?

RODGERS: Oh, he was fine. He was fine.

Q: No Metropolitan temperament?

RODGERS: None. None at all. He couldn't have been nicer. The one difficulty was with his English, which is very bad. At one point Josh Logan was ready to quit, not quit the job but quit trying to work with Pinza, try to replace him, and we talked him out of that, talked him into continuing and trying to get a performance out of him, and of course eventually did. But to the last day he was in the show, there were words that you couldn't understand. But you got the meaning just the same. He was magnificent in it.

Q: How did he react to being this matinee idol of the decade?

RODGERS: Oh, I think the way he always did. He'd been an operatic idol for many many years. It wasn't very different.

Q: But not the volume, I'm sure.

RODGERS: Oh, yes, he had a much bigger public, of course, but I think that he was used to those groups of people waiting at the stage door. That didn't seem to bother him. The only thing that bothered us was the pressure that was put on him the minute the show opened to get out of the show as soon as possible and get out where the real money was.

Q: You mean, night clubs?

RODGERS: No, movies. And his contract was for a year, and I don't think

314 The Composer Speaks, 1939–1971

the show was open three days before he had a contract to make two movies at the end of his year in *South Pacific*. And the minute the year was up he left the show and went right to the Coast, and made two enormous failures.

Q: Yeah. You told me last time about calling Mary Martin and about her dubiousness about singing with Pinza, and that you solved it by having them not sing together.

RODGERS: That's right. Yes.

Q: Ewen I guess refers to the fact that when she was cast, there were of course all sorts of billing problems and percentage problems to be ironed out, having two big stars like this. Did the two of them get along?

RODGERS: Oh, yes. Sure. Sure. There were no temperament troubles that I can recall with that show at all. All went very smoothly, and things fell into their place. No, there was no trouble like that. As a matter of fact, both Pinza and Martin did something almost unbelievable. They each wanted a very high percentage of the gross, and we told them that it wasn't possible, and that if they wanted to work with each other, and by that time they wanted to very much, they would both have to cut. And they did. Which did make it possible, as it wouldn't have been otherwise, wouldn't have been feasible. They were very good about it, and it turned out well for everybody.

Q: In the Ewen book, this is just one of many similar anecdotes. Someone brings you a lyric, leaves the room for five minutes and you've got the song written. The one I'm thinking of specifically is "Bali Ha'i" which according to Ewen was written in five minutes when some-body's back was turned. Is this really true? Do you work that fast?

RODGERS: Well, you see, it's true as far as it goes, but it doesn't go the whole way.

Q: Some songs, not others?

RODGERS: No—well, let's take "Bali Ha'i" as an example. Oscar comes into Logan's apartment. It's lunchtime. And he hands me a piece of paper with typewritten words on it. And I say, "Excuse me," and I go into the other room where the piano is, and sit alone for a few minutes, and then go to the piano and develop an idea I got sitting in a chair, and I think the whole process didn't take more than five minutes. That's true.

Now, what's been left out? What's been left out is the months before that day that I knew we were going to have a song about Bali Ha'i, about that island; that I knew Bloody Mary, who had to be a contralto, was going to sing it; that I knew it had to have an island flavor. I knew all the conditions surrounding the composition of that tune. Absolutely everything. And I'd had the title for months.

Now, I think any writer will tell you that you carry an idea around for months before it's crystallized. Then the moment "of truth" comes and he sits down to make something. This leaves out all the months of gestation, thinking about it.

Q: But these months and gestation is mental, you hadn't sat down at a piano?

RODGERS: No, nowhere near a piano, didn't have two consecutive notes. You see, the business of writing for the theatre is writing descriptive music. Now, what you write when you're writing for the theatre is conditioned by the character singing the song, the situation, the song that went before it, the song that follows it, the climate you're work- ing in—is it Oklahoma, is it Siam, is it West Side or is it an island in the South Pacific? All these things condition your thinking, and your thinking can go on for months. Then a man comes in and hands you some words that are very very good and absolutely correct, and over three-quarters of your work is done for you. And you go, and if you have your trade, you know how to apply it, and it can come very quickly. It can be slow, too, but that you don't hear about because it's not remarkable.

The same thing with "Oh, What a Beautiful Mornin'." You've known, after long discussion, how you want to open your show, what you would like the thing to smell like. You know everything about who's going to sing it, to whom. You know it should be a waltz—it should be in three-quarter time anyway. And in comes a man with a set of lovely words, and the hair starts to rise on the back of your neck and you're off to the races.

But the story that you read in the magazine interview leaves out all the preparatory work. It just goes to those few minutes of actual composition. It's like saying, "She had a baby in a half an hour." Well, she didn't have a baby in a half an hour at all. She had a baby in a minimum of nine months, and maybe 29 years. Because the whole personality goes into it. So does her husband's. Everything about that kid is pre-arrived at. And then she actually goes to work and has the kid. Well, this isn't very different, unless you're an awfully sloppy worker.

Q: That's very interesting. I'm glad we got to that. There was a departure in the usual rehearsal procedure, I gather. Instead of breaking the thing up and having dances in one place, and somebody—in another—

RODGERS: Yes—for a very good reason. There were no dances.

Q: True. I shouldn't have mentioned the dancing. Isn't the procedure sometimes to have various members of the cast working in different places on different scenes?

RODGERS: Oh, sure. Different buildings, usually.

Q: Why was the decision made here to work in one place?

RODGERS:—Because they were all part of the book.

Q: Because the thing was so closely integrated.

RODGERS: Closely integrated, and there was no dancing. There's some singing by the ensemble, but a thing like "Nothing Like a Dame" had a great deal of movement in it, but it wasn't dancing, and had to be directed as though it were dialogue, which Logan did brilliantly. So you got the feeling that you were almost looking at a ballet. But that had to be rehearsed by the Seabees who also played small parts in the show. The thing was rehearsed very much the way a dramatic show is.

Q: It's not fair then to say this procedure was done as a departure because you wanted the show and the people in it to feel that—

RODGERS: Oh, no. There was no other way to do it. There was no other way to do it. There'd be no sense in sending the boys and girls, the Navy nurses and the Seabees, off to another building to rehearse something. There was nothing for them to rehearse that didn't involve the principals. So everything had to be done in one building.

Q: Anyway, *South Pacific* was of course a fantastic success in New York. Why do you think, when it opened in London, the reviewers were less than enthusiastic? Just a question of too much buildup in advance?

RODGERS: That could have had something to do with it. I have always felt that the London press was very chauvinistic about their theatre and particularly their musical theatre, because the English have been amazingly inept at doing musical shows. They haven't done any really fine ones in my lifetime. And there's a jealousy there, and I think it gets into the press. *Oklahoma!* when it went there at the end of the war took them by surprise, and the notices were wonderful, but that was the last show of Oscar's and mine that got good notices in London.

Q: They didn't like *Carousel*?

RODGERS: Oh, no. It was "over sentimental." Everything we did was over sentimental. "Treacle" is the word they love to use. This is the worst thing they can say about anything, and they used that extensively. About everything we did. We never got a good set of notices again. And the worst set of notices we ever got in London was *The Sound of Music*.

Q: Yes, I think we mentioned that in our first interviews, how cruel they were to Mr. Hammerstein.

RODGERS: Oh, yes, they were terrible. And I think I must have mentioned too that it ran in London for almost six years.

Q: The movie version of *South Pacific* came quite some time later. Was this another case where you were not involved at all in the filming?

RODGERS: I myself was not involved at all, although I was one of the producers. Oscar and I owned the company that produced it. I was ill and didn't get out for any of the shooting at all. Oscar did, some of it.

Q: That too was successful financially, I gather, but there were critical barbs about its being overproduced, comments about the use of various color lenses for various scenes which seemed unnecessary and so forth. What did you think of the final product?

RODGERS: I thought it was awful. I thought it was over-produced. I thought the use of color was atrocious.

Q: Who directed it?

RODGERS: Logan. And he ran wild. If you remember the little show that the Seabees and the Navy nurses put on at the beginning of the second act, it's a pathetic little thing. Their costumes were made of comic strip pages from the newspapers that had been sent to them, and you got the feeling that they might have played to an audience of, oh, at most 100 men. That was the way the whole show was done. In that particular part of the film, it was an enormous vaudeville show that they put on. You saw soldiers that went back to what looked like to miles, watching the show. This is an example of over-elaboration. So the picture lost all personal contact, and didn't do much good to see the girl's face turn from natural color to yellow when she started to sing.

Q: Did Josh Logan ever tell you what he had in mind with this peculiar use of color? Did he ever talk about it?

RODGERS: Yes, he talked about it, when we said we thought it was awful. By then he discovered the whole theory, and said it simply wasn't possible to go back to ordinary photography, that somebody had told him it would be possible if he didn't like it, but he was committed and couldn't change. Well, I don't know. There it was, at least, that way. And it was successful. It did make money. But I think somebody once said, "That isn't everything."

Pipe Dream

Q: When we last spoke, Mr. Rodgers, we were in the mid-fifties, just about up to the time when you started to do *Pipe Dream*. Is it true that Feuer and Martin were originally planning to do *Pipe Dream* with Frank Loesser?

RODGERS: I don't remember that now.

Q: Well, in the Ewen book, he says that they had the rights and they were going to use Frank Loesser. Somehow that fell through and they came to you and Mr. Hammerstein and asked if you would do the show. Were they associated with it in any way?

RODGERS: No. Not at all. It's possible, of course. We knew them. But I don't remember that. Certainly they weren't in it in any way.

Q: What is your recollection then of how the idea of doing *Sweet Thursday* came about?

RODGERS: I'm not sure about how it did come about, except that we were very friendly with John Steinbeck, who wrote *Sweet Thursday*, and it could have come about through him very easily.

Q: What kind of guy is Steinbeck personally?

RODGERS: Oh, he's fine. A very nice man. Certainly as intelligent a man as you'd like to meet. Very good to be with. We still see him and his wife.

Q: Was he enthusiastic about the idea of making a musical out of it?

RODGERS: Yes.

Q: What do you think it was that attracted you to the book?

RODGERS: I think, the writing and the characters. Because of course that was where we made our big mistake—we were seduced by the writing and the characters, and didn't recognize the fact that the characters were not right for Oscar and me. We shouldn't have been dealing with prostitutes and tramps.

Q: *Pal Joey* was a disreputable character.

RODGERS: Yes, but that wasn't Rodgers and Hammerstein, you see.

Q: That was Rodgers and Hart.

RODGERS: The public didn't expect the same thing. I'm not using that as an alibi for the failure of the show.

Q: And you do feel it was a failure.

RODGERS: Oh, it was.

Q: I'm not talking about financially, but you regard it as an artistic failure.

RODGERS: Yes. I think these things are epidemic within a show. You start out with a bad idea, and everything seems to become infected.

Q: How did you hit on the idea of casting Helen Traubel? Wasn't she a Madame in it?

RODGERS: Yes, she was. And that was a big mistake. We had seen her on television a great deal and of course knew her from the opera, and we didn't know that there'd been a good deal of disintegration as far as the voice was concerned, and my wife and I stopped off in Las Vegas to see her work in one of the hotel nightclubs, when we were on our way back from California. And that was misleading, because she had a microphone within six inches of her face, and she was jolly and there was no acting. But it all looked fine. This looked like the woman we'd seen and enjoyed on television. And when we got her in the theatre, we found out that it was a different woman entirely. She couldn't have been nicer, but the voice had gone, to a great extent, and she didn't know how to act. And we had made a vital mistake in taking a woman without a thorough audition in the theatre—which is a mistake I haven't made since then.

Flower Drum Song

Q: How do you feel about *Flower Drum Song* in retrospect? It was a success, [but] not of the caliber of your greater shows.

RODGERS: I like it. I liked the show when it was done. Beyond its success, I liked the movie. I felt they did it quite well. But I've always liked that show.

The Sound of Music

Q: Of course the next one, *Sound of Music*, was a fantastic smash, behind only *Oklahoma!* and *South Pacific* in the number of performances on Broadway. How did you come to do the Trapp family story?

RODGERS: Just how Leland Hayward and Dick (Richard) Halliday got the idea, I don't know.

Q: They came up with the scheme first and brought it to you, was that it?

RODGERS: Yes. Yes. And their original idea, the reason they came to see me—Oscar wasn't terribly well then—they asked me to look at the German film about the Trapp family, and their idea was to do it with Mary Martin as a straight play. And they wanted me and Oscar to write one number that Mary could sing someplace in the show. I watched the film, and after it was over, we sat around talking. Lindsay and Crouse had been approached and were willing to write the play. I said that I thought it was a mistake, that they should do it without songs, do it as a straight play, or do it as a full musical, go all out. And they agreed, they thought it was a good idea.

Our trouble there was that we were committed to do *Flower Drum Song*, and that was all set. The people were engaged, the theatre was arranged for, and it had to be done first. I told them it would take a year before we would be free. It was very flattering— they said they would wait, if we would do it as a full musical. And Oscar saw the film shortly after and liked it, liked the idea, and we all agreed to do it and we did do it.

Q: It seems strange to consider a story about a singing family in terms of a straight play rather than a musical.

RODGERS: That's right. You'd have to have all your singing off stage.

Q: Do I gather from this that Mary Martin was interested in doing a straight play rather than a musical?

RODGERS: I gathered that from our conversations. Her husband [Holliday] was there talking for her.

Q: It certainly would not have been a really dramatic part to show off a new facet of her talent. Do you think just simply doing a straight play is easier and less exhausting than doing a musical? Do you think that's why she wanted to?

RODGERS: No, I don't think so. I think it just appealed to them in that way. The German picture had very little singing in it, was more or less a dramatic story about the Trapp family.

Q: Were there any particular problems in getting some of the music to work?

RODGERS: No. No, from the musical point of view, it lent itself very readily, comfortably, to music. It's easy enough once you've made up your mind that nuns could sing, to let them sing, and as long as you accept the fact that singing in the theatre is part of the book, and if you keep it part of the book, you have no trouble. No reason why the Mother Superior can't sing, and she sang the second and third

number in the show and again later, of course. There were no troubles at all. You had the family itself. It was easy enough to make
them sing, and to accept the fact that they sang.

Q: Of course, the show was a fantastic smash, and the movie wound up
being the biggest grossing movie in history. What do you think of the
movie version?

RODGERS: I thought it was wonderful. I thought they did everything well.
From the very start of the picture, that fantastic swooping down
through the mountains to the meadow, and picking up Julie
Andrews. That began it and I think it never stopped.

Q: When we first started doing these interviews we talked a bit about the
reaction to or of the critics of how cruel they could be sometimes.
You mentioned specifically the London critics, regarding *Sound of
Music*, cruelty directed mostly at Mr. Hammerstein, I guess.

RODGERS: No, it was the whole thing. I think I came off less badly than
the others, with the music, although there was not great enthusiasm.
But they were terrible to the book and even worse to the lyrics.

Q: How do you account for this? Critics of course are going to be more
sophisticated than the average theatregoer. There's plenty of music in
the show that the average person obviously loves and adores. How
do you account for the fact that there seemed to be some undue
hostility towards this show?

RODGERS: I don't know, unless it's a native resentment towards anything
that is simple emotionally as *The Sound of Music*. They are much
more inclined to be good to something that's new, which is reasonable, that's fine, but has no connection with sentiment whatsoever,
and I think that is unreasonable. Surely vast numbers of the theatregoing public and the motion picture public are deeply interested in
sentiment. And I'm tired of this semantic nonsense about the difference between sentiment and sentimentality. I still don't know what
that means. But most of us live on sentiment. We feel it towards our
parents when we're very young. We feel it toward our wives and
husbands and certainly toward our children. It's a way of life all over
the world. And to reject this, I think is ridiculous. And this is what
they're doing. They will accept something that doesn't even make
sense, much less sentiment, like *Hair*.

Q: I take it you've seen *Hair* recently?

RODGERS: Yes, I've seen *Hair* recently, and I admired its muscle. I don't
know where all that energy came from, and I don't know where it
went. Certainly it went into nothing.

Q: So then you did not like the show?

RODGERS: No. I didn't like the show. I don't know why it was produced,
and I don't know what it accomplished. When I was there, there was
very little audience reaction. Fair applause. Very little laughter. And

to see a few naked people in very dim light is not my idea of an evening.

No Strings

Q: Last time, Mr. Rodgers, we were talking about Mr. Hammerstein, and we reached the point where he died and your very fruitful collaboration with him was over. At that time, how did you envision your future in the theatre at that point?

RODGERS: I wasn't sure about it. The theatre is a collaborative enterprise. You never work alone, you never work in a vacuum, and I knew I would have to work with somebody, although not necessarily a lyric writer. I felt that I could do my own lyrics if I had to. I would have been happy then, as I am happy now, to work with some vigorous young person of talent. But at that time, I didn't feel able to adjust myself to a new personality. I'd only worked with two men in my life, and while I was very lucky with Oscar because there was no adjustment there, I knew that it was luck and that I couldn't expect that kind of relationship twice, at least not at the beginning, and I felt that I'd be better off trying to go it alone, for a while at least. Which is exactly what I did.

From a personal viewpoint, there's an enormous sense of loss because as I told you we were very close friends, and then there was the professional sense of loss, because we got on very well working together, and I really didn't know what was going to happen, felt that I had to play it by ear.

Not too long after, I got the idea for the show that turned out to be *No Strings*.

Q: The original idea for the show was yours?

RODGERS: Yes.

Q: What was the nutshell idea?

RODGERS: The nutshell idea was seeing Diahann Carroll on TV one night, and she was well-dressed, and her hair was attractively done, and I felt that it might be a wonderful idea to take a colored girl and put her in a stratum of society that you weren't used to seeing colored people in—to dress her extremely well, and let her lead a much more sophisticated and intellectual life. In other words, to get them out of the bandanna and gingham stage. And before I did anything else, I phoned Diahann, whom I knew and whom I'd admired tremendously, ever since *House of Flowers* when she was in her first part and was a very young girl. And we met, and she thought it was a wonderful idea and wanted to do it.

The next step was to get a book. Now, I'd had experience with Samuel Taylor. Oscar and I have produced a play of his called *The*

Happy Time which was based on a novel, and it had been a very fruitful and very pleasant relationship. I called Sam in, and he liked the idea, liked Diahann, and wanted to work with me. He did some preliminary work, and then Dorothy and I went up to his place in Maine and spent a week or ten days up there, laying out the show, getting ideas for numbers, putting them into a fairly loose general synopsis that we had, and from there on just proceeded the way you'd expect.

Q: When you got into this, you knew you were going to be doing the lyrics?

RODGERS: For that show? Yes. Yes.

Q: As I recall, the show is about a white American writer and his romance in Paris with Diahann Carroll.

RODGERS: That's right.

Q: She of course is a Negress, but is there much in the actual dialogue of the show about this problem, about the fact that she is a Negro?

RODGERS: No, it's never verbalized at all in the play.

Q: A white girl could actually play the part?

RODGERS: No, she couldn't, because where the man gets hung up eventually is when he realizes that he's been wasting his time and his talent and his energy running around Europe having fun, and he knows that the only way he'll ever concentrate and write a second book is to go back to the United States and go back to Maine, where he came from, and sit down and concentrate. Then the race thing becomes perfectly evident and looms very large. He knows he can't take this girl into a small Maine community. It would be impossible for her, and therefore impossible for him.

Q: It isn't just her race, though. Isn't it also that she's such a sophisticated worldly person that she would have difficulty adjusting to a small town in Maine regardless?

RODGERS: Yes. Yes, but I don't think that would be enough, for two people of the same race, to break up a marriage.

Q: All this is very subtly implied, mostly by the fact that you look at her and you see she's a Negro.

RODGERS: That's right.

Q: But there are no actual words at any point.

RODGERS: No, it is not said. No, but we know what she is, even in one song, where the boy sings about his boyhood in Maine, and she sings about her childhood "North of Central Park," and we didn't have to tell the audience that she was a Negro. It's perfectly obvious.

Q: What was your own working system when you were writing the songs and the lyrics?

RODGERS: It varied. I had no set method of working. You mean, in writing the songs? No, I would do it any way that I felt. I'd get an idea for a song, and from that a title, and then possibly write the whole tune, and then finish the lyrics, or occasionally write a whole lyric and set it to music, as though somebody else had written the words. I had no set plan at all.

Q: The idea of having the orchestra without strings and having it offstage but not in the pit, the whole concept of the show—how did it evolve? I mean, for instance, even the title—I mean, it couldn't have been called *No Strings* until you decided not to have strings.

RODGERS: That's right.

Q: What was the timing and how did that evolve?

RODGERS: Well, the title came before anything else. I mean, when the book was finished, the title came before the songs were written. As a matter of fact, the song, "Sweetest Sounds," was the first one I did, and then I think the second one was the song called "No Strings," which was in the second act of the play. The idea of not having musicians in the pit, but offstage, evolved out of long talks with Joe Layton, the director of the show. It was an idea that I liked very much. I wanted to see how practical it was, and it turned out that it was extremely practical. But the one thing that I wanted more than anything else was to involve the musicians with the players, and actually we started the play off that way. There was no overture. The curtain went up, and Diahann Carroll sang a duet with a flute, and the flute player was onstage with her, but he was to be disregarded, except by the ear. He didn't exist as a character. There was no flute player. But he was there playing a flute.

Then we went from there to Dick (Richard) Kiley, who sang with a clarinet. And this was before the two characters met in actuality. Later on, I used a small combination onstage, used a solo trumpet, and the first act ended with the drum solo, and you saw the drummer, and that was all you saw, because the boy and girl were in the bedroom. The drummer simply played what you knew was going on, between the boy and girl. That had never been done before and hasn't been done since.

Q: All this evolved collaboratively between you and Mr. Layton?

RODGERS: Yes, and Sam Taylor as well, but these basic ideas were mine.

Q: How do you feel about the show in retrospect?

RODGERS: Very happy about it.

Q: It was a success, as I recall.

RODGERS: Not a big one. Not a big one. It got by, but barely.

Q: What were the reviews like?

RODGERS: The *Tribune* was bad, the *Times* was wonderful, and the rest of the papers (because we had a few then) went from pretty good to very good. We had all in all quite a good press.

Q: I remember loving it.

RODGERS: Well, from the way people talk to me about it now, it isn't really far enough back for an awful lot of nostalgia to set in. People did like it.

Q: It was glamorous, which is something you miss in theatre today.

RODGERS: Yes. And it was new. It may have been too new. I'd like to see it done again in another five years, let us say. It might be the same thing that happened to us with *Pal Joey*, which had a great many passionate fans, and not an enormous public, until it was revived, ten years after it was done first.

Q: There's one question I should ask you, from the point of view of what's going on in the country today. During the course of rehearsals of the out of town try-outs, was there anything in the way of unpleasant incidents or pressure because of the fact that this was a relationship between a white and a Negress?

RODGERS: Not once. Not one single incident. Nobody ever walked out. Nobody ever objected to it. And I don't think there were more than three letters objecting to the idea, or to what went on in the play, and you can tell by reading letters about the person who's written them. You can tell the personality. And these were what one refers to as crank letters. Had no meaning whatsoever. But in general the public was wonderful about it.

Q: Did you enjoy the process of writing your own lyrics for the show?

RODGERS: Yes. I did. It was difficult, but lyric writing is extremely difficult anyway. Any lyric writer will tell you that.

Q: You also wrote a couple of lyrics for the remake of the movie *State Fair*.

RODGERS: *State Fair*, yes. Oh, very often I had to write lyrics for updated versions of shows, and when I was working with Larry, very often I had to do his work for him, and that meant lyric writing. I'd had more experience than most people knew. And besides that, I worked in very close proximity to both lyric writers, Larry and Oscar, and I had to learn a good deal about the trade.

Q: And yet for your next show, you did first get I think Alan Jay Lerner for a while, which didn't work out, and Stephen Sondheim, so you decided that you'd prefer to have a lyricist if you could find one who was appropriate?

RODGERS: I'd always be delighted to work with a lyric writer who's better than I am. I felt that way then. I felt that Alan wrote a better lyric than I could, and the difficulty there was that he wouldn't write any lyrics.

Q: This was the show that eventually became *On a Clear Day*.

RODGERS: Yes.

Q: How did you get involved in it? Did he come to you with the idea or did you have the idea?

RODGERS: I'm trying to remember who called whom. I think this was all a matter of exchanging underground messages. You know, the way politicians approach each other. Nobody picks up a telephone and says frankly, "How'd you like to work with me?" You send out feelers, and I think we were both feeling around, trying to find each other, and we did. The only unfortunate thing was, it didn't work. He's a brilliant lyric writer. He's fine. You can see that in *On a Clear Day*, which eventually reached the stage, and that was a failure, but the songs were great. He found a very good composer, Burton Lane, whose tunes were lovely. Did a very good job. Where the play failed was in the book, but not in the songs.

Q: The association between the two of you, when this show was in mind, dragged on quite a while, didn't it, before you decided it just wouldn't work?

RODGERS: Oh, yes, two or three years of struggling and trying to get the work done. Finally I knew it would never happen and I gave up.

Do I Hear a Waltz?

Q: Who came to you with the idea of doing *Do I Hear a Waltz?*

RODGERS: Arthur Laurents, the author of *Time of the Cuckoo*, on which *Do I Hear a Waltz?* was based, and I had been talking about this for a few years, and eventually we decided we'd better do it as a musical, and Steve Sondheim, a great friend of Arthur Laurents, and also a first-rate lyric writer, and the three of us got together to do the show. It's a matter of conference [Ed. probably coincidence], really, that got us all together.

Q: The show I believe was not a financial success.

RODGERS: No, indeed.

Q: What do you think went wrong?

RODGERS: Well, again, I think what went wrong was in the book.

Q: It was a bad idea in the first place?

RODGERS: No, I think it was a good idea, but I think the insistence on the part of the author in making the heroine unsympathetic just made it impossible for that show to be received by the public. Women hated it, and that's always bad. The character of the girl was very unpleasant, and the love affair in the play was abortive, and unpleasant in its own way too. I think this all hurt it. I don't think it was a terribly good score, either. There was one song called "Do I Hear a Waltz?" which is still played quite a lot, but that's about all. The lyrics were brittle, and not loving at all. I don't think that helps.

Q: That was what he was aiming at, though it didn't work.

RODGERS: Yes. Yes, surely, and the music has to reflect the content of the lyrics and the book. I'm not trying to cop out, as they say, and blame the fact that the score wasn't terribly good on somebody else. I know it wasn't very good. But it was preceded by a good score, perhaps a number of good scores.

"The Broadway Audience Is Still There, Waiting for More Good Shows"

During the run of *Two by Two* Rodgers discussed "the state of the theater" in an interview in *Dramatists Guild Quarterly*. At the outset, Rodgers states categorically that the problems with Broadway can be attributed to the absence of first-rate new material. He then offers his opinions on the current scene, expresses his antipathy to rock (which he calls hard rock and devoid of melody and harmony), and his appreciation of the sole nonrock component of Burt Bacharach's *Promises, Promises*, the song "I'll Never Fall in Love Again." Acknowledging the difficulties he had over an extended period of forced amateur labor from 1920 to 1925 and the resulting desperation that placed him on the verge of abandoning the theater (to sell underwear), Rodgers offers encouragement and advice to those who dream of a professional career: get your work performed anywhere and by anybody. As Rodgers put it, "If I were starting out and the Astor Hotel [home of Columbia's Varsity Show of 1920, *Fly With Me*] was still in existence, I would be satisfied to have my stuff shown in its men's room. Any place."

The following is an edited transcript of a recent question-and-answer session with Richard Rodgers about the state of the theater, held at the request of the Dramatists Guild Quarterly, *expressly for publication in these pages. We are grateful to Mr. Rodgers for his generous cooperation in this project, whose questioners were the* Quarterly's *editor and reporter.* [Tagline by *Dramatists Guild Quarterly* editor.]

Q: You have just celebrated fifty years in show business by doing a new show and it, like most of your others, is a resounding success. How does bringing in a show differ from when you first began?

RODGERS: *Two by Two* was fun in spots and murder in others.

Q: Was it more of a chore—more murder—than it would have been ten years ago?

RODGERS: I don't think so. Your trouble in producing any show arises out of the confrontations with the people you are working with. You have your difficulties with writers and actors as people rather than as craftsmen or performers. This is where you have your trouble, just as you do in a club you belong to or a bar you go to. It's the guy on the stool next to you who's almost as neurotic as you are.

Source: Richard Rodgers, "The Broadway Audience Is Still There, Waiting for More Good Shows," *Dramatists Guild Quarterly* (1971), 6, 11–17.

Q: Does the result still seem worth the effort?

RODGERS: Certainly. You'd have to be terribly sick not to enjoy it.

Q: Do you find it gives you as much pleasure to bring in a successful show as it did, say, thirty years ago?

RODGERS: I'm not sure that it does. I think it would be fatuous to say that you don't get a little used to it, but I guess you get a little used to trouble too. Still it's essentially the same. You go down there and see a lot of standees and you say, "Oh, Ma, look at me," and it's great. A number at the end of the first act stops the show, and again, it's great. Or you read a bad notice and it hurts like hell.

Q: What about audience reaction, now and then?

RODGERS: The audience reaction is just what it always has been to any successful show that I have had anything to do with. They're just as enthusiastic; they applaud as often. They laugh as much.

Q: What about the general debilitation of the city itself—the rising incidence of crime, the dirt, the disrepair? What is this going to do to the Broadway theater?

RODGERS: It is going to hurt. All these things, strikes, whatever, hurt us but I don't think this is our main trouble. I think the trouble lies with us, in the shows we are producing, the shows we are writing.

Q: Do you mean that we are doing bad work, or doing the wrong work?

RODGERS: Doing wrong work is doing bad work. We aren't doing enough good shows—shows good enough to bring people down from Scarsdale and in from New Jersey. Every time we do get a hit on Forty-fifth Street all the other shows on Forty-fifth Street start to do well.

Q: That is still true?

RODGERS: That still is absolutely true.

Q: In other words, you think that all the Broadway theater really needs is better material.

RODGERS: That's right. That's right.

Q: There are about thirty theaters on Broadway. Do you think that if we could come up with thirty good shows the public in New York would support them?

RODGERS: Yes, I do. I do. I often meet people who say they would love to go to the theater but don't know what to go to see. Then they ask me to recommend something. Hell. They shouldn't have to ask me to recommend something. Who am I? I'm a guy who works in the theater.

Q: Do you think they mistrust the critics?

RODGERS: That's what the politicians call a good question. I don't know. I only know the way I feel about them. Certain of the critics I do trust, and certain of them I do not. Certain of them I trust in certain areas, and not in others.

Q: How do you think today's critics compare with those of, say, twenty years ago?

RODGERS: Twenty years ago you could think of critics as a group, but you can't today, unless you want to throw in radio and television where they devote about sixty seconds to reviewing a show that has taken two years to produce. I suppose they are critics because they criticize.

Q: Is there any radio or television critic whom you regularly listen to and like?

RODGERS: No. If I happen to be home I listen to the eleven o'clock news, and very often I hear this one-minute review.

Q: Does any one radio or television reviewer stand out in your mind?

RODGERS: I think Newman is outstanding. He seems more serious, less casual. But I don't know how uncasual you can be in a minute. And incidentally this is a man who panned hell out of *Two by Two*.

Q: Do you think you got a fair shake from today's critics on *Two by Two*?

RODGERS: On the whole it got a very good press. I think it was a good press. From where I sit it had to be a fair press. You're not going to fight with a good notice.

Q: You say we're not creating the right material today, and that if we were we could keep thirty playhouses open—that there is an audience. What is the nature of this "right" material? What should a young playwright try to write for the Broadway theater?

RODGERS: That depends entirely on what he likes to write, or what he is capable of writing. You can't tell him to write comedies or write tragedies. We know that in times of stress people want to forget their troubles, so I suppose comedies have a better chance. I am not even sure of that. I think what they want more than anything else is to see good work.

Q: Why is there a dearth of good work?

RODGERS: I don't know. I don't know where the writers have gone. A number of years ago we had a very good alibi. We said they were all in Hollywood writing pictures. Well, they aren't making any pictures, so that can't be where they are, and television doesn't use them. Maybe they are afraid to spend the couple of years that it takes to write a play and get it produced, provided they are well enough known to get it produced. Producers aren't inclined to take chances at today's prices.

Q: If you were starting out now, would you be satisfied to have your work shown in Minnesota or Los Angeles or New Haven or some place other than New York?

RODGERS: If I were starting out and the Astor Hotel was still in existence, I would be satisfied to have my stuff shown in its men's room. Any place.

Q: Would a Milwaukee men's room have the same significance to you as a New York men's room?

RODGERS: Perhaps not. I think there would be a poorer chance of breaking into the commercial theater by way of Milwaukee than by way of Forty-fourth Street. But nevertheless I would rather be shown in Milwaukee than not shown, and I think this is the only way for young people to get started. It doesn't have to be Milwaukee. It doesn't have to be big. It can be somebody's club. It can be somebody's church. I say this with a great deal of feeling because that's the way I started—doing amateur shows.

Q: Where was this?

RODGERS: In New York. Larry (Hart) and I used to write shows for anything. We wrote a show for a girls' school. Our first success was what would now be called an off-Broadway show. In 1925. It was a revue called *The Garrick Gaieties*. It played at the Garrick Theater on Thirty-fifth Street, between Sixth and Broadway. It was just a little bit of a revue. Twelve kids in it, and it caught on and put us on our feet. It was just a little more professional than the amateur shows that we had been doing right along. We wrote a show for a girls' school—a musical version of *If I Were King*—and the lead was played by Dorothy Fields with a beard. I think you'll do anything to be heard.

Q: With the goal of eventually being heard in New York.

RODGERS: I think eventually, as the theater runs today, New York has got to be your target. Apparently there is increased activity regionally—I know something about that because I know how often these theaters do our stuff.

Q: Is the Broadway theater—as it exists today—a worthy arena for the young composer who has goals similar to those you aspired to as a young man?

RODGERS: It has to be. I don't think he has any choice. They aren't producing.

Q: They are not producing the musical shows the kids go to on Broadway. The kids—the forthcoming adult audience—are at Fillmore East. What's going to happen to the Broadway musical when these kids—having grown up on rock—become the expense account audience?

RODGERS: I can tell you more about that when I find out how much acceptance the score of *Two by Two* has with the kids.

Q: To what extent have you accommodated the arrangements, orchestrations, melody lines, and so forth, of *Two by Two* to the rock revolution?

RODGERS: Not at all.

Q: Not in the least?

RODGERS: Not in the least. When I studied music at Juilliard, I was told that music is composed of three elements: melody, harmony and rhythm. To an enormous degree, what they are hearing at Fillmore East includes only one-third of these: it has rhythm. It has very little in the way of harmony and nothing in the way of melody. You can, I suppose, tear up the old definition and say that rhythm is music. But I don't believe it. I don't think that anybody else does either.

Q: Then you don't see the music of *Hair*, or of *Promises, Promises*, as the precursor of the new Broadway music?

RODGERS: I think that both *Hair* and *Promises* as scores try to be hard rock. Whether they succeed in this respect or not, I am not expert enough to know. But I know where I would place my money, if there were some way of betting on it. I would bet that the song "I'll Never Fall in Love Again," from *Promises*, will be around when everything in *Hair*, and all of the "hard rock" portions of *Promises*, are forgotten. That's a song song. It's the only thing in the score that anybody knows and I think the reason is that it has melody and harmony, and the rhythm falls naturally. It's a lovely rhythm, but this isn't what it is based on. It is a very good song.

Q: You seem to be saying that the Broadway theater is the only musical theater we have—just like this is the only planet we have—and so we'd better take care of it. How are we to make it more viable, economically as well as artistically?

RODGERS: I think you get back to basics. It's all in the writing, to begin with. Then you need professional producers, and they exist. Mr. Merrick finds a good piece of material, and produces it superbly, and he gets a hit. But first he has to have the good material. Of course, the more expensive it becomes to produce, the less chance the marginal show has. We're into a feast or famine situation where you have a big hit or you close. There's no such thing as a musical that does fairly well.

Q: A kid who has the book and the score of a new musical pretty well along—what is he to do?

RODGERS: I guess he does the same thing I did. He sits on a lot of benches and gets turned away by all the publishers. He sends stuff in the mail and it is returned, usually unopened. He is confronted with a completely impossible situation. In some way, one out of I don't know how many thousands breaks through this. While he's waiting for it to happen he has a job at Macy's, or he's going to school. In the meantime he writes, and that he has to do. He has to write. If he doesn't write, then he will certainly get no place.

Q: Does the man who really has it make it?

RODGERS: I don't think so. He can be closed out and become discouraged. I felt discouraged when I was 22, and almost went into another business, and then *The Garrick Gaieties* came along. It was another semi-amateur show. I was pretty weary of amateur shows by the time I was 22, but I tried one more, and it was the one more that worked. For myself, and for many of the people I know, the unprofessional show was the answer—it's what got the cork out of the bottle. Sometimes, hard as it is, they come out of the colleges. Cole Porter did. Deems Taylor came out of NYU. Oscar (Hammerstein) and I came out of Columbia, not together. Both Oscar and Larry were seven years ahead of me. But the colleges are a very good proving ground for a composer, for a lyric writer, for a playwright.

Q: Have you ever wished that you hadn't gotten so tied to one particular genre of music, and had, instead, explored other veins?

RODGERS: I took a little time. I tried. But the one thing I have always found interesting is writing for the theater. I never wanted to be a "serious" composer. Symphonic work is not for me, and what else is there? I certainly don't want to write grand opera. Even if I knew how, I wouldn't want to.

Q: What comes first, the lyric or the melody line?

RODGERS: Either, or both. In all the years with Larry Hart I had to give him the melody. Otherwise he wouldn't work. He had to have music. But Larry had to be trapped in a number of ways before he would work. Music was one of the ways. We had to work very closely, together in the same room. He wouldn't pick up a pencil unless I was there. With Oscar it was just the other way around. We would discuss the show at great length and decide on various spots where we wanted to have a certain kind of song, and Oscar would disappear to his farm and come back three weeks later with a lyric. Then I would write the music for it.

Q: You hadn't so much as discussed the meter, the beat, the mechanics?

RODGERS: Occasionally, yes. Yes, I think we knew, for example, that "Oh, What a Beautiful Mornin'" was going to be a waltz. We knew, in general, what all of the songs were going to be like in complexion.

Q: When you are composing to words already in front of you, do you tend to kind of one-finger a melody line to which chords get fitted, or do you do a chord progression to which a melody line gets fitted? Which?

RODGERS: I do it all sorts of ways. I don't usually finger a melody anyway. I usually get the approach sitting in a chair or walking around, outdoors.

Q: You hear it, mentally.

RODGERS: Yes—the approach to it. The kind of tune it should be. Then I'll do the tune, on a piece of paper, or at the piano. If it is on a piece of paper, I'll eventually take it to the piano to hear it.

Q: What do you turn over to the orchestrator or arranger?

RODGERS: I give them a piano part that is so full that it cannot be played by one person.

Q: You yourself put in the nuance?

RODGERS: Of everything. Very often with further suggestions: a flute should do this, etc. I make a three-staff piano part, melody and the two lower ones for harmony and rhythm. The staves are very full. They could not be played on the piano by any one person, and this procedure works out very well because when I get the orchestration there are no surprises. Usually there are a great many additions by the man who does the orchestration, and if he is a good man the additions are good.

Q: Do you tend to work with the same man?

RODGERS: I worked with Russell Bennett more than anyone else. Various people before that and a few others as well. The good ones know what you are trying to say musically and they don't violate what you are doing. They enhance it.

Q: How many times have you been asked these same questions?

RODGERS: It seems like forever. And they always start with: "Which comes first, the lyric or the music?"

Q: What is the fascination? Why do so many people ask you the same questions?

RODGERS: I think this is the nearest they can come to getting into your mind. People are intimidated, mystified by the business of writing music. They can't imagine how you do it. They are sure that you wake up in the middle of the night and grab for a pencil—which has never happened to me in my life.

Q: But how *do* you do it?

RODGERS: The only way I have ever been able to explain this is by saying that music is my medium—my language. A painter's medium is color, in a composition on canvas. I use sound. A good example is a thing I did for television a number of years ago called *Victory at Sea*. I had to write themes for all sorts of activity. There were no lyrics—no words. But there were pictures, which made it the same as having words. How do you make a noise like a submarine? Well, you make it your way. You've got your tool—which is sound—and you come up with sounds that, to you, are appropriate to a submarine. This actually happened. I had a submarine theme.

Q: Which is your best score?

RODGERS: *Carousel*, and that applies to the whole show. It isn't easy to explain why I think so. I have more respect for it; I think the music has more to say, and that the book has more to say. Maybe I like it best because to me it was the most important—in terms of quality. It dug deeper.

Q: Over your fifty years in show business, which was the most frustrating time?

RODGERS: You sound like David Frost. The most frustrating time—that would have to be Hollywood. Larry and I weren't able to find anybody who understood us. We knew what we were trying to say, but in the end we were not even allowed to write. We were under contract and I tried to get the agent to break the contract for us and let us come back East. But he didn't do it, and they kept us there. Our final job was writing the lyrics—both of us were assigned to writing the lyrics—for a new version of *The Merry Widow*. That was the last thing Rodgers and Hart did in California, and the day the contract was up I took my child and the child's mother and Larry and got on the Chief and came back here. In a way I have always been a little grateful to them. If they had been a little easier to work with—a little nicer—we might have stayed.

Q: So *State Fair* wasn't an attempt to go back?

RODGERS: Oh, no. This was a thing that we were in love with. Fox called us up and asked us to look at the old picture—the one with Will Rogers. We did, and we were crazy about it and said we would be happy to do it. I am very glad that we did—but you see Rodgers and Hammerstein were two different fellows. We had written *Oklahoma!* and every time one of us blew his nose it was a symphony.

Q: You did a stage version of *State Fair*. Was this ever intended for Broadway?

RODGERS: No. It was intended for stock. It was originally done in St. Louis—and was not too spectacular a success. Oh, it was a much better picture than it was a stage show. It was meant to be a picture.

Q: How about TV? You've done *Cinderella* and *Androcles*. Were these experiences satisfying? Is TV a good place for a person to work?

RODGERS: As in pictures, it depends entirely on who you are working with, whether you have a meeting of minds, and whether you understand one another. *Cinderella* worked wonderfully. They do it every year. *Androcles* was not successful—it didn't work very well. I am perfectly willing to share in the blame.

Q: Do you have any idea as to what you are going to do next?

RODGERS: Not the vaguest. For the moment, I don't want to do anything. I am tired of going through the long siege of getting *Two by Two* on the stage—it has been difficult, as all shows are—and having just run a mile, I don't feel like running another three blocks.

Q: Why did you do this latest one? Why didn't you rest on your laurels. You had it made. Why risk possible embarrassment—possible failure?

RODGERS: Well, damned if I know. I don't have to do it for the bread, but I think I have to do it for myself. I like to work. I like to write. I like the theater. I am energetic. I probably am pretty young physically for my age. But that isn't it. Maybe I am doing it in spite of the fact that I was very ill. A little over a year ago I almost died, with a very bad coronary. With good treatment and good behavior I got over it completely. Now maybe this is ego talking—you know, "I'll show them. I'll not only get well, I'll do a show." There might be a more pleasant way of saying it. Maybe it's simply a will to live. And if you have lived in the theater as long as I have, to quit would be a kind of not living—which doesn't intrigue me very much. I should say not.

Q: *Life* ran this picture of Frederick Loewe on the Mediterranean with about twenty bikinied beauties around him . . .

RODGERS: Yes, I remember that . . .

Q: And Loewe is asked when he is going to do another Broadway show. He looks around himself, at the yacht, at the beauties, at the Mediterranean, and replies, "Whatever for?"

RODGERS: But unlike Dick Rodgers he doesn't say that music is his means of expressing himself. Loewe is expressing himself in other ways. I have a different kind of life. I have a wife I am delighted to live with and six grandchildren who please me enormously because they kiss me a lot.

Q: No generation gap there?

RODGERS: No, apparently not. My children are good to me. That's the stodgy kind of old-fashioned life I happen to enjoy. And I like the actual work. I like being given a lyric, and taking it and trying to work out the problem, trying to get a good idea for a song—the music—that pleases me. Rehearsals please me. I enjoy the transfer from my head to somebody else's throat—the whole process. Even the terror of taking the thing out of town. It looks awful then, even if it's good. You don't know whether you're going to get it fixed or not. I like the whole process.

Q: Opening nights, too?

RODGERS: If it is a *good* opening night.

credits

"Hammerstein: Words by Rodgers" by Richard Rodgers. From *The New York Times Magazine*, 10 July 1960, 26, 54. Copyright © 1960 by Richard Rodges. Used by Permission of The Rodgers and Hammerstein Organization.

"Opera and Broadway" by Richard Rodgers. From *Opera News*, 25 February 1961, 8–11. Copyright © 1961 by *Opera News*. Reprinted by permission of *Opera News*. Used by Permission of The Rodgers and Hammerstein Organization.

"Now the Musical Theater is Enshrined" by Richard Rodgers. From *The New York Times Magazine*, 21 June 1964, 20–23. Copyright © by Richard Rodgers. Used by Permission of The Rodgers and Hammerstein Organization.

"A Composer Looks at His Lyricists" by Richard Rodgers. Reprinted from *The Dramatists Guild Quarterly* © 1967. All rights reserved. Used by Permission of The Rodgers and Hammerstein Organization.

From *Reminiscences of Richard Rodgers* by Richard Rodgers. Copyright © 1969 by Columbia University. Reprinted by permission of the Oral History Collection of Columbia University. Used by Permission of The Rodgers and Hammerstein Organization.

"The Broadway Audience Is Still There, Waiting for More Good Shows" by Richard Rodgers. Reprinted from *The Dramatists Guild Quarterly* © 1971. All rights reserved. Used by Permission of The Rodgers and Hammerstein Organization.

Librettos and Plays

A Connecticut Yankee: © 1927 by Herbert Fields. International Copyright Secured. Used by Permission of the Estate of Dorothy Fields. All Rights Reserved.

Green Grow the Lilacs: Copyright © 1930 by Lynn Riggs. Copyright Renewed © 1957 by Howard E. Reinheimer. Copyright © 1931 by Lynn Riggs. Copyright Renewed 1958 by Howard E. Reinheimer. Used by Permission.

I Married an Angel: © 1978 by Richard Rodgers individually and as Trustee under the Last will and Testament of Lorenz Hart and as Trustee u/d/t/ with Winifred Kron Galef and Lucille K. Fitzmaurice. International Copyright Secured. Used by Permission of The Rodgers and Hammerstein Organization. All Rights Reserved

Oklahoma!: © 1942 and 1944 by Oscar Hammerstein II. Copyright Renewed. International Copyright Secured. Used by Permission of The Rodgers and Hammerstein Organization. All Rights Reserved.

South Pacific: © 1949 by Richard Rodgers and Oscar Hammerstein II. Copyright Renewed. International Copyright Secured. Used by Permission of The Rodgers and Hammerstein Organization. All Rights Reserved.

Lyrics

With Oscar Hammerstein II

"All Er Nothin'," "I Can't Say No," and "Kansas City" (from *Oklahoma!*): Lyrics by Oscar Hammerstein II. Music by Richard Rodgers. © 1943 by WILLIAMSON MUSIC. Copyright Renewed. International Copyright Secured. All Rights Reserved. Used by Permission.

"A Cockeyed Optimist," "Twin Soliloquies (This Is How It Feels)," and "You've Got To Be Carefully Taught" (from *South Pacific*): Lyrics by Oscar Hammerstein II. Music by Richard Rodgers. © 1949 by Richard Rodgers and Oscar Hammerstein II. Copyright Renewed. WILLIAMSON MUSIC owner of publication and allied rights throughout the world. International Copyright Secured. All Rights Reserved. Used by Permission.

"A Hundred Million Miracles" (from *Flower Drum Song*): Lyrics by Oscar Hammerstein II. Music by Richard Rodgers. Copyright © 1958 by Richard Rodgers and Oscar Hammerstein II. Copyright Renewed. WILLIAMSON MUSIC owner of publication and allied rights throughout the world. International Copyright Secured. All Rights Reserved. Used by Permission.

"Suddenly Lovely" (from *South Pacific*): Lyrics by Oscar Hammerstein II. Music by Richard Rodgers. © 2001 by WILLIAMSON MUSIC. International Copyright Secured. All Rights Reserved. Used by Permission.

"You'll Never Walk Alone" (from *Carousel*): Lyrics by Oscar Hammerstein II. Music by Richard Rodgers. © 1945 by WILLIAMSON MUSIC. Copyright Renewed. International Copyright Secured. All Rights Reserved. Used by Permission.

With Lorenz Hart

"Any Old Place with You" (from *A Lonely Romeo*): Words by Lorenz Hart. Music by Richard Rodgers. © 1919 (Renewed) Warner Bros, Inc. Rights for Extended Renewal Term in U.S. controlled by The Estate of Lorenz Hart (administered by WB Music Corp.) and The Family Trust U/W Richard Rodgers and The Family Trust U/W Dorothy F. Rodgers (administered by WILLIAMSON MUSIC). All Rights outside U.S. controlled by Warner Bros. Inc. International Copyright Secured. All Rights Reserved. Used by Permission. WARNER BROS. PUBLICATIONS U.S. INC., Miami, FL 33014.

"Bewitched" (from *Pal Joey*): Words by Lorenz Hart. Music by Richard Rodgers. © 1941 (Renewed) Chappell & Co. Rights for Extended Renewal Term in U.S. controlled by The Estate of Lorenz Hart (administered by WB Music Corp.) and The Family Trust U/W Richard Rodgers and The Family Trust U/W Dorothy F. Rodgers (administered by WILLIAMSON MUSIC). All Rights outside U.S. controlled by Chappell & Co. International Copyright Secured. All Rights Reserved. Used by Permission. WARNER BROS. PUBLICATIONS U.S. INC., Miami, FL 33014.

"Come With Me," "Dear Old Syracuse," and "He and She" (from *The Boys from Syracuse*): Words by Lorenz Hart. Music by Richard Rodgers. © 1954 (Renewed) Chappell & Co. All Rights Reserved. Used by Permission. WARNER BROS. PUBLICATIONS U.S. INC., Miami, FL 33014.

"Falling In Love with Love" (from *The Boys from Syracuse*): Words by Lorenz Hart. Music by Richard Rodgers. © 1938 (Renewed) Chappell & Co. Rights for Extended Renewal Term in U.S. controlled by The Estate of Lorenz Hart and The Family Trust Dorothy F. Rodgers (administered by WILLIAMSON MUSIC). All Rights outside U.S. controlled by Chappell & Co. International Copyright Secured. All Rights Reserved. Used by Permission. WARNER BROS. PUBLICATIONS U.S. INC., Miami, FL 33014.

"Love's Intense in Tents" (from *Poor Little Ritz Girl*): Words by Lorenz Hart. Music by Richard Rodgers. © 1920 (Renewed) Warner Bros., Inc. Rights for Extended Renewal Term in U.S. controlled by The Estate of Lorenz Hart (administered by WB Music Corp.) and The Family Trust U/W Richard Rodgers and The Family Trust U/W Dorothy F. Rodgers (administered by WILLIAMSON MUSIC). All Rights outside U.S. controlled by Warner Bros. Inc. International Copyright Secured. All Rights Reserved. Used by Permission. WARNER BROS. PUBLICATIONS U.S. INC., Miami, FL 33014.

"Manhattan" (from *The Garrick Gaieties, 1925*): © 1925. By Lorenz Hart and Richard Rodgers. Carlin American, Inc. owner of publication and allied rights throughout the world. International Copyright Secured. All Rights Reserved. Used by Permission.

"Mountain Greenery" (from *The Garrick Gaieties, 1926*): Words by Lorenz Hart. Music by Richard Rodgers.© 1926 (Renewed) Warner Bros. Inc. Rights for Extended Renewal Term in U.S. controlled by The Estate of Lorenz Hart (administered by WB Music Corp.) and The Family Trust U/W Richard Rodgers and The Family Trust U/W Dorothy F. Rodgers (administered by WILLIAMSON MUSIC). All Rights outside U.S. controlled by Warner Bros. Inc. International Copyright Secured. All Rights Reserved. Used by Permission. WARNER BROS. PUBLICATIONS U.S. INC., Miami, FL 33014.

"Shortest Day of the Year" (from *The Boys from Syracuse*): Words by Lorenz Hart. Music by Richard Rodgers. © 1938 (Renewed) Chappell & Co. Rights for Extended Renewal Term in U.S. controlled by The Estate of Lorenz Hart (administered by WB Music Corp.) and The Family Trust U/W Richard Rodgers and The Family Trust U/W Dorothy F. Rodgers (administered by WILLIAMSON MUSIC). All Rights outside U.S. controlled by Chappell & Co. International Copyright Secured. All Rights Reserved. Used by Permission. WARNER BROS. PUBLICATIONS U.S. INC., Miami, FL 33014.

"There's a Small Hotel" (from *On Your Toes*): Words by Lorenz Hart. Music by Richard Rodgers. © 1936 (Renewed) Chappell & Co. Rights for Extended Renewal Term in U.S. controlled by The Estate of Lorenz Hart (administered by WB Music Corp.) and The Family Trust U/W Richard Rodgers and The Family Trust U/W Dorothy F. Rodgers (administered by WILLIAMSON MUSIC). All Rights outside U.S. controlled by Chappell & Co. International Copyright Secured. All Rights Reserved. Used by Permission. WARNER BROS. PUBLICATIONS U.S. INC., Miami, FL 33014.

"Thou Swell" (from *A Connecticut Yankee*): Words by Lorenz Hart. Music by Richard Rodgers. © 1927 (Renewed) Warner Bros. Inc. Rights for Extended Renewal Term in U.S. controlled by The Estate of Lorenz Hart (administered by WB Music Corp.) and The Family Trust U/W Richard Rodgers and The Family Trust U/W Dorothy F. Rodgers (administered by WILLIAMSON MUSIC). All Rights outside U.S. controlled by Warner Bros. Inc. International Copyright Secured. All Rights Reserved. Used by Permission. WARNER BROS. PUBLICATIONS U.S. INC., Miami, FL 33014.

"Where or When" (from *Babes in Arms*): Words by Lorenz Hart. Music by Richard Rodgers. © 1937 (Renewed) Chappell & Co. Rights for Extended Renewal Term in U.S. controlled by The Estate of Lorenz Hart (administered by WB Music Corp.) and The Family Trust U/W Richard Rodgers and The Family Trust U/W Dorothy F. Rodgers (administered by WILLIAMSON MUSIC). All Rights outside U.S. controlled by Chappell & Co. International Copyright Secured. All Rights Reserved. Used by Permission. WARNER BROS. PUBLICATIONS U.S. INC., Miami, FL 33014.

Music and Lyrics

Rodgers and Hammerstein

"It Might As Well Be Spring" (from *State Fair*): Lyrics by Oscar Hammerstein II. Music by Richard Rodgers. Copyright © 1945 by WILLIAMSON MUSIC. Copyright Renewed. International Copyright Secured. All Rights Reserved. Used by Permission.

"The Surrey with the Fringe on Top" (from *Oklahoma!*): Lyrics by Oscar Hammerstein II. Music by Richard Rodgers. Copyright © 1943 by WILLIAMSON MUSIC. Copyright Renewed. International Copyright Secured. All Rights Reserved. Used by Permission.

"A Wonderful Guy" and "Younger Than Springtime" (from *South Pacific*): Lyrics by Oscar Hammerstein II. Music by Richard Rodgers. Copyright © 1949 by Richard Rodgers and Oscar Hammerstein II. Copyright Renewed. WILLIAMSON MUSIC owner of publication and allied rights throughout the world. International Copyright Secured. All Rights Reserved. Used by Permission.

Rodgers and Hart

"My Heart Stood Still" (from *A Connecticut Yankee*): Words by Lorenz Hart. Music by Richard Rodgers. © 1927 (Renewed) Warner Bros. Inc. Rights for Extended Renewal Term in U.S. controlled by The Estate of Lorenz Hart (administered by WB Music Corp.) and The Family Trust U/W Richard Rodgers and the Family Trust U/W Dorothy F. Rodgers (administered by WILLIAMSON MUSIC). International Copyright Secured. All Rights Reserved. Used by Permission.

Music

Rodgers and Hammerstein

"Boys and Girls Like You and Me" (from *Cinderella*): Lyrics by Oscar Hammerstein II. Music by Richard Rodgers. Copyright © 1943 by WILLIAMSON MUSIC. Copyright Renewed. International Copyright Secured. All Rights Reserved.

"A Lovely Night" (from *Cinderella*): Lyrics by Oscar Hammerstein II. Music by Richard Rodgers. Copyright © 1957 by Richard Rodgers and Oscar Hammerstein II. Copyright Renewed. International Copyright Secured. All Rights Reserved. Used by Permission.

"Out of My Dreams" (from *Oklahoma!*): Lyrics by Oscar Hammerstein II. Music by Richard Rodgers. © 1943 by WILLIAMSON MUSIC. Copyright Renewed. International Copyright Secured. All Rights Reserved. Used by Permission.

"That's For Me" (from *State Fair*): Lyrics by Oscar Hammerstein II. Music by Richard Rodgers. Copyright © 1945 by WILLIAMSON MUSIC. Copyright Renewed. International Copyright Secured. All Rights Reserved. Used by Permission.

Photographs

Photographs on page 2 (Richard Rodgers, 1953), page 85 (Richard Rodgers and Oscar Hammerstein II, 1943), page 191 (Richard Rodgers and Stephen Sondheim, 1965), and page 259 (Richard Rodgers, 1950) are courtesy of The Rodgers and Hammerstein Organization.
Photograph on page 9, Richard Rodgers and Lorenz Hart, *Time* cover, September 26, 1938, is courtesy of TIMEPIX.

Every effort has been made to contact copyright holders of original material contained in this volume.

index of Rodgers's works

general index

Michener, James, 91, 135, 142, 148, 311
Mickey Mouse, 74
Middle of the Night (Chayefsky), 133
Midler, Bette, 248
Mielziner, Jo, 69, 125, 132, 142, 198
Milestone, Lewis, 73
Milk and Honey (Herman), 222
Miller, Marilyn, 15, 48
Minnelli, Vincente, 102
Mister Roberts (Logan, Heggen), 133, 137, 148
Mr. Sycamore (Frings), 114
Mitchell, David, 248, 250
Molnár, Ferenc, 121, 122, 123, 125, 157, 180, 292
Montresor, Beni, 238, 251
The Moon Is Blue (film), 219
Moore, Victor, 72
Moran, Polly, 74
Mordden, Ethan, 5, 6, 11, 88, 98, 100, 102, 105, 224
Mordente, Tony, 237
Morgan, Frank, 74
Morgan, Michele, 76
Morgenthau, Henry, Jr., 121
Morley, Victor, 13
Morning's at Seven (Osborne), 133
A Mother's Kisses (Adler), 241, 243
The Most Happy Fella (Loesser), 171
Mozart, Wolfgang Amadeus, 168, 172, 194, 204, 290
Munsell, Warren, 114
Munson, Ona, 72
Murray, Ken, 72
Music in the Air (Kern, Hammerstein), 269, 271, 291
Music Is (Adler), 241
The Music Man (Willson), 237
My Fair Lady (Lerner, Loewe), 4, 7, 89, 169, 171, 210, 211, 212, 213, 223, 237, 293, 298
Myrtil, Odette, 111

Nana (film), 74
Nathan, George Jean, 7, 162–63, 294
Nelson, Portia, 161
The New Moon (Romberg, Hammerstein), 104, 286
Nichols, Mike, 242
Nixon, Marni, 78
No, No, Nanette (Youmans, Caesar), 106
"Nobody Knows the Trouble I've Seen" (African-American spiritual), 53, 67

The Nutcracker Suite (Tchaikovsky), 46
Nype, Russell, 245

Oakie, Jack, 35
Odets, Clifford, 165
Offenbach, Jacques, 18, 194, 204
Of Thee I Sing (G. and I. Gershwin), 291, 297
O'Casey, Sean, 162, 295
O'Hara, John, 69, 158, 159, 272, 273, 304–5
O'Neil, William J., 13
O'Neill, Eugene, 162
Oh, Boy! (Kern, Bolton, Wodehouse), 296
Oh, Kay! (G. and I. Gershwin, Bolton, Wodehouse), 12, 169
Oh, Lady! Lady! (Kern, Bolton, Wodehouse), 296
"Old Black Joe" (Foster), 92
"Old Folks at Home" (Foster), 51, 74
"Ol' Man River" (Kern, Hammerstein), 104, 185, 270
On a Clear Day You Can See Forever (Lane, Lerner), 212, 324, 325
On Borrowed Time (Osborne), 133
On the Town (Bernstein, Comden, Green), 168
Once Upon a Mattress (M. Rodgers, Barer), 7, 253, 255
One Touch of Venus (Weill, Nash, Perelman), 124, 132, 146
"Onward, Christian Soldiers" (Sullivan), 64
Oppenheimer, George, 224, 228
Osborne, E. W., 13
"Our Heroine" (Michener), 135, 156

Paar, Jack, 218
Pacific Overtures (Sondheim, Weidman), 242
Pajama Game (Adler, Ross), 7, 240, 247, 276, 298
Parsifal (Wagner), 195, 211
Patience (Gilbert, Sullivan), 16
Payson, Charles Shipman, 52
Peerce, Jan, 76
Pennington, Ann, 48
Perkins, Ray, 285
Peter Pan (Charlap, Styne, Leigh, Comden, Green), 146
Pickford, Mary, 79
Picnic (Inge), 133
Picon, Molly, 222